M

DATE DUE

JUL 3 1 2005	
AUG 2 9 2005	
DEC 0 9 2005	
JUL 1 1 2006	
SEP 2 9 2007	
NOV 0 3 2007	

DEMCO, INC. 38-2931

MAY 0 5 2005

HOT PROPERTY

PAT CHOATE

HOT PROPERTY

THE STEALING OF IDEAS
IN AN AGE
OF GLOBALIZATION

ALFRED A. KNOPF NEW YORK 2005

THIS IS A BORZOI BOOK
PUBLISHED BY ALFRED A. KNOPF

www.aaknopf.com

Knopf, Borzoi Books, and the colophon are registered
trademarks of Random House, Inc.

Library of Congress Cataloging-in-Publication Data
Choate, Pat.
Hot property : the stealing of ideas in an age of
globalization / Pat Choate.—1st ed.
p.   cm.
Includes bibliographical references and index.
ISBN 0-375-40212-8
1. Intellectual property—Economic aspects. 2. Intellectual
property—United States. I. Title.
K1401.C48575 2005   346.7304'8dc22
2004059440

Manufactured in the United States of America
First Edition

To Jerome and Dorothy Lemelson

CONTENTS

Ideas are the purest product of the mind . . . the greatest, most stable source of the wealth of nations.

—Joan M. Bernott, author of *Bright Ideas at Risk*

Knowledge has become the key economic resource and the dominant, if not the only, source of competitive advantage.

—Peter Drucker,

The Atlantic Monthly, November 1984

The primary cause of economic development is the mind. The cause of wealth is invention, detection, enterprise.

—Michael Novak, political scholar

[Patents] . . . added the fuel of interest to the fire of genius, in the discovery and production of new and useful things.

—Abraham Lincoln, "Lecture on Discoveries and Inventions"

The Congress shall have power . . . to Promote the Progress of Science and useful Arts, by securing for limited Times to Authors and Inventors the exclusive Right to their respective Writings and Discoveries . . .

—Article 1, Section 8, of the Constitution of the

United States of America

HOT PROPERTY

MY FAKE ROLEX

I n the summer of 1990, my corporate employer and I separated "without ceremony," as the term goes, which meant I got no good-bye dinner and no parting gift. As consolation, Michael Barker, a friend for many years, invited me to lunch at Billy Martin's Tavern, an old-fashioned steak house in the middle of Georgetown, one of Washington, D.C.'s best neighborhoods. After the meal and with a bit of fanfare, Michael presented me with a gaudily wrapped box, along with a few impertinent comments. Inside the box was a big, chunky, fake gold Rolex watch with a broken band—what he called an "appropriate memento."

As we were leaving the restaurant, I asked Michael where he had purchased my gift. He pointed to a sidewalk vendor who was sitting behind a tacky little card table covered with cheap jewelry and trinkets. We walked over and asked the man to show us any watches he had for sale. He reached under his table and pulled out a small display carton containing maybe a dozen watches, some of which were poor imitations of famous brands and others that looked like the real thing, though, of course, none was.

Fast-forward to the spring of 2004. The two of us return to Billy Martin's, but now two big vending tables are outside the restaurant, each at its own corner location. (Apparently, the sidewalks on the other corners were too narrow.) The vendors have decked the booths with faux luxury items— elegant handbags, leather wallets, beautiful silk scarves, belts, perfume, and, of course, watches. Louis Vuitton and Chanel handbags, purportedly indistinguishable from the originals, are there for $65. Have a particular Rolex model in mind? Here it is. Want a Cartier tank watch? There are two models—one with a silver band, the other in leather. Prefer a Movado? They are all available. All fake.

Michael picks up a faux designer belt. He is wearing the real thing (he thinks). He paid $250 at the designer store, but this goes for $20. After inspecting the counterfeit, we cannot tell the difference between it and the genuine item. The vendors, of course, will process any credit card, using wireless technology to get a quick approval. Gift-wrapping is available for a small fee.

We take a cab downtown, where we see similar booths. In two places, we have trouble crossing the street because the booths and the customers crowding around them spill into the crosswalks. Apparently, the booths with the best knockoffs are found on and near the famed K Street corridor, where Washington's richest and most powerful lobbyists, lawyers, and former public officials have offices. Throughout the day, you can see Washington's political and legal elites stop at the booths, make their purchases, and then move on.

These sales are illegal, violating the laws of the federal government and the District of Columbia, both of which forbid sales of pirated and counterfeit merchandise. Still, in the early morning of most days, Michael says that you can see the vendors double-park their vans while they set up and stock their stands. He also claims that if you are patient, you can see a police car glide up to a booth and stop, a window go down, the vendor hand in a purse or some other luxury item, the window go up, and the car ease away.

Three blocks from the heart of downtown Washington, 17th Street crosses Pennsylvania Avenue. Step across the avenue and on the east side are the White House and the Old Executive Office Building. On the west side is the building that houses the Office of the United States Trade Representative and America's top trade negotiators.

Evidently, the irony of the situation seems lost on our public leaders. Yet a principal thrust of U.S. trade negotiations is to stop the global pirating and counterfeiting of goods even as a bazaar featuring such U.S. and foreign-made products operates openly in the very heart of Washington. Any diplomat or trade negotiator staying at the Mayflower Hotel in downtown Washington would have to walk around or through this bazaar of fakes to reach the White House or the Trade Negotiator's Office.

Ultimately, this blatant peddling of fake goods is not about municipal corruption in Washington, though that exists. Rather, it is about a global crime of immense proportions—the stealing of ideas, creations, and products—that is becoming so common that we accept it, even as we condemn and outlaw it.

Consider this: the Chinese government has a quota on the number of Hollywood films that can be legally imported, now twenty per year. Yet, throughout China, customers can buy pirated digital copies of most American-made movies for as little as 75 cents. Subtitles, of course, are available. To get a copy of a first-rate movie before Hollywood releases it in the United States, Chinese buyers may have to pay as little as $1 to $3 per disc. Pirated copies of *The Matrix Reloaded, Kill Bill: Vol. 1, Star Wars II,* and the *Lord of the Rings* trilogy, among dozens of other recent hits, were widely available in China, often before they were in U.S. theaters. China's largest legal distributor of Hollywood films reports that he sold 300,000 legitimate copies of *Titanic* but that pirates sold between 20 and 25 million. On average, the country's knockoff vendors outsell the legal movie distributors about 35 to 1.

In Pakistan, illegally duplicated CDs constitute almost 100 percent of total music sales. In Russia, music thieves operate with such impunity and so dominate the market that three of every four recordings sold are unauthorized copies.

In China and Vietnam, more than 90 percent of the packaged business software installed in computers is pirated. In Eastern Europe, more than 71 percent of such software comes from illegally produced copies; in Latin America, the figure is 55 percent. When Microsoft introduced its Windows 95 software in 1995, it sold for $85 in the United States. Only days after it was introduced in the U.S., counterfeit copies of the package, including both the software and the manual, could be bought in China for only $5. A decade later, the current version of Microsoft's operating system sells in China for less than $2 a copy. Apparently, even pirates face market pressures.

In Italy, counterfeiting is an established industry with a long, discreditable history. Buyers can easily find top-quality copies of luxury-brand shoes, belts, bags, dresses, and scarves. Three out of four Italian producers of designer wear suffer from counterfeiting. Also, more than 80 percent of Italian consumers say they willingly buy fake goods. Indeed, fake is fashionable there.

Admittedly, finding sympathy for Bill Gates, the world's richest man, over any economic losses he might endure from the piracy of Microsoft products may be difficult. Also, most consumers and politicians do not automatically empathize with the makers of expensive luxury goods when their high-end products are copied and sold at street prices.

But piracy and counterfeiting are about more than software, music CDs, movies, and designer goods. For instance, anyone who flies on passenger airlines should consider this: while the lifetime odds of dying in a car accident are sixteen times greater than those of perishing in an airplane mishap, planes sometimes crash because they contain bogus parts that fail in flight. The Federal Aviation Administration (FAA) reports that counterfeit parts played a role in 174 aircraft accidents or crashes in the United States between May 1973 and April 1996, resulting in 17 deaths and 39 injuries. And while the FAA is responsible for certifying every parts manufacturer, inspecting their production and the parts themselves to ensure flight safety, most of the world's 2,000 to 5,000 parts dealers are unregulated. This is a major loophole. It enables counterfeiters to sell fake parts to these unregulated dealers, who in turn supply the world's aircraft repair stations, which service the planes of U.S. airlines. Consequently, equipment that is counterfeit, stolen, too old, or improperly reconditioned—what is collectively called "bogus" but is tagged as airworthy—finds its way into the airplanes we fly. In its 1996 study of counterfeit airline parts, *Business Week* reported that 2 percent of the 26 million parts installed annually may be bogus.

Strandflex, an FAA-approved manufacturing company located in upstate New York, admitted in May 2001 that for almost a decade it had been selling substandard airline cable to companies and the U.S. government for use in commercial and military aircraft. Airline cable connects cockpit controls to the engines, landing gear, rudders, and wing surfaces. When tested by the U.S. Air Force, the Strandflex cable snapped at barely half the load it was supposed to carry. Air Force investigators found Strandflex cable in the engine start and throttle controls on Air Force Two, which transports the vice president and other high-ranking U.S. officials. The plane was grounded in August 1999 and recabled before it was allowed to fly again. Southwest Airlines found and replaced the same bogus cable in forty-seven planes that it operates.

Or consider the case of Air-Pro, a Florida company that sold 1,900 defective aircraft hoses to companies that supply the U.S. government and passenger airlines. These "flight-critical" parts carry fuel, oil, and hydraulic fluids. Because hoses deteriorate as they age, the FAA sets time limits on their use after manufacture. But Air-Pro falsified the manufacturing dates on its hoses so they could be sold by dealers as being years newer than they actually were. Investigators also found that the Florida firm had substituted polyolefin for Teflon in the protective sleeves on hoses used in the landing gear of commercial jets, an act that substantially increased the risk of over-heating and fire. Finally, investigators discovered that Air-Pro had sold companies that supply airlines contaminated oxygen hoses, which are used during emergencies by the crew and passengers.

Or consider West Coast Aluminum Heat Treating Co., located in La Miranda, California, which for sixteen years sold suppliers aircraft and space vehicle parts certified as genuine, but that break under pressure. In April 2001, the FAA notified the government and airlines that more than 12,000 suspect parts sold by this company were now in the following aircraft:

- Boeing Company models 737, 747, 757, DC-8, DC-9, DC-10, MD-11, MD-80, and MD-90

- Bell commercial helicopters

- The U.S. Navy's P-3 aircraft, F/A-18, and Phalanx missile

- The Marine Corps' AH-1 Cobra attack helicopter

- The U.S. Army's Kiowa Warrior and Apache helicopters

- The U.S. Air Force's C-9, C-17, KC-10, F-15, F-16, F-22, and AWACS

- NASA's space station

Now imagine this. You are on an airplane six or seven miles up in the sky with your seat reclined, happily reading a book or watching a movie, when the pilot comes on the loudspeaker and announces:

> Your attention, please. We are experiencing some flight difficulties because (a) one of the cables needed to fly the plane has snapped; (b) an essential [fuel, oil, or hydraulic] hose has ruptured; or (c) a key structural part has just broken in two. Our flight crew will help prepare you for an emergency landing. Please stay calm.

Then, an emergency oxygen mask drops from the ceiling and you just hope that yours is not one of those contaminated hoses sold by Air-Pro. At such a moment, pirating, counterfeiting, and bogus goods may take on an entirely new importance.

· · ·

If you take prescription drugs and travel, consider this: worldwide, mosquitoes infect 300 million to 500 million people with malaria annually. More than one million die each year, of which 90 percent are children under five. One reason for these deaths, according to World Health Organization investigators, is that in the seven African countries where malaria is most prevalent, 20 to 90 percent of the antimalarial drugs distributed are counterfeit or have no medical value whatsoever. The International Federation of Pharmaceutical Manufacturers Associations estimates that 25 to 50 percent of all medicines distributed in Africa are counterfeit, with no curative value.

Closer to home, Mexican border towns across from California, Arizona, New Mexico, and Texas have changed dramatically over the past decade. Many of the shops that once sold tourist T-shirts, handicrafts, matadors painted on black velvet, pottery, tin goods, and assorted pictures of cute little Chihuahuas with enormous eyes are now pretending to be pharmacies, targeting American consumers seeking bargain-priced medicines. Tijuana, for instance, has more than 1,700 pharmacies—one for every 1,300 residents. In contrast, the entire neighboring city of San Diego has about 125—one for every 10,800 inhabitants.

Many of these Mexican pharmacies look exactly like ones found in the United States: a well-groomed person in a neat white jacket with pens in the pocket stands in front of fully stocked shelves, ready to help. Whether these people really are trained and licensed pharmacists is largely irrelevant since most of their American customers come not for medical advice but to purchase specific bargain-priced medicines, which sell for 30 to 85 percent less in Mexico.

No prescription? No problem. Roughly a fifth of these stores will sell medicines without a prescription, while most of the rest will steer you to a nearby Mexican physician to write one out.

The threat to those who need real medicines is that almost 25 percent of what is coming into the United States from Mexico is counterfeit, substandard, contaminated, or poisoned. Many, including birth control pills, have no active ingredients. Many fakes are stamped with forged company logos and are packaged in blister packs that are indistinguishable from the real thing. Often, counterfeiters buy real medicines that are past their expiration dates, repackage them with "new" dates, and sell the goods to unsuspecting American customers.

The value and the volume of these counterfeit medical products entering the U.S. from Mexico are huge by any measure. A University of Texas study reports that the sales of fifteen specific pharmaceutical products coming into the United States from Nuevo Laredo each year exceed $134 million. Thus, this one border town has a sales output roughly equal to 6 percent of the entire Mexican pharmaceutical market. The Texas study found that 11,000 Valium tablets per day enter the U.S. through Nuevo Laredo.

Even if the border pharmacies did not exist, more than four hundred Internet sites, half of which are in the United States, would still exist, shipping medicines directly to American consumers. In early 2001, the Customs Service and the Food and Drug Administration (FDA) did a five-week pilot study in Carson City, Nevada, a small city, where they intercepted incoming shipments of medicines from foreign sites. Of the 1,900 packages examined by the FDA, more than 700 contained drugs unapproved for use in the United States or medicines that were mislabeled or required a U.S. prescription. The study's principal conclusion was that neither Customs nor the FDA had the capacity to monitor international shipments of illegal or counterfeit drugs into the United States. The *Washington Post* reported in its 2003 landmark five-part study of counterfeit medicines ("Rx Roulette") that "Overwhelmed customs workers inspect less than 1 percent of an estimated 2 million packages containing medicine shipped into the country each year. Virtually all of these shipments are illegal."

Today, many Americans assume that drugs bought over the Internet and sent to them from Canada meet that nation's stiff regulatory requirements and thus are safe. However, the Partnership for Safe Medicines reports, "Not all medicines that claim to be from Canada are really from Canada— approximately one-third of websites that purport to be from Canada are not from Canada." These Internet drug sellers, regardless of whether they claim to be Canadian or not, increasingly are transshipping their goods to the U.S. from other nations—notably Singapore, South Africa, Argentina, and Pakistan.

Of equal significance, Canadian law exempts from regulatory oversight any imported pharmaceuticals intended for export. More alarming, Canada's trade agency reports that between September 2002 and September 2003, imports of pharmaceuticals surged from several nations long associated with counterfeiting—China (43 percent increase), Iran (2,753 percent), Thailand (52 percent), Argentina (221 percent), Ecuador (198 percent), and South Africa (84 percent). Since none of these nations has a mutual recognition agreement on good manufacturing practices with Canada, none of these imported drugs can be sold to Canadian citizens. But they can be transshipped from Canada to customers in the United States, and many are.

Although the U.S. drug and manufacturing system is one of the world's safest, globalization has made it more difficult to protect. Federal officials are unable to precisely estimate the portion of all medicines consumed in the U.S. that are counterfeit, but various estimates put the number at 5 to 8 percent. Most important, the Food and Drug Administration reported in 2004 that there has not been a single U.S. fatality "causally linked to specific counterfeit drugs in the last decade." This is an extraordinary achievement. By contrast, half or more of the medicines sold in China are counterfeit; in 2001 these counterfeits resulted in the deaths of more than 190,000 Chinese. Other parts of the world, including Africa and South America, are similarly victimized, largely because their pharmaceutical supply chains lack integrity.

In contrast, three primary wholesalers distribute 90 percent of the prescription drugs sold in the U.S. They buy directly from the manufacturer and sell directly to the various dispensers, such as hospitals, pharmacies, and secondary wholesalers, a practice that allows for strict control. Yet counterfeiters still slip fake medicines into those networks.

Despite the FDA's remarkable success in protecting the integrity of U.S. medicines, the agency reports that the sale and use of counterfeit medicines are an expanding problem, made worse by the growing amount of unregulated imports through Mexico, Canada, and the Internet. The result is predictable: counterfeit ulcer medicines that result in internal bleeding, bogus antibiotics that cause severe ear infections, and sham AIDS and cancer drugs, contaminated with nonsterile tap water, that enter patients' bloodstreams. The FDA list of such counterfeits is long and growing.

Even our babies are being victimized. The sale of counterfeit baby formula is one means. The FDA requires that all infant formulas sold in the U.S. contain specified minimum amounts of twenty-nine nutrients, maximum amounts for nine of those, and that the product be made under strict manufacturing guidelines.

Counterfeiters elude these FDA mandates in several ways. One is by duplicating the labels. In 1999, FDA agents arrested individuals in Southern California who were taking a $7 can of basic milk- and soy-based infant formula and relabeling it as an $18 can of Mead Johnson's Nutramigen, a product given to infants sensitive to milk. According to the FDA, babies who required hypoallergenic infant formula were likely to have mild to severe allergic reactions to the mislabeled product, including fever, vomiting, skin rash, and diarrhea. Likewise, in 2002 the federal government convicted a Californian who posed as a wholesale grocery distributor for buying bulk quantities of a basic and inexpensive infant formula, manufactured for export to the Middle East, and packaging it for sale in California as Similac, a higher-priced formula produced by Abbot Laboratories. FDA agents seized nineteen tons of counterfeit powdered formula; in addition, they removed six thousand cans from retail and wholesale stores throughout California.

Less-developed countries have it much worse. In May 2004, the Xinhua News Agency described how at least two hundred Chinese babies had died because they had been fed fake infant formula sold in the Anhui and Shandong provinces. Chinese investigators report that they found 141 counterfeit production facilities, selling forty-five types of substandard infant formula through five wholesalers, who supplied village grocery stores. One popular formula contained only one-sixth of the nutrients required to meet a baby's daily needs. Those fake formulas caused the baby's head to swell as the rest of its body withered, a symptom of starvation. Hundreds of others suffered severe malnutrition and brain damage.

Counterfeit toys covered with a lead paint that can poison young children, counterfeit toys with weak small parts that babies can swallow and choke on, fakes with unsafe stuffing, pajamas with phony labels made with cheap, non-flame-retardant cloth —all these and more are found in every city of every country of the world. In the United States and Europe, with their stringent child-safety standards, governments locate and recall many of these dangerous goods every year but still do not get them all. Certainly, counterfeiting takes on a new meaning when it harms our children.

The topic of intellectual property might seem dull, at least initially. It is sometimes technical. It often involves complex legal concepts. It is deeply mired in obscure politics, dominated by people and bureaucratic organizations known primarily to the involved lawyers, bureaucrats, and technicians.

Nonetheless, intellectual property issues matter for many reasons. They are important because counterfeit and pirated goods can be disastrous to the health and safety of people. Fake aircraft parts, phony medicines, and counterfeit children's goods are only part of that menace. Today, global commerce is inundated with fake and defective auto parts, medical equipment, sunglasses, ladders, tools, ropes, shampoos, cosmetics, and apparel. Each represents a particular danger, and all are the source of numerous deaths and injuries to unsuspecting users.

Piracy and counterfeiting impede innovation: thieves do not invest in research, design, production, development, or advertising. They create nothing. Rather, they steal revenues from legitimate inventors and producers and thus limit investments for additional development. The result is fewer new medicines, fewer advances in science, fewer new products, fewer new music CDs, fewer new movies, less new software, and higher prices for whatever is created. For these reasons, all of us are indirectly harmed even when thieves steal from Microsoft and Disney.

Pirates and counterfeiters also frustrate creativity. Their actions deny incentives—whether they be money, recognition, fame, or power—to the creators of new ideas who do the work and take the risks that innovation demands.

Fakes destroy good jobs. Music piracy is so rampant in Mexico—three in every five recordings are pirated copies—that it threatens the future of local artists and legitimate record companies. The European Union reports that pirating and counterfeiting cost its member nations more than 100,000 jobs per year. The sale of knockoff vehicle spare parts has created a loss of 30,000 jobs in the European Union. One of every five firms in France with fifty or more employees admits to being a victim of counterfeiting and piracy.

The absolute financial value of global piracy and counterfeiting is unknown, and most of the conjectures must be viewed with some caution. Yet the fragmentary evidence that exists outlines a global crime wave of massive proportions. The Federal Bureau of Investigation, for instance, reports that U.S. companies lose $200 billion to 250 billion annually due to worldwide copyright, trademark, and trade secret infringement. The European Commission (EC) reckons that legitimate European companies lose between $43 billion and $61 billion annually to counterfeiters. The EC also calculates that 5 to 7 percent of world trade is composed of counterfeit goods. If that estimate is correct, the cost to lawful companies around the world in 2003 was between $363 billion and $509 billion. Significantly, the EC reports that the value of counterfeiting as a percentage of world trade is growing. Between 1990 and 1999, it doubled, from 3.5 percent to 7 percent—a growth rate that reflects the rapid globalization of the world's economy and a corresponding lack of anticounterfeiting protections.

The natural response to a crime wave so overwhelming is "there ought to be a law." Well, there are laws, treaties, and agreements aplenty. Some, such as those of the United States and Europe, are very strong and provide powerful protections. But the laws of many other nations are weak. In some countries, laws exist, but they are meaningless shams because they are never enforced. Other nations, notably China, are pursuing national development strategies based on the uncompensated, unapproved stealing of other nations' best ideas and technologies. Altogether, regardless of its form or motivation, this global theft of ideas is now so massive that it threatens innovation and creativity everywhere, as well as the industries and jobs they support.

The starting point for any examination of intellectual property laws, here or abroad, is when someone creates an idea.

Ideas are intangible, even ephemeral, things. Yet they are the wellspring of all advances in literature, science, technology, agriculture, music, medicine, designs, and even mousetraps. Ideas catalyze the birth of a book, invention, song, movie, or any other creation. And although ideas cannot be owned, the right to exclude others from producing the creations that flow from them can be—at least for a set time. Intellectual property law is about classifying the form an idea takes, the right to exclude others from its use, the enforcement of that right, the penalties for any infringements of that right, the assignment of responsibility for imposing that punishment, and, equally important, the attendant obligation of the intellectual-property owner to society.

With potentials so vast, financial values so great, and security so tenuous, an idea—especially a commercial idea—is particularly vulnerable to theft and misuse. Thus, many societies, over a period of centuries, have developed a body of law to protect the ownership rights to these products of the mind.

Although the protections take many forms, as a body they are called "intellectual property rights." Fundamentally, such rights, wherever they exist, are a basic social contract between society and someone who creates an idea—a golden covenant, by which the public grants that creator the right to exclude others from using his or her creation for a specified period in exchange for the disclosure of its details and ultimately the surrender of that property right by allowing the creation to enter the public domain. The hope is that by giving the author or inventor a property right for a limited time, while also making public the creation's most intimate details, the general state of knowledge will be advanced.

In the United States, such protection is a "right" that flows directly from the U.S. Constitution. Specifically, Article 1, Section 8, grants Congress the power "to promote the Progress of Science and useful Arts, by securing for limited Times to Authors and Inventors the exclusive Right to their respective Writings and Discoveries." This is the only place in the Constitution where the word "right" is used explicitly. The constitutional amendments that became known as the Bill of Rights were not ratified until almost the end of the third year of George Washington's first presidential term and almost nineteen months after passage of the U.S. Patent Act in 1790.

This twenty-seven-word clause is the legal basis of every patent and copyright ever issued in the United States. Congress may change the terms and duration of patents and copyrights, thus rendering the contemporary definition of what is the proper balance between the public and private interests, but the Constitution guarantees every American's right to such protections.

Over time, four basic types of intellectual property protections have been created: copyrights, trademarks, patents, and trade secrets. Each contains its own bundle of rights, backed by a body of law that is appropriate for specific types of intellectual products. Lawrence J. Siskind, a San Francisco intellectual-property lawyer, has created a useful typology for distinguishing these four types of protection. Imagine, he says, that Thomas Edison wrote a book about the process of incandescence. A copyright would protect Edison's literary or artistic creation, barring others from either copying or distributing his words or any illustrations in his book. But a copyright would not forbid others from using the ideas in the book to create their own electric lights.

If Edison held a patent, however, he would possess "the right to exclude others from making, using, offering for sale, or selling" his invention in the United States or importing the invention into the country. Thus, a patent would give Edison the right to exclude others from using his idea for a set period—in exchange, of course, for publicly disclosing its details. Edison's incentive is that he gets a chance to develop his idea and reap the financial reward during a prescribed period. The public's incentive to make such a grant is that knowledge is advanced by Edison's disclosure.

If Edison wanted to call his lightbulb the "Edison Bulb," he would seek a trademark. That could be either a word, a name, a symbol, or a device to distinguish his idea or product from all others. While others could make and sell lightbulbs if they did not violate Edison's patent, they could not call their product an Edison Bulb. That right would belong to him. Edison could also package his bulb in a distinctive way, and that too would be protected as "trade dressing." Thus, when others sold their bulbs, they could not make or package them to appear as the Edison Bulb.

If Edison chose to keep secret the details of how he made his lightbulb, his customer list, his manufacturing processes, and any special formulas or designs, laws on trade secrets would protect him. But as Siskind points out, if he marketed the product and someone independently took it apart and figured out how his creation was made or worked, Edison would probably lose any legal rights. Coca-Cola has kept its formula secret, but relying on trade secret protections is risky.

Of course, there is much more to each of these basic protections. For instance, there are several types of patents. Utility patents protect useful inventions, methods, and processes. Design patents safeguard unique and ornamental shapes and designs. Patents also are given to those who invent or discover and asexually reproduce a distinct and new variety of plant.

Congress sets the length of protection for each type of intellectual property. Utility and plant patents are generally valid for twenty years from the date of application. Design patents last fourteen years from the date the patent is granted. Copyrighted works registered after 1978 are authorized for the life of the author plus 70 years. Those registered before 1978 are secured for 95 years from the date the copyright was originally granted. For works made for hire—that is, work done by an employee or contractor as part of his or her job—the copyright endures for 95 years from publication or 120 years from creation, whichever is shorter. Trademark rights can exist indefinitely if the owner continues to use the mark and reregisters it every ten years.

These are powerful shelters. The logical question, of course, is that if these rights exist, are embodied in law, and are so powerful, then why is pirating and counterfeiting such a large business?

One answer is that pirating and counterfeiting are largely anonymous crimes. Who knows or can trace the producer, distributor, or even retailer of the counterfeit medicines, faulty aircraft parts, mislabeled clothing, or purloined movies, software, and music CDs? Most often, pirates and counterfeiters try to be phantoms—unseen, unknown, and undetected. In many instances, the FBI reports, they are part of organized crime. One Colombia drug cartel operative supposedly claims that there is more money and far less risk in trafficking counterfeit drugs than in selling cocaine.

Also, the advent of the Internet, cellular phones, and powerful computers has vastly expanded the means and opportunities for intellectual property crimes. Digital production, for example, makes possible the mass manufacturing of optical products (music CDs, computer software, and DVD movies) that are indistinguishable from the original and at a tiny cost per copy. The Internet allows stolen movies, software, and CDs to be shipped intact and speedily anywhere in the world with virtually no chance of detection.

Computer-aided manufacturing helps thieves replicate almost any kind of good and make it appear indistinguishable from the real thing, even if substandard materials and processes are used. Advances in digital imaging and printing, which make even counterfeit currency difficult to detect, are then used to conceal counterfeit goods in bogus packaging identical to the original.

Delivering phony goods, moreover, is no longer a major impediment to the world's intellectual-property pirates. Global shipping is inexpensive and easily available, generally with no questions asked. Customs inspections are rare, and with the end of the Cold War, the rich industrial nations have opened their borders to a massive inflow of legal goods behind which bogus products hide as they move to market. And when counterfeiters and pirates are caught and convicted, the penalties are generally but a tiny cost in a highly profitable business: the seizure of the contraband and maybe a small fine.

Counterfeiting and pirating thrive in many nations in part because intellectual property is alien to their cultures. In India, writing and publishing have long been considered as charitable pursuits and scholars as engaged in a selfless endeavor; their work is created to be freely shared and copied.

This particular crime thrives in many nations because their governments are active participants, willfully blind to the offense. In other instances, national intelligence services steal proprietary information that they pass on to domestic corporations. Several governments require foreign companies to license the use of their technology to domestic firms in exchange for access to their markets. The variations on and opportunities for such coercion seem limitless.

Much of the theft of intellectual properties, however, is committed by individuals and corporations acting for profit, often without the help of their governments. As we will see, few products and industries today are immune to such criminal acts. Nor are these crimes limited to any geographic region or particular groups of nations—though rates vary among countries. It is a global problem, involving virtually every product, every industry, hundreds of millions of customers worldwide, and many billions of dollars annually. More disturbing, such crime promises to be one of the twenty-first century's growth industries.

The growth potential for this crime exists, in large measure, because of a distinctive feature of intellectual property protections: they are of national origin, issued country by country. Consequently, having the protection of a patent, copyright, or trademark in your home country does not automatically mean that your creations are safeguarded elsewhere. Rather, owners of intellectual properties must generally seek protection country by country.

Nor does holding a patent or copyright in another nation mean that its shields are the same as those found in the United States and Europe. Most important, many nations do not provide the means to enforce their trademarks, patents, and copyrights. Their laws are legal niceties, as fake as the goods whose production they facilitate. A few large nations, notably China, that have intellectual property laws on the books promise to enforce those laws, then allow, even encourage, violations. These national differences create major problems for patent, copyright, and trademark holders and major opportunities for pirates and counterfeiters.

By contrast, America's system of intellectual property protections is the strongest in the world, largely because the U.S. has a political culture that emphasizes these rights and provides ample private means to defend them. Though strong, the U.S. system of intellectual property protections did not emerge completely or immediately. The Founding Fathers had false starts, and the system evolved over several decades. It also involved America's theft of other nations' ideas and inventions, the machinations of rapacious entrepreneurs, and bitter, seemingly endless lawsuits. To defend his telephone patent, Alexander Graham Bell and the Bell Telephone System fought more than six hundred lawsuits, all of which they won.

In the American experience, intellectual property is the heart of national development and security. From 1790 until the end of the Cold War, U.S. policy was explicitly directed toward industrial, military, and economic self-sufficiency, all of which depended on the acquisition, creation, and application of innovative technologies. To jump-start America's development process, the Founding Fathers expropriated ideas and technology from the rest of the world without embarrassment, apology, or compensation. A century and a half later, Japan did the same. Today, China is taking that path to development.

In response to this ongoing and massive foreign taking of U.S.–owned intellectual properties, the United States has championed the creation of a new body of international laws and protections, called the Trade Related Intellectual Property System (TRIPS), which is administered by the World Trade Organization (WTO). The initiative for creating TRIPS came from two U.S. corporate CEOs, John R. Opel of IBM and Edmund T. Pratt Jr. of Pfizer pharmaceuticals, more than twenty years ago. Working together and behind the scenes, these two visionaries led a decade-long campaign that in the mid-1990s imposed a U.S.–style system of intellectual property laws on almost all other nations.

If this new global regime works, the protection of intellectual properties owned by Americans and creative people everywhere will be strengthened. It will be one of the twentieth century's great successes in international law and foreign relations. But to be effective, the new system must be developed through use, which is not happening.

Ironically, after leading the long, historic fight to put these global protections into place, Washington is now strangely unwilling to use them. Since June 2000, the U.S. has not filed a single intellectual property case at the World Trade Organization, although the United States Trade Representative has repeatedly documented how, when, and where foreign pirates and counterfeiters, often with the support of their governments, are ravaging U.S.–owned intellectual properties. At the same moment, the domestic federal enforcement of U.S. intellectual property laws has been reduced to the vanishing point as the resources of federal law enforcement agencies were transferred to the war on terrorism and never replaced. Consequently, U.S. intellectual-property owners now stand alone in the fight against what one observer calls "the crime of the twenty-first century."

In a development as significant as TRIPS, the United States sharply transformed its domestic patent and copyright laws in the late 1990s. In a protracted legislative patent war, large corporate interests tried to eliminate vital protections that small inventors relied upon to defend their patents, remove the U.S. Patent and Trademark Office from congressional oversight, eliminate civil service protections for patent examiners, and vest control of the patent function in a private corporation whose directors would be appointed by the president.

Simultaneously, advocates of copyright change worked to lengthen the duration of copyrights and expand corporate control of the Internet. One unintended consequence of the copyright battle is that much of the knowledge created in the last seventy-five years of the twentieth century is now locked up in copyrighted works whose ownership is unknown, that produce few if any royalties, are not digitalized, and thus remain largely unavailable to most potential users. Were the commercially inactive portions of that knowledge base released into the public domain, existing computer technology could easily deliver it to the fingertips of anyone connected to the Internet.

Intellectual property issues are far from dull. They involve some of the most interesting and creative ideas and people in the world. More important, these issues lie at the very core of today's global power politics—the endless contest for wealth and influence.

Americans, who make up less than 5 percent of the world's population, create a majority of its innovations. The experiences of these creative, fascinating, and sometimes odd people have shaped much of what is called the "American system of innovation."

PART I

THE AMERICAN
EXPERIENCE

CHAPTER 1

THE GOLDEN COVENANT

Manhattan's 30,000 citizens were awakened on the morning of April 30, 1789, by the roar of cannons. But this day the gunfire was not for war, but to celebrate George Washington's inauguration as the first president of the United States.

Soon after 10:30 a.m., the president-elect, led by a joint congressional committee, appeared in Lower Manhattan at Federal Hall (formerly City Hall), which was serving as the new nation's temporary capitol. Washington was dressed in a brown suit of homespun broadcloth—a gift from the Hartford Woolen Manufactory, a small mill in Connecticut. Before the Revolutionary War, this wealthy Virginia planter had had his suits made of silk and velvet by London's finest tailors. But now he wore a simple American-made suit—his personal gesture of support for domestic manufacturing. Yet the new president's appearance was far from drab. His suit was adorned with brass buttons embossed with the new national symbol, the bald eagle, and his cuffs had a row of studs, each marked with thirteen stars, symbolizing the founding states. Washington's overture was widely noted in the nation's newspapers, which reported that everything he wore that day had been made in the United States.

George Washington's support of domestic manufacturing was not some passing political sop to a special interest group. Rather, his position had been forged by eight hard years of Revolutionary War experiences and huge debts to European suppliers and financiers.

Several times, Washington's army almost lost the war because ammunition was in short supply. In the first year, soldiers often went into battle with no more than nine cartridges each. At the battle of Bunker Hill, the Americans quickly ran out of ammunition, finishing the fight by clubbing the English troops with the butt ends of their muskets. Thousands of Washington's troops spent the winter of 1777–78 at Valley Forge, Pennsylvania, with no shoes for their feet, few clothes, and not enough blankets to keep out the cold. In a letter dated December 23, 1777, a desperate Washington wrote to the Continental Congress that he had "no less than two thousand eight hundred and ninety-nine men in camp unfit for duty, because they are barefoot and otherwise naked."

From the beginning of the war, Washington's army lacked guns, gunpowder, rope, sails, shoes, and clothes, among many other military necessities, largely because Great Britain had long prohibited most manufacturing in its American colonies. Instead, the mother country restricted colonial production to timber, furs, minerals, and agricultural goods. Thus, the U.S. economy was overwhelmingly agricultural when war came, with more than 94 percent of the population living on farms. After independence was declared, the new nation had to buy its war matériel from the Dutch, French, and other European suppliers, and do that largely on credit. Any nation that sold goods to the American colonials risked a conflict with Britain, then the world's foremost military power. And when British leaders said they would hang any of the revolutionary leaders they captured, the threat was real, making government service a bit riskier than it is today.

In late 1776, a distressed Continental Congress sent Benjamin Franklin, the best-known American, to Paris to seek French support and goods. His list of purchases in 1777 illustrates just how little manufacturing capacity America had. He bought 80,000 shirts, 80,000 blankets, 100 tons of powder, 100 tons of saltpeter, 8 ships of the line, muskets, and 100 fieldpieces. Then Franklin arranged for smugglers to carry the goods across the Atlantic Ocean in a 4,000-mile, three-month journey to St. Eustatius, a Dutch island in the Caribbean, where smugglers received the supplies and slipped them through the British naval blockade and into the colonies, a 1,400-mile trip that consumed another five to six weeks.

For eight years, Washington and the Continental Congress struggled to obtain enough materials for their troops. By war's end, the need for U.S. military and industrial self-sufficiency was seared into their consciousness. For Washington, wearing a plain brown suit of American-made broadcloth on Inauguration Day was a small sacrifice that sent a large message to his fellow citizens.

Before taking office, Washington informed Thomas Jefferson, the man who would soon be secretary of state, that the development of manufacturing and inland navigation would be his greatest concern as president. As the historian Doron S. Ben-Atar reveals in his 2004 book *Trade Secrets*, Washington was a strong proponent of importing European technicians, and in his first State of the Union message, he also encouraged the introduction of foreign technology. In his many speeches, Washington "voiced the widespread expectation that the federal government would devote its energies to industrial development."

After assuming the presidency, Washington and the Congress moved quickly to reduce America's dependence on other nations for its national security needs. Action was imperative, because as the Revolution's leaders had seen, today's allies often become tomorrow's enemies. In that quest for self-sufficiency, Washington turned to Alexander Hamilton, a loyal, brave, and brilliant aide who had led a bayonet attack at Yorktown. Far more foresighted than most of his contemporaries, Hamilton envisioned an economic and political structure for a post-Revolution America. When Washington appointed him secretary of the Treasury, Hamilton was ready with recommendations. In January 1790, he presented Washington and Congress a white paper titled "Report on Public Credit," which outlined the actions necessary to make the new nation appear creditworthy to foreign investors, including a controversial recommendation to pay off all the state debts incurred during the Revolution. At almost the same time as it received Hamilton's credit report, Congress ordered him to prepare a report on manufactures that would "render the United States, independent on foreign nations, for military and other essential supplies."

On December 5, 1791, Hamilton submitted to Congress his "Report on Manufactures," which outlined why and how the United States could achieve economic equality with Europe and an industrial self-sufficiency. Building a strong U.S. industrial base, he wrote, " 'tis the next great work to be accomplished."

To become a true equal of Europe, Hamilton proposed that the United States follow Europe's lead and erect a tariff wall behind which the American market could develop and American manufactures could prosper. This, he argued, was the only way to confront Europe's manufacturing subsidies, its high tariffs on U.S. imports, and its repeated pattern of dumping goods at artificially low prices in the U.S. market to kill America's infant industries. Without his proposed actions, American manufacturers could never compete fairly, either in Europe or in their own domestic market, Hamilton reasoned.

Behind this tariff wall, the government could provide the protections of a strong patent system, giving inventors and investors a government-guaranteed right to the exclusive use of their innovations for a fixed period. To accelerate national development, Hamilton also wanted to encourage the migration of skilled foreign workers to America. They would bring badly needed abilities and state-of-the-art technology to the new nation. In his report, Hamilton commented favorably on the actions of Samuel Slater, a twenty-one-year-old mechanic who in 1789 had slipped out of England with one of the British textile industry's crown jewels: the secret of how to build and operate a machine that could spin cotton and wool into thread.

Hamilton's message to potential immigrants was loud and clear: bring your nation's industrial secrets to America, gain citizenship, get a patent, be honored, and become wealthy.

One irony of the American Revolution is that most of its leaders were Anglophiles. In the French and Indian Wars, Washington sought a regular commission in the British army but was rejected because of his colonial status. Franklin was the delight of London society until he defended the colonists' rights. And in the years leading up to the Declaration of Independence, Jefferson, Madison, and Monroe, among other revolutionary leaders, thought of themselves as loyal British citizens and sought a course that would allow the colonies to remain a part of Britain.

Even after the Revolutionary War, with all the bitterness it generated, many English traditions and assumptions remained embedded in the hearts and minds of Americans. One of those fundamental notions was that patent and copyright protections encouraged innovation and national development. The appeal of those ideas is understandable, in part because they had an extended history. By the late 1700s, Britain had the longest continuous patent tradition in the world, one whose origins traced back to 1449, when Henry VI issued John of Utynam a letter patent (an open letter with the king's seal) granting the Flemish glassmaker a twenty-year monopoly on the process that produced the windows at Eton College. In exchange, the foreign glassmaker was required to teach English artisans his process.

As former subjects of the English king, the newly minted Americans were familiar with the doctrine of the public interest, as incorporated into Britain's Statute of Monopolies (1624). It gave a fourteen-year monopoly to "the true and first inventor" of new manufactures—a law in effect for more than 150 years before the American Revolution. Likewise, the colonists were familiar with Britain's copyright law, the Statute of Anne, which was enacted in 1710. Under that act, the monopoly power of publishers was weakened and the rights of authors of new works were strengthened with copyright protection for fourteen years, with the possibility of a fourteen-year renewal. And while the Statute of Monopolies did not apply in the colonies, the various colonial governments enacted patent laws that imitated it. After independence and before the ratification of the U.S. Constitution, twelve of the thirteen colonies enacted copyright laws based on the Statute of Anne.

For the leaders of the new nation, the basic concept was simple: patents and copyrights encouraged inventors and authors to produce more new and useful creations. These innovations could help the U.S. progress. And as the details of these creations became public, the general knowledge of the nation would be expanded. The process as a whole could only make life better for most Americans and would help the new nation grow richer and stronger faster. The concept was so fundamental that the Founding Fathers integrated it into the Constitution, believing that the public good fully coincided with the claims of individual authors and inventors. When the "authors and inventors clause" (sometimes called the "progress clause"), drafted by James Madison and Charles Pinckney, was presented for consideration at the Constitutional Convention on September 5, 1787, there was no debate and not a single dissenting vote.

Creating a working system of patents and copyrights was a top priority for George Washington. In his first State of the Union message (January 8, 1790), he recommended that Congress enact legislation to encourage the introduction of new inventions from abroad and foster their creation domestically.

Congress acted quickly, and the president signed the first Patent Act into law on April 10, 1790, and the first Copyright Act less than two months later, on May 31, 1790.

The Patent Act made the issuance of a patent a matter of the highest importance—a function administered by the president and three senior cabinet officers. There was no patent office. Rather, a patent petition was submitted directly to Secretary of State Thomas Jefferson. Then Secretary of War Henry Knox and Attorney General Edmund Randolph reviewed it.

These three constituted a patent board. They established strict rules for obtaining a patent, and on the last Saturday of every month, they met to review applications. If two of the three approved, a patent letter was prepared for the personal signature of President Washington, who then sent it back to Jefferson who, as secretary of state, also signed the letter and then had the Great Seal of the United States affixed. The patentee then had a fourteen-year period during which to exclude others from using the creation. The total cost was roughly $5, which went not to the Treasury but to the clerks who copied and processed the paperwork. Those early patent grants are greatly valued today for their historic signatures.

Jefferson was surprised by the number of innovations inspired by the prospect of a patent. Soon after passage of the 1790 act, more applications and models of inventions were appearing at his office than he and his two colleagues could handle.

As often happens with something new in government, the first patent act was a false start, and Jefferson knew it. He urged Congress to alter the "whole train of business and put it on a more easy footing." To that end, he drafted legislation and sent it to his congressional allies in February 1791. Jefferson's escape from the patent board, however, was delayed for more than a year as Congress repeatedly postponed any vote on his or any other patent reform proposal. Meanwhile, the board was obligated to carry out its duties.

In 1792 Jefferson wrote his old friend Congressman Hugh Williamson of North Carolina that of all the duties ever imposed on him, reviewing patent applications consumed his time the most and gave him the most "poignant mortification."

By early 1793, only 57 patents had been issued and 114 applications were pending, while dozens of others had been denied. Inventors hated the system; it delayed consideration of their applications and imposed such scrutiny that for every one approved, another was denied. The board abhorred the process because it had neither the time nor the resources to meet its obligations.

Eventually, Congress enacted the Patent Act of 1793, without most of Jefferson's recommendations. What emerged was legislation that sharply changed the patent system from one with strict rules to one with virtually no rules. Congress allowed inventors to register their inventions with the State Department without an examination. The courts were assigned the responsibility of sorting out which patents were legitimate and which were not.

Not surprisingly, with such lax rules the number of applications and issuances rose. Between 1793 and 1836, when the patent laws were next altered, more than 9,500 patents were issued. In such a lenient environment, piracy flourished.

Many applicants went to the State Department, where models of inventions were found, bought a copy of a patent, duplicated it, and then filed an application for the same invention. Often, the same idea was patented multiple times. The owners of the later grants would enter business, telling others they had the exclusive use of an innovation, or take the official documents to unsuspecting licensees and investors for money. In other situations, an inventor would create an innovation, unaware of the advances of others, secure a patent, and sincerely believe that the conception was his alone. The result was a patent holder's nightmare and a lawyer's dream. The courts were soon clogged with lawsuits.

In the end, the most important feature of the Patent Act of 1793 was what it did not provide: protections for foreign inventors. Only American citizens were eligible for a U.S. patent. Thus, any American could bring a foreign innovation to the United States and commercialize the idea, all with total legal immunity.

In 1800, the law was amended to allow foreigners who had resided in the United States for two years to obtain patents, subject to an oath that the ideas they were attempting to patent had not previously been known or used in the United States or abroad. The oath, of course, was meaningless. In 1832, the law was changed to permit the issuance of a patent to those resident aliens who gave an oath declaring their intention to become U.S. citizens. They also had to work the patent inside the United States within twelve months, or it would be voided.

Because of these discriminatory laws, between 1793 and 1836 the U.S. government issued patents only to foreign citizens who worked in America, had alien status, or swore an oath to take citizenship. In 1836, Congress finally gave foreigners the right to obtain a U.S. patent without such restrictions. But even then, the system remained discriminatory. By law, a U.S. citizen, or an alien declaring his or her intention to become a citizen, paid a patent application fee of $30. Citizens of all other nations, except those of the British Empire, were charged $300. Subjects of the king of Great Britain paid $500. Apparently, some old wounds had not yet healed.

Hamilton and Congress wanted to rapidly industrialize the United States and do so by whatever means necessary—a practice we now call "nation building." America thus became, by national policy and legislative act, the world's premier legal sanctuary for industrial pirates.

The benefits of sanctuary, moreover, were not limited to foreign technicians and craftspeople willing to bring technology to America. It also worked well for those Americans bold and capable enough to steal foreign industrial secrets and bring them back to the United States. Among the foremost of these spies, and certainly one of the most influential in early American history, according to industrial espionage expert John Fialka, author of *War by Other Means: Economic Espionage in America,* was Francis Cabot Lowell, a cultured Boston entrepreneur.

In 1810, the thirty-five-year-old Lowell set out to steal one of the foremost industrial secrets of that age: the plans of the British textile industry's Cartwright loom. In such locales as Edinburgh, Lancashire, and Derbyshire, textile makers were spinning cotton and wool into thread and then weaving the thread into cloth with water-powered, mechanical looms—an economic alchemy that transformed cotton and wool into gold for England. The secrets of this technology were so precious that British law forbade the export of the machinery, the making or selling of drawings of that equipment, and the emigration of the skilled workers.

Thanks to Samuel Slater, who brought the secret of England's automated spinning machines across the ocean, America knew how to turn cotton fibers into thread mechanically. But the nation did not know how the power loom worked or how to machine-weave thread into cloth in the vast quantities that it made possible.

No *Mission: Impossible* adventure was better planned or executed than Lowell's caper. First, he developed a cover story for his trip to England: his health was bad, and his doctor prescribed a foreign tour for relaxation and recuperation. While the idea of touring cold, dank nineteenth-century British mills where the air was filled with lint might seem an improbable cure for any affliction, Lowell was a major American merchant shipper, and his Boston pedigree was impeccable. To allay the suspicions of his intended victims, he took his wife and young children with him to England, stayed in the best hotels, and toured the countryside in an elegant rented carriage.

British textile producers welcomed the touring American importer, proudly showing him whatever he wanted to see in their factories— something they never did for their local competitors. The idea of a proper Bostonian, a Harvard graduate, a rich shipping merchant being an industrial spy out to steal their manufacturing processes was simply ridiculous.

What his British hosts did not realize was that Lowell possessed an almost photographic memory and that he shared their avaricious economic attitudes. Nor did they know that after each day's tour, he would return to his room and carefully draw out what he had just been shown and record the details of his conversations. Eventually, Lowell accumulated from his British hosts all the technical information he needed to build a fully integrated textile mill—one that could take cotton bales in one end and ship finished cloth out the other. How he got the plans out of England remains unknown. His bags were searched twice, but nothing was ever found.

On returning to Boston, Lowell and his brother-in-law, Patrick Tracy Jackson, raised $100,000 in capital and created the Boston Manufacturing Company. They then bought an existing building just outside Boston near Waltham, a facility with a ten-foot waterfall, to power their first mill. Working with a hired mechanic, Lowell constructed a prototype mill and a power loom that were superior to the British versions he copied. His company was an immediate success. Lowell then built a group of mills at a village that eventually was named after him. Soon the Boston Manufacturing Company was weaving more than one-third of a mile of cloth per day, a feat that was as extraordinary then as going to Mars would be today.

By the time Lowell began to build his first factory, America was again at war with the British. Instantly, he became a hero for bringing America England's most valuable industrial secret. After the war, the British moved to destroy their new U.S. competitors, using the old technique of selling their goods in the U.S. market for far less than Lowell's production costs—a predatory practice called "dumping." The British used cotton produced in India with cheap labor, brought it to England, mechanically spun it into thread and wove the thread into cloth, and then shipped it to America. The English product was not only less expensive; it was of better quality, reflecting greater experience.

Lowell and his U.S. colleagues responded as Hamilton had foreseen. In 1815, they enlisted the political help of Massachusetts Senator Daniel Webster, who was not a strong supporter of protective tariffs. But he did believe that the United States required self-sufficiency in manufactured goods if it was to prosper. That could not be if English and European producers were allowed to dump their goods on the U.S. market and kill America's infant industries. In 1816, Webster, working with Senator John Calhoun of South Carolina, who represented a major cotton-producing state, pushed through Congress a protective tariff on cotton and woolen imports of 30 percent for two years, 25 percent for another two years, and 20 percent thereafter. This gave the infant U.S. textile industry a market all its own and the time to grow. American cotton producers were also given a market: American textile makers. And those who truly wanted foreign goods could continue buying them, but at a higher cost and with the import duties going to the U.S. Treasury. It was Webster and Calhoun's legislation, but it was Hamilton's plan in action.

Apparently, Lowell's health was indeed bad, for he died in 1817 at age forty-two, but by then he and his partners had established larger and better factories. Today, Lowell is primarily remembered for installing the first power loom in the United States; where and how he got the plans is largely forgotten. Yet he improved on something else he acquired in England, something even more important than the Cartwright loom: a culture of manufacturing.

When Samuel Slater opened his factory in the early 1790s, he transplanted the English industrial culture that he knew, one in which women and children were employed in the most miserable of circumstances. Slater's first mill was staffed with children ages seven to twelve, who worked from sunrise to sundown in an unheated factory for less than $1 per week. While most Americans were pleased to have the English technology, few admired England's manufacturing culture, which was seen as degrading, immoral, and fit only for the lowest class of people.

Lowell was shrewder than Slater. He refined the manufacturing culture in a way that made it attractive to Americans. In what is still called "the Lowell Experiment," he staffed his factory with young farm women, but not just any farm women. Lowell announced that he hired only women of good moral character. The company, moreover, fired any worker guilty of "smoking, drinking, lying, swearing, or any other immoral conduct." He built dormitories for his workers, provided them with nourishing meals, offered lectures and other cultural events, required that they attend church, and closely chaperoned them. Fathers were invited to inspect the operations. The mill girls, as they were known, were paid in cash, not company store credit as British workers were, and their tenure was usually limited to three years. Most farm girls of that era were accustomed to long hours, and for most, work at the Boston Manufacturing Company meant a distinct improvement in their lives. Many used the money they saved as dowries. Others supplemented the income of their families. And most did not wish to leave at the end of their three years.

America was fertile ground for the type of manufacturing culture that Lowell introduced. Large farm families often needed the supplemental income that the mill girls provided, and few comparable opportunities existed for women. The work was honorable and the environment respectable to a people who were deeply religious. Francis Cabot Lowell understood all this, which allowed him to break the American prejudice against factory work.

In England, with its rigid class system, a working-class person, even one with a superior idea, had little chance to secure capital and build a thriving business. America was different. Talented, ambitious people of whatever class were admired and manufacturing came to be seen as a route to riches. And for capitalists, Lowell furnished a model of how to raise money through limited-risk investment in a corporation and the potentials of mass production. With Francis Lowell and the Boston Manufacturing Company, the industrial revolution truly came to America, and the world thereafter would never be the same.

Within a quarter century of Lowell's tour of English mills, America was well on its way to becoming a major industrial power. Its inventors were creating one innovation after another and manufacturing was by then well established, though often it was not practiced as wisely or humanely as in the Lowell Experiment. Moreover, by the 1830s American inventions were being pirated in other nations. The time had arrived to tighten America's patent laws.

Any new patent law had to be more flexible than the 1790 act but at the same time more rigorous than the 1793 act, under which a patent was simply registered. And patents needed to be made available to foreigners, if for no other reason than that their governments would provide reciprocal protections to American inventors. What emerged out of that necessity was the Patent Act of 1836, which became the foundation of the modern system. Congress authorized the appointment of a commissioner of patents, who was empowered to reject applications that lacked novelty, and gave inventors the right of appeal that would be heard by impartial but skilled arbitrators. The act also provided for a major library of scientific works and clerks, technicians, and examiners who could compare applications with existing technology to ensure that they were truly advances. Also, the patent went to the first person to create the advance, and with it the right for the exclusive use of that creation for fourteen years from the date the patent was issued. In 1842, the system was strengthened further when Congress expanded the laws to cover new and original "designs for manufacture." Finally, the United States had a patent system that truly encouraged novelty and rewarded merit. With a patent on a commercially attractive idea, inventors could assure investors that for a set time only they could exploit their new creation.

Looking backward, the Patent Act of 1836 marked another divide in U.S. economic history. By making patents real, the legislation unleashed the innovative capacities of an entire nation on a scale never before attempted. Regardless of social position, education, or economic condition, any citizen who invented something novel and useful could be awarded exclusive rights for its use and commercialization. Many of the ideas that were pouring forth represented fundamental breakthroughs that profoundly changed the way the U.S. economy worked. For example:

- In 1837, Thomas Davenport built an electric motor that could power shop machinery, thus creating power tools.

- In 1840, John Rand invented the collapsible metal squeeze tube, which could be used to hold and dispense liquefied materials such as toothpaste and artist's pigments.

- In 1842, Crawford Williamson Long performed the first medical operation using an ether-based anesthesia—painless surgery.

- In 1844, Charles Goodyear was granted a patent on a process for "vulcanizing" rubber, creating a pliable material unaffected by temperature.

- In 1846, Richard Hoe invented the cylinder printing press, revolutionizing printing.

- In 1854, Elisha Graves Otis demonstrated, at the Crystal Palace Exposition in New York, his new safety braking system by cutting the cables on an elevator as it reached the top of a three-hundred-foot tower. Otis was on the elevator. The brakes worked, and Otis lived to create a successful elevator company that transformed urban design worldwide.

Each advance led to a host of improvements and a demand for other goods and services that, in turn, produced entirely new industries. In 1832, Samuel Morse, a portrait painter and professor of literature of art at New

York University, conceived the first practical telegraph, after a trip to Europe where he saw demonstrations of electromagnets, batteries, and the transmission of signals over wire. Morse filed his patent application in 1838, got the patent in 1840, and in 1843 persuaded Congress to appropriate $30,000 to fund construction of a forty-mile experimental telegraph line. On May 11, 1844, from a chamber in the U.S. Supreme Court, Morse sent the now famous message to a small group in the Mount Clair train depot in Baltimore. The message, chosen by the daughter of the U.S. patent commissioner, was the biblical quotation "What hath God wrought."

How appropriate. Before Morse, the fastest way to transmit a message between Washington and Baltimore was by rider on a fast horse or by pigeon. But after the telegraph was put into place, communications were almost instantaneous. The telegraph was the Internet of the nineteenth century, but even more so. It revolutionized business, newspapers, war, shipping, and life. Morse's invention also created a new industry. Within ten years, more than 23,000 miles of telegraph lines crisscrossed the United States, creating a demand for copper wire, poles, insulators, and telegraphs, and for thousands of telegraphers trained in Morse code. By October 1861, the West and East coasts were connected, putting the Pony Express out of business. With the telegraph, news was available within minutes anywhere in the world, including quotes for commodities and stocks. A newspaper reader in California had access to the same late-breaking information as one in New York City, London, Paris, or Calcutta.

Along with the telegraph, advances in steamboats, canals, hard-surface roads, and railroads were transforming transportation and the U.S. economy. Swiftly and with self-assurance, America industrialized.

The British, who created and led the industrial revolution during the first half of the nineteenth century, did not clearly recognize that they had a major economic rival across the Atlantic until the Great Industrial Exhibition was staged in 1851 at London's Crystal Palace. The exhibition was created to highlight British industrial prominence. The surprise, however, was how far American producers had advanced. Among the more than 13,000 items displayed, hundreds were made in the United States. Reapers, threshers, pistols, rifles, machine tools, and locks were among the dozens of products that impressed the British not for their quality, but for the way most were constructed: they were produced with machine-made, interchangeable parts. Five pistols could be disassembled, the parts put into a bin, and five fully workable pistols could be reassembled. Mass production had arrived. Using machinery that often had been invented, patented, and produced in the United States, Americans by the late 1850s were making in volume clocks, watches, furniture, plows, and a host of other goods. Moreover, as the volume increased, prices dropped, making the fruits of innovation accessible to a wide market, which was protected from foreign competition by high tariffs.

British industrialists and their government wanted to know the secret behind what they called the "American system of manufactures." Throughout the 1850s, British delegations regularly came to the United States on inspection tours. As James McPherson writes in *Battle Cry of Freedom,* the British identified four explanations.

First, the United States had a large domestic market, composed of a people who were upwardly mobile, and operated behind a high wall of tariffs, what became known as the "American system of trade." Second, skilled labor was limited, thereby creating a demand for machines that could perform precision work that in Europe was done by artisans. Third, the United States had a plentiful supply of natural resources, particularly wood and water, which provided virtually unlimited industrial power. Wood was also an inexpensive material that Americans could use for production. In addition, the skills needed to make and use woodworking machines were easily transferred to tools that could work metals. Finally, the British concluded, U.S. efficiency and productivity were grounded in the country's education system, which encouraged widespread literacy. People who could read their Bibles and newspapers could read instruction manuals. McPherson reports that "even counting the slaves, nearly four-fifths of the American population was literate in the 1850s." In the New England states, the literacy rate among adults was almost 95 percent.

There was also a fifth reason. As one British observer noted, every American "seems to be continually devising some new thing to assist him in his work, and there is a strong desire . . . to be 'posted up' in every new improvement." Americans were tinkerers. In America, inventions, patents, and commercialization provided a path to riches for those with merit. And the patent system protected their rights, allowing them time to secure financing. Samuel Colt, for instance, traveled the lecture circuit giving demonstrations of laughing gas to finance the development of his revolver, until the War Department gave him an order. Charles Goodyear worked for years in absolute poverty until he perfected his process for vulcanizing rubber. Samuel Morse was literally down to his last dollar by the time Congress approved the Washington-Baltimore demonstration project. Each of these inventors not only created major innovations but subsequently became wealthy and famous.

In these early years of the twenty-first century, when most people are unable to identify any individual inventors, it is difficult to imagine the fame and adulation enjoyed by inventors such as Robert Fulton, Eli Whitney, and Samuel Morse, among dozens of others. Life in the early nineteenth century was hard, even for those with wealth, and the inventions that began to pour forth markedly improved the lives of most Americans. Progress was visible, touchable, and experienced by most Americans. That progress created a spirit, an expectation that each generation of Americans would live better than its predecessors. That prospect, in turn, created an attitude that America was limited only by its imagination, that for the country and its individual citizens almost anything was possible. And it was.

Ultimately, and without quite realizing it, the Founding Fathers and those who later improved the patent system created an "American system of innovation." It worked beyond anyone's imagination. In the span of a lifetime, from the time of the Constitutional Convention to that of the Civil War, the United States went from an agricultural nation, barely advanced from its colonial status, to Britain's principal industrial rival. Moreover, the Civil War accelerated America's industrialization, creating an unprecedented burst of innovation. In those four war years, the U.S. Patent Office in Washington granted more than 16,000 patents, while the Confederate Patent Office in Richmond issued 266.

Throughout the Civil War, the foremost U.S. advocate of inventors was Abraham Lincoln, who remains the only president to practice patent law and the only one to be issued a patent: no. 6469, for a device to lift boats over river shoals. As president, Lincoln worked aggressively to advance telegraphy, railroads, agriculture, artillery, and naval armament. He was the principal advocate for an American steel industry. Under his leadership, the United States authorized the transcontinental railroad, the Land-Grant College Act, and the building of one of the world's first two steel battleships. Lincoln also extended the patent term from fourteen to seventeen years, where it remained until the concluding years of the twentieth century.

When the Civil War ended, America was well on the way to becoming the world's leading industrial power. In the following hundred years, U.S.

inventors revolutionized life and work not only for their own country but also for most of the world with literally millions of new inventions. These innovations, moreover, came in an expanding array of fields, many of which did not even exist in the early nineteenth century, reflecting the growth of basic knowledge. Accordingly, the patent system was severely challenged over time to modify its protections to cover new types of innovations. (It has largely managed to do this.) Since the Civil War, the system has been overhauled more than sixty times, sometimes in important ways.

In 1870, the requirement that inventors submit a working model along with their patent applications was dropped. That same year Congress enacted the Trade-Mark Act, which authorized federal registration of private trademarks. As the name suggests, a trademark is a sign that distinguishes one good or service from another. It can be a picture, such as a "golden arch"; a name, such as "Coke"; a logo, such as a swoosh sign; or some combination of these. The idea of trademarks is not new. Cave drawings show bisons with marks on their flanks like brands indicating ownership. Bricks from First Dynasty Egypt were marked to identify the maker. Ceramics from ancient Greece bear the potter's seal. And, more recently, silver goods made by Paul Revere carried his own special mark.

The 1870 act created the world's first Trade Marks Registry. But in 1879, the Supreme Court ruled the act unconstitutional because it did not distinguish between intrastate and interstate commerce. The Constitution allows regulation of commerce between the states, but not within states.

Immediately after the Supreme Court decision, trademark holders, with liquor producers showing the way, pressured Congress to enact a new trademark bill that would be constitutional. Since the difference in taste between hard liquors is often indistinguishable—at least by inexperienced consumers—the distillers used the shape of their bottles and packaging to differentiate their goods. Absent a trademark, piracy flourished. Other interests faced the same problem. In 1881, Congress responded by enacting a new trademark law, but applied it to export goods only. But that gave no domestic protection.

Trademark owners organized an association and began lobbying the president and the Congress for legislation. The advent of mass advertising was a driving force behind this effort. Beginning in the early twentieth century, companies were spending tens of millions, then hundreds of millions of dollars on style changes, special packaging, and individual logos, all for the purpose of differentiating their products from those of their competitors. But piracy undermined all that.

Eventually, Congress responded by passing the Trademark Act of 1905, which gave Americans their first substantial set of constitutional trademark provisions; these were further strengthened in 1920. In 1946, Congress passed the Lanham Act, which created the modern U.S. trademark system, providing certification for the first-use date, renewal requirements, defensive registrations, and enforcement provisions.

Even as Congress strengthened protections for trademarks, it was also expanding the patent laws to include innovations in new fields. In 1930, the Plant Patent Act was enacted to provide patents on new varieties of asexually produced plants and varieties.

Beginning in the early 1980s, the Patent Office started issuing patents for computer software. Previously, it had viewed software as mathematical algorithms that could not be patented. That view changed after 1981, when the Supreme Court ruled in favor of a patent applicant, paving the way for the Patent Office to grant patents on software. Soon, thousands of software patents were being issued annually.

The idea of patenting software remains bitterly controversial, which reflects the various corporate interests involved as much as any ideology. Before the 1981 decision, for example, IBM, which held more than 70 percent of the U.S. computer market, opposed software patents. It argued that software was such a dynamic field that patents would actually retard innovation. Absent software patents, IBM benefited from what was in the 1950s, '60s, and '70s open source software—that is, software available to all at no charge. Its position was adopted and lobbied for by the various computer and software associations. IBM's stance also came to permeate the thinking of a generation of industry leaders.

However, after the Supreme Court made legal the patenting of software, IBM reversed its strategy. It aggressively moved to patent its innovations in the software field. Annually, IBM is the world's largest recipient of patents, with the most computer-related patents, including software. In the calendar year 2003 alone, IBM was awarded 3,415 patents, more than any other company in history. Altogether, IBM holds more than 40,000 patents worldwide. It is one of the largest non-European patent holders in Europe and one of the largest foreign patent holders in Japan.

In January 2004, the company announced that in the previous eleven years its inventors had received more than 25,000 U.S. patents. In this period, 1993–2003, IBM was awarded more patents than the next nine largest information technology companies combined, including Hewlett-Packard/Compaq, Intel, Sun, Microsoft, Dell, Apple, EMC, Oracle, and EDS. IBM over those eleven years was awarded almost three times more patents than any other information technology company in the world. Bill Gates and Microsoft may attract the most attention, but IBM gets the most patents.

Through its software patents, IBM is able to maintain its strong role in the computer industry. Others must license from IBM or risk lawsuits. Moreover, it is willing to cross-license its technology in exchange for a license on other technology. IBM makes more than $1 billion annually from the proceeds, an amount that is increasing over time, reflecting its growing portfolio of patented software. The only way for competing computer companies to confront such political and economic power is to purchase IBM's licenses while aggressively seeking their own patents, which can then be used as barter with IBM and others in the industry.

America's copyright laws have a more roguish history than those dealing with patents. In part, this is because the Articles of Confederation provided no copyright protections—that responsibility was left to the individual states. Noah Webster, a young schoolmaster and author, led the efforts that filled that national void.

Webster, whose father was a weaver and farmer, was a prodigy, entering Yale at the age of sixteen in 1774. Upon graduation and with no money, he became an educator, first teaching in Connecticut schools. During the Revolutionary War, his students were largely without books, and securing more from England was both expensive and difficult. Webster's ambitious response was to create a new system of education, one that would provide all Americans with the intellectual skills they needed to govern themselves.

But first Webster had to create educational materials that Americans could use. Between 1783 and 1785, he published *A Grammatical Institute of the English Language,* a three-part collection of a spelling book, a grammar, and a reader. The spelling book was known as the "Blue-Backed Speller" or the "Old Blue Back" because of the color of its cover. For more than a century, a vast number of Americans learned their ABCs from Webster's books. Webster's problem was how to keep pirates from making unauthorized duplicates of his books. America had no copyright laws immediately after the Revolutionary War, which meant that Webster had no recourse whenever his ideas and creations were stolen.

Webster responded by getting on his horse (literally), going to the capitals of the thirteen newly formed state governments, and lobbying for enactment of copyright protections. He took with him model legislation, which imitated Britain's Statute of Anne. Connecticut adopted the first state copyright law in 1783. By the time of the Constitutional Convention in 1787, all of the states except Vermont had enacted copyright laws. The state laws in Maryland and Pennsylvania, however, never took effect because they contained a provision that required "all and every of the States" to pass similar laws before theirs became active. The chaos surrounding the enactment of twelve different state copyright laws highlighted the need for a uniform federal statute.

Noah Webster is truly the father of U.S. copyright. His motive was self-interest, but it resulted in widespread benefits to authors. The royalties from his three textbooks and his dictionary, which amounted to about one penny per book, sustained him and his family for the rest of his life.

While lobbying for passage of the state copyright laws, Webster became acquainted with many national leaders, particularly Benjamin Franklin. He also evolved into one of America's foremost pamphleteers, defining for the public the principles that should be incorporated into a new constitution. Naturally, he strongly advocated inclusion of a copyright provision and, later, legislation to bring that protection to life. The result of his efforts is the first Copyright Act, signed into law on May 31, 1790, which provided federal protections for copies of maps, charts, and books, and to the authors and proprietors of such copies. As with Britain's law, the act gave fourteen years of protection, with the right of renewal for another fourteen years. Notably, only the works of U.S. citizens were protected until 1891, when U.S. copyright coverage was expanded to foreign authors and publishers. Ironically, the first copyright issued in the United States was for *The Philadelphia Spelling Book* by John Barry, one of Webster's principal rivals.

While the Copyright Act of 1790 prohibited the piracy of works copyrighted by U.S. citizens, it also encouraged the theft of copyrighted foreign materials. In part, such overt discrimination reflected a certain duality: Americans wanted to build their own culture, one based on their own books, art, and creations, and they wanted foreign copyrighted works on the cheap. In the early nineteenth century, congressional refusal to extend copyright protection to foreign works was not highly controversial in the United States. Readers got access to European writers at a cheap price, and U.S. publishers could establish themselves with modest costs. Conversely, in the absence of a copyright agreement between the two nations, British publishers issued the works of U.S. writers without paying either the author or the American publisher, though the flow of literary works from the U.S. to England was small at this time. The attitude of many British readers then was summed up in the sneer of one wit: "And just who would want to read the works of an American author?"

British and other foreign authors, of course, had a different view about this absence of U.S. protections. Charles Dickens and Anthony Trollope, whose works were immensely popular in the United States, felt perpetually robbed by American publishers, and they were. Pirated copies of Dickens's *A Christmas Carol* sold for as little as 6 cents in the U.S. at the same time as they were selling for the equivalent of $2.50 in Great Britain. Dickens lobbied his American audience and the U.S. Congress for an international copyright, ironically noting "the exquisite justice of never deriving sixpence from an enormous American sale of all my books." Trollope ridiculed the argument made by those who opposed the parochial U.S. position that American readers were the gainers when U.S. publishers appropriated the works of others because they came "not from the people, but from the book-selling leviathans, and from those politicians whom the leviathans are able to attach to their interests."

Gradually, American attitudes changed. By 1837, Henry Clay was actively advocating the idea of an international copyright. His argument was that allowing U.S. publishers to deny payments to foreign authors encouraged them to ignore talented American writers to whom they would be legally obliged to pay royalties. By then, America had produced its own literary class, writers of consequence whose works foreign publishers were pirating. Henry Wadsworth Longfellow, Horace Greeley, Ralph Waldo Emerson, and Louisa May Alcott, among many others, had proceeds from sales of their books stolen because their country refused to accept an international copyright.

The cost to American authors was staggering. Harriet Beecher Stowe's *Uncle Tom's Cabin* was a worldwide best seller. The book was published in April 1852; more than 300,000 copies had been sold in the U.S. by the end of the year. Yet 1,500,000 pirated copies were sold in Great Britain and the British colonies in 1852 alone. Eventually, pirated copies were also sold in more than twenty other nations. Stowe received not a penny for those foreign sales; she lost more than $200,000 in royalties—a fortune then. Samuel Clemens, who published as Mark Twain, was particularly incensed by this piracy, both because it encouraged U.S. publishers to ignore American writers and because those Americans talented enough to be published were having their works stolen by foreign pirates. In the fall of 1872, Twain reported that while traveling by train from Liverpool to London he sat across from a man reading a pirated copy of *Innocents Abroad.* According to Fred Kaplan, author of *The Singular Mark Twain,* despite being uncompensated, the American humorist was pleased to see a fellow traveler reading his book, though he found it odd that the expression on the man's face never changed.

Twain developed a special loathing for Canada's pirate publishers. In 1876, Toronto publisher Charles Belford printed and distributed *Tom Sawyer* before the American edition came out, costing Twain his British royalties on the book. Fortunately for Twain, British law allowed foreign authors to obtain a British Empire copyright if they were physically on British or British Commonwealth soil for two specific days: the day of publication and the day before. Though the trip was a burden, Clemens went to Montreal for a couple of days in 1881 to get British Empire copyright protections for *The Prince and the Pauper.*

Despite petitions to Congress from prominent writers, such as Benjamin Disraeli and Mark Twain, legalized literary piracy was U.S. policy. Rather than adopt an international copyright, Congress added insult to injury at the end of the Civil War, imposing a 25 percent tariff on imported books, thereby increasing revenues for the government while paying foreign authors nothing. Literary piracy remained U.S. policy until 1891, when Congress enacted legislation authorizing copyright relations with other nations— and even that step had its limits. Congress confined copyright protections of foreign works to those manufactured in the United States, largely because of pressure from the printing unions. This "manufacturing clause" remained law until 1986.

In the more than two hundred years between the founding of the United States and the elimination of the manufacturing clause, the scope of U.S. copyright laws was repeatedly deepened and broadened as Congress expanded its protections for domestic owners and finally for all copyright holders.

- In 1802, prints were added to the protected works.

- In 1831, music was included and the term of copyright protection was extended to twenty-eight years with the privilege of renewal for another fourteen years.

- In 1856, dramatic compositions were covered.

- In 1865, photographs received protection.

- In 1870, works of art were added. Also, the copyright functions, including registration, were shifted from the courts to the Library of Congress, where they remain today.

- In 1891, authors got the right to certain derivative works, including translations and dramatizations.

In the early twentieth century, copyright protections were expanded even further to keep pace with technology. Thus, Congress extended the copyright to movies, sound recordings, and nondramatic literary works.

In the late 1970s and early 1980s, piracy of U.S.–produced semiconductor designs flourished. Again Congress acted, creating the Semiconductor Chip Protection Act of 1984, which permitted the copyrighting of the three-dimensional images or patterns fixed in the product—that is, the mask. While others are permitted to reverse engineer the work embodied in the mask and incorporate that knowledge in another original work, they are prohibited from duplicating and commercializing it. Once again, original works are protected, while practical knowledge is advanced.

In 1990, Congress passed several major copyright bills. One gave the owners of copyrighted computer programs the exclusive right to authorize and set the terms for the rental, lease, or lending of their programs. Consequently, most software today is made available as a "lease" or "rental" with severe penalties for unauthorized duplication. Another bill extended copyright protection to architectural designs and granted visual artists moral rights of attribution and integrity.

In 1998, two historic changes were made in U.S. copyright laws. In the Digital Millennium Copyright Act, a far-extending global copyright treaty was ratified. Together, that legislation and treaty provide substantial protections for copyright holders, even as they sharply limit domestic fair use standards and expand the means to collect fees from copyright users. In the Sonny Bono Act, copyright protections on both new and existing works were extended for twenty years. Both acts were, and remain, highly controversial, as we shall see in later chapters.

In retrospect, the logical question is just how important technological advances were to America's development over the past two centuries. The answer is that they were vital. The cotton gin, interchangeable parts, the telegraph, electricity for the home and factory, mass production techniques, the airplane, and the television, among millions of innovations, each profoundly changed the nature of work and life, not only in the United States but throughout the world. And while two centuries seems to be a long time, it is short in the context of world history. More than 50,000 Americans now living, those 100 years and older, have been here for half that time, experiencing the benefits and costs created by the American system of innovation.

But we do not have to rely wholly on anecdotes. Economists have attempted to measure the effects of technology on the American economy. The studies are distinguished by the use of differing techniques, different periods, and different parameters. The constant in most of these studies is that each used three basic factors—labor, capital, and technology—apportioning to each its relative contribution.

Nobel Prize winner Robert Solow of Harvard University found in his work that technological advancement, coupled with increased human capital improvements in the labor force, accounted for between 80 and 90 percent of the annual productivity increase in the U.S. economy between 1909 and 1949. Edward Dennison of George Washington University concluded that in the period 1929–1982 more than two-thirds of the productivity gains were due to advances in science and technology.

Whether the precise numbers of those studies are correct, the important point made by each is that progress in knowledge and innovations was the primary factor behind the growth of America's economic productivity. And while quarrels continue among economists, historians, lawyers, and politicians as to the details of the American system of innovation—that is, Are patent terms too long or short? Is copyright coverage too broad or narrow? Are trademarks useful or not?—the fact remains that the Founding Fathers created a system of innovation that has worked better than any other in the history of the world.

CHAPTER 2

THE AMERICAN SYSTEM

W‌hat are the three greatest inventions and discoveries in world history?

In 1859, Abraham Lincoln, a prominent Illinois railroad lawyer and unsuccessful politician, said they were "the arts of writing and of printing, the discovery of America, and the introduction of Patent-laws." Writing, coupled with printing, he said, allowed us to communicate across time and space, preserve and spread the seeds of invention, and bring thousands of minds to a field where once there was but one. The discovery of America, he said, swept away "the dust of ages—real downright old-fogyism" that seemed to "settle upon, and smother the intellects and energies of man." America was different, for here, thought was emancipated, the advancement of civilization and arts was encouraged, and its creators were rewarded. Finally, patents secured to the inventor, for a limited time, the exclusive use of their invention and "thereby added the fuel of *interest* to the *fire* of genius, in the discovery and production of new and useful things."

When Lincoln gave his "Lecture on Discoveries and Inventions" in 1858, the United States had a fully functioning patent system and the concept of intellectual property rights was deeply engrained in the national consciousness as natural and beneficial.

Yet there was a catch, both then and now. For these rights to have meaning, Congress must define them with legislation that sets bounds, obligations, procedures, and penalties. While the "authors and inventors" provision of the Constitution remains unaltered more than two centuries after its ratification, those rights have been repeatedly redefined by legislation—and the courts have continued to redefine the meaning of that legislation. The result is a vibrant U.S. intellectual property "system," one constantly evolving in response to changed circumstances and unexpected innovations.

Importantly, in America the primary responsibility for enforcement of intellectual property rights resides with the holder of such rights. Neither the Patent Office nor the U.S. attorney general assumes or has that duty. Rather, the government provides a set of laws defining such rights, a body of precedents, and an open federal court system where disputes may be tried, and police who enforce the court's decisions. This is a most potent combination. And unlike trade and other laws that assign government the power to decide whether, when, and how to initiate action and decide what is an acceptable outcome, for domestic cases this "American system" puts that authority with the holder of the patent, copyright, trademark, or trade secret. That, too, is potent. As the U.S. economy has become increasingly entwined with the global economy, American diplomats and trade negotiators have worked to persuade other governments to adopt the American system of intellectual property protections, which ultimately depends on the right of private action.

This intellectual property structure and division of powers did not spring forth whole; it has evolved over more than two centuries. The experiences of three great nineteenth-century American inventors—Eli Whitney, Alexander Graham Bell, and Thomas Edison—illuminate that evolution. Each made enormous contributions to life and knowledge, and all were deeply involved with patents and patent litigation. Their experiences illustrate the intent of those who put the "authors and inventors" clause into the Constitution, the difficulties of transforming that intent into reality, the fundamentals of America's intellectual property laws, and the various patent strategies inventors and companies devised to defend their rights and gain advantage.

The legend about Eli Whitney is that he invented the cotton gin, the milling machine, and the "American system of manufacturing," which uses interchangeable parts. The real Whitney story is different but far more interesting. Whitney did invent the cotton gin, but he went broke trying to enforce his patent on it. He kept his creditors at bay with monies from a large government contract to produce muskets made from interchangeable parts. But he delivered the arms more than seven years late and the factory he built to produce them could not make interchangeable components. And he adapted milling and assembly techniques invented by others. Nevertheless, Eli Whitney revolutionized U.S. manufacturing in ways that persist even today.

Whitney was a tinkerer and a skilled mechanic. He was Mark Twain's model for the Connecticut Yankee in King Arthur's court, a nineteenth-century "MacGyver" who could fix or invent anything. During the Revolutionary War, the teenaged Whitney, son of a prosperous Connecticut farmer, made money by forging and selling nails, a product previously imported from England. He did well in that business but wanted more from life. At the age of nineteen, he decided to become a lawyer. He prepared himself for college by attending Leicester Academy for almost four years. He entered Yale in 1789 at the age of twenty-three.

Whitney paid for his Yale schooling with cash gifts from his father, by borrowing money from others, by manufacturing hat pins for women and walking sticks for men, and by coloring the outlines of divisions on maps for other Yale students. Not unlike many of today's college graduates, Whitney finished Yale in debt, but his prospects were good. Yale president Ezra Stiles found Whitney a position as a teacher in New York City, but during graduation week, the offer was withdrawn. Fortunately for Whitney, Stiles knew of another job. He had been asked by Yale alumnus Phineas Miller to locate a private tutor for the children of a Major Dupont, a wealthy South Carolina plantation owner. The position was offered to Whitney, and he quickly accepted. Miller, the overseer of a large Georgia plantation, was in New York with his employer, Catharine (Kitty) Greene, the thirty-six-year-old widow of Revolutionary War hero Nathanael Greene. Whitney knew neither, nor had he ever been to the South. Miller graciously invited him to come to New York, from which the three travelers would sail together to Savannah.

The trip was a nightmare for Whitney. He left New Haven on the regular packet for New York City and immediately became seasick. Worse, in the middle of the night, the ship floundered on the rocks at Hell's Gate, about six miles from the city. Whitney and five other passengers rented a wagon that took them the rest of the way. Once they arrived, Whitney saw an acquaintance, hailed him, shook hands, and then realized that the man had an active case of smallpox, a highly communicable disease that killed roughly 30 percent of its victims.

Fortunately for Whitney, his traveling companion, Kitty Greene, was a caring woman well acquainted with adversity. She refused to leave Whitney alone in New York. She found him a doctor, who inoculated the young teacher with a tiny amount of smallpox spores taken from someone else— an ancient process called variolation that kills only one of every hundred people infected. The technique produces a mild case of the disease, but also makes the patient immune to smallpox for life. Greene and Miller cared for Whitney during the two weeks it took for the spores to do their job. Finally, the three travelers boarded the ship to Savannah. Whitney, a poor sailor, was seasick during the entire seven-day trip. Once again, Greene supervised his care.

When they arrived in Savannah, Kitty Greene invited Whitney to visit her plantation before proceeding to South Carolina and his teaching job. Whitney, who had been raised in a Puritan society, knew no one like Kitty Greene—vivacious, charming, warm, witty, generous, and sweet-tempered— who had been brought up in Rhode Island under the care of an aunt who had taught her all the social graces of that era. She also had courage and grit. When her husband went to winter camp at Valley Forge, Kitty Greene accompanied him and shared the burdens, like Martha Washington. Whitney's biographer, Constance Green, writes of Kitty: "Her gallantry of spirit during the gloomy winter at Valley Forge had fortified her husband and his fellow officers and won her the admiration of General Washington himself. She commanded the devotion of countless friends." One of those was Martha Washington, who nursed Kitty back to health after the difficult birth of her fourth child in January 1780. The young woman's spirit is illustrated by her challenge to the commanding general, a legendary dancer, to a dance-until-you-drop marathon. To the delight of the officers and their wives attending the party at Bound Brook, the winter encampment in 1779, Washington danced with Kitty Greene for a solid three hours. Bruce Chadwick, a Washington biographer and a discreet scholar, does not reveal which of the dancers called a halt, which suggests that it was Washington.

During the war, Nathanael Greene, scion of a wealthy Rhode Island family, had liquidated most of his fortune, even selling his home, using the monies to feed, arm, and clothe his troops—expenses Congress refused to reimburse. The state of Georgia was more grateful. After the war, it gave the general a plantation near Savannah named Mulberry Grove. The gift, however, was a mixed blessing; after ten years of war-related neglect, the estate was dilapidated. Faced with the need to make a living, the war hero took possession of the estate. Refusing to own slaves, Greene worked himself to death, dying of heatstroke at the age of forty-four in 1786, leaving his thirty-one-year-old widow with five children and a debt-ridden, money-losing plantation. When Whitney arrived in 1793, Phineas Miller, overseer of the estate, was trying to pay the plantation's debts by pulling out the mulberry trees, which were once used to produce silk, and using the land to grow corn and rice.

Whitney, who intended to stay with his new friends for only four or five days, made Greene a special house gift: a new tambour, a frame to hold her needlepoint. A clever and observant person, Greene asked her new friend if he could design and make a machine that could clean raw cotton of its seed.

The problem faced by southern cotton producers was that the green cotton they were raising had short strands with seeds firmly attached to the fiber. The fiber was valuable, but only without the seeds. Moreover, removing the seeds had to be done laboriously by hand: one worker could produce about one pound of fiber per day. Machines from India, called charkas, pulled cotton through two wire rollers to dislodge seeds from long-staple cotton, but even that was a hard, slow process.

The challenge Greene put before Whitney was an ancient one. More than 3,500 years ago, weavers in India were producing closely woven, sheer cotton textiles. Alexander the Great introduced cotton into Europe; he called it the "vegetable wool." South American producers may have been growing cotton even before there were weavers in India. All had faced the same insolvable problem: the cotton plant was easy to grow and easy to harvest, but the fiber was difficult to separate from the seeds. Consequently, textiles in late-eighteenth-century Europe and America were composed mainly of wool (77 percent) and flax (18 percent), with cotton making up only 5 percent.

Whitney, who had never seen cotton before his visit to Savannah, was immediately captivated by Greene's request. In only ten days, he devised a small, hand-turned model that solved the problem that had baffled cotton producers for more than three millennia. Whitney's triumph came at almost the same moment that he learned Major Dupont intended to pay only half the promised wage for tutoring. Miller offered to pay Whitney's expenses if he would stay at the plantation and built a full-size commercial gin. The three friends struck a deal. Whitney would produce the machine, Miller and Greene would provide the capital, Miller would manage the newly formed company (Miller and Whitney), and profits would be split evenly between the two sides. Thus, Whitney remained at Mulberry Grove, where his next step was to make a production model. He completed it in six months.

Whitney's hand-cranked cotton engine, a name soon shortened to gin, had metal pins protruding from a rotating cylinder that slipped the pins between small slits in a fixed wooden board. The pins pulled the fiber through the slit, leaving the seed on the board. Then another roller, operating in the opposite direction, swept away the fiber with cross-sweeping brushes, keeping the teeth unclogged. Later, other inventors would replace the pins with notched metal disks similar to the blade of a circular saw, thereby making the machine more rugged.

The gin was simple and easy to make. Any blacksmith and carpenter could create a duplicate. Most important, the machine and one man could produce fifty pounds of fiber per day, using waterpower or a horse to turn it. Though the machine sometimes cut the cotton fiber, thereby lessening its value, the quantity produced was so great that the loss of quality did not matter. Almost overnight, cotton was on its way to becoming the king of southern agriculture, totally altering the fortune of an entire region.

Whitney filed a patent application on June 20, 1793. Secretary of State Thomas Jefferson was greatly intrigued. Jefferson, a Virginia plantation owner and farmer, wrote Whitney asking how much cotton the gin cleaned per day, the cost, whether the device was tested, and whether he could buy one. In February 1794, Whitney sent the Patent Office a model gin. Less than a month later, on March 14, 1794, he got his patent.

Unlike the long delays generated under the Patent Act of 1790, the Patent Act of 1793 enabled Whitney's claim to move from application to award in less than nine months. But under this new law, there was no Patent Board to test the invention for novelty or identify who first invented the gin. Whitney's patent was more a registration than a legal guarantee for his right to fourteen years' exclusive use of the invention. Now it was the federal courts that had to sort out any questions about novelty and who was the first to invent—a job they were unprepared and unqualified to perform.

Young Eli Whitney had stumbled into an economic and legal trick bag. His invention was enormously useful. No cotton planter could prosper without it. The gin allowed one man to do the work that previously had required fifty. But his invention was easily and cheaply duplicated, and his patent protections were weak.

While waiting for his patent to be registered, Whitney clearly understood the need for secrecy. In a letter to his father on September 11, 1793, he described the machine and his plans. In conclusion, he asked his father not to show the letter to anyone but his brother and sister and to enjoin them "to keep the whole a profound secret." Foolishly, Greene and Miller were not as discreet, for they demonstrated the prototype gin to other planters. Soon after, a neighboring grower named Edward Lyon somehow stole the secrets of the gin. Legend offers three possibilities. One is that Lyon and a small group broke into the workshop at Mulberry Grove and stole one of Whitney's models. Another is that Lyon dressed himself as a woman, entered the workshop, and copied the design. The most probable is Lyon's own account that he hired an industrial spy to get the secrets. Regardless of which tale is true, Lyon became a major producer of pirated Whitney cotton gins.

Whitney and Miller's greed encouraged such piracy. The young entrepreneurs wanted to own all the cotton gins, gin all the cotton, and be paid two of every five pounds of cotton they processed. Such a monopoly and price seemed so reasonable to Whitney and Miller that they dashed headlong into making and installing their gins.

However, the price appeared unreasonable, even rapacious, to the cotton planters, who did all the work to grow cotton, provided all the money, took all the risks, but were being asked to pay the Miller and Whitney Company 40 percent of their production in exchange for ginning the remaining 60 percent. The planters could easily, and inexpensively, buy or make a pirated copy of the gin, keep all their profits, and use the extra money to battle the two Yankee inventors in the federal courts, which is precisely what most planters did.

The southern planters expanded their cotton plantings and then ginned them with pirated copies of Whitney's invention. Production soared almost immediately. The price of cotton land tripled in value. The year before Whitney invented the gin, U.S. growers harvested 1.5 million pounds of cotton. Two years after the gin's introduction, they brought in more than 6 million pounds. By 1810, the South produced more than 93 million pounds of cotton. In 1825, the year of Whitney's death, America shipped 171 million pounds to England. By 1845, the U.S. was growing almost 90 percent of the world's cotton. By 1861, cotton constituted almost three-quarters of the value of all U.S. exports. In the 1920s, the U.S. was selling abroad more than 3 billion pounds of cotton per year; cotton was the nation's largest export. Whitney's invention made it all possible.

Whitney and Miller filed lawsuits against those pirates they could identify, but there were too many. Even the first year that Whitney manufactured his engine, more than nine out of every ten gins in use were pirated copies. The two Yale graduates, moreover, had pitted themselves against the center of the southern establishment, the plantation owners and cotton growers, whose wealth and political influence were increasing rapidly. In Georgia, the inventors lost sixty federal lawsuits between 1798 and 1806. The plantation owners had no incentive or intention to share their gains. Instead, they demonized Whitney and his patents, claiming that the pirated models had actually been invented first. Eventually, several states licensed the use of Whitney's machine for a fee—a sop by any measure with monies that came from the pockets of taxpayers.

Whitney and Miller collected almost $90,000 from the states of North and South Carolina, Georgia, and Tennessee, but only with great difficulty. South Carolina paid Miller and Whitney $20,000 in 1802 but in 1804 demanded that it be repaid. When Whitney arrived in Columbia, South Carolina, to appear before a special legislative committee considering the payment, state law officials arrested him, demanding the disputed $20,000. In a raucous hearing, Whitney so effectively faced down his accusers and the pirate gin makers that the legislature reinstated its previous payment. Despite such victories, Whitney spent $40,000 to get the states to pay for licenses, and the cost of fighting more than sixty lawsuits in Georgia alone consumed the rest of the money the partners received from the states. Denison Olmsted writes in his *Memoir of Eli Whitney* (1846) that a lawyer well acquainted with the cotton gin patent lawsuits observed that "in all his experience in the thorny profession of the law, he has never seen such a case of perseverance, under persecution. . . . Even now, after thirty years, my head aches to recollect his narratives of new trials, fresh disappointments, and accumulated wrongs."

Surprisingly, the federal court in Savannah finally validated Whitney's patent in 1806, leaving him one year of protection. He asked Congress for an extension, but southern lobbyists persuaded a majority of members to reject Whitney's petition. With that, he gave up trying to make any money out of his gin. He coined a maxim out of his experience: "An invention can be so valuable as to be worthless to the inventor."

Although Whitney fought for his royalties until 1807, he was essentially defeated a decade earlier. By 1797, Whitney was broke and back in Connecticut. He and Miller lacked the resources—political or economic—to protect their gin patent.

Miller married Catharine Greene in 1790. In 1799, to pay their debts, they put Mulberry Grove up for auction and moved to Cumberland Island, another Greene estate, where they raised long-staple cotton. The great plantation sold in 1800 for only $15,000. Psychologically and financially crushed by the patent wars, Miller died in 1803. Whitney remained a frequent visitor to the Greene-Miller family until the British army occupied the island plantation during the War of 1812. According to the curator of Whitney's papers, the correspondence between Whitney and Kitty from that period "records the life of a woman managing a plantation on her own." In 1814, Kitty died, leaving her plantation to her daughter Louisa Shaw. In the caring tradition of her mother, Louisa in 1818 nursed until his death a special cancer patient: her father's former military aide and her mother's admiring friend, General "Light-Horse" Harry Lee, father of future Confederate general Robert E. Lee.

At the age of thirty-two, Eli Whitney started over. Though broke, he was famous for his invention of the gin. He was educated and he had unusual access to influential people. The French government presented him his next opportunity—not directly but by its aggressive acts, which almost triggered a war between the two former allies. In the late 1790s, the newly created U.S. Navy fought several battles in the West Indies with French ships it caught pirating American commercial vessels. When in 1797 U.S. diplomats visited the French Foreign Ministry in Paris to discuss a peace agreement, they were asked to pay a $250,000 bribe before the French government would even deal with them, what became known as the XYZ Affair. Delegation chairman Charles Pinckney's response was "No, no, not a sixpence," which quickly was transformed into the famous political epigram "Millions for defense, sir, but not one cent for tribute." An outraged American public demanded war, which President John Adams just barely averted.

Adams's diplomacy averted a possible disaster, for in the late 1790s America lacked the arms needed to fight another war. As late as 1794, the United States still purchased its muskets and rifles from European producers. But after Napoleon took control of France, the European countries needed all the arms they could produce to fight what became known as the Napoleonic Wars. Although the U.S. government, at George Washington's insistence, had established armories in Springfield, Massachusetts, and

Harper's Ferry, Virginia, in the mid-1790s, those two new facilities still did not produce enough muskets or cannons to meet U.S. needs. In three years of operation, the Springfield Armory had turned out barely a thousand muskets. War was imminent and America needed additional arms quickly. Thus, in 1798, Congress appropriated $800,000 for the purchase of weaponry from private manufacturers and suppliers.

Whitney saw his opportunity. Though he had no arms factory, no arms machines, no arms workers, and no arms experience, he persuaded fellow Yale graduate Oliver Wolcott Jr., secretary of the Treasury, to issue him a contract of $134,000 to produce 10,000 muskets within twenty-eight months. The contract was issued in January 1798. Wolcott also gave Whitney a $5,000 advance, which saved the failed gin manufacturer from ruin. Most important, Whitney contracted with the government to manufacture these muskets by using machines that could speed production and improve quality. It was a novel idea. Although unknown to Wolcott at the time, he had created the forerunner of the Defense Advanced Research Projects Agency. To produce this many muskets quickly, Whitney had to develop the required machinery and processes.

Year after year, he also had to invent reasons and political diversions to explain his repeated delays on a twenty-eight-month contract that ultimately took ten years to complete. One stunt that assisted him enormously in securing political forbearance took place in January 1801, when he met in Washington with President Adams and his old friend president-elect Thomas Jefferson, plus senior congressional leaders. As the meeting opened, Whitney placed a large bag on the table. He pulled out a hundred musket locks, took them apart, put the parts into a pile, mixed the pile, and then reassembled each lock, each of which worked perfectly. He invited his audience to join in the demonstration—disassembling the weapons and then reassembling them from a pile of parts. Elizur Goodrich, a participant in that demonstration, wrote a friend that Whitney's muskets were superior to all others and "are considered as evidence that this Country need not depend on a disgraceful recourse to foreign markets for this primary means of defence."

Unfortunately, such perfection was not the norm at Whitney's factory. The historian Merritt Roe Smith claims that Whitney staged the demonstration with individually fashioned pieces. And he probably did so because, as the economist Vernon W. Ruttan reports, "At that time Whitney's factory did not yet have the capacity to produce interchangeable parts for the rifles that he manufactured." What he actually demonstrated, though deceptively, was the concept of mass production using interchangeable parts. And the attending audience of influential politicians accepted as desirable what they thought they had been shown.

Whitney completed his musket contract almost eight years late. His total profit was $2,500, less than 2 percent of the contract's value. All that was unimportant. Using machinery invented by others, plus some by Whitney and his staff, the factory eventually did make weapons with interchangeable parts. In the end, Whitney championed a system of manufacturing that ended America's dependence on foreign arms makers. For that, he was celebrated as an American hero. And the mass production techniques and equipment eventually used to make muskets could be adapted to make dozens of other items by machine. That, too, was widely understood and appreciated.

As for Whitney the inventor and businessperson, the musket contract saved his career. By the time it was completed, he had a fully functioning factory, valuable expertise, and a market for his weapons. Using machines, low-skilled workers could make technically complex arms. Eventually, Whitney became wealthy producing weapons.

After his experience with the cotton gin, Whitney never filed another patent application. Whatever other inventions and improvements he created, he kept as trade secrets. Whitney had learned that those who invent something valuable are destined to a life in court, particularly when the patent laws are weak and vague.

Whitney, of course, was not the only early inventor victimized by the weak Patent Act of 1793, only the most famous. Eleven years after his death, Congress finally passed patent legislation that created a modern patent system. That new act established a distinct Patent Office, managed by a full-time commissioner. It also resulted in an excellent patent library, specialists being hired to examine applications for originality, and inventors being given much stronger legal means to defend their creations.

A half century after Whitney's death, another inventor's experiences demonstrated just how powerful a legal defense the new Patent Act provided. On the morning of February 14, 1876, the attorney for Alexander Graham Bell—a twenty-eight-year-old Scottish immigrant and Boston University speech instructor—paid the U.S. Patent Office a fee of $15 and filed Bell's application covering "the method of, and apparatus for, transmitting vocal or other sounds telegraphically." Two hours later that same day, the attorney for Elisha Gray, a rich Chicago inventor and rival of Thomas Edison, paid the Patent Office a fee of $10 and filed Gray's caveat, which announced his intention to file a patent on a device that would send speech by wire.

By that two-hour gap, Bell became the first person to register a claim for a patent on the telephone. Three weeks later, the Patent Office granted him a patent that recognized him as the sole inventor of the telephone and gave him the exclusive right for its commercialization for seventeen years. U.S. Patent No. 174,465 eventually became known as "the single most valuable patent ever issued in the history of the world."

Today we remember Bell, if at all, as just another name on a long list of nineteenth-century inventors and their inventions. Yet what he accomplished and how he did it is the very essence of the Founding Fathers' intent when they put the patent provision into the Constitution. Bell had an idea, developed it into an invention, got a patent, beat back a robber baron's challenge to that patent, and used his limited-term exclusive right to commercialize his invention, and in the process vastly, and forever, improved life and knowledge in the United States and the rest of the world.

Bell, moreover, was not some two-dimensional cardboard creature. His life was a series of adventures, filled with spectacular timing, amazing coincidences, and breathtaking luck. For example, he completed and signed his telephone patent application almost four weeks before his attorney filed it with the Patent Office. Neither Bell nor his lawyer was aware that Elisha Gray would be submitting a caveat (a brief description of an invention for which a patent application will soon be filed) in the same field, the same day. By luck, Bell's full application arrived at the Patent Office first. History seems to pivot on such events.

Even Bell's presence in the United States was by happenstance. Born in Scotland, he came from a family of distinguished academics. His grandfather, father, two brothers, and uncle all taught speech in the universities of Edinburgh, Dublin, and London. Bell's grandfather invented a system to correct stammering. His father, Alexander Melville Bell, was the foremost British elocutionist of his time—a real-life version of Professor Henry Higgins. Eliza Symonds Bell, his mother, was an accomplished painter of miniatures. She was also deaf. Young Bell's specialty was teaching the deaf, for whom he developed special learning techniques while in his early twenties.

Bell left Scotland because within a span of four months a tuberculosis plague in Edinburgh killed his two elder brothers, after which the twenty-three-year-old Bell also suddenly became infected. Scottish doctors decided that only a total change of climate could save his life. In 1870, his father quickly retired and migrated with Alexander and his mother to the tiny village of Brantford, Canada. While recovering, Bell taught his father's system of "visible speech" to the local Mohawk Indian tribe. In 1871, now in good health, Bell was hired by the newly created Clarke School for the Deaf, a pioneering facility in Boston, with which he remained affiliated in various capacities until his death in 1922. Once on the job, his work so impressed the community that Boston University soon hired him to teach there as well.

In Boston, Bell supplemented his teacher's pay by instructing private patients. One was Mabel Hubbard, a fifteen-year-old girl who could neither hear nor speak. Her father was Gardiner G. Hubbard, a prominent Boston attorney and entrepreneur, and her grandfather had sat on the Massachusetts Supreme Court. Though almost completely forgotten today, Gardiner Hubbard was one of the first "superlobbyists"—someone with influential political contacts in Washington, Boston, and New York. He helped Cambridge, Massachusetts, get gas lighting, pure water, and a street railroad to Boston in the 1850s. In 1871, he persuaded the Massachusetts legislature to fund the Clarke School for the Deaf, which recruited Bell from Canada.

More important to the evolution of the telephone, Hubbard was one of the principal champions behind the post–Civil War political movement to nationalize Western Union and the other telegraph companies, and make them part of the United States Post Office, which would then be named the U.S. Postal Telegraph Company. During and after the Civil War, Western Union and a handful of smaller companies controlled telegraphic communication throughout the United States. Like the railroads, they abused their monopoly power, putting profits ahead of serving the public. They charged so much for sending a short message that only well-off businesses and a handful of wealthy individuals could use the service. Most people could afford to send telegrams only in emergencies.

At the same time, Western Union charged the Associated Press a very low rate for transmitting its news nationwide. In exchange, the AP never criticized, questioned, or distributed articles that disparaged the telegraph companies. Those newspapers that did reveal telegraph company practices, such as the *Herald* of San Francisco and *Petersburg Index* of Virginia, suddenly experienced a doubling or tripling of their rates or a cutoff of Associated Press news dispatches. This monopoly on fast communications gave a handful of telegraph executives life-and-death control over virtually every newspaper in the United States, and thus great political power.

Hubbard fought to break this private concentration of power. He backed legislation that emulated Britain's policy—in 1870, the British government had bought the private telegraph companies and converted the service into a publicly owned utility. In quick succession, the British cut their telegraph rates almost in half, provided access to all users, and charged everyone the same rate. Hubbard flooded Congress with documentation from Great Britain and other European nations, which showed how rate cuts and universal access were stimulating a vast increase in volume, including private correspondence. In some nations, usage increased by almost 250 percent within two or three years of nationalization. Best of all, the British system offered more reliable service than did the U.S. companies, and it paid for itself.

Largely forgotten now, that political fight raged from the end of the Civil War until the Forty-second Congress adjourned in March 1873. Western Union, the leading U.S. telegraph company, invested hundreds of thousands of dollars to kill the Hubbard legislation. One of Western Union's most effective lobbyists was Uriah Hunt Painter, chief clerk to the House Postal Committee, which handled all telegraph legislation. Western Union's payments to Painter were nothing less than bribes. But it got value for its money. Ultimately, Western Union and its principal stockholder, Cornelius Vanderbilt, prevailed in Congress. By the end of that fight in 1873, Vanderbilt and his minions loathed Hubbard, but at least they were free of him. Then suddenly in 1875, over dinner one evening, this young speech instructor confided to his patient's father that he believed he could make a device that could transmit speech over wires. At first Hubbard thought it was nonsense, but he soon changed his opinion.

Of all the people in the United States to whom Bell could take an idea for the telephone and find practical business and political advice, Hubbard was the best one. He understood wire communication and what it meant. He knew in detail where Western Union and others had the right-of-way to string wire. He knew the hotels, offices, and companies where Western Union had a service monopoly. He understood the economics and politics of how Western Union operated. Most of all, Hubbard knew that Bell's invention, if it worked, would give him a second chance to take on the greatest telecommunications monopoly of its time.

Bell had no money, no political connections, and no business experience, but Hubbard did. Thus, Bell allowed Hubbard to make the appropriate arrangements for ownership of the patent and creation of a new company to develop it. Hubbard organized a trust, which he headed, that issued 5,000 shares of stock. Thomas Watson, Bell's assistant, got 499 shares. The balance was split among Bell, Hubbard, and Thomas Sanders. Sanders, a manufacturer who helped finance Bell's experiments, had a deaf five-year-old child who also was one of Bell's private students. Bell lived with the Sanders family, which allowed the young teacher to use their home basement as a lab.

Another factor also influenced Hubbard's interest in Bell. Mabel Hubbard and Alexander Bell had fallen in love. They married in July 1877, when she was nineteen years old. On their wedding day, Bell's matrimonial gift to his bride was all his telephone stock, except ten shares. They adored each other for life.

Even after Bell was awarded his patent, few people immediately recognized its potential. Bell and Hubbard's challenge, therefore, was to build public enthusiasm for the strange idea of talking to someone over a piece of wire. Again, Bell was lucky. Hubbard was one of the commissioners for the 1876 Centennial Exposition in Philadelphia, which opened two months after Bell received his patent. The exposition was the first world's fair in the United States. The exhibits from all over the world covered more than 260 acres and included 13 acres of new inventions and devices, as well as a half mile of sewing machines, each different from the other.

The spectacle was grand, dominated by the giant Corliss engine that drove five miles of shafting and moved power throughout the building. One man attended the engine, sitting beside it in a chair and casually reading the local newspapers and drinking his coffee.

The first typewriter was one of the novelties on display, as was a prototype slice of the cable for the Brooklyn Bridge, a wonder-to-be. Plows, cooking ware, and thousands of other inventions filled the hall. The exposition had a panel of judges and scientists to evaluate the inventions for their uniqueness and utility. Today, the Smithsonian Institution in Washington still displays many of those exhibits, including the Corliss engine.

Hubbard used his influence to get Bell a small space for his telephone exhibit. The only place available at that late date, however, was a narrow area between a stairway and wall. Hubbard set up a table there and mounted an exhibit arranged by Bell, who was too poor to attend the exposition. The telephone exhibit attracted less attention than the packaged card tricks on sale at the adjoining table. However, Bell's luck continued. On a Friday afternoon at the end of June 1876, Bell took Mabel to the train so she could join her father in Philadelphia. She coaxed Bell to come with her, but he refused. She persisted, and again he pleaded poverty. Finally, just as the train began to leave the station with Mabel on it, Bell saw tears easing down her cheeks. He started to trot alongside the train, waving good-bye. Then, impulsively, he jumped on board without either a ticket or baggage.

Of all the weekends Bell could have been in Philadelphia, this was the most important because Hubbard had persuaded the exposition judges to look at Bell's invention. The judges and scientists arrived late on Sunday afternoon. At almost the same moment as they got to Bell's little table, whether by an accident of timing or arrangement by Hubbard, the emperor of Brazil, Dom Pedro II; his wife, Empress Teresa; and their entourage walked up there as well. The emperor stretched out his hands and said, "Professor Bell, I am delighted to see you again." The judges, scientists, and other observers were stunned. How did the emperor of Brazil know this obscure Boston teacher of the deaf? Unknown to them, two years earlier, Dom Pedro and his wife had visited Bell's Boston classroom to study his teaching techniques. Afterward, the emperor had been so impressed that he had established a school for the deaf in Rio de Janeiro using Bell's system.

Bell immediately involved the emperor and his wife in the demonstration. Earlier, he had connected a wire from a transmitter in a distant part of the hall to a receiver at his table. After the greetings, Bell went to the transmitter at the other end of the building and recited Hamlet's soliloquy. The emperor put the receiver to his ear and suddenly called out, "My God, it talks!" For six hours, the judges, scientists, and others took turns speaking and listening over the wire. With that, the telephone suddenly became one of the Centennial Exposition's star inventions.

Paradoxically, Elisha Gray was part of Dom Pedro's entourage and witnessed Bell's demonstration. As one observer noted, "How disenchanting for Gray."

After the exposition, Bell gave public lectures and staged a series of demonstrations. The first of these was in Salem, Massachusetts, where he connected a telephone to a telegraph wire that ran to a room in Boston from which Thomas Watson sent messages to people in the Salem audience. The *Boston Globe* reported the event, proclaiming the success of "a feat never before attempted, the sending of news over the space of sixteen miles by the human voice." Immediately, many newspapers across America reprinted the *Globe*'s story, stimulating public interest in the telephone.

Despite all the publicity created at the Centennial Exposition and by the *Globe*'s article, the business community saw no commercial prospects in the invention. Thus, the Bell Telephone Company's sales of telephones were low, leaving the new company with virtually no money. A year after the exposition, the London *Times* denounced Bell's telephone as "the latest American humbug" and declared that it "was far inferior to the well-established system of speaking tubes."

Almost eighteen months after the exposition, a discouraged Hubbard met with William Orton, the president of Western Union, and offered to sell all the rights to the telephone patent for $100,000. It was surely a difficult meeting, since both men despised each other.

Orton rejected the offer, asking, "What use could this company make of an electrical toy?" Who, he wondered, would want to talk over a wire when they could use a telegraph and get a printed message? He was not alone. Vanderbilt, Hubbard, Sanders, and even Bell did not appreciate the telephone's social implications. As Ruth Schwartz Cowan noted in *A Social History of American Technology*, they all knew that the telegraph and telephone were technologically similar. Yet none of them understood that in social terms the two devices are very different. A telegraph relies on intermediaries. A telephone offers person-to-person voice communication. With the telephone, people could socialize with each other, something they could never do with the telegraph.

After Orton's rejection, Hubbard, Bell, and Sanders's only choice was to persevere alone. Lack of capital was one obstacle. Lack of experienced management was another. Hubbard's solution was to hire the best man in the nation to manage the new company. That man turned out to be Theodore Vail, then the superintendent of the Postal Service's Railway Mail Service, a man respected by U.S. postal officials and Congress.

Fortuitously, Sanders's family included several wealthy Bostonians, many of whom provided the new company with loans and capital. To attract even more capital, Hubbard devised a clever franchise arrangement, not unlike that used by McDonald's and dozens of other companies a century later. Under the Bell franchise, a licensee got a charter to provide telephone service in a designated area. The licensees had to finance the erection of telephone poles and wire. They also had to lease the phones and switching equipment from the Bell Telephone Company. Each franchise lasted for five years but was renewable. A permanent franchise was also available. The cost was 35 percent of the local company's stock. Hubbard's idea was an instant success.

By 1879, the Bell Telephone Company had 185 franchisees spread throughout the United States. Today, Hubbard would patent that idea as a business process much as Amazon has done with one-click shopping and Dell Computer has with its just-in-time, anyway-you-want-it ordering.

Eventually, Orton and Vanderbilt realized they had a potential competitor. They responded like robber barons: they set out to crush the Bell company. With great dispatch and energy, Western Union established its own telephone company and hired Thomas Edison and Elisha Gray to develop a better phone.

Fortunately for Bell, Gardiner Hubbard knew exactly how to handle Western Union and others who violated his son-in-law's patent. He recruited Chauncey Smith and James J. Storrow, two of Boston's most experienced and best-connected patent attorneys. They sued the violators, thereby initiating a national patent war that lasted for more than a decade. Most deliciously for Hubbard, the first to fall were Commodore Vanderbilt, Orton, and Western Union. In their hubris, Vanderbilt and Orton had wandered into a two-front business war. One was with the Bell Telephone Company, which was proving unexpectedly difficult. The other was with Jay Gould, an unscrupulous financier, who had created a competing national telegraph company largely for what we now call "greenmail"—that is, Gould would go away if Vanderbilt would pay him an exorbitant price.

Ultimately, the deciding factor in the fight was the validity of Bell's patent. After a trial of more than a year, George Gifford, one of the nation's premier patent attorneys and Vanderbilt's lawyer, informed his client that the case would probably be lost. Gifford recommended settlement. Meanwhile, at Bell, the financiers had taken firm control, sharply limiting Hubbard's actions as president—an unwanted but substantial blessing for the company. The board recognized that Orton and Vanderbilt so hated Hubbard that any settlement involving him was unlikely. After limiting Hubbard's authority, the Bell board authorized William Forbes, leader of the Boston financiers investing in the company, to negotiate a settlement with Western Union. Forbes concluded a deal in the fall of 1879.

The Bell Telephone Company bought the Western Union telephone system, got all its telephone customers, and agreed to stay out of the telegraph business. Western Union received royalties of 20 percent on all telephone rentals on the equipment it had sold for a period of twenty years. Most important, Western Union acknowledged that Alexander Graham Bell was the original inventor of the telephone and that his patents were valid, and it agreed to stay out of the telephone business. With this settlement and Western Union's acknowledgment of Bell's patents, the value of the telephone industry soared. Soon, commercial competitors across America began to organize their own local and regional companies, raise money, and challenge Bell's patents.

Americans loved the telephone. Rather than send an expensive twenty-five-word message, they picked up a receiver and talked directly with virtually anyone, anywhere in the U.S. The Bell company took to heart Hubbard's desire for inexpensive, reliable, and universal service. Indeed, meeting that goal became an almost religious mission for the people at "Ma Bell." By 1920, the first year a telephone census was taken, the United States had nearly 75 percent of the world's phones, which provided service to nearly 35 percent of all U.S. households. New York City alone had more telephones than six European countries combined—Belgium, Norway, Denmark, Italy, the Netherlands, and Austria. And while rural telephones were almost nonexistent in most other countries, they quickly found their way to farms throughout the United States, breaking the isolation of rural Americans. Even before World War I, almost 75 percent of the farms in Iowa had a telephone. By the time the Bell System was broken up in the mid-1980s, more than 92 percent of U.S. households had telephone service. Today, almost 95 percent do.

In the late nineteenth century, many inventors who had worked on various aspects of the telegraph convinced themselves that they had created the telephone or significant elements of it. There was so much money at stake, a situation today akin to deciding who owns the Internet, that speculators of that age were willing to finance lawsuits against the Bell company. Winning just one of these lawsuits would be worth a king's ransom. In the long legal war over the invention of the telephone, Bell company attorneys fought 13 lawsuits of national significance, 5 of which went to the Supreme Court. In addition, they contested 587 lesser lawsuits. Bell won every case.

In part, Bell's lawyers won because they were skilled and the company financing them had sufficient capital to pay their costs. But in the final analysis they won because they were defending a clear, well-written patent that met all the constitutional and legal tests. In 1910, Herbert N. Casson, in *The History of the Telephone,* described how remarkable the Bell patent was:

64

It was a Gibraltar of security to the Bell Company. For eleven years, it was attacked from all sides, and never dented. It covered an entire art, yet it was sustained during its entire lifetime. Printed in full, it would make ten pages of this book, but the core of it is in the last sentence: "The method of, and apparatus for, transmitting vocal or other sounds telegraphically, by causing electrical undulations, similar in form to the vibrations of the air accompanying the said vocal or other sounds." These words expressed an idea that had never been written before. It could not be evaded or overcome.

Elisha Gray always believed that he had invented the telephone first, and he continued to contest the Bell patent until his death in 1901. His former business partner said, "Of all the men who DIDN'T invent the telephone first, Gray was the nearest."

Bell's patent wars were a rite of passage common to the more successful inventors of that era. In the nineteenth century, having a superior patent attorney was as essential to an innovative company as having an honest accountant. Eli Whitney fought more than sixty suits, and sixty-two persons besieged Samuel Morse with lawsuits claiming that they were the true inventors of the telegraph.

In that age, U.S. companies had to have a patent strategy. Otherwise, they disappeared. Larger, well-financed corporations, such as Western Union, often infringed on patents held by others, knowing that smaller rivals and individual inventors could ill afford litigation. Small companies with capital, such as Bell's, used their patents to muscle their way into markets or even create entire industries. Many firms generated revenues from patent licenses. Others produced a horde of patents they then used for cross-licensing purposes with other firms, both to defend core technologies and gain access to the technology of others. Finally, many inventors, notably Thomas Edison, gained personal fame, social position, and public attention, even immortality, from their inventions and the sheer number of patents awarded in their name.

Most modern patent strategies are little more than imitations of business practices developed in the nineteenth century by long-forgotten inventors, lawyers, and robber barons. The principal changes over time have been the personalities and industries in conflict, plus a battlefield that is now global, rather than national.

Of all the inventors' pursuits of the nineteenth century, the career of Thomas Edison perhaps best illustrates the maxim that an inventor's best protections are a strong patent and a good lawyer. The genius inventor devised many, if not most, of today's corporate patent strategies, including some that were clearly illegal, if not criminal. Others were simply sleazy, still others brilliant, and some were both.

Ultimately, Edison's inventions and business strategies brought him world fame but surprisingly little wealth. Eli Whitney, Alexander Graham Bell, William Kellogg, and Henry Ford, among dozens of other American innovators in the nineteenth and early twentieth centuries, converted their creativity into extraordinary riches, leaving their families fortunes that endure today. Of all these creators, moreover, Edison was the most prolific. Between 1869 and 1931, he submitted an estimated 1,600 to 1,700 applications to the U.S. Patent Office, which granted 1,093 singly and jointly—the historic record for any inventor. In addition, he was awarded more than 1,200 patents in thirty-four other countries.

Yet, it is not just the sheer number of patents awarded Edison that is amazing but the diversity of fields. Among his creations were the automatic, duplex, and quadruplex telegraphs, a superior telephone transmitter, the electric typewriter, text-printing telegraph machines, the dictating machine, the mimeograph, the phonograph, the incandescent lightbulb, movie cameras, movie projectors, the alkaline battery, modern portland cement, and a superior rubber-producing plant.

Despite his creativity, Edison's net worth upon his death in 1931 was approximately $12 million, a large sum but a pittance considering what he created. Henry Ford called Edison "the world's greatest inventor and its worst businessman." Moreover, Edison would likely have been penniless by the end of his career had it not been for his patents and his lawyers.

Even Edison's critics, and there were many during his lifetime, grant that he was a creative genius; even his admirers must grant that he was an incompetent entrepreneur. Yet he invented team research, took commercial development straight from the lab to the marketplace, and devised a host of patent strategies that have been used for so long and by so many that their origin is obscured. Of all Americans, Edison did the most to popularize the idea that life could be improved through technology, and by that, he generated vast public support for inventors and patents, plus fame for himself. Edison's story is as much about his patents, their protective force, and his publicity as it is about his inventions.

In 1868, the twenty-year-old Edison, an itinerant telegrapher, submitted his first patent application, for an electric vote recorder. The device was an immediate commercial failure. As Edison soon learned, the last thing legislative bodies of that day wanted was an instant vote count; generally, they preferred a slow count to enable politicking and last-minute deals. This little machine had no market, leading Edison to issue a maxim that he would invent only things that he could sell. Profits from inventions that sold enabled him to establish his own shop and devote his time fully to inventing.

Early in his career, Edison became, in effect, a consulting inventor. Anyone who had a technical problem or who needed something practical invented could hire him and his team. They worked for fees, bonuses, and royalties. Often, what Edison called the Money Interests cheated him badly. In an age of scoundrels, he did business with two of the worst: Jay Gould, owner of the Atlantic and Pacific Telegraph Company, and William Orton, president of Western Union, who refused Hubbard's offer to buy the Bell telephone patents. These rival companies were today's equivalent of Microsoft and Cisco. They were at the cutting edge of electronic communications; Gould and Orton were private enemies whose companies were perpetually seeking to best each other.

Edison's first money as an inventor came from his enhancements of the telegraph, including a stock ticker and gold price reporter, for which the Gold and Stock Telegraph Company paid him $40,000. In 1870, under contract with the newly created Automatic Telegraph Company, Edison invented a superfast printing telegraph that could transmit and record one thousand words a minute at a time when a top telegrapher could send forty to fifty by key. He further refined the machine, allowing it to record messages in script instead of dots and dashes. In one experiment, the machine recorded and printed three thousand words a minute. This machine allowed typists to put many messages on a paper strip that would then be sent in a burst to a similar machine that printed the text in script. The automatic telegraph could send dozens of messages in the time it previously took to send one.

In addition to inventing printers and what became the Remington typewriter, Edison was awarded more than a hundred patents for improvements in telegraphy. They ranged from galvanic batteries to devices that could perforate telegraph paper. In addition to high-speed printers, Edison's other major invention was the quadruplex telegraph, a revolutionary device that could send four messages over the same line simultaneously—two going each way. The prospective savings to a telegraph company in the cost of lines alone were estimated to be at least $15 million. Yet the money-desperate Edison squandered his patent rights to this valuable invention. In an argument with George Harrington, co-owner of the Automatic Telegraph Company, Edison impetuously assigned that company a two-thirds interest in all his inventions and patents on telegraphy for the period 1871–76. Then, in exchange for the use of Western Union's experimental shop, Edison agreed to list the company's chief electrician as a co-inventor of the quadruplex, even though this broke his agreement with Harrington.

In the summer of 1874, Edison demonstrated the quadruplex to Commodore Vanderbilt, the owner of Western Union, and William Orton, the company president. Subsequently, the telegraph company successfully installed several experimental units. Reeling from the financial panic of 1873, Edison asked Orton for a $10,000 advance in order to forestall foreclosure on his shop, but Orton would provide only $3,000. Orton wanted Edison's patent on the quadruplex, which he thought he could buy cheaply if Edison became sufficiently desperate for money.

By December 1874, Edison was broke. Orton offered to advance Edison $5,000 against the purchase of the patent but would not agree to a final price. Edison made three offers, each less than the last, none of which Orton accepted. Without concluding the negotiations, the Western Union president left for Chicago, promising Edison to "think about it." Meanwhile, Edison was paying a sheriff in New Jersey $5 a day to withhold a foreclosure judgment that had been entered against him.

While Orton was away on Christmas holiday, General T. T. Eckert, Western Union's general superintendent, told Edison he knew someone interested in buying his portion of the quadruplex patent. Eckert was secretly negotiating to leave Western Union and assume command of Gould's Atlantic and Pacific Telegraph Company. Gould, known as "the Great White Shark of Wall Street," met Edison, and a deal was struck quickly. Edison accepted $30,000 and 3,000 shares of A&P stock for his portion of the quadruplex patent. He also took the position of company electrician. At the same time, Gould bought the Automatic Telegraph Company and its portion of the patent rights. Instantly, Gould had technologically quadrupled the capacity of his system without investing a penny in new lines. Even better, he thought, he was keeping the technology from Vanderbilt and Western Union.

When Orton learned of the sale, he was furious. Western Union immediately sued Gould and his Atlantic and Pacific Telegraph Company. Meanwhile, Edison used the $30,000 to pay his debts and finance the creation of other inventions, including an electromotograph switch, which allowed a branch telegraph to tap into the main line. His invention was an improvement over the Paige relay, a switch on which Western Union held the patent and which all other telegraph companies, including Gould's, had to license.

Orton canceled A&P's license to use the Paige relay, thus trying to put Gould out of business. Edison's new invention, however, could replace Western Union's Paige relay. To stave off the disaster Orton was trying to create, Gould offered Edison $250,000 for his patent on the electromotograph. Edison accepted. Gould saved his company by replacing the Paige relays with Edison's invention.

Gould never paid Edison a dime for the electromotograph. Nor did he ever deliver Edison the promised 3,000 shares of stock in his telegraph company. Edison sued. As L. J. Davis notes in *Fleet Fire,* paralyzing rivals with lawsuits was Gould's favorite tactic. Paying attorneys and bribing judges was generally cheaper than paying litigants. Edison's lawsuit against Gould took almost thirty years to complete, but in the end he won. In 1906, the court appointed a master to determine how much Gould owed the inventor. In 1913, Edison got $1. The log of that telegraph litigation consumes five volumes at the Rutgers University Library, where many of Edison's papers are stored.

Though crafty and corrupt, Orton and Gould's tactics were far from unique in that era. Edison soon determined that the only way he could avoid theft by the Money Interests was to manufacture his inventions with his own company. For others, this was the right answer, though it proved wrong for Edison. Nevertheless, self-production was the business model Edison used the rest of his life, with only a few exceptions.

Among the dozens of companies that Edison organized were the Edison Electric Lamp Company, the Edison Machine Works, the Edison Ore Milling Company, the Edison Electric Light Company, the Edison Phonograph Company, the Edison Phonograph Works, the Edison General Electric Company, the Automatic Phonograph Exhibit Company, the Edison Portland Cement Company, the Edison Storage Battery Company, the Edison Manufacturing Company, the Edison Business Phonograph Company, and the Edison Botanic Research Company. By separating these companies, he ensured that failure of one would not affect all the others. This was wise, because Edison repeatedly moved from industry to industry, leaving bank-rupt business shells in his wake.

When starting up a new company, Edison would have invented some-thing unique, plus hold the seventeen-year exclusive-use right granted with his patent. Some of the monies generated by the new venture would be used for research and the creation of other inventions, which then became the center of another company. As time passed, competitors would emerge for the older company and the patent would expire. Edison would have long ago moved on to whatever was next and lost interest in that particu-lar device or invention. Though he occasionally returned to an invention to make improvements, as he did with the phonograph, this pattern of creating, manufacturing, marketing, and going on to something new was repeated throughout Edison's career.

The one constant in Edison's business operations was his patents. The patents, or even the prospect of a patent, enabled him to attract investors and secure private capital. As the list of his patents and successes grew, so too did the number of investors willing to put money into his ventures. Eventually, the great New York banker J. P. Morgan became one of Edison's patrons. That was fortuitous since Morgan was a man of character and one of the nation's foremost executives. He despised people such as Gould, who looted corporations. He was a builder who headed the most important bank of his time. He was so influential that the Morgan bank effectively served as the nation's central banking system until 1913, when the Federal Reserve System was created to regulate U.S. banks and the nation's money supply.

Morgan helped finance Edison's work to provide electric lighting. Indeed, Morgan's house and the *New York Times* both got electric lighting the day that Edison first turned on the power in New York City. Ever practical, Edi-son realized the benefits of helping a banker and a newspaper to be the ini-tial participants in something truly historic.

To make those electric lights work, Edison had to develop six essential systems. One was a lightbulb that would last. Another was a dynamo that was reliable. To move electricity from the dynamo to the customer, Edison created an underground conductor network. New York City streets then had an overhanging maze of telegraph wires that was so impenetrable that moving electricity by wire was almost impossible. Edison also had to create safety fuses, insulating materials, and light sockets that could be turned off and on. Almost single-handedly, he invented an entire industry.

On September 4, 1882, from a power station on Pearl Street in lower Manhattan, Edison flipped a switch and provided electric lighting for buildings in a one-third-square-mile area of downtown New York. One measure of Edison's ingenuity is that he eventually received 424 patents for the different interlocking features required to complete this remarkable achievement.

With those patents, Edison erected an intellectual property fortress. Competitors had three choices: license Edison's technology, provide Edison a technology of some comparable value, or leave the field. This fortress was extended by trade secrets and the expertise Edison and his team gained by being first.

Still, Edison's patent stronghold was vulnerable, because he had used the wrong type of current in his power system for mass distribution. Direct current, used by Edison's system, can be transmitted only over short distances—at that time, a half mile. This meant that an Edison power system required generators at regular half-mile intervals. Moreover, Edison was adamant that direct current was the future.

An eccentric Croatian-born genius named Nikola Tesla had a different vision. Tesla, who stood more than six feet, six inches tall, weighed less than 140 pounds, and often dressed in formal clothes at work, fashioned the theory of polyphase alternating current electricity—what we know as alternating current (AC)—an advance as significant as Edison's.

Alternating currents allowed a company to build a generating plant and transmit electricity great distances over wires. Even in some of the initial demonstrations, Tesla was able to efficiently transmit power more than a hundred miles. At the customer's site, a transformer reduced the electricity into a form that powered lights and appliances. Tesla briefly worked for Edison. Yet Edison was unmoved by Tesla's ideas about alternating currents, thinking he could overcome direct current's basic disadvantages by other means.

Discouraged by Edison's indifference, Tesla created his own company and patented his ideas. Eventually, George Westinghouse, inventor of the automatic air brake and an engineer of great skill, came to Tesla and offered to buy his patents. Westinghouse recognized the potential of AC-generated electricity and wanted to be part of that future. He also understood the advantages of Tesla's alternating current system over Edison's. Tesla offered Westinghouse his patents on alternating currents for cash and royalties.

Soon Tesla and Edison were in a race for patents, and Edison and Westinghouse were in a race for customers. It was the nineteenth-century version of the Beta-versus-VHS videotape format fight of the 1980s, and Westinghouse was winning. In December 1887, Edison filed eleven lawsuits against Westinghouse for infringing the patents on Edison's system of illumination. Westinghouse was undeterred. Edison attempted to secure legislation in New York and Virginia limiting electric currents to 300 volts, thereby destroying Westinghouse's system. That plan also failed.

Edison's last step was to frighten the public. He hired publicists to raise the specter that AC was dangerous. He granted Harold P. Brown, a self-taught engineer, the use of the Edison labs to run experiments on the "death points" of AC and DC currents. In one of the first such demonstrations before a crowd of invitees, Brown muzzled and tied down a seventy-six-pound dog named Dash. Then he put electric contacts on Dash's foreleg and left hind leg, and began to apply the current. Starting at 300 volts, Brown administered increased amounts of electricity. Dash was in acute pain, howling and trying to escape. The audience was soon screaming for Brown to stop. Instead, he administered a deadly final burst of electricity. In response to the reports of outraged citizens, the head of the Society for the Prevention of Cruelty to Animals stopped Edison's grisly demonstrations.

Perhaps Edison's most ghoulish trick was to lobby the state of New York to use an electric chair for executions. Edison assisted in the design and recommended Westinghouse's AC current. Westinghouse responded to Edison's macabre public relations ploy by financing legal appeals for the first person facing death by electrocution. Ultimately, the electric chair ploy did not harm the reputation of Westinghouse's system. The Westinghouse Company beat out Edison's in the competition to light the 1893 Chicago World's Fair and soon after won the contract to construct a hydroelectric plant that could harness the power of moving water at Niagara Falls.

J. P. Morgan, repulsed by Edison's antics, ended the AC-DC currency wars. All Morgan wanted was a company that could dominate the market and make money for his investors.

In 1889, Edison needed money. He went to the railroad tycoon Henry Villard, one of the few financiers he trusted. Villard put several of Edison's manufacturing companies and a competitor into a new company named Edison General Electric Company and became its CEO. Villard, a naturalized citizen born in Germany, sold 62 percent of the new company to Deutsche Bank, which wanted to create a German-controlled electric cartel based on the Edison patents.

Morgan, an Anglophile, would not tolerate a German bank controlling America's electric industry. It wanted the reins in the hands of those indebted to the House of Morgan. Thus, Morgan encouraged Thomson-Houston, another Edison competitor, to consolidate the two companies into what became General Electric. In 1891, Edison General Electric under Villard had returns of 11 percent on its capital. Thomson-Houston under Charles Coffin was producing 26 percent returns. Once the companies were merged, "Edison" was dropped from its name. As lead banker, Morgan dismissed Villard and picked Charles Coffin to run the new corporation.

Coffin, the first of GE's many legendary CEOs, soon arranged a détente with Westinghouse. GE needed Westinghouse's AC patents. Westinghouse needed Edison's patents on power and lighting. The two companies cross-licensed each other, forming a patent pool that enabled both of them to proceed as they wished, while forming a major barrier to newcomers.

By then, however, Edison was entranced by another of his inventions, machines to reduce and extract low-grade iron ore in New Jersey for use in steel mills. As Edison was ushering in an age of electricity, Andrew Carnegie was pioneering the steel age. Edison sold his stock in General Electric and used the money to mine low-grade ore in New Jersey. He devoted years of effort and millions of dollars to the attempt but failed miserably.

By the time the iron ore venture collapsed, he was on to other inventions and other businesses. He made a success of the phonograph but failed spectacularly in cement. He devised a way to improve the centuries-old method of making portland cement, a name acquired from the way the product resembled limestone found on the isle of Portland, England. As with his foray into electricity and lighting, Edison built an intellectual property fortress around his cement business, securing forty-nine separate patents. To market cement, Edison, working with architects, designed a three-story house built entirely of concrete—sides, roofs, partitions, cupboards, and bathtubs would all be poured. Neil Baldwin writes in *Edison: Inventing the Century* that the inventor could market each house complete for only $1,200, including plumbing, heating, and lighting because he envisioned doing them as low-cost housing, another new idea. Cement was the future. But again the business failed, though Edison's company did build Yankee Stadium with cement.

In the movie business, Edison held only nine patents, the most important of which was for a camera, but with them he dominated the field. As with other of his inventions, the initial novelty of moving pictures attracted patrons, making great profits for Edison's company, while his monopoly discouraged most competitors. Still, there were rivals. Foreign filmmakers, particularly those from France, were offering good products to U.S. distributors at a reasonable rate. Absent a U.S. copyright on foreign works, Edison simply swiped copies of the overseas films and distributed them himself. Thus it was that Auguste and Louis Lumière, and Georges Méliès, true pioneers, withdrew from the U.S. market, because their films were being pirated by America's most admired inventor.

In 1897, Edison was awarded an important motion picture patent for the kinetographic camera. He immediately used that patent to create another monopoly. The method: bringing lawsuits against rival moviemakers, their agents, and exhibitors who displayed their films. One of those Edison sued in 1898, American Mutoscope and Biograph Company, challenged his suit. In a 1907 decision, the U.S. Circuit Court of Appeals found for Edison, upholding his camera patent.

By then Americans had fallen in love with motion pictures, but most of those that Edison produced were dull and pedantic. Biograph and other companies were obviously here to stay. Edison's next move was to bring his principal competitor into the monopoly. Thus, in 1907, he organized the Motion Picture Patent Company with Biograph, his main rival. Anyone using the patents of the new company paid a substantial fee; those who refused to pay were destroyed. The raw capitalism of that time was not for the fainthearted.

Altogether, Edison and Biograph licensed only nine U.S. producers and one importer. Using his monopoly power, Edison standardized the release of movies, determining when, where, how, and by whom films were shown and the fee imposed on theater owners.

His control of the movie industry was strong, profitable, but stifling. Ultimately, Universal Film challenged his control. Again Edison sued, but this time infelicitously. In 1917, the U.S. Supreme Court ruled that the license agreements issued by the Motion Picture Patent Company were illegal. A year later, Edison sold his movie company and left that business forever. As always, he was into something else.

Edison's last great quest began in the late 1920s: for a plant that produced rubber. America was then dependent on foreign plantations to supply its raw rubber, a commodity most keenly needed in the automobile industry. Edison led a massive, multiyear search to find the right plant, examining thousands of samples from all over the world. From the plant he eventually chose (the goldenrod), Edison was able to produce only a few pounds of rubber per acre. By the time of his death, he had the yield up to 150 pounds per acre. Later, John Miller, Edison's brother-in-law, got the yield up to 300 pounds. With that, the Edison family stopped its research, turning the project over to the U.S. Department of Agriculture.

When World War II erupted and the predicted rubber shortage emerged, chemists devised a carbon-based substitute, which was cheaper and easier to produce. Nonetheless, Edison had made another discovery, though one for which patents did not then exist. One of his last political forays was to urge Congress to expand the patent laws to include plants. Congress enacted that legislation, the Plant Patent Act, in 1930. The first such patent went to Henry Rosenberg, who on August 18, 1931, received plant patent number 1 for his champagne-colored "climbing" rose.

Edison died in October 1931. His son Charles took control of Edison Industries, though he also served as secretary of the navy (1937–1940) and governor of New Jersey (1941–1944). In 1956, the company gave the Edison laboratory to the National Park Service. In 1957, Edison Industries merged with McGraw Electric, becoming McGraw Edison, where Charles served as chairman of the board. Fittingly, that company's best-known product was the Toastmaster, a popular toaster. The filament used to brown toast was the same as the one in Edison's first working lightbulb.

Though Edison died three-quarters of a century ago, the intellectual property practices and strategies he devised are exemplary even today. With some inventions, such as those in phonographs, his patents were so simple, so elegant, and so comprehensive that they stood alone as a defense for his creation. Others, such as those in electricity and lighting, required a fortress approach, patenting all and everything related to that invention and the surrounding systems. Edison repeatedly used patents to attract investors and to promote himself.

But Edison did not rely solely on his patents to protect his intellectual property. When trademarks were available, he reinforced his patents with them. In the movie and phonograph business, he also followed a strategy, filing applications for all of his creations on disk and film. By this, he devised a layered defense—using patents, copyrights, and trademarks to secure his inventions. If one form of protection was penetrated, he could rely on others as a defense.

For his alkaline battery, cement, and other ventures, Edison established license arrangements, as he did in motion pictures. He was thus able to maintain a degree of control in the industry, while drawing royalties and creating a basis for cross-licensing arrangements.

Finally, Edison was a fierce litigator. To pirate his patents, copyrights, or trademarks was to invite a wrathful response in the courts. Many did, and many lost substantially. Regardless of whether he won or lost in court, all knew that Edison aggressively defended his intellectual property, thereby discouraging interlopers. In retrospect, his successes with inventions and creations, coupled with his failures in business, reveal that he inadvertently created what was, in fact, the first modern intellectual property company—that is, an organization whose real business is the creation of intellectual properties that can be successfully commercialized through a variety of strategies.

Edison's world was filled with pirates, counterfeiters, and infringers. He understood how they worked and he took appropriate action, not always legally but generally effectively. With the rising globalization of the world economy in the latter part of the twentieth century, new opportunities have been created for these old crimes. Indeed, piracy and counterfeiting are well on their way to being one of the growth industries of the new century. Thomas Alva Edison would have understood perfectly the inadequacies of the old defenses and the need to create new ones for today's global economy.

CHAPTER 3

A WORLD OF PIRATES

Lynn Brown's ingrown toenail was inflamed, so Brown, a US Air flight attendant from Pell City, Alabama, went to her doctor, who prescribed a common antibiotic named gentamicin. She took the prescription to her pharmacy, got it filled, and began her treatment. Almost immediately, she lost her balance and could barely walk. Unknowingly, Brown's pharmacist had filled her prescription with a contaminated, counterfeit antibiotic that destroyed her vestibular function—her ability to balance. The damage was permanent.

Lynn Brown is lucky to be alive. She is also lucky not to be deaf or have damaged kidneys, as happened to others who got some of this same polluted medicine. CBS News reports that counterfeit gentamicin "may be to blame for hundreds of severe reactions and at least 66 deaths in the U.S." In 1996, Flavine International, a company owned by a German executive, admitted that for years it had been importing nine counterfeit drugs into the United States, including gentamicin. Flavine acquired these drugs from Long March Pharmaceuticals, a Chinese producer.

The U.S. Justice Department indicted Flavine International and its German owner. Eventually, a deal was struck: a $1 million fine was paid, the owner was sentenced to jail for two years, and Flavine promised never to violate U.S. drug regulations again.

Despite the damage to Brown and others, the Food and Drug Administration allowed Flavine to continue importing gentamicin and other drugs. In 1999, California and Colorado hospitals reported that patients taking gentamicin were having strange reactions. The FDA then wrote Long March, the supplier, a letter complaining of its defective manufacturing processes but inexplicably allowed the Chinese company to continue exporting its products to the U.S.

Despite the FDA's demand, the complaints from U.S. patients increased. Finally, in June 2000, the FDA blocked imports from Long March. In December 2000, Long March changed its name to Leshan Sanjiu. In May 2003, the FDA stopped shipments from Leshan Sanjiu into the U.S. If Long March/Leshan Sanjiu is not exporting into the United States under some new corporate name, it would be surprising. Meanwhile, Lynn Brown and the six hundred other identified victims are rebuilding their lives and alerting others to the dangers of counterfeit medicines (www.wobblers.com).

Samuel Johnson said, "No man has yet become great by imitation." "Perhaps not," the *Economist* notes, "but many have become rich that way."

The business model for counterfeiting is simple: identify a popular product, preferably a well-known brand, copy it, sell it, and keep all the profits. Though the model is simple, the nature of pirating varies significantly. Some pirates are little more than petty thieves, making unauthorized downloads of music and movies from the Internet for their own pleasure. Still, several million petty crimes can add up to massive losses if the theft occurs in a particular industry, such as pirating music online.

Other pirates are major criminals, working in enterprises that systematically steal the patented, copyrighted, and trademarked products of others on a grand scale. These "enterprise pirates" are found in every nation, and their operations range in size from a blacksmith shop hammering out fake bolts for airplane landing gear to multinational crime syndicates.

Finally, state-sanctioned piracy is theft in its most costly manifestation. It is one thing to steal a copy of a song from a CD but quite another to steal the entire consumer electronics industry from another nation. Today, several governments are actively engaged in efforts to do just that: seize the entire industries of other nations. Often, their efforts are nothing less than piracy on a worldwide scale.

"Petty" and "enterprise-level" pirating are almost the perfect crimes because governments everywhere, including that of the United States, refuse to adequately enforce their laws against such activities. American efforts to stop product pirates are so small relative to the size of the crime wave that they are little more than tokenism. Consequently, a counterfeiter's risk of detection is tiny, the jeopardy of indictment is even smaller, and the hazard of imprisonment is almost zero. Not surprisingly, Colombian and Mexican drug dealers find that product counterfeiting is far safer than drug smuggling—a white-collar crime with fewer penalties and laxer enforcement. Counterfeiting also involves a better-educated class of criminals.

The U.S. Justice Department's 2001 annual performance report reveals what a smart career choice counterfeiting is for those considering a life of crime. That year, the department filed only 106 cases involving 162 defendants trafficking in counterfeit goods, services, audios, movies, sound recordings, music videos of live performances, and the criminal infringement of copyrights. Of the 76 defendants the courts convicted or who pled guilty, only 25 did prison time. By contrast, in 2001, the Justice Department filed charges in 8,471 drug cases, involving 7,007 defendants, and had a 90 percent conviction rate that year. For every 280 people sent to jail for dealing drugs, only one goes for trafficking in counterfeit goods.

The profit potential in counterfeiting is enormous. The business requires no research, no development, and no warranties; it allows shoddy materials and substandard production practices. In digital counterfeiting, the knock-off is as good as the original, and often the phonies are difficult to detect. Small costs and large profits are the very essence of pirated and counterfeit goods.

As for the size of the market, the Federal Bureau of Investigation reports that counterfeiting costs the U.S. economy between $200 billion and $250 billion annually. The FBI data comes from the International AntiCounterfeiting Coalition, which calculates the losses from worldwide copyright, trademark, and trade secret infringement. That does not include losses created from the theft or infringement of U.S. patents, which are substantial.

Absent global detection and enforcement of intellectual property rights, pirating and counterfeiting touch all nations and nearly all goods. They steal business and profits from legitimate owners. They rob taxes and revenues from governments at all levels. They trick consumers into buying products such as fake medicines and phone parts, which can be life threatening. They are largely anonymous crimes, enabling seemingly lawful people and businesses to participate invisibly in this most profitable of corruptions.

Unfortunately, Lynn Brown's experience with a bad medicine is not unique. Despite the efforts of the Food and Drug Administration, counterfeiters such as Long March continue to slip their fake medicines into the U.S. market. In March 2003, the FDA discovered that counterfeit versions of Procrit, a stimulant of red blood cells used in cancer treatment, had been slipped into the U.S. supply. The FDA says the fake is contaminated with bacteria and has no active ingredient. The pharmaceutical maker Serono has twice located supplies of phony Serostim, an anti-AIDS drug, on the market. In February 2002, the FDA warned consumers to immediately stop using PC SPES and SPES, two dietary supplement/herbal products. The California Department of Health Services found that PC SPES contained warfarin, a prescription anticoagulant, and SPES contained alprazolam, a habit-forming tranquilizer. BotanicLab, the maker of SPES and PC SPES, voluntarily issued a national recall of both products. A company representative said it believed the contamination had occurred with one of its suppliers in China.

These fakes get into the U.S. pharmaceutical market via several routes. One is when corrupt distributors or pharmacists "repackage" wholesale drugs into retail packages. At that point, the fake medicines are mixed with the real. Another way is through bulk purchases of defective active ingredients. In this method, the counterfeiter blends substandard ingredients into real medicines, a deadly swindle that is difficult to detect. Sometimes drugs that are diverted out of the U.S. market are returned illegally. Often, these drugs are past their shelf life and thus ineffective, but the counterfeiters prepare false labels, containers, seals, and certificates of analysis that fool legitimate pharmaceutical distributors. No matter the technique, counterfeit medicines are getting into the U.S. market and doing so on a substantial scale.

How big is the problem? No one really knows because, as the World Health Organization (WHO) points out, counterfeiting is an underworld activity and many countries, particularly developing nations, neither investigate nor report counterfeit operations. However, other data sources exist. Harvey Bale, the director general of the International Federation of Pharmaceutical Manufacturers Associations, estimates that 1 to 2 percent of the worldwide pharmaceutical supplies are counterfeit, which is probably too conservative an estimate. The problem, Bale says, is far worse in the developing nations, such as those of Africa, where the overall fake rate is between 25 and 50 percent.

WHO data reveal why counterfeit drugs are so dangerous. Between December 2000 and December 2001, WHO scientists analyzed forty-two different types of substandard medicines sold in twenty countries. They divided them into five categories:

1. Products without active ingredients (43 percent)

2. Products with inadequate quantities of active ingredients (21 percent)

3. Products with incorrect active ingredients (24 percent)

4. Products produced by copying someone else's medicines (2 percent)

5. Products with correct quantities of active ingredients but with the wrong name of manufacturer and/or country of manufacture on the label (7 percent)

The WHO data revealed that roughly 9 out of every 10 medicines are either without any active ingredients, have too few, or have the wrong ingredients altogether. Thus, the patient either gets no useful medication, or too little, or something perhaps even harmful, as Lynn Brown did. What makes these drugs lethal is that they are made so they cannot be distinguished from the real thing.

Clearly, producing and selling substandard medicines as the real thing are more serious matters than simply operating a fraudulent business; sometimes they are nothing less than murder. The WHO reports repeated instances of counterfeiters mixing glycerol with diethylene glycol and passing the concoction off as a legitimate medicine. The WHO documents how this has killed 109 children in Nigeria (1990), 223 children in Bangladesh (1992), 23 patients in Argentina (1992), and 89 children in Haiti (1996). During Niger's 1995 meningitis epidemic, more than 50,000 people were inoculated with fake vaccines containing no antigen, resulting in the death of 2,500.

In underdeveloped nations, the sale and distribution of counterfeit medicines take place on such a scale and is of such consequence that they almost amount to genocide. In Latin America, for instance, 15 to 20 percent of the entire drug market is counterfeit. In Russia, at least 5 to 10 percent of the medicines are fake. In the developing nations of Southeast Asia, approximately 10 percent of the medicines are counterfeit. In Pakistan, the counterfeit rate for medicines is 50 percent. In China, the rate is 50 percent and in certain brands up to 85 percent. In these nations, a physician has no assurance that the medicine taken is what has been prescribed. Thus, patients often die.

In Africa, an estimated one million people die of malaria each year because they do not get lifesaving treatments. More than 71 percent of the casualties are children under five years of age. The WHO claims that prompt diagnosis and treatment with real medicines could save at least 200,000 of these lives annually.

The risk of sickness in developing nations is enormous. Some simple arithmetic illustrates the situation. Malaria remains the world's major killer. The WHO reports that between 300 million and 500 million people are carrying the disease. The infection rate in countries such as Guinea is extraordinarily high, roughly 75 out of every 100 people. In Botswana and Angola, it is more than 48 percent. The WHO reports that more than 38 percent of the malaria treatments sold in such developing nations are counterfeits with no medicinal value.

Producing and selling counterfeit medicines to poor and ignorant people are an unscrupulous business, but they are profitable. The sales potential exists largely because most nations do not regulate the production, distribution, import, export, or use of medicines. The WHO reports that fewer than 40 of its 191 member states have a strict regulatory regime. More than 60 have no regulations at all. The others have varying levels of regulatory capacity. Even where rules do exist, the counterfeiters have unlimited chances to slip their fake goods into the long supply line that stretches from production through multiple layers of distribution and on to final consumption by patients.

Another reason that counterfeiting is so prevalent in the developing world is that most people must pay for their own drugs. Unlike Europe, Japan, or even the United States, where there are major health insurance programs and government support, there are no ways to enforce quality control in those nations. Poor, sick people are easy victims.

Without honest oversight, corruption finds a fertile field. In nations such as Taiwan, China, India, and Russia, mighty criminal enterprises produce, move, and market counterfeit medicines. Their governments protect them.

Before globalization, citizens of the developed world could smugly view the possibility of counterfeit drugs entering the U.S. market as something far from their lives. Now that is no longer true. The FDA, in its 2002 Performance Plan Summary, states, "The agency is unable to assure the U.S. public that it can prevent unsafe imports from entering the country." This is an honest and brave statement.

In hearings held by the House Commerce Committee in 2001, the FDA reported that international mail brings into the United States more than two million unregulated parcels a year that contain regulated drugs. However, that agency lacks the personnel to inspect virtually any of these packages. The FDA also is able to inspect very few of the drugs coming from Mexico, which serves American consumers from thousands of pharmacies just inside its border cities, such as Tijuana. Much of this Mexican medicine comes from Colombia, China, and India and is counterfeit.

More recently, the FDA has reported that hundreds of Internet sites are offering to Americans counterfeit medicines from foreign factories. The agency catches and closes some of these sites, but others pop up to take their place. The FDA's problem, of course, is that the U.S. government has long starved it of enforcement funds. In 2000, the FDA had only 68 people to monitor 310 points of entry into the United States.

Perhaps most worrisome, FDA officials tell Congress that more than 80 percent of the bulk active ingredients that go into U.S. prescription drugs are imported. Worse, the agency has information on only 18 percent of the companies supplying these ingredients. Consequently, it has never inspected the facilities of more than 4,600 foreign companies that supply most of the ingredients used in U.S. prescription medicines. More troubling, the FDA reports that 623 firms from China and 409 from India that manufacture drugs for export to the United States have never been inspected to determine if they meet required current good manufacturing practices (GMPs). Of all nations, China and India are the world's two main counterfeiters of medicines.

Congressman Fred Upton (R.-Mich.), who chaired sessions during the House Commerce Committee's hearing on counterfeit medicines, explained the danger:

> A bulk quantity of as little as 50 kilograms can be used in the production of millions of tablets or capsules. Thus, only one counterfeit bulk that contains an impurity or is synthesized improperly could cause immediate death or injury to numerous people.

Simply put, the FDA does not know, nor can it guarantee, that the active ingredients used in U.S. pharmaceuticals meet the nation's standards. Nor can other governments do the same for their citizens. This is a spectacular and dangerous failure.

The cost of counterfeiting pharmaceuticals is so small and the interdiction efforts of the world's governments so weak that the major medicine makers decided in 2001 to mount their own anticounterfeiting programs, creating the Pharmaceutical Security Institute (PSI). This new institute works closely with U.S. and European trade negotiators, local law enforcement officials, health care authorities, and customs services.

At the same moment that the pharmaceutical industry is trying to strengthen patent protections, the less developed nations in the WTO are seeking to weaken them. In August 2003, the WTO reached an agreement by which poor nations can compel the patent owners of medicines to license production to a local manufacturer. If a country lacks the necessary manufacturing capacity, it can import the drugs from other nations that produce them, such as South Africa, India, or Brazil.

Three WTO conditions are imposed on nations when they issue compulsory licenses. First, the exporting nation is required to notify the WTO when it issues a compulsory license, plus its terms and conditions, which the WTO then posts on its Web site. Second, importing nations, other than the least developed countries, such as Uganda and Ethiopia, are also required to list on the WTO site their intention to use this compulsory licensing system, which is also posted on the Web. Finally, companies making drugs under a compulsory license are prohibited from diverting them to developed countries and are required to use special labels, colors, shapes, and sizes to differentiate these medicines from the originals.

The WTO gives several examples of such differentiation that local manufacturers should follow. Bristol-Myers Squibb, for instance, uses different markings and imprints on capsules supplied to sub-Saharan Africa. Novartis employs a different name and packaging for the antimalarial drug it provides developing countries. GlaxoSmithKline, Merck, and Pfizer use one combination of coloring, packaging, and numbering for the developed world and another for medicines sold in developing countries. The expectation is that if Brazil or India issues a compulsory license for a medicine for its domestic market, any exports to other nations would be marked differently.

The promise of WTO's compulsory licensing program is that it will reduce the costs and increase the availability of real medicines for the sick and dying people of the developing world. The danger is that pharmaceutical makers in Brazil, India, and elsewhere, which have long pirated the patented medicines of the U.S., Europe, and Japan, will simply use this WTO provision as a back door to slip their products into those rich markets, while ignoring the poor.

Before the creation of the patent accord, countries such as Brazil and India arbitrarily used foreign patents without notification or payments of royalties. Now such takings must come through a global forum, with more transparency. For patent holders, that alone is an important improvement. Unfortunately, compulsory licensing does not guarantee lower prices, a reduction in counterfeiting, or even better-quality products because many local pharmaceutical manufacturers in the developing world are the world's principal source of defective drugs. Their notoriously corrupt local governments show little willingness to police production, distribution, pricing, and black market operations. More discouraging, almost all of the 316 drugs on the WHO's model list of essential medicines are generic, in the public domain, freely available to any country or company for manufacture. The WTO patent accord does nothing to relieve the shortage of those drugs, or even to protect them from counterfeiters using fake components.

The good news is that prices for real drugs can be cut substantially through negotiations between health ministries and the major pharmaceutical makers. The Pan American Health Organization reports that the average prices of a one-year treatment with antiretrovirals in ten countries of Latin America and the Caribbean were cut by 54 percent in one year through bulk purchase negotiations between those governments and the pharmaceutical companies. In Argentina, for instance, the price for a year's treatment fell from $5,100 in 2001 to $1,300 in 2002.

A paradoxical aside to these nations' success is that the Medicare Act passed by the U.S. Congress in November 2003 explicitly prohibits the federal government from negotiating with pharmaceutical companies to get similar bulk price cuts for U.S. Medicare beneficiaries.

While stealing and counterfeiting others' property is as old as commerce itself, globalization of the world's economy, with all of its impersonal tools of international commerce, is facilitating a rapid expansion of this crime. People are now doing massive amounts of business with individuals and groups they do not know and will never meet again, thereby removing centuries-old practices and relationships that once encouraged integrity in the marketplace. In the absence of private means, public scrutiny becomes ever more important.

To be sure, some governments attempt to catch these pirates and counterfeiters. In the United States, the agency principally responsible for intercepting phony goods entering the U.S. market is the Customs Service. Created in 1789, it was the first federal law enforcement agency. Its duties then were to collect import and tariff duties and to prevent smuggling.

Today, Customs still has those traditional missions. Over two centuries, however, there has been mission creep. Customs is now responsible for enforcing four hundred different laws administered by forty separate federal agencies. When Congress placed Customs in the new Department of Homeland Security, it also expanded the agency's mission to include the investigative and enforcement functions of the Immigration and Naturalization Service—a major task involving millions of people illegally slipping into the United States annually.

Of the four hundred laws, enforcing those on counterfeiting is not Customs' top priority. Because of mission overload and understaffing, Customs apprehends only a tiny fraction of the counterfeit goods flowing into the United States. In 2002, its staff apprehended a total of $60 million in phony goods. The Federal Bureau of Investigation (FBI) estimates that counterfeiting imports cost the U.S. economy $200 billion to $250 billion annually, thus Customs is catching barely two ten-thousandths of one percent. Weighing the risks of capture against the rewards of success, counterfeiting is a crime where the chance of detention is so small as to be negligible. Here, crime does pay.

Some U.S. industries heavily targeted by global pirates, such as pharmaceuticals, software, and digital products, rely primarily on their own detectives and lawyers to catch the pirates stealing their intellectual property. Those industries do not disdain the law enforcement efforts of the U.S. government; they just cannot depend upon them.

These businesses secure enforcement aid from the government mainly by diplomatic means: they lean on nations to enact and then enforce strong national intellectual property protections. So far, most other governments, particularly those of the developing nations, have not responded especially well.

To put the spotlight on foreign intellectual-property pirates, the U.S.

Trade Representative (USTR) issues annually the *Special 301 Report,* which reviews the adequacy of other nations' intellectual property protections. Congress also requires the USTR to identify those nations that are the worst violators of U.S. intellectual property laws or that refuse to engage in good-faith negotiations over those acts. The worst offenders are blacklisted as priority foreign countries.

Being a priority foreign country is not a compliment; it means that the USTR must negotiate a change in that nation's practices or else take some remedial action, such as imposing trade sanctions. Countries with lesser intellectual property offenses are on a "priority watch list" or a "watch list." The USTR is also required to negotiate an end to their errant ways.

In 2004, the agency identified fifty-two violating nations. The list is skewed by political considerations. Some chronic violators, such as Japan, are omitted.

Many countries on these lists, such as Argentina, Brazil, India, Colombia, the Philippines, Saudi Arabia, Venezuela, and Vietnam, are notorious repeat offenders. These violators are not all poor and developing nations. Italy and other members of the European Union seriously infringe on patents, copyrights, trademarks, and trade secrets of American owners.

The intellectual property violations of three nations identified in the 2004 *Special 301 Report* demonstrate how their governments enable these crimes, making counterfeiting nothing less than state-sanctioned theft. Brazil, for example, is one of the world's largest pirate markets. In 2003, the value of copyright piracy there exceeded $785 million. Counterfeiting is so rampant that virtually every audiocassette sold in Brazil is a pirated copy. Yet the government arrests few of these pirates and convicts almost none.

Taiwan's criminal organizations make so much money from counterfeiting that they are now financing pirate operations in Hong Kong, Malaysia, and mainland China. The piracy rate for movies in Taiwan is 44 percent; for entertainment games, it is 42 percent; and for software, it is close to 41 percent. Movie and game pirating in Taiwan alone costs U.S. companies more than $300 million annually. Music pirating is so pervasive there that it has driven most legitimate producers into bankruptcy.

The Philippines is now one of the world's "safe havens" for organized pirates and industrial-scale counterfeiting. Its many counterfeit products include clothing, medicine, consumer electronics, automotive products, cosmetics, toys, books, American television programs, and software. Philippine pirates ship these bogus goods throughout Europe, Asia, Africa, and the Middle East. They act with impunity because the government in Manila refuses to enact remedial legislation, let alone capture and prosecute local pirates.

Of all nations, intellectual property theft by Japan and China is the most important to the United States. It is so sophisticated, massive, and damaging that it merits a separate examination in Part II of this book.

Soon after the 9/11 terrorist attacks, Cranston Print Works produced a men's patriotic necktie whose copyrighted design subtly blends the red, white, and blue stripes and stars of the flag into an attractive pattern. A few weeks after Cranston began distributing its ties, pirated copies suddenly became available from China. Cranston, which was founded in 1824, traces its roots back to Samuel Slater through its 1936 purchase of the Slater East Village mill in Webster, Massachusetts, making it the oldest textile-printing company in the United States. Slater, of course, is the person who in the late 1780s brought to America England's secret of how to spin thread mechanically.

Cranston employs forty designers to develop its patterns. George Shuster, CEO of the employee-owned Rhode Island company, says the theft of a pattern is "just like a thief coming into our business and stealing a pile of money." And it is. As part of the company's efforts to catch the pattern pirates, Shuster established a bounty program in which employees are urged to look out for rip-offs. If they see a pirated design, they are asked to buy it. If they are wrong, they are reimbursed for the purchase. If they are right, they get a percentage of any legal settlement that Cranston Print Works may receive from the infringers, which can range from a minimum of $250 up to $2,500.

Schuster reports that the Cranston "bounty" program results in one or two copyright infringement discoveries per month. Whenever the company catches a pattern pirate, it sends a cease-and-desist letter. Often, that does not work. At any given moment, Cranston has between twenty-five and thirty copyright infringement lawsuits under way. In the United States, Shuster says, such lawsuits are very effective. Cranston merely presents its copyright and puts its design beside that of the pirate. That is usually sufficient. Shuster also says that Cranston has filed a lawsuit in China, but the effort was worthless. China does not have functioning judicial procedures to deal with such theft.

The big surprise, Shuster says, is how Canada handles pattern pirating.

Canadian law requires plaintiffs in such cases to hire an artist, who makes a black-and-white drawing of the copyrighted item and then produces a similar drawing of the contested pattern. The two are placed one over the other. If the pirated version deviates even slightly, it is considered an original work. Shades of color are ignored. Thus, proving pattern piracy in Canada is difficult if not impossible: smart pirates there know to vary, just a little, their rip-offs from the originals.

Pattern theft, which costs U.S. textile companies more than $100 million each year, is only one of the ways profits, stability, jobs, and even the very existence of the textile and apparel sector, America's largest manufacturing employer, is now threatened by foreign-based pirating and counterfeiting. The International Trademark Association reports that 22 percent of all apparel and shoes sold worldwide are counterfeit. The portion of the U.S. market taken by fakes, 22.8 percent, is slightly higher than the world average. Another measure of the threat is that the U.S. Customs Service reports that counterfeit apparel constituted 15 percent of all illegal goods it seized in 2003. This theft is massive, in excess of $20 billion annually in the U.S. market alone.

Not only is the U.S. textile and apparel industry one of the world's largest victims of counterfeiting, the United States is also the world biggest market for counterfeit apparels and textiles. The existing black market has two elements. The first is clothing that bears sham labels of leading producers such as Ralph Lauren, Calvin Klein, Guess, Levi's, Coach, and Donna Karan. The second are goods made in one nation, such as China or Pakistan, but labeled and shipped as if they were made in another. Such false labeling and transshipment violates U.S. trade laws. American retailers often sell transshipped goods with counterfeit labels, thereby violating both these laws.

Apparel with spurious labels comes to America from all over the world. Often, the factories that produce the originals also fabricate the fakes. They have the patterns and simply continue making the goods. Most U.S. buyers are unaware when such production overruns are made. In recent years, American companies have increasingly gone to Hong Kong and China, where they contract their work to agents. These agents in turn subcontract the production to others. Today, China and Hong Kong have more than 44,000 apparel factories and four million apparel workers available for such contracting.

While Washington has an agreement with China and Hong Kong that allows its customs inspectors to investigate these factories for evidence of transshipping and counterfeiting, it is done only sparingly and rarely at night, when much of the pirated production is accomplished. In the four-year period 2000–2003, U.S. Customs textile production teams made only forty-two visits to twenty-two separate countries, where they inspected almost 1,700 factories. Although six visits were made to Hong Kong, there were none made in China. A majority of these twenty-two nations received only one visit during that period.

The results from those visits, however, are dramatic. Based on information developed on those trips, customs officials targeted for inspection almost 2,500 foreign apparel shipments entering the U.S. They found that a quarter of them contained illegal imports. Despite such successes, the Customs Service performs few foreign on-site reviews because it has only a handful of textile inspectors: barely three hundred people to staff more than three hundred entry points and visit at least two dozen major textile-exporting countries. More than 3 million apparel shipments, worth more than $85 billion, enter the U.S. every year. The Customs Service has enough people to inspect about one-hundredth of one percent of them. Viewed another way, the odds of a shipment of counterfeit or transshipped apparel being caught as it enters the U.S. are about one in ten thousand.

The General Accountability Office reports that Customs will lose its authority to make visits to foreign factories in all those nations that send textiles and apparels into the United States under quota. Consequently, it projects that the already weak interdiction efforts will be further eroded.

The problem is enormous. As long ago as 1992, the Customs Service estimated that Chinese transshipments into the U.S. market exceeded $2 billion annually. In 1994, Customs reported that China could not account for almost $11 billion of its apparel exports. Most of these phantom products likely came to America. Put into perspective, $11 billion buys almost 3 billion pieces of Chinese-made apparel, or roughly ten garments for each person in the United States.

The Customs Service catches very little of this massive inflow, because leaders of the U.S. government do not want some laws strictly enforced. Immigration laws are one. Laws against textile counterfeiting and trans-shipment are another. The question, of course, is why the government allows an illegal activity to overwhelm legal producers and destroy the jobs of hundreds of thousands of U.S. citizens.

One reason is China. The interdiction of between $3 billion and $11 billion in counterfeit or smuggled garments would be seen as hostile and surely precipitate a major diplomatic crisis. A succession of U.S. presidents has refrained from protesting in view of larger geopolitical objectives, such as securing China's help in dealing with North Korea's nuclear program and its purchases of U.S. Treasury bonds, which finance a major portion of the U.S. budget deficit.

Another key factor is the logistical reality that selling several billion pairs of black market pants, blouses, dresses, and shirts requires a massive distribution and marketing system in the United States. Thus, exporters of counterfeit textile and apparel products cannot, and do not, operate alone; they require U.S. outlets able to handle massive volume. Many American retailers and importers make their stores available, blending legal and illegal goods on their shelves. Then they lobby behind the scenes, generally through their retail and import associations, to weaken U.S. interdiction efforts.

Most of these retailers and importers are neither dupes nor victims. Inevitably, they know the source of their illicit goods. Three billion pieces of hot clothing do not just accidentally fall off the backs of trucks at their backdoor loading docks.

Months before the apparel arrives at their stores, some major retailers and designers go to the foreign producers or their agents, show their patterns, look at material samples, place orders, establish timetables, and agree on terms and methods of payment. If these retailers and importers buy something in China and it arrives from Nigeria, they know it has been illegally transshipped, to avoid the quota on importing. For most of these outlet owners, the illegality of this swindle is irrelevant because the profits are so great.

Ultimately, transshipping and importing counterfeit goods are as much about politics as about production, marketing, and distribution. It is a crass relationship. Today, U.S. retailers and importers are a principal source of campaign funds for presidential and congressional candidates. One of the quid pro quos for these contributions is that the beneficiaries diminish the Customs Service's interdiction efforts with short funding.

This low political theater has its own particular logic. In Act I, a few members of Congress from the ten largest textile- and apparel-producing states publicly press the president to increase the number of customs agents assigned to capture counterfeit apparel.

In Act II, the congressional leadership enacts legislation that authorizes the employment of additional customs agents. This causes a rash of political announcements that the government will finally stop illegal transshipment and imports of counterfeit apparel.

In Act III, the funding for these new hires mysteriously disappears in a budget and appropriation process that generally occurs late at night, in the final moments of a congressional session, far out of sight of C-Span cameras—sometimes on unrecorded voice votes. Consequently, Customs is again left with only a handful of people to do a job that requires thousands.

Cutting Customs' funding is the job of some elected officials and lobbyists who receive the retailers' and importers' political contributions. Accepting those cuts silently and passively is the price required of others. Some members of Congress refuse to participate in this corrupt political kabuki, but they are not a majority and thus their votes do not matter in the larger scheme of things. A few members are unaware of what is happening.

As these political games suggest, textile and apparel counterfeiting and transshipments are crimes that pit one interest against another—producers versus retailers. Ultimately, the side that demonstrates the greater capacity to provide campaign funds holds the upper hand. In this, retailers and importers dominate, reflecting their greater wealth and larger political contributions.

Using that strength, retailers and importers have persuaded Congress to ratify trade agreements that eliminated all U.S. quotas on textile and apparel imports after January 1, 2005. After that date, China, India, Pakistan, or any other nation will be able to legally ship as many textiles and articles of clothing into the U.S. market as they wish and retailers will be able to legally stock those goods. Even so, the counterfeiting of apparel and textiles will remain a major crime.

Smuggling fake goods into the U.S. market is a trifle compared to the loss overseas of stolen intellectual properties.

According to the International Intellectual Property Alliance (IIPA), a private-sector coalition of six trade associations, the core "copyright industries" are music and book publishing, radio and television broadcasting, cable television, newspapers and periodicals, records and tapes, motion pictures, theatrical productions, advertising, computer software, and data processing.

These large, rich industries are important to the U.S. economy. Stephen E. Siwek, a principal in the Washington-based firm Economists Incorporated, reported that in 2001 copyright-based industries contributed more than $535 billion to the U.S. gross domestic product (5.24 percent of the total GDP) and employed more than 4.7 million people (3.5 percent of total jobs).

Siwek also disclosed that in 2002 foreign sales and exports of the copyright-based industries exceeded $88 billion. Copyright-based companies had more exports in dollar value than any other sector of the U.S. economy in 2002, including agriculture, textiles, apparel, electronics, aircraft, motor vehicles, and chemicals. While the U.S. economy as a whole had a trade deficit of almost $500 billion that year, American moviemakers ran a trade surplus with every other nation, a unique performance.

Taken together, America's copyright industries are one of the U.S. economy's few growth sectors. These industries are particularly vulnerable to counterfeiting because of the wide availability of inexpensive digital copying technologies and the growing capacity of the Internet to transmit large files quickly. Most new computers, for instance, can make perfect digital copies, including of DVDs. Thus, literally anyone with a modern computer, operating from virtually anywhere, can exactly duplicate software, music, and movies. The Motion Picture Association of America (MPAA) reports that pirated DVDs were not a problem for the industry in 1999 but by 2002, the MPAA had seized more than 7 million pirated DVDs worldwide. Equally significant, the MPAA said that with the rapid introduction of broadband, high-speed Internet connections, Net users as of 2003 were downloading between 400,000 and 600,000 movies *every day*, all illegally.

The Business Software Alliance (BSA), the major trade group for software makers, stated that the global piracy rate for software in 2002 was 39 percent, and in the U.S., it was 23 percent. The economic cost of this theft is high. In the U.S. alone, the software industry lost an estimated $2 billion in profits, more than 105,000 jobs, approximately $5.3 billion in lost wages, and more than $1.4 billion in lost tax revenues that otherwise would have flowed to the various levels of government.

Overall, the IIPA asserts that worldwide digital piracy costs America's copyright industry $20 billion to $22 billion annually, and that approximation excludes illegal Internet downloads. Optical disc technology makes digital theft easy. Laser discs (LDs), video compact discs (VCDs), and digital video discs (DVDs) are simple to make, inexpensive to produce, and easy to distribute. The digital copies are perfect duplicates of the original, and tens of thousands of perfect counterfeits can be made daily.

In testimony before the House Judiciary Committee in March 2003, Jack

Valenti, president of the MPAA, reported that there were twenty-six large-scale optical production facilities in Russia. These plants have the capacity to produce 300 million DVDs and CDs a year, though the legal demand in Russia is only 18 million units annually. Valenti told Congress that as of early 2003 pirated Russian DVDs were showing up in Europe, Russia's target market. He warned that "if bold actions are not taken quickly to shut down this piracy, American sales of copyrighted works to Western Europe—our most lucrative market in the world—will be demolished by these pirated imports from Russia."

Actually, Russia is only just catching up with other nations, many of which have older, larger, and more diversified counterfeiting industries. In Indonesia, for instance, the IIPA reports that the piracy rate for U.S. movies is 92 percent, music 87 percent, and business software 81 percent. In India, the world's second most populous nation and a major producer of legitimate copyrighted goods, the piracy rates for U.S. products are high: movies 60 percent, music CDs 40 percent, business software 69 percent, and books 36 percent. Even higher piracy rates exist in China and a handful of new nations, such as Ukraine, that once made up the old Soviet Union.

Of course, such theft is not limited to foreign consumers. Americans also steal. In 2002, the Business Software Alliance released a study that measured software piracy state by state for the year 2001. The rate ranged from a low of 12 percent in New York State to a high of almost 49 percent in Mississippi. Seemingly, the denser the population, the less software crime there is.

Another factor favoring the digital pirates is the ease of shipment in today's global economy. Even after the 9/11 terrorist attacks, the Customs Service had only enough personnel to inspect roughly one percent of the containers entering this country. Pirates often pack their digital goods inside bulkier legal cargo or put hidden compartments in shipping containers. Acting on tips, police have found fake DVDs in bags of asphalt, stacks of cardboard boxes, secret compartments in cars, and just about everywhere else.

Jack Valenti reports that Macau marine police, working with Hong Kong Customs, caught two specially built smugglers' submarines. These boats could submerge and surface using compressed air tanks. When they were underwater, fishing boats towed them. One contained 174,000 pirated optical disks; the other had 73,000.

Closer to home, the largest counterfeit software seizure in U.S. history illustrates the sophistication and scope of modern digital pirating. In November 2001, a task force of federal, state, and local law officials in Los Angeles arrested software pirates shipping phony goods to the United States from Taiwan through the Port of Los Angeles. The retail value of these fakes would have been more than $60 million. The inventory of fake Microsoft products apprehended included the following:

- More than 30,000 copies of Windows Millennium Edition software

- More than 4,300 counterfeit Windows XP manuals

- More than 93,000 certificate of authenticity labels

- More than 25,000 counterfeit end user license agreements

Although the raid broke this one pipeline, others continue to operate. The BSA estimates that there are 840,000 Internet sites offering illegal software as the genuine thing. With easy, quick downloads and vendors pretending to be legitimate sellers, many purchasers are unaware that they are buying stolen goods. The net result is that the U.S. has a software piracy rate of 23 percent, which means that one of every four installed computer programs in this country is a counterfeit or pirated copy.

Clearly, producers of digital products of all types have every incentive to reduce this piracy, and they try. Despite the scale and scope of counterfeiting and the harm it does to the rightful owners of the stolen intellectual property, capturing these criminals is a low priority for most governments. Sometimes corruption is the reason. For the United States and European governments, interdiction of terrorists and drugs has precedence over interdicting pirated movies and music.

By default, therefore, the principal responsibility for confronting the digital pirates resides with the copyright owners and their trade associations. As we have seen, this is nothing new. In the late nineteenth century, the federal government did little to catch stagecoach and railroad bandits, so the stage and rail companies hired private detectives like the Pinkerton Detective Agency. The scene from the movie *Butch Cassidy and the Sundance Kid* where the two robbers are chased by skilled private detectives is typical of the times.

One of the modern detectives' most basic tools is more than a century old:

the telephone. The BSA operates and publicizes toll-free hotlines, which it operates in sixty nations. Much as with the Internal Revenue Service's tip line, these hotlines allow the honest, the vengeful, and the disgruntled to report those who are infringing on others' software copyrights.

When a tip comes in, the BSA contacts the company and arranges a software audit. Since one out of every four pieces of software used nationally is counterfeit, these audits often result in user companies having to pay for unlicensed software use. Upon settlement, the BSA usually issues a press announcement that serves as a public warning to others.

The BSA also operates a global Internet crawler system. Because the Net is largely unrestricted, anonymous, and unregulated, it allows legitimate copyright owners to send electronic "spiders" quickly crawling through Internet sites to identify any infringing software offered for sale. When the BSA catches an infringer—and it catches thousands annually—it sends a notice of violation to the offender with a demand for removal of the infringing software. Most often, violators halt their activities. For those that refuse, the BSA launches highly visible legal action, including working with government authorities to secure criminal prosecution. BSA representatives go into offenders' offices with U.S. marshals armed with search warrants or sometimes court orders to seize their computers.

The Motion Picture Association of America operates an even larger antipiracy program. Each year, MPAA launches 600 investigations into suspected movie piracy and on average has 400 active cases pending at any time. MPAA has an even larger presence in other countries. In 2000, the trade association initiated 60,000 investigations into alleged pirate operations around the world and participated in 18,000 raids with local authorities. In 2002, it seized and destroyed more than seven million pirated videocassettes and optical disks. MPAA also operates a hotline, and it pays rewards to those whose tips lead to successful raids on pirate DVD factories.

While the piracy of music, movies, and software is a major problem and seems to attract most of the public attention, the piracy of books—an ancient crime—continues, made easier by the same digital technology that plagues the other copyright industries. The IIPA reports that the piracy rate for books in nations such as Russia, Pakistan, and the Philippines exceeds 40 percent of the books sold annually.

The *Chronicle of Higher Education* reports that the piracy of U.S. textbooks is running rampant in developing nations, costing publishers and authors millions of dollars. In many technical fields, such as medicine, engineering, and physics, U.S. scholars and leaders are the best in the world, and their subjects are taught in English around the world, using the same textbooks as those assigned in the United States. In many of these countries, enterprising pirates will wait outside classrooms on the first day of a semester and take orders for textbooks. Using digital techniques, many of these pirated books have covers that precisely duplicate those of the original works; they are printed on the same type of paper and have text that is literally indistinguishable from that of the real book.

In 2003, U.S. publishers lost more than $550 million to textbook piracy. Not surprisingly, foreign students think that the illegal copying of U.S. textbooks is acceptable. An Association of American Publishers survey of students in Singapore, Taiwan, and Hong Kong revealed that more than 94 percent had no qualms about buying pirate textbooks.

The principal complaint from students both in the U.S. and abroad is that textbooks cost too much. Consequently, U.S. publishers have long offered special discounts in poorer nations. Yet the crime continues. As in so many other areas where pirating flourishes, China represents a special problem. Publishers report that the Chinese government is uncooperative in stopping piracy, even going so far as to prevent U.S. publishers from hiring local experts to do research on the problem.

In 2003, publishers' chief Washington lobbyist, former U.S. Representative Patricia S. Schroeder, brought the textbook piracy problem to the attention of Robert B. Zoellick, the U.S. Trade Representative. The *Chronicle of Higher Education* reports that Zoellick "advised her that U.S. publishers need to lower their prices further in foreign markets to undercut the pirates." Fighting a price war with the thieves who stole their book does not seem an attractive solution for authors and publishers.

Despite all their efforts, authors, artists, software writers, publishers, software companies, moviemakers, and all the copyright industry trade associations can never stop global pirating on their own. Government help is required. This will be discussed in subsequent chapters.

For W. R. Grace & Co. officials, 1995 was not a good year to be in India. At dozens of mass rallies, some of which turned into riots, enraged Indians burned effigies of the Florida-based chemical company's executives. The rioters were protesting proposed changes in India's patent law that would give Grace exclusive rights there to manufacture and sell a pesticide made from seeds of the neem tree. The product would extend the shelf life of the juice from the neem tree by several weeks to several years.

To millions of Indians, the Grace patent, which was validated in the United States in 1992, is tantamount to international piracy. For many centuries, Indians have used neem bark, leaves, flowers, and seeds for everything from birth control to toothpaste. The branches even serve as a toothbrush. Oil from neem seeds is also a natural pesticide that repels more than two hundred species of insects, including beetles, boll weevils, and mosquitoes, but has no effect on the environment or helpful species such as bees. The same oil is used as fuel for lamps, facial cream, and nail polish and as a treatment for a variety of illnesses, including leprosy, diabetes, ulcers, skin disorders, and constipation.

In 1995, Grace tried to patent its enhanced neem product in India. But public opposition was so strong to foreign control of what is considered a national heritage that patent reform legislation was stalled in the Indian Parliament until 1999. Subsequently, India lodged opposition to Grace's neem patent both in the United States and in Europe. In 2000, the European Patent Office revoked Grace's patent in its entirety, saying that it lacked novelty. But more than eighty other patents on various medicinal properties of the tree remain active.

"Biopiracy" is of particular concern to India, which has a rich variety of 47,000 plant species and 81,000 species of fauna, and at least 15,000 unique plant varieties. Over the centuries, Indians have developed uses for many of these species. The Indian government recognizes more than 3,000 plants as having medicinal value, while more than 6,000 are the basis of folk and herbal treatments. Drug, biotechnology, and seed companies from the developed nations have taken some of this traditional knowledge, supplemented it with research, and obtained patents in their home countries that give them the exclusive use of their patented products for up to twenty years.

Western pharmaceutical makers, for instance, patented the wound-healing properties of India's turmeric and bitter gourd; the Indian government successfully persuaded the U.S. Patent Office to cancel the patent. Rice Tec, Inc., a U.S. company, received a patent on a hybrid of basmati rice, a delicacy that has been available in India for centuries. A Colorado firm has a patent on the yellow beans grown for centuries in Mexico and has successfully sued Mexican farmers and seed companies for infringing on its intellectual property. A Swiss company is attempting to patent the rice genome data and require royalties from those who get access to it. All that these concerns do is legal. Under existing global treaties, once the U.S., Mexico, Canada, Japan, or a European nation issues a patent, the company has exclusive right in that country for up to twenty years. The nation where the genetic material or traditional knowledge originates is not obligated to issue its own patent or enforce one issued in the U.S., Europe, or Japan. But for a developing nation to contest a patent in the developed world, an extraordinary expenditure of money and time is required. It took India five years, for instance, to persuade the European Patent Office to revoke Grace's neem patent. India has proposed at the World Trade Organization that patent applicants be required to disclose the origin of any biological materials used in their inventions and obtain the informed consent of the country of origin.

The United Nations Convention on Biological Diversity, to which 182 nations are parties, has gone several steps further. In April 2002, it adopted voluntary guidelines to protect developing nations from having their native species seized and exploited by foreign corporations. These guidelines are a first step toward national legislation by participating countries and eventually a global treaty. In the U.N. guidelines, "prior informed consent" of all stakeholders is recommended. The guidelines require that genetic materials from developing nations be developed only in ways and for purposes that are formally agreed to by that country. Those terms and conditions, moreover, cannot preclude traditional uses in the host nation. Product developers would also be required to ensure a "fair and equitable" sharing of benefits. Finally, the guidelines encourage each host nation to "avoid the imposition of arbitrary restrictions on access to its genetic resources."

To the developing world, the unauthorized use of a nation's genetic resources and traditional knowledge is as egregious a form of pirating as the digital ripping, burning, and mixing of movies and music are to the developed nations.

The global counterfeiting business includes more than textiles, apparel, medicines, books, digital music, movies, and other optical works. Literally hundreds of other goods are also being pirated, including children's toys, auto parts, airplane parts, furniture, paintings, computers, bolts, watches, tools, and luxury items, among an almost endless list.

While some of this is the work of individual thieves or criminal syndicates, the most destructive and most costly pirating is that organized by national governments. In this, the United States has dirty hands. Early in its history, a succession of presidents, beginning with George Washington, John Adams, Thomas Jefferson, and James Madison, oversaw industrial expansion programs that heavily relied on the theft of foreign-owned technology. Many nations claim that this U.S. tradition continues with its support of biopiracy. But America was, and is, not alone in this tradition. Germany did the same in the late nineteenth and twentieth centuries.

PART II

THE BUSINESS
OF NATIONS

CHAPTER 4

THE GERMAN METHOD

When World War I broke out in August 1914, Britain's Royal Navy was ready. It quickly blockaded the German Imperial Fleet in its ports, forcing 734 German and Austrian merchant vessels to seek refuge in neutral harbors. By early 1915, only a third of Germany's merchant fleet remained active, and even that was restricted to the Baltic trade with neutral Sweden and Norway.

The blockade eventually cut off Germany's food supplies, but it also created an immediate economic crisis in England. When the war began, Britain depended on Germany for 90 percent of its optical glass; 75 percent of its electric light glass; most of its semifinished steel; almost 80 percent of its textile dyes; and most of its precision bearings, engine magnetos, machine tools, medical instruments, synthetic medicines, and chemicals, not to mention dozens of other German-made goods. Suddenly and almost completely, these supplies were cut off.

The British people were surprised, then distressed to realize how dependent they were on German factories, for few had understood that Britain was no longer industrially self-sufficient. Even more upsetting, the U.S. did not have substitute sources of supply to which they could turn. The U.S. also relied on German factories for nearly 90 percent of its synthetic dyes, most of its optics, scientific machinery, and medical tools, and almost all of its chemical-based pharmaceuticals. By 1914, Germany dominated those industries worldwide.

The British blockade of Germany disrupted life and work in the United States, though the country remained neutral until April 1917. As the blockade took hold, U.S. hospitals, doctors, and dentists soon exhausted their supplies of German-made "miracle" drugs. Laminal, which was needed to treat epileptic seizures, became unavailable, as did Salvarsan, the "magic bullet" that cured syphilis. Chloral hydrate, the hypnotic, and beta eucaine, the local anesthetic, were suddenly no longer obtainable. Even aspirin, a German product, was in short supply. Limited amounts of novocaine and other German-made local anesthetics forced U.S. doctors and dentists to undertake "Bulgarian operations"—surgery without any painkillers. When U.S. companies tried to fill the void, German-held patents that remained valid in neutral America were used to thwart them by German companies' U.S. lawyers.

Although many U.S. textile manufacturers had a substantial store of German-made dyes on hand in 1914, none anticipated a long war. Soon supplies were exhausted and prices soared. In a desperate move to breach the blockade, Germany built an experimental cargo submarine, the *Deutschland*. The squat, wide-beamed, 2,000-ton U-boat, under the command of an old merchant marine captain, arrived at the Port of Baltimore the morning of July 9, 1916, with 163 tons of concentrated textile dyes. The captain and crew were honored with a parade, Baltimore's mayor hosted an official dinner in their honor, and the local German-American society distracted the crew with numerous parties over the next two weeks.

At midnight on August 2, the submarine, loaded primarily with 789 tons of natural rubber and other raw materials badly needed in Germany, moved outside the harbor, slipped into the Atlantic Ocean, silently eased under the eight British warships waiting for it outside the Chesapeake Bay, and returned safely to Germany. Despite their success, German officials judged the risks too great for another foray, making this the last large shipment of German dyes to reach the United States until after the war. The *Deutschland* survived the war, but Great Britain took the ship as part of its postwar reparations from Germany. Captain Paul Koenig's account of that daring 1916 trip, *Voyage of the Deutschland,* became a best-selling book and a huge propaganda coup for Germany. Despite this daring foray, Britain's naval blockade of Germany held firmly throughout the war.

When the United States declared war in 1917, it seized more than 12,000 German patents, almost 5,000 of which covered chemical inventions and processes. The government made these patents available to U.S. producers;

however, many were useless since the German patent owners had filed either misleading or incomplete information in their applications. Others were of no use because U.S. manufacturers and scientists lacked the skills and expertise required to use them. Even by the end of the war, the United States hadn't closed all the gaps created by the loss of German-made imports.

The sudden shortage of dyes, medicines, and other German-made products caused many protests against the British blockade. The breadth and depth of the U.S. dependence also startled America's political elites. How had the United States, whose long-standing policy was industrial self-sufficiency, become so reliant on Germany for goods and medicines that were obviously so vital to the economy and national security?

After the war, Congress examined this issue. Congressional investigators concluded that the U.S. dependence on German imports in 1914 had been no accident of history or economics. Rather, imperial Germany, its banks, and its corporations, working closely together, had systematically monopolized global markets for dozens of technology-based goods. The reviews concluded that Germany's patent policy was central to its strategy of monopolizing world trade in those products. Germany preferred patents to tariffs as a means of protecting its industries, thereby avoiding the risk of provoking other nations into raising tariffs and stifling German exports.

The German method revealed in these inquiries remains a distinctive and systematic approach to technology-based, government-subsidized national development. In fact, many nations today, including Japan, Korea, and China, are using the German method to guide their development.

The most complete expression of the German method was a giant global cartel, IG Farben, which would become notorious for Germany's employment of poison gases against soldiers in World War I, its use of slave labor in World War II, and its role in the Holocaust. This story of Germany's industrial ascendancy, including a description of the German approach to research and technology-driven national development, begins in 1906 in the most unusual of circumstances: at an elegant dinner in New York City, featuring a German industrialist whose speech honored one of the nineteenth century's greatest chemists, an Englishman.

Sir William Henry Perkin anticipated that the dinner in his honor would be grand, for it was to be at New York City's famed Delmonico's, arguably

America's finest restaurant at the start of the century. The four hundred guests included some of the world's foremost research and industrial chemists, many of whom were Sir William's friends. What he did not know, until he reached the head table and looked out over the assembled group, smartly dressed in their formal wear, was that every gentleman would be wearing a mauve bow tie.

The ties were a tribute to the man who had, fifty years earlier, invented the first aniline synthetic dye, colored mauve, and thus forever changed industrial chemistry. After several champagne toasts and seemingly unending tributes, Sir William was named the first recipient of the Perkin Medal, the highest award given by the American division of the Society of the Chemical Industry. The medal recognized a lifetime of achievement in applied chemistry and remains, a century later, the highest professional award for America's industrial chemists.

Paradoxically, it was a failed research project that set Sir William on a path to professional greatness and immense personal wealth. In 1856, the seventeen-year-old William Perkin was a lab assistant and student of the famed German chemist August Wilhelm von Hofmann, whom Prince Albert, consort of Queen Victoria, had personally recruited from Germany to head England's Royal College of Chemistry. In 1841, Hofmann discovered that aniline could be extracted from coal tar, an odious, worthless industrial by-product created in enormous quantities during the making of steel that was left in huge, smoking piles around steel mills.

Hofmann assigned Perkin the task of deriving synthetic quinine from coal tar anilines. For such a young student, the task was ambitious by any measure. In the nineteenth century, quinine produced from the bark of cinchona trees was the best treatment for malaria, then and now one of the world's most lethal diseases. Since the demand for quinine far outstripped the supply of cinchona bark, Hofmann reasoned that if synthetic quinine could be manufactured, millions of lives could be saved annually.

The project proved to be beyond the teenager's skills. It was also beyond the skills of every other chemist for almost a century. Harvard professor Robert Burns Woodward, the 1965 Nobel Prize winner in chemistry, finally unraveled the organic structure of quinine in 1944.

Like many chemistry students in the 1850s, Perkin had his own private laboratory, a makeshift affair on the top floor of his father's London house. Working there the Easter weekend of 1856, Perkin mixed an aniline-based compound that resembled an oily black sludge. He then reworked the sludge in various ways: purifying, adding other chemicals, heating, cooling, and suspending it in various liquids, all the while carefully taking notes.

What Perkin created was not quinine; rather, it was a beautiful powder. When he dampened the powder and spread it on a small patch of silk, the fabric turned a pale, light purple. By accident, he had created the first synthetic aniline dye—a product far superior to the natural dyes then used. Perkin named his dye "Tyrian purple," a color of royalty and wealth for centuries.

Fortunately, Perkin realized he had invented a dye. But he knew nothing about dyes, textiles, fashion, finance, manufacturing, or distribution. His dye worked only on silk and wool, not on cotton, the fabric that dominated bulk sales. Four hundred pounds of coal were needed to produce one ounce of dye, and the cost was prohibitive. An ounce of Perkin's dye cost three times more than an ounce of platinum. However, only a tiny amount of the dye had to be put into a large vat of water to create a permanent color. Perkin's father, a businessman, saw the commercial potential of the discovery and sent his son to an established dye manufacturer in Scotland, who confirmed that the young man had discovered something of great value, but only if his dye was consistent, inexpensive to make in bulk, and would not fade with repeated wear, washing, or exposure to the sun. The dye met all those requirements.

Against Hofmann's advice, Perkin left the Royal College, took a British patent on his process, and created a company with his brother and father, who invested his life's savings in the new venture. Initially, Scottish and English dyers were indifferent to Perkin's product. Perkin and his family also had to create their own manufacturing processes. They designed large-scale commercial techniques for making aniline by nitration of benzene, reducing it, oxidizing it, harvesting it, removing impurities, and then squeezing out the dye. They delivered their first commercial batch to the largest silk-dyeing firm in London just before Christmas 1857.

Perkin's synthetic dye became a glorious success because of two factors that had nothing to do with either the inventor or his invention. As Simon Garfield describes in *Mauve*, in the summer of 1857, Empress Eugénie, the young wife of Napoleon III and the most fashionable woman in Europe, decided that her eyes were a pale violet and that her clothes should match the color of her eyes. Thereafter, pale violet was her favorite color, and she used it extensively in her dresses and decorations. Then, only months later, in January 1858, Queen Victoria wore a pale violet velvet train at the London wedding of her daughter Victoria, the Princess Royal, to Prince Frederick of Prussia—the future parents of Kaiser Wilhelm II. The wedding was perhaps the most important social event of the decade. Queen Victoria's use of pale violet elevated pale violet to the color of choice for fashionable women.

In a shrewd marketing move, the young Perkin changed the name of his dye from Tyrian purple to "mauveine," a French term that honored Empress Eugénie. Faced with an English aversion to using a French name on a British product, Perkin soon switched the name again, calling the dye "mauve." Overnight, European fashion degenerated into what one critic described as "mauve madness"—any woman who was anybody wore mauve. Only Perkin could produce the dye in large volumes, and his was superior to the old plant-based purple dyes. The twenty-one-year-old manufacturer was soon selling his synthetic dye to English, American, and European textile makers as quickly as he could produce it. Perkin then discovered a way to make a red dye called alizarin. It was an instant success. The next season his green dye quickly became the rage. One after another, new colors emerged, each becoming the favored hue.

Fashion changed with the invention of the new synthetic colors. Imagine a motion picture of the Victorian age in which the color of dresses, umbrellas, hats, cushions, drapery, wallpaper, and upholstery is dull, almost sepia-like, or black. Then imagine that the movie suddenly shifts to Technicolor and the screen explodes with hundreds of bright, opulent shades. Almost that abruptly, fashion in London, Paris, Berlin, Brussels, and all the other major cities of Europe was quickly transformed from drab to vibrantly colorful.

The new colors were not only beautiful, they were enormously profitable to produce. Though a successful entrepreneur, Perkin was at heart a researcher and teacher who eagerly shared his knowledge and expertise with others, willingly explaining the intricate process required to make aniline dye. Soon, German, French, and Polish businesspeople and scientists were coming to England to hear his lectures, work in his factory, and study his production techniques.

Perkin was naïve: he believed that his British and European patents protected him from intellectual property theft. They did not. In 1858, the French government denied Perkin a patent on technical grounds—he had not registered his invention in France within six months of his British patent. Perhaps more significantly, a French firm stole his technique about the same time and went into competition with his company. Almost without exception, the foreigners who studied with Perkin returned to their home countries with the knowledge he had shared, created their own companies, and became Perkin's competitors. Among the most famous of these student-entrepreneurs was Carl Martius, who co-founded the giant German dye maker Agfa.

Inevitably, Perkin became snarled in costly and protracted patent disputes. On June 26, 1869, for instance, he was granted a British patent for his alizarin red production process. But two German scientists also discovered a way to make the red dye. Their patent was granted in Berlin one day before Perkin's. If their patent had prevailed, Perkin would have been ruined. Eventually, a compromise was reached. Both patents were issued and a deal was made between the parties by which the scientists' company, BASF, controlled the market for the red dye in Europe and the United States and Perkin controlled it in the British Empire.

Tired of business and litigation and now faced with well-financed European competition, Perkin sold his company for cash in 1873 to another British dye maker. He then retired at the age of thirty-five, a famous and wealthy man.

By then, the manufacture of synthetic dyes had already evolved into one of the world's most promising industries. The principal beneficiary, however, was not England but Germany. As Perkin reflected in later years, British leaders focused on short-term results, while the Germans looked into the future. In mid-nineteenth-century England, British textile firms wanted a quality dye at a cheap price—a commodity. British companies and their government didn't much care where that commodity came from. By contrast, the German companies and the German government envisioned something bigger: global control of an indispensable product with vast collateral potential.

The German vision was quickly realized: the German chemical industry rose to world domination long before World War I. In 1863, for instance, the Hoechst chemical firm had 5 workers; by 1912, it employed more than 7,700, including 380 chemists. BASF began with 30 employees in 1865 but employed 11,000 by 1914. By 1900, six German companies dominated the world's synthetic dye industry—Bayer, BASF, Hoechst, Agfa, Cassela, and Kalle. By then, the revolution in organic chemistry, triggered by Perkin's accidental discovery, had created hundreds of synthetic dye colors and many other chemical-based products, including herbicides, aspirin, cough suppressants, local anesthetics, cures for supposedly incurable diseases such as syphilis, and industrial goods such as paints and soaps.

As the Germans anticipated, chemicals proved a most profitable business. By 1900, German dye companies were exporting 75 to 85 percent of their annual production, which yielded profits of 25 percent or more on sales, making dyes Germany's largest, most profitable export. The result was a massive flow of wealth into Germany for its corporations, investors, and workers.

The growth of German industry in the late nineteenth century and the rising strength of imperial Germany were entwined phenomena. In the late 1860s, Otto von Bismarck, whom Kaiser Wilhelm I made chancellor, triggered a series of brutal wars against Denmark, Austria, and France, and then unified several small German states with Prussia, creating Germany in 1871.

Bismarck believed that Germany's military strength ultimately depended on its industrial and economic capacity. Under Bismarck, and after 1888 Kaiser Wilhelm II, German bankers, industrialists, academics, and the military worked together to make Germany Europe's most advanced industrial nation. They succeeded brilliantly. Within thirty years of unification, Germany was Europe's major economic and military power, surpassing the British Empire.

In large measure, Germany grew so quickly because its government provided the necessary leadership, plus the physical and political infrastructures. The state, for instance, built and operated the nation's communication network—the postal service, the telegraph, and the telephone. It also owned the railroads, financed an advanced technical education system, and sponsored cutting-edge scientific research. It provided a system of social welfare, including pensions, which made workers beneficiaries of its economic policy. It established a discriminatory patent system that stripped foreign inventors of their rights while protecting German inventors. After an economic depression in 1873, the government also adopted a mercantilist trade strategy, raising tariffs against imports while providing cash bonuses to industries that exported German-made goods.

Germany also built a great merchant fleet, which by 1914 was the second largest in the world. In the late nineteenth century, German engineers designed the most advanced, safest, and fastest commercial ships of that era, in German shipyards, with German workers, using German steel. In 1897, the *Kaiser Wilhelm der Grosse,* a 14,000-ton, four-funneled passenger ship, seized the transatlantic speed record—the legendary "Blue Riband" long held by Great Britain. The first Atlantic liner fitted for commercial wireless telegraphy, it held the Blue Riband until 1900, when the prize was taken by an even faster German ship, the *Deutschland*. German ships held the Blue Riband for a decade. With their safety, speed, and reliability, the four-funneled German ships so dominated the Atlantic passenger trade that England's White Star Line placed dummy fourth funnels on the *Titanic* and the *Olympic* so they would appear equal to the German ships.

Most important, Germany was a "bank economy" where the line between the public and private sectors was so indistinct that it was barely visible. The kaiser, for instance, appointed the management of Germany's central bank (the Reichsbank), even though it was privately owned. Through the Reichsbank, policy was set for Germany's giant private banks. These banks, in turn, were major stockholders in German industries, financed their operations, and sat on their boards. The banks also operated branches throughout Europe, Great Britain, and the United States, where they opened markets by providing loans to pay for German imports. The banks, and the corporations they financed and controlled, also collected foreign economic and political intelligence for their German clients and the German government, thus giving Germany deep insight into the workings of its foreign competitors. Even today, German banks hold more than 25 percent of the voting capital in a quarter of Germany's major corporations and 28 percent of all seats on corporate supervisory boards. The bankers sit on the boards of every major German corporation and are empowered to vote the stock of their clients. As a group, German banks still have voting authority over at least three-quarters of the stock of all major German firms. In the past, they had even greater control.

As German trade expanded, the banks forced the companies they ruled into cartels; that is, similar businesses were brought together to control the production, pricing, and marketing of products. By eliminating domestic competition, the banks were able to reduce costs, lower business risks, and raise prices. This move also facilitated incursions into foreign markets. Not surprisingly, organizing cartels became a popular way to streamline operations, and unlike in the United States, cartels were legal there. In 1900, for instance, Germany had 275 cartels; by 1908, it had more than 500. By World War I, the nation had cartelized virtually every German industry of any significance.

In 1919, the U.S. Office of the Alien Property Custodian released a report that examined Germany's pre–World War I private-public nexus. Using an extensive set of documents that office had seized from various German operations in the United States, the custodian concluded:

> The relations between the German Government and the great German chemical houses were so close that representatives of the industry were naturally almost direct representatives of the Government.... It was, perhaps, difficult before the war [World War I] to know where to draw the line between purely commercial and actual governmental German activities. The outbreak of war left no doubt.

The ironic sidebar to Sir William Perkin's dinner at Delmonico's is that one of the featured speakers was Germany's most prominent dye maker, Dr. Carl Duisberg, the general manager of Bayer and leader of the German industry that by then had taken much of the British dye market. Duisberg had married into Friedrich Bayer's family, but he controlled the Bayer Company and the German chemical cartel not because of his family relationship but because of his skills as a chemist, manager, and politician. Although Duisberg praised Sir William's achievement in his speech, he also lectured his audience as to why Germany's chemical industry was superior to England's and, by implication, to America's. England, Duisberg explained, had a wide array of industries, but Germany had specialized in a few. Germans, he claimed, had a special talent for chemistry, which suggested, again by implication, the English and Americans did not. Richard Sasuly, in *IG Farben*, discusses Duisberg's speech:

> Duisberg failed to mention much of his story. He did not tell of the way in which German industry had borrowed (stolen) the work done in other nations and protected its own with a special patent system set up in 1877. And above all, he did not tell of the way in which Germany, a nation without colonies and therefore without assured sources of raw materials, had turned to chemistry as a means of making raw materials. For Germany synthetics were the wealth of the Indies.

Sasuly's assertion about Germany's lack of resources was much to the point. Its industry had specialized because Germany had few resources. It had coal, air, water, potash, low-grade iron ore, land, and Germans. Moreover, any strong foreign navy could easily block German supplies and exports. Worse, one German border was shared with Russia and another with France, both of which were hostile. The fortunes of geography and the uneven distribution of natural resources meant that in any protracted war, Germany had to grow its own food, create its own raw materials, and produce its own weapons—or do without.

Because Germany lacked natural resources, the country's most important asset was the knowledge, skills, and talents of the German people. Thus, Germany specialized in those industries where its scientists, engineers, and skilled workers could transform the nation's limited resources into the goods it needed. That meant synthetic fertilizers to increase food production; steel for rails, machines, and armaments; machine tools to make precision goods; optics for science and commerce; electro-technical products for home and industry; chemicals for industrial and consumer goods; and pharmaceuticals for health care. Any surplus production of these goods was exported, boosting the country's wealth. Most important, the factories that produced these domestic goods could also make the tools of war when the need arose; thus, German factories were the ultimate arsenals.

Contrary to Duisberg's haughty observation that the Germans were better at chemistry than the British because of some national characteristic, the Germans were superior because their country valued the sciences and engineering more than Britain did. The British spent relatively little on science and technical education, and the country's social system relegated most scientists to the sidelines with other British eccentrics. Consequently, the great British universities and companies lacked the scientific-industrial linkages found in Germany. There, by contrast, scientists and engineers held an elevated position in society, and the public considered them heroes, much as the U.S. revered its inventors. Germans saw science as the path to the future. By 1900, science had become an honorable "calling" in Germany, much as religion and medicine were elsewhere.

Under Bismarck and the kaiser, Germany invested heavily in scientific research and science education, realizing that basic advances in the laboratory often led to commercial applications, which in turn could have military uses. Synthetic dyes were just one such success. Steel, machine tools, and optics were others. Factories that made those commercial goods could quickly be converted to produce the chemicals, weapons, and poisons that would be needed by Germany's military forces if war broke out. In 1911, the German government and German industries created a national science establishment, the Kaiser Wilhelm Society. (In 1948 it was renamed the Max Planck Society, after the famed German physicist.) Between 1911 and

1948, the society created thirty-five separate institutes that did cutting-edge research in disciplines such as physics, chemistry, mathematics, biology, anthropology, metallurgy, neuropathology, genetics, psychiatry, and law.

In the late nineteenth century, America lagged far behind Germany and most other industrial nations in the sciences. U.S. universities had few scholars—only 10 percent of Harvard's professors had PhD degrees in the 1870s. Princeton's library was so inadequate that it was open only two hours per week. Systematic medical research did not exist in the United States until the Johns Hopkins Medical School opened in 1893. Thus, between 1870 and 1914, an estimated 15,000 American doctors studied in Austria or Germany, where the best science was practiced.

For all these reasons and more, Germany dominated the sciences a century ago. The most important measure of that dominance is that between 1901 and 1919, one-third of the Nobel laureates in physics did their work in Germany, as did half the laureates in chemistry. Almost all the rest worked in Austria, England, France, Sweden, or Italy.

Germany's investment in science produced results that literally changed the world. By 1906, for instance, German scientists were using coal to produce synthetic rubber, oil, fuels, lubricants, fibers, light metals, and dozens of chemical-based biological and medical discoveries. Science provided Germany what nature had not.

An example of Germany's ability to use science to compensate for its dearth of natural resources was the way it discovered how to manufacture the synthetic nitrates essential for the production of fertilizers and explosives. Before World War I, Germany depended on shipments of natural nitrates from Chile, which were shut off by the British naval blockade in 1914. After this rude awakening, Germany made itself self-sufficient in nitrates; the groundwork for this achievement had already begun. First, in 1909, Fritz Haber, an academic chemist working on an industry grant, had discovered how to create ammonia out of air and water. For this, he won a Nobel Prize. Then German engineers translated the "Haber process" from the laboratory to full production. In July 1914, Carl Bosch, a thirty-four-year-old BASF engineer, opened a full-scale chemical plant, using the Haber process, which produced forty tons of synthetic ammonia a day. Finally, Bosch devised a way to transform ammonia into synthetic nitrates. He perfected the method by May 1915, just in time to save the German army from defeat, since Germany's supply of natural nitrates was exhausted. In 1931, Bosch received a Nobel Prize in Chemistry.

The creativity of German scientists and engineers seemed boundless. The descriptive slogan of that pre–World World I era is that Britain and France had colonies, but Germany had science and chemistry. Its scientists, laboratories, and factories were able to produce the resources that nature denied Germany, giving the nation the self-sufficiency required by a great military and economic power.

Yet Germany was a comparatively small nation and the capital investments needed to meet its economic and military aspirations were far greater than its domestic market alone could ever support. To gain the scale of research and production it needed, the nation had to dominate the global markets its industries supplied, which often meant nothing less than mounting a coordinated attack on rival foreign producers. To succeed, German technology and production processes had to be superior to any competitor's. When other nations had better technology, the German government assisted its companies in stealing it, as it did with the British dye industry. If another nation's nascent industry threatened a vital German interest, German economic forces had to quickly destroy it.

"Cutthroat" is an apt description of how German businesses and government operated a century ago. Kickbacks, bribery, predatory litigation, theft of industrial secrets, price-cutting, secret rebates, sabotage, and thuggish actions—German corporations used all these tactics and more against one another and their foreign competitors. America's robber barons, of course, did the same. The difference is that the Germans acted with the full knowledge and support of their government, while the Americans did not.

The most powerful cartel controlled the German dye and chemical industries. With its superior science and technology and an arsenal of patents, it also dominated the world's chemical industry. An investigative team commissioned by General Dwight Eisenhower at the close of World War II concluded that the dye and chemical cartel's extensive production facilities, far-reaching research, deep technical experience, and concentration of economic power had been "indispensable for the German war effort and must be broken up."

Beginning in the late 1930s, U.S. investigators gained access to many of that cartel's records and, after the war, to many of its executives. Their research revealed a maze of relations, often illegal, with leading companies in the United States, Britain, and elsewhere that in a few instances existed through both world wars. Perhaps most important, those investigations—as documented in books such as Joseph Borkin's *The Crime and Punishment of IG Farben,* Sasuly's *IG Farben,* and Robert Franklin Maddox's *The War Within World War II*—provide glimpses into how Germany's cartels manipulated competition, politicians, and governments worldwide for decades. Those cartels are the heart of the German model now being emulated in nations such as China and Japan.

IG Farbenindustrie Aktiengesellschaft was the full name of Germany's most powerful cartel. IG is a German abbreviation of Interessen-Gemeinschaft, which means "community of interests." In German, the full name translates as "Community of Interests of the Dye Industry, Inc." In Germany, it was simply IG—*the* cartel. The rest of the world knew the organization as IG Farben. Sasuly described this German creation as "the most advanced specimen of cartel organization" in the world. It became Germany's major business model.

IG Farben's founder was Carl Duisberg, the featured speaker at Sir William Perkin's Delmonico's dinner. In the early twentieth century, he recognized the need to eliminate rivalry among German chemical companies, and in 1904 he suggested that all German dye makers form a single, giant trust where they would share research, divide markets, operate plants at maximum efficiency, jointly attack foreign competitors, and split profits. Their model was John D. Rockefeller's Standard Oil Trust, which controlled the U.S. petroleum industry. In itself, Duisberg's suggestion was that most rare of nineteenth-century compliments: one robber baron imitating the dirty work of another.

By 1916, domestic competition for dye ended in Germany as IG Farben members jointly determined acquisitions, capital allocations, production, employment reductions, and technological exchanges. Each company had a set number of votes for decisions, and each received profits according to a formula. Withdrawing would have meant commercial suicide.

From its beginnings, IG Farben was a ruthless competitor. Before World War I, the combine reduced its prices in the United States and other foreign markets to make them 25 percent less than they were at home. Whenever U.S. or other foreign competition emerged, it lowered its prices for however long it took to drive the competitors out of business or into bankruptcy. IG Farben used this dumping strategy so extensively and well that it became an industrial art form. Virtually unlimited capital from German banks and deep subsidies from the German government gave the cartels all the resources required to outlast foreign competitors. In 1903, for example, the U.S. had five companies producing salicylic acid, which is used to make medicines, dyes, and photographic chemicals. In 1913, only one remained and IG Farben owned it. The cartel drove all the others out of business with predatory price cuts.

Whenever possible, the cartel cornered and diverted vital raw materials needed for its products, often creating artificial shortages, which were then used to raise prices and deny finished goods to others. When the British blockade of Germany stopped the flow of phenol to the United States in 1914, the cartel acted quickly to buy any new excess U.S. production, thereby denying Britain a vital raw material. Phenol was used by Thomas A. Edison to make synthetic resins for the gramophone industry. Once blocked from German supplies, Thomas Edison built his own facilities to produce all the phenol he required, plus a large surplus. But phenol had uses other than for gramophones: it was also vital for the manufacture of munitions.

In early 1915, IG Farben had Dr. Hugo Schweitzer, a U.S.-based German executive of the Bayer Company, establish an American front company that bought all of Edison's extra phenol. Edison never knew the true identity of his customer. After the United States entered the war and seized German corporate files, the Alien Property Custodian discovered a letter from a German diplomat congratulating Dr. Schweitzer on his purchase, comparing it with "a military coup accomplished by an army leader in destroying three railroad trains of forty cars (each) containing four and a half million pounds of explosives."

The German approach to patenting provided another particularly important weapon of market control for IG Farben. The patent protection scheme was both simple and complete. Beginning in the mid-1870s, the German government issued fifteen-year patents on chemical innovations, but only to those who built and operated a facility in Germany that incorporated the patented improvement. By this method, the Germans effectively denied patents to virtually every foreign chemical maker, none of which wanted to take on the cartel in its home country. At the same time, German corporations could take a foreign technology not patented in Germany, even if it might have been patented elsewhere, and use it with impunity in their German factories.

Sir William Perkin, in his later years, often complained about how British patent law inadequately protected his work and that of others. He pointed out that he had repeatedly won patent suits against infringers but received only a few hundred pounds in compensation, plus a public apology. The lofty attitude of the upper-class-dominated British government was that an apology was a great penalty and embarrassment, as "gentlemen do not steal the ideas of others."

As Simon Garfield notes in *Mauve,* until 1907 British patent law allowed German firms to take a patent in England without having any corresponding obligation to work it there. By this, German dye makers "sealed their monopolies" on a technology. Between 1891 and 1895, not one of the six hundred foreign patents issued by the British government was being worked in Great Britain. The British government maintained its indifference until David Lloyd George reformed English patent law in 1907, forcing foreign companies to work their patents in England or lose them, thereby saving Britain's chemical industry from total destruction by the Germans.

In the United States, German companies used a fourfold patent strategy. First, they refused to license their patented technology to any U.S. companies except under the most extraordinary circumstances. Nor did the Germans share their technology in any way. They erected corporate and government barriers to industrial espionage, used only German workers in their key positions, and only rarely built factories in other nations. Clearly, Germany knew the value of its technology.

Second, the Germans hired skilled and politically well connected American lawyers, who filed thousands of U.S. patent applications on behalf of their clients. Anyone who infringed on one of those German-owned, U.S.–issued patents faced protracted, expensive litigation in the United States. By this, the Germans "sealed" their monopoly inside the United States, as they had in Great Britain.

Third, even when the German companies described their technology in their patents, they generally omitted vital details, identified false steps, or concealed key ingredients that often could be purchased only in Germany. This violated the legal requirement that a patent contain sufficient information that someone skilled in the field could replicate whatever was patented. The Germans even filed bogus patents whose sole purpose was to misdirect research and investment by competitors. Occasionally, the discouragement was severe. In 1919, the U.S. Alien Property Custodian reported to Congress that "anyone who attempted to repeat the method for manufacturing a dyestuff in the German patent No. 12,096 would be pretty certain to kill himself during the operation." In other words, the Germans cheated.

Because the Germans held a virtual monopoly on the global production of dyes, their government used their patents instead of tariffs for protection against imports. Again, the scheme was simple. Germany set low tariffs on imported dyes, while seeking reciprocally low tariff concessions in the United States and elsewhere for the export of German dyes. But the German patent scheme so smothered foreign producers that they had no product to export into Germany's domestic market. When a U.S. chemical maker independently invented a new way of making an existing product and secured a U.S. patent, the Germans would try to lure the inventor or company into a consortium, often with the threat of ruinous dumping if the U.S. manufacturer refused. Few did, although there was one notable exception.

Herbert Dow was an American chemist who loathed English and German chemical cartels and fought them vigorously. Dow's story really began eons ago, when a great ocean receded from the area below the plains of central Ohio, leaving a vast storehouse of minerals in the brine. In the early and middle nineteenth century, geologists knew that this brine had absorbed many of the underlying minerals, but they had few means of removing the chemicals from the foul-smelling liquid. The most common approach was to dig a well, pump up the brine, boil it down, and then remove the salts and a small amount of bromides, which then were used to make up patent medicines and film-developing chemicals. The process was inefficient, and the business was very unprofitable.

In 1888, Dow, a twenty-one-year-old scholarship student at the newly created Case School of Applied Science in Cleveland, Ohio, became interested in brines while doing his senior thesis on boiler fuels. As part of his research, Dow visited a local oil rig to get a natural gas sample. The driller showed Dow the liquid oozing up from the drill casing and asked him why it tasted so bitter. Dow did not know, but he took a sample back to his college lab for testing.

What he discovered was that the brine contained extraordinarily large quantities of lithium and bromine, which explained the bitter taste. Dow then did some simple calculations that revealed that each barrel of brine contained about $3 worth of lithium, plus a few pennies' worth of bromine. By contrast, a barrel of oil was worth $1. The brine waste held the real value of the well. With that analysis and a little arithmetic, Dow became fascinated with brine, igniting a professional obsession that lasted his entire life.

In 1889, young Dow, now a college graduate, formed a small chemical company to extract bromines from the Ohio brines. The company soon failed because Dow's techniques were too primitive. He then raised capital, created a second company, and patented an electrolytic process for extracting chlorine out of the brine. In the spring of 1895, Dow's new company built a chlorine factory in Midland, Ohio, that featured rows of electrolytic cells through which the brine would pass. An hour before lunch the day the new plant opened, the cells filled with brine and Dow turned on the current. All seemed to be working well.

At noon, he and his crew left the electricity on and walked down the street for a celebratory lunch. As they moved away from the factory, the chlorine cells exploded. When Dow and his crew turned to look, they saw a ball of fire pushing out the factory walls. The roof then collapsed into the flames, which badly damaged surrounding buildings. Firefighters were barely able to control the chemical-driven fire. An investigation revealed that the electric current had released hydrogen, a highly explosive element, which a spark had ignited.

After the plant explosion, Dow's corporate directors removed him from control of the company's affairs. Later that year, he created his third company, using capital drawn heavily from faculty members at Case. He named it Dow Chemical. Though Case was a small school—Dow was in its third graduating class of six students—its faculty members were intellectual superstars. One of those was Albert A. Michelson, the first person to measure the speed of light and, in 1907, the first American recipient of a Nobel Prize in Physics. Albert Einstein later said that Michelson's work had opened the way for his theory of relativity. Another professor was Edward W. Morley, whose work provided the key to creating a reliable atomic weight scale. The Case faculty understood Dow's work. Some of its members joined the board of the newly formed Dow Chemical and worked with their former student to find a safe way to extract minerals from brine.

By 1900, after ten years of failure, Dow was beginning to make money, and he had perfected and patented his process to extract chlorine from brine. The chlorine was transformed into a bleach used to make newsprint for the rapidly expanding newspapers of that era. In 1901, United Alkali, a group of companies from England, Scotland, and Wales, controlled the U.S. bleach market, selling more than a hundred million pounds of powder annually, using its own techniques. The British cartel had split the world market with the Germans. The bleach "pool" set its price at $1.75 per hundredweight, established production figures for its members, and allocated markets. It also squeezed the life out of U.S. newcomers, such as Dow.

In 1902, the British combine decided to eliminate Dow Chemical and the handful of other small American bleach makers. It announced that the 1903 price of bleach would be $1.25 per hundredweight, down 40 cents from $1.65 in 1902. Dow Chemical met the price. The British then dropped it to $1.04, which was less than their production costs. The other small American companies dropped out of the business. Dow Chemical remained, though it was nearing bankruptcy.

In late 1903, the British announced that the 1904 bleach price per hundred weight would be 88.5 cents. Herbert Dow raised the stakes: he reduced his price to 86 cents and was able to contract for a large volume of sales. Once Dow was financially committed to these sales, the British raised their price back to $1.25, leaving him on the hook to deliver bleach at a rock-bottom price. The combine anticipated that Dow would sink or fail to fulfill his contracts and get sued. But although Dow Chemical went deeply into debt, it fulfilled its contracts, enhancing Herbert Dow's reputation as a trustbuster and reliable supplier. By 1905, the bleach war was over. Herbert Dow had bet everything against the British combine and won.

The practices used by the British—dumping, price gouging, and coordinated actions—were little different from those of German cartels. But Germany's banks and government openly supported the German cartels while the British banks and government offered far less financial and political support for theirs. Thus, the Germans could persist where the British had to concede defeat.

After Dow Chemical defeated the British monopolists, IG Farben moved in. The Germans' goal was to gain a global monopoly on the production of bromines, which were then produced in only Germany and the United States. Refined bromine is a key ingredient in the production of various medicines and photographic chemicals. Bromine also can be combined with nitric gases to make a highly deadly poison gas, suitable for warfare. Dow owned the patents on his bromine process, so the Germans could not drive him out of business with patent suits. Since he also had an unlimited supply of brine in Ohio, the Germans could not cut his supply of raw materials.

Farben elected to dump its bromines in the U.S. at a price so far below the cost of production, for such a long period, that the American company would either have to leave the business or go bankrupt. The Germans would then buy its patents and remaining assets, locking in their hold on the market. Such dumping was not outlawed in the United States until 1916, which did Dow little good in 1904. He stood alone against IG Farben.

In late 1904, Herbert Dow received an unscheduled visit from Hermann Jacobsohn, the cartel's representative. Dow Chemical had been "caught" selling bromine in England and Japan, said Jacobsohn. He then lectured Dow that this was a serious violation of the rules imposed on U.S. producers by the German cartel. He issued Dow an ultimatum: either obey the German rules and withdraw from the European market, or the cartel would put two pounds of bromines on the U.S. market for every one Dow exported. The meeting ended quickly when Dow ushered his visitor out the door.

Dow wrongly thought the Germans were bluffing. Within days, a New York bank called Dow to demand payment on a note it held—a financial shot across the bow. In early 1905, the German cartel suddenly cut its U.S. price for bromines in half, from 30 cents to 15 cents, while holding its European price at 40 cents per pound.

Dow learned of the German price cut while visiting clients in Texas. He immediately took a train to the St. Louis office of another U.S. chemical maker, where he met with Jacobsohn. Again, Jacobsohn lectured Dow on how Germany owned the bromine markets in Europe, Japan, and the rest of the world. Dow would be punished severely if he continued his folly—U.S. bromine sales in the European and Japanese markets, even small quantities, were forbidden. If Dow refused to be sensible, the cartel would flood the U.S. market. Money was no object, Jacobsohn explained, for German banks backed the cartel, and their government supported German banks.

Dow stood up after Jacobsohn's tirade, told him there was no need for further discussion, and left. He prepared for yet another cartel war, and he was smarter this time about what to do. He knew the German price of 15 cents contained a tariff of 3 cents. This left 12 cents for the Germans to produce, ship, and distribute their bromine in the United States.

Dow also thought his patented production technique was superior to the Germans', his supply of raw materials was inexhaustible, and his costs were predictable. Moreover, he had a new strategy. He ordered his salespeople to drop his U.S. price on bromines to 12 cents a pound and to sell 120,000 pounds at that price in the U.S. market. He wanted the Germans to think Dow Chemical intended to match them price drop for price drop, as it had done in the bleach war with the British.

Meanwhile, he secretly ordered his British and European salespeople to take all the orders they could at 27 cents a pound, roughly a third lower than the Germans' price there. Dow ordered his factories to produce a stockpile of 300,000 pounds of bromines. Finally, he placed orders through intermediaries to buy all the 15-cent pounds of German bromines they could. Dow intended to fill his European orders with bromines made by IG Farben. It was a risky strategy that depended on keeping his German purchases secret.

In 1905, Dow Chemical effectively dropped out of the U.S. bromine market, slowly pulling down its stockpile with sales at 12 cents a pound, thereby convincing the Germans they were in a price war. Simultaneously, Dow repackaged the 15-cent pounds of German-made bromines and shipped them back to Europe, where he fulfilled his 27-cent-a-pound contracts. Dow's European operatives confidently assured their European customers that the bromines they were getting were equal in quality to anything produced by the Germans—which, in fact, they were.

The cartel representatives anticipated that their price drops would quickly destroy Dow Chemical or that Dow would capitulate. Yet he persisted through 1905, and then through 1906. Meanwhile, German sales in the United States seemed to explode because of the artificially low price. In 1907, Dow was still in business. The Germans cut their U.S. price to 12.5 cents and then to 10.5 cents per pound, selling as much as they offered, all below the cost of production and shipment. Dow continued to make token U.S. sales, keeping up the appearance that he was waging a price war. Meanwhile, he was making a profit with his transshipments, but not much. Consequently, his company was in constant peril. Herbert Dow was determined to beat the Germans, although his bankers and directors were urging surrender.

In 1907, Dow took his family to Europe, ostensibly for a vacation but actually to visit the facilities of his German competitors. The Germans thought a tour of their factories would impress Dow with the futility of competing against the world's largest chemical combine. The Germans' hospitality to Dow was a strategic mistake. Dow immediately saw that his process was superior to theirs in every way that mattered. He also learned from the Germans that the world market for bromines was far greater than he and his corporate directors had thought. The visits gave Dow extra incentive and resolve to continue his fight.

During his visit, cartel representatives offered to end the bromine war by withdrawing from the U.S. market, leaving it to Dow alone, if he would withdraw from Europe, Japan, and the rest of the world. Dow politely refused and returned to the United States, where he continued to ship the cartel's bromines back to Europe. By then, the cartel knew Dow was reselling its product. Its members even grew suspicious that one of their own was secretly working with Dow against the group, though none was.

In the early spring of 1908, the Germans requested another meeting with Dow. In May, a delegation met him in St. Louis. Once again, the Germans demanded that Dow take the U.S. market and leave them the rest of the world. Dow countered, "My proposition is this. Germany for the Germans. The United States for American manufacturers and the rest of the world on an equal footing." The Germans refused Dow's proposal and returned home. Their visit and offer had been merely a negotiating gambit to test Dow's resolve, which remained unbreakable.

Several months later, the Germans asked for yet another meeting. Dow agreed but left the negotiations in the hands of H. E. Hackenberg, the company's corporate secretary. Hackenberg agreed to meet the Germans in London on November 24, 1908. He advised Dow, who was also going to London, to travel under a pseudonym because if rumors spread that the bromine war might be ending, other U.S. companies might enter the business.

Once in London, Dow, Hackenberg, and a quartet of German negotiators, including Jacobsohn, met for three days at the Savoy Hotel. Both Dow and the Germans were unyielding, but some progress was made. The negotiators shifted their discussions to Stassfurt and Berlin, where they could involve IG Farben's corporate leaders. The Germans relented somewhat but insisted that they should control two-thirds of the bromine market outside of Germany and the United States. Once again, Dow refused their offer.

What happened next? The story is that Dow made no deal and the Germans silently capitulated. Despite the absence of public agreement, in 1909 the German cartel began slowly to withdraw from the U.S. market. Dow Chemical then slowly abandoned the German market. Eventually Dow's proposal ruled: the Germans controlled the German bromine market; American manufacturers, which meant Dow Chemical, controlled the U.S. market. Dow and the Germans competed everywhere else. In 1909, prices began to rise to world market levels.

Dow won the bromine war. I speculate that Herbert Dow and IG Farben's representatives reached a quiet understanding, along the lines of Dow's proposal, while avoiding publicity that might have triggered an antitrust suit from President Roosevelt's or President Taft's trustbusters, who were aggressively pursuing many U.S. corporations engaged in monopolistic activities.

The bleach and bromine wars had a profound effect on Herbert Dow. His company could not have survived without the safeguard provided by his patented processes, making intellectual property protection a major issue for him. He also came passionately to believe that the United States should never depend on another nation, particularly Germany, for vital chemical goods, such as dyes and pharmaceuticals.

His fears about U.S. supply dependence became a nightmarish reality during World War I. Suddenly, the U.S. was dependent on a domestic organic chemical industry that was decades behind the Germans' in most areas, such as dyes and medicines. As the war progressed, U.S. leaders came to understand that Germany's global dominance in organic chemistry had a strategic military consequence as well. In 1920, British army major Victor LeFebure, in his book *Riddle of the Rhine: Chemical Strategy in Peace and War,* carefully drew out those implications. LeFebure's thesis: "Organic chemical factories have proved to be not only arsenals in disguise but endowed with the flexibility of their parent, the science itself."

In 1920, chemical warfare was what atomic warfare is to our own time: a frightening prospect that had been tried and found highly effective. And just as nations now believe they require nuclear weapons for their deterrent value, the United States concluded then that it absolutely had to possess an independent organic chemical industry—not just to fill domestic needs but for quick conversion to wartime use if needed.

In 1919, President Woodrow Wilson and House Speaker Nicholas Longworth convinced Congress that the United States should never again be dependent on Germany or any other nation for the goods created by an organic chemistry industry. Congress responded by erecting a high tariff against the import of any dye or other organic chemical products not made in the United States. A quasi-public corporation, the Chemical Foundation, was created to administer the German chemical patents, which had been seized in 1917 and now were licensed on a royalty basis to those companies that applied them in the United States. The royalties were then used to foster the U.S. organic chemical industry. It took almost a decade to build it.

DuPont bought a license to use the German dye patents and invested millions of dollars in new facilities. Yet Irénée Du Pont, the CEO of the company bearing his family name, concluded, after losing a great deal of company money trying to make the German patents productive, that they were unusable. The information in the patents was incomplete, and the Americans lacked the knowledge to fill in the gaps.

Yet DuPont was determined to enter the dyestuff business in a major way.

In November 1919, a DuPont executive went to Paris, where he met Carl Bosch and proposed a joint IG Farben–DuPont dyestuff venture. But Bosch would not share the German technology with the U.S. company—though the French government did force the Germans to share it with France's leading dye producer. The U.S. reluctance to follow France's lead and use such strong-arm tactics reflected IG Farben's legal and political influence in the United States, despite the war.

As much as private companies wanted to be in the dye business, the U.S. Army may have wanted an American-based capacity even more. The War Department agreed with Major LeFebure's analysis that organic chemical factories were nothing less than advanced arsenals in camouflage and that America needed them.

Unable to get cooperation from IG Farben, DuPont resorted to industrial espionage. In 1920, it secretly contracted with four senior German chemists from Bayer to work in the United States. The Germans would be paid an up-front cash bonus, be brought to the United States with their families, and be given U.S. citizenship. In return, they would reveal the German dye secrets and work at DuPont. In late 1920, a DuPont agent whisked the German chemists, their families, and a trunk full of Bayer's technical drawings out of Germany to Holland. However, Dutch authorities in Amsterdam detained the scientists and discovered their trove of stolen engineering drawings. When the German press learned what had happened, a minor international incident ensued over the attempted theft of Germany's most valuable industrial secrets.

Despite all the negative publicity, DuPont got two of the chemists and their families out of Holland and into the United States. The Dutch authorities sent the two other chemists and their families back to Germany, where they were placed under police surveillance. But neither the U.S. Army nor DuPont was to be thwarted.

After World War I, Allied military forces occupied parts of Germany. But the two German chemists and their families were held in an unoccupied area. In May 1921, a DuPont lawyer arrived in occupied Germany to arrange their escape. He met the commanding general of the U.S. forces, and the general ordered his intelligence chief to rescue them. Army intelligence did its job. Two months later, the chemists and their families arrived in New Jersey on the U.S. Army transport *Somme*. Soon the four German scientists were at work in Delaware and the DuPont Corporation was finally on its way to mastering the dyestuff industry, which it finally did by 1930. In her study of the U.S. efforts to create a domestic organic chemistry industry, Professor Kathryn Steen at Drexel reports that U.S. companies eventually developed a domestic dye industry, but never one that could compete with the Germans'. After tariffs on dye imports were dropped in the early 1960s, the U.S. dye industry withered. But the struggle to master dyes expanded the knowledge of U.S. chemists and manufacturers, allowing them to develop aliphatic organic chemistry, which depends for its base on petroleum rather than coal. In turn, this led to other discoveries in polymer chemistry and elsewhere. Thus, America developed an organic chemistry industry and the scientists to staff it.

During World War I, Herbert Dow came to believe that airplanes would play a decisive role in future wars and that magnesium and aluminum would be the metals that America would need to build them. Magnesium is strong and weighs a third less than aluminum. Before World War I, Dow had discovered a way to draw magnesium from Ohio's brine. Even before the United States entered World War I, Dow was trying to find a way to produce magnesium in quantity at a low price. The work continued for more than two decades at a financial loss to the company every year. Herbert Dow died in 1930, but his son Willard, who succeeded his father as CEO of Dow Chemical, continued the company's obsessive quest to pull magnesium out of the Ohio brine and later out of the ocean.

The Aluminum Company of America (Alcoa) and IG Farben held patents on some of the technology that Dow used. In 1931, Alcoa and IG Farben created a jointly owned company to hold their patents: the Magnesium Development Company, called "Alig." Germany's goal throughout the 1930s was to expand its production and hold back America's. As part of the deal with IG Farben, Alcoa agreed to make Dow Chemical limit its magnesium production to 4,000 tons a year. Alcoa threatened Dow with unlimited litigation if it produced more than the German-set limit or shipped more than 150 tons a year to Great Britain.

As World War II approached, Dow Chemical was America's sole magnesium producer. In early 1940, Willard Dow openly challenged the Alcoa–IG Farben limits on U.S. magnesium production, daring them to sue. In January of that year, Dow Chemical bought one thousand acres of land in Freeport, on the Texas coast, and began building a huge plant that would extract magnesium and other chemicals vital in wartime from the ocean. Britain was one of the first customers; Dow agreed to supply its desperate aircraft industry with 8.4 million pounds of the precious metal per year.

Dow then went to the U.S. War Department, which was proposing a massive airplane construction program, and offered to expand, at the company's expense, its magnesium production by another hundred million pounds per year—if the U.S. would buy the output at a preset, low price. Foolishly and inexplicably, the War Department rejected Dow's offer.

Dow's Freeport plant produced its first magnesium ingot on January 21, 1941. Historian E. N. Brandt, author of *Growth Company* and Dow's company historian, rates Dow's large-scale mining of the ocean as one of the "greatest chemical engineering feats of all time." Nine days after starting production at the world's newest, most advanced, and largest magnesium production facility, the U.S. Justice Department indicted Dow Chemical, charging that it had conspired with Alcoa and IG Farben to constrict production of the vital metal. Willard Dow was justifiably furious: his father and he had invested in magnesium production for more than two decades, all at a loss, and had built a massive new facility, despite the lack of government interest. The charge added insult to injury: it was based on the "Alig" contract between Alcoa and IG Farben, and neither Dow nor his employees were participants in that arrangement.

In March 1944, the Senate Special Committee Investigating the National Defense Program—which was known as "the Truman Committee"—held a hearing on the Justice Department's allegation. After taking testimony from Willard Dow, Justice Department officials, and others, Senator Harry Truman and his committee issued a report that totally exonerated Dow Chemical.

After the Japanese attack at Pearl Harbor, the U.S. ordered thousands of airplanes, creating a magnesium shortage. Suddenly, price was no object and ten other companies wanted to participate in what would become a cost-plus business—that is, these producers were paid their cost plus a guaranteed profit. Dow shared its technology and knowledge with them, while keeping its own price low. Still, it took time for those companies to build their new plants and bring them up to maximum production. Consequently, Dow supplied 84 percent of all the magnesium produced in the U.S. in 1942, a critical time when air supremacy over Europe and the Pacific islands was being bitterly contested. Because of Herbert and Willard Dow's foresight and determination, America had all the magnesium it needed to build the airplanes and other weapons used to win World War II.

.   .   .

IG Farben and most German industries actually ended up after World War I with more and better facilities than they had had in 1914. While the war and harsh peace terms cost German industry its almost total global monopoly in the chemical and medical industries, German companies remained technologically advanced. Faced with political unrest and economic instability at home and plagued by reparation demands, particularly from France, many German industries consolidated in the 1920s and cut production. The largest such revamping was in chemicals.

In 1925, the IG Farben cartel members merged into a single corporation and kept the old name. Carl Bosch—the Nobel Prize winner and an aggressive German nationalist—was named its leader. At its creation, the new IG Farben was the largest corporation in Europe and the largest chemical company in the world. After General Motors, U.S. Steel, and Standard Oil, it was the world's fourth largest corporation. Domestically, it included more than 380 German firms. It produced all of Germany's dyes and explosives, two-thirds of its nitrogen, and more than 40 percent of its chemicals and pharmaceuticals. It owned banks, coal deposits, metal companies, and sales organizations. It operated the largest private research labs in Germany, employing 1,000 qualified chemists among its 120,000 workers.

IG Farben worked furiously in the 1920s to reestablish its global market holds. A different technique was required than that used before 1914. In the prewar era, German companies had totally dominated key industries, such as dyes, and the old IG Farben had been able to pull together those companies and set a common policy that Germany then imposed on world markets. But after World War I, other nations, especially England and the United States, created their own organic chemical companies, so they could have an assured industrial capacity if war broke out again.

After World War I, therefore, IG Farben's challenge was to bring all these national companies into a global cartel through which it could once again dominate the world's dye and chemical industries. As usual, Carl Bosch succeeded brilliantly. He began with France, Germany's historic enemy before, during, and after World War I. After a series of maneuvers, including a failed attempt to buy the giant French dyestuff producer Kuhlmann, the Germans agreed to stay out of the French market if the French would agree to leave the rest of Europe to the Germans. The two companies then agreed on a price-fixing scheme, market splits, joint sales, and technology sharing.

IG Farben brought virtually all the world's major chemical makers into its cartel with similar agreements, all largely hidden from view. Ultimately, it had 500 foreign partners, operating through 200 distinct cartel agreements. Among those partners in the era between the two world wars were DuPont, Imperial Chemical Industries of Great Britain, Japan's Mitsui, and Alcoa. Through these agreements, IG Farben retained Germany's control of the global chemical industry.

Perhaps the most controversial of these deals, and certainly one of the most illustrative, was between IG Farben and Standard Oil of New Jersey. In the mid-1920s, Bosch set out to replicate his prior success of creating synthetic nitrates on a grand scale, but this time he intended to produce synthetic oil and synthetic rubber. He needed a partner, and no company was richer than Standard Oil.

In 1926, the giant U.S. oil company sent Frank A. Howard, head of its research and development division, to inspect IG Farben's capacity to make synthetic oil out of coal. What Howard found in Germany was Standard Oil's worst nightmare. Howard quickly wrote back to New Jersey that Bosch's technology constituted the greatest threat to Standard since the U.S. government had broken up the Standard Oil Trust in 1911. The Germans, he reported, were going to be able to make half a ton of oil out of a ton of low-grade coal. "This means," Howard wrote, "absolutely the independence of Europe in the matter of gasoline supply. Straight price competition is all that is left."

Walter C. Teagle, president of Standard Oil, immediately booked passage to Germany, arriving a few days later. Bosch and the German scientists impressed him as much as they had his research director, and soon Bosch and Teagle were negotiating. Though Bosch was generally unwilling to compromise, Germany was in deep recession by the late 1920s and IG Farben lacked the ready capital it had once possessed. Bosch needed cash for IG Farben's research and development; Teagle needed control of Farben's synthetic oil patents and technology. The world had far more coal than oil. A cheap coal-based conversion process, which the German scientists and engineers were on the verge of creating, would make Standard's oil wells, pipelines, and refineries worthless.

The ultimate deal reached by the two industrial giants in 1928 was that each agreed to respect the sovereignty of the other. IG Farben agreed to stay out of the oil business and Standard agreed to stay out of IG Farben's chemical businesses. IG Farben transferred the world patent rights for its coal-to-oil process to a new corporation, named the Standard–IG Company, though it kept the patent rights for Germany. Standard Oil got 80 percent of the stock and IG Farben got 20 percent. In addition, Farben received 2 percent of Standard Oil's common stock, then worth $35 million.

In this deal, Standard Oil gained world control of a threatening technology, while Bosch kept the unlimited right for its use in Germany. IG Farben got the money it needed to develop the coal-to-oil process further.

In 1930, Bosch established the Joint American Study Company (JASCO) to develop synthetic rubber. Its stock was held 50-50 between the two companies. Under the terms of various contracts, the two companies were to share their knowledge and patents with each other, and neither was to use that knowledge without the approval of the other.

The synthetic rubber effort eventually became a major embarrassment for Standard Oil. Once Adolf Hitler took power in Germany, his Nazi government refused to allow the transfer of IG Farben's technology for making synthetic Buna rubber to JASCO. However, Farben insisted that Standard transfer to Germany its new technology to make Butyl rubber, which the U.S. company did. Meanwhile, in 1940 several U.S. tire and chemical makers, including Dow, tried to get Standard Oil to join them in developing synthetic rubber for the United States. Standard Oil stalled the U.S. effort, hoping to acquire IG Farben's technology and approval to share it with the other American companies. It never got either. Consequently, the U.S., which had previously received virtually all of its rubber from areas Japan had seized, had an acute rubber shortage when it entered the war, forcing the national rationing of tires.

In 1942, the United States Congress learned of the Standard Oil–IG Farben deal, largely from German documents seized by the Alien Property Custodian. Members were outraged. Soon Standard Oil made another deal, this time with the Justice Department. Standard agreed to offer all its synthetic rubber patents and technology to any U.S. company royalty-free. The Justice Department agreed not to press what would amount to industrial treason charges against the responsible executives, who were in any case quickly retired from the company.

Sharing the secrets of synthetic rubber is only one of the mistakes U.S. executives, operating through secret agreements, made with IG Farben. When Germany began to rearm in the 1930s, its engineers lacked the knowledge needed to produce tetraethyl lead, used in fuel for high-performance engines. The principal developers of that technology were Standard Oil and General Motors, which jointly owned the Ethyl Gasoline Corporation. Farben approached Ethyl in the mid-1930s about a joint venture to produce leaded gas in Germany. General Motors was willing, as was Standard Oil. The proposal was twice reviewed by the War Department, which inexplicably had no objection to the transfer of such vital knowledge to Hitler's Germany. Only the president of DuPont, then GM's largest stockholder, objected. DuPont's position was that "under no condition should you or the Board of Directors of the Ethyl Corporation disclose any secrets or 'know-how' in connection with the manufacture of tetraethyl lead in Germany."

GM and Standard Oil ignored DuPont's warning, and the deal was made. The jointly owned Ethyl-Farben plants in Germany were almost complete when Hitler marched into Czechoslovakia. To fill the supply gap before that invasion, IG Farben bought $20 million worth of tetraethyl lead from its new partner, Ethyl, and shipped that war matériel to Germany. As a result, the Luftwaffe had its leaded gas before Czechoslovakia was carved up. Afterward, using the American technology, IG Farben was able to manufacture leaded fuel for its fighter planes throughout World War II.

Other U.S. industries and their executives also ignored the dangers of strengthening a potential enemy nation. Zeiss, the German optical instruments maker, had a long-standing secret patent and technology arrangement with Bausch & Lomb, the U.S. optical producer. In the early 1920s, Zeiss agreed not to build a plant in the United States, and Bausch & Lomb agreed to restrict its production of military optics. When Hitler took power, Zeiss refused to share its technological advances with its U.S. partner, while Bausch & Lomb foolishly kept Zeiss informed of its projects and advances it had made on behalf of the U.S. military. Thus, the U.S. entered World War II with only those militarily critical optical instruments that Nazi Germany had allowed Bausch & Lomb to provide: inferior range finders, periscopes, bombsights, telescopes, and binoculars.

In 1934, the Sperry Gyroscope Company, then the leading airplane instruments maker in the world, entered a deal with Askania, a German firm, to license its technology for automatic pilots. There was to be a sharing of information, but under Hitler's regime, it all went one way—to Germany. By 1939, Askania had Sperry's technology. In the early days of World War II, using its contracts and its patent position, the German company tried to block Sperry from supplying Britain's Royal Air Force with its most advanced navigation products.

The Robert Bosch Company of New York was created in 1906 to produce and sell magnetos, pumps, and other products of the Robert Bosch Company of Stuttgart, Germany, an old-line enterprise founded in 1887. By 1930, the American company had a virtual monopoly on the U.S. production of magnetos and fuel injection systems. Though American Bosch posed as an independent U.S. company, in fact it had a contract with its German parent that required its permission as to what it produced, how much it produced, and to whom it sold its products. In the months leading up to U.S. entry into the world war and throughout 1942, American Bosch choked the U.S. production of diesel engines needed by the navy and others by delaying its production and delivery of essential fuel injection systems. In 1941 before the attack on Pearl Harbor, the navy desperately asked American Bosch to license its fuel injection technology to the Caterpillar Company. No answer was forthcoming. As soon as U.S. authorities understood that American Bosch was under German control; the Alien Property Custodian took over the company. The shortage was soon eliminated.

Equally outrageous, the German pharmaceutical cartel used its patents to withhold medicines from the U.S. market. In the early days of World War II, American soldiers fighting the Japanese in places such as Guadalcanal were ravaged by malaria. Soon U.S. supplies of quinine were exhausted and could not be replenished because the Japanese had captured Java, which held most of the world's cinchona trees, from which the medicine is made. Unable to get quinine, the U.S. had to use a second-best medication called Atabrine, which had been invented and patented by IG Farben. The German cartel licensed the manufacture of Atabrine to only one U.S. company, Winthrop Chemical, which had once been part of Farben. Under German pressure, Winthrop refused to violate its contract with Farben and expand production until it was forced to do so by the U.S. government.

Similarly, the Remington Arms Company would not sell tetrazene-primed ammunition to Great Britain before Pearl Harbor because its contract with an IG Farben subsidiary prohibited such sales. Dozens of similar examples were revealed by various congressional investigations and in several books. As Richard Sasuly wrote in his investigation of IG Farben:

> Aluminum, and atabrine, machine tools and periscopes: for all of
> them the pattern was the same. Cartels produced critical shortages
> in the United States when rearmament began. IG Farben and the
> other German firms had done their work well.

As it happened, the United States, on balance, gained far more technology and knowledge from Germany in the 1930s and 1940s than the Germans got from naïve U.S. CEOs and their companies. The principal transfer came in the form of refugees from Germany, the consequence of what British authors Jean Medawar and David Pyke called "Hitler's gift."

In March 1933, Adolf Hitler, the new German chancellor, and Carl Bosch, still head of IG Farben, met for the first time. Hitler assured Bosch of his government's full support for Farben's synthetic oil project. Against the advice of his friends, the plainspoken Bosch told Hitler that his intention to expel Jewish scientists from German universities would set German physics and chemistry back a hundred years. In *The Crime and Punishment of IG Farben,* Joseph Borkin recounts that Hitler shouted, "Then we'll work a hundred years without physics and chemistry." He dismissed Bosch, never to speak to him again or even permit him to be in the same room. Bosch, undeterred, continued his public defense of Jewish scientists, but with little success.

A month after that meeting, the ninety-day-old Nazi-led government adopted a law that forbade anyone of "non-Aryan descent" from working in the German civil service, including state-run universities. Whatever their background, whatever their prior service to Germany, even the most distinguished Jewish scientists and scholars were forced out of their jobs and humiliated. Within a year, almost 20 percent of Germany's mathematicians and physicists were dismissed from university positions. Entire university departments were decimated. Most Jewish scholars were not forced by the new government to leave Germany, though most did. Altogether, Medawar and Pyke estimate in *Hitler's Gift* that almost 2,600 Jewish scientists and scholars left Germany within one year of Hitler's edict. In a stunning departure of talent, German universities almost instantly lost 25 percent of their physicists.

The United States and Great Britain were the principal beneficiaries of the Nazis' racial hostility. Of the twenty-seven German scholars who were forced out of their universities and had won or would win a Nobel Prize in science, fifteen moved to the United States and eight to England. One of these scientists was awarded a Nobel Prize as a co-discoverer of penicillin; another uncovered the atomic structure of the hemoglobin molecule; and another got his Nobel Prize for creating a new treatment for paraplegics. Thousands of lesser-known scientists, scholars, and artists made their way to America. Several of these German scientists eventually formed the core of the U.S. and British effort to build an atomic bomb. That story and the Jewish émigrés' role in it are well known. Many others settled in colleges, universities, and research organizations throughout the United States, where they soon took prominent roles in research and teaching, helping their adopted country become the world's science leader. Medawar and Pyke conclude that although the anti-Semitism of Nazi Germany and the resulting loss of so many distinguished German Jewish scientists squandered talent and led to an immediate falling-off of standards in Germany university teaching and research, Germany was not paralyzed.

Under their Nazi leaders, German scientists and engineers manufactured enormous quantities of synthetic oils, lubricants, rubbers, and other materials during World War II. They developed stereo magnetic recording, operated a state television system, and produced many of the most advanced weapons of World War II, including more than two thousand operational jet fighters, the V-1 ramjet bomb, and the V-2 rocket.

Eventually, the United States gained full access to all that technology. After the U.S. declared war against Germany in December 1941, it seized all the patents and patent applications belonging to citizens of nations it was fighting, including those from Germany, Italy, Japan, Romania, Hungary, and Bulgaria. The U.S. also took over patents and patent applications from the enemy-occupied countries, including France, Belgium, the Netherlands, and Norway. Altogether, the U.S. appropriated almost 46,000 active patents, 4,800 patent applications, 800 inventions, 400 trademarks, and 200,000 copyrights, including Adolf Hitler's U.S. copyright on his book *Mein Kampf.* In early 1942, the Alien Property Custodian, who held and administered this large treasure house of intellectual property, licensed the items on a nonexclusive basis to any U.S. company or user for a flat fee of $50, which eventually was reduced to $15. The patents included everything from the IG Farben–Standard Oil patents on synthetic fuels to patents on radios and household appliances. Among these were 8,000 active chemical patents, mostly German.

To promote the use of the foreign patents, the custodian created patent libraries around the United States staffed with skilled patent librarians. Of the 4,600 patent applications on file when the war began, almost 3,200 were eventually issued. The U.S. Patent and Trademark Office maintains a complete set of those seized patents in its Patent Search Room in Arlington, Virginia.

Germany, Italy, Japan, and the other Axis powers, of course, also seized U.S. patents and copyrights registered in their countries. The result was a great sharing of technology, license-free, between the warring powers. Ultimately, the United States was the primary beneficiary, as it won the war and could keep whatever technologies it wanted.

In addition, America systematically sought out key scientists and engineers in Germany and the rest of Europe after the war. The most famous of those were Wernher von Braun and his team of rocket scientists. They and their families were brought to the United States, where they continued their work for decades. Many scientists in other fields, including chemistry, telecommunications, and metallurgy, also came to the United States, particularly after the beginning of the Cold War, bringing Europe's best technologies with them.

After World War II, much of German industry was destroyed, but IG Farben sustained little damage. U.S. Army officials estimated that as of October 1945, at least 87 percent of the chemical cartel's capacity was ready for production and most of its management and talent remained in place. Farben's main office in Frankfurt also survived the war and served as the headquarters for the Supreme Allied Command; it was occupied until 1994 by the U.S. Army.

From November 1945 to October 1946, the International Military Tribunal at Nuremberg tried the senior officials of the Third Reich, including Hermann Göring and Albert Speer. Between the end of that tribunal and April 1949, the U.S. also indicted and tried dozens of German bankers, military leaders, industrialists, politicians, and judges for war crimes. Among those defendants were twenty-four senior officials from IG Farben, including the chairmen of its management and supervisory committees. Of these defendants, thirteen were found not guilty of any crime. Five were found guilty of plundering the facilities of other nations. Four were found guilty of using slave labor. One defendant was found guilty of both plundering and slave labor. Not one was found guilty for contributing to IG Farben's participation in the Holocaust.

The Nuremberg trials came at the beginning of the Cold War, as U.S. officials were deciding that Germany's industrial capacity was vital to the West. Restoration proceeded quickly, largely because Germany retained its most important asset: the knowledge and skills of its remaining people. In early 1953, the Allied High Commission divided IG Farben into five companies: Bayer, BASF, Hoechst, Cassela, and Huels.

After West Germany regained its independence in 1955, Bayer acquired Huels and Cassela, leaving the nation with three big chemical companies. In 1965, the U.S. government sold at auction General Aniline and Film (GAF), one of IG Farben's principal U.S. operations, which had been seized during

World War II. GAF was sold for more than $329 million. On April 1, 1978, BASF bought GAF's giant dye works at Rensselaer, New York, bringing it back under German control. Bayer's U.S. operations had been seized in 1917 and sold to Sterling Drugs for $5.3 million. In 1994, Bayer reacquired those operations, plus the right to exclusive use of the Bayer trademark in North America. The price was $1 billion cash.

The Big Three have prospered since the 1950s. Each has long been far larger than IG Farben was at its peak. In 2003, BASF was the world's largest chemical company ($42 billion in sales), far ahead of Dow ($32 billion) and DuPont ($27 billion), America's two largest chemical companies. Bayer also was larger than Dow and DuPont, with sales of $36 billion in 2003. In the late 1990s, Hoechst merged with France's Rhone-Poulenc, creating Aventis, which had $22 billion in sales in 2003. In 2004, another French drug maker, Sanofi-Synthélabo, acquired Aventis. Sanofi-Aventis will have annual sales of around $33 billion in 2004.

Despite losing two world wars and being split from East Germany for almost forty-five years, West Germany prospered. Although its economic growth in the 1950s was called the "German miracle," it was nothing more than an accommodation of the German method to new circumstances. Today, the unified Germany is Europe's economic powerhouse. And once again, the old IG Farben companies dominate their industries.

More than a century ago, Japan's leaders noted the effectiveness of the German way of industrial organization and technology-based growth. As with so many other Western creations, the Japanese took the essence of that method and adapted it to their needs. What emerged is the offspring of the German method and Japanese style.

CHAPTER 5

JAPAN'S WAY

The story of Japan's post–World War II revival, including the role of foreign intellectual property in that process, begins in one of that nation's darkest hours: the sixteen days between the emperor's surrender announcement on August 14, 1945, and General Douglas Mac-Arthur's arrival at the end of the month. The bureaucrats who had brilliantly organized Japan's wartime economy were deeply worried about their fate.

Early in the war, the Japanese government had separated the control of industry from its ownership, putting real power into the hands of those bureaucrats. In 1943, that control, which was split among several agencies, was consolidated into a newly created Munitions Ministry, staffed by the smartest, most competent graduates from Japan's most prestigious universities. As Germany had a brilliant general staff to guide its military, Japan had an equally brilliant staff of bureaucrats to oversee its wartime industrial economy. Under their guidance, Japan's industrial production during World War II hit its peak in 1944, despite the U.S. Navy's devastation of the country's merchant fleet and the U.S. Army Air Corps's destruction of its factories.

As World War II ended, those bureaucrats, fearing that the Americans would arrest anyone associated with munitions, secured an imperial edict that changed the name of the Munitions Ministry to the Ministry of Commerce and Industry (MCI) as of August 26, 1945, only four days before General MacArthur landed in Japan. In 1949, the name was changed once again, to the Ministry of International Trade and Industry (MITI)—an acronym that eventually gained world fame. Today, it is called the Ministry of Economy, Trade, and Industry (METI). Regardless of the name, this ministry has long provided the thinking and vision that guides Japan's economy.

To the munitions bureaucrats' surprise, their wartime powers over Japanese industry were strengthened by MacArthur's staff, many of whom were ardent New Dealers who thought the owners of Japan's giant prewar holding companies—the *zaibatsu* (family-owned holding companies)—had pushed the nation into war and thus must be stripped of their powers. Consequently, the occupation authorities confirmed the Tojo government's wartime decision to separate more than a hundred private owners from their properties and put control in the hands of the government. Thus the same bureaucrats who had run Japan's wartime production were left in charge of Japan's postwar industrial development. It is as if General Eisenhower had placed Albert Speer, Hitler's armament minister, and his Nazi staff in charge of Germany's postwar development.

The American occupation authorities also strengthened Japan's Ministry of Finance, which controlled Japan's banking system and the Bank of Japan. The single most important step was the reorganization of industry, not around the old zaibatsu but around the banks in those conglomerates. Such a power shift was greatly significant because in that era Japanese corporations obtained their capital in the form of loans from the major city banks, which regularly loaned more money than they possessed. In turn, the banks depended on guarantees from the Bank of Japan, which the Finance Ministry controlled. Most important, the bureaucrats in the Ministry of Finance gained enormous power over all of Japan's industries through controlling the banks that provided their capital. With this reorganization, Japan became a bank economy; that is, banks played a major role in deciding the strategy of the corporations they helped finance. Bureaucrats in the Finance Ministry oversaw the banks.

Thus, MITI determined the industries that would be nurtured, the Ministry of Finance allocated the capital, the banks provided corporations the funds they required, and the companies did the work of building and selling products and services. If a Japanese company wished to deviate from the plan, its capital would be cut off. If it complied, capital was available.

The power of MITI and the Ministry of Finance was further strengthened by the corresponding loss of influence by the Foreign Ministry and the military after Japan's surrender. Henceforth, Japan's influence in the world would come from economic rather than military conquest. But before that could be, the war-torn nation had to be rebuilt.

The first years of the Allied occupation were a desperate time for most

Japanese. Six million Japanese troops in faraway places had to be repatriated; the major cities, including Tokyo, lay in ruins; almost 4 million people were still homeless in 1948, and the average caloric intake was just over 1,000 calories a day, just enough to sustain a 100-pound person. Black markets thrived openly. At the same time, the occupation forces were arresting war criminals, conducting trials, even executing a few wartime leaders, and all the while trying to impose foreign ideas on an ancient culture.

After the Communists took control of China and Stalin blockaded Berlin, remaking Japan in America's New Deal model suddenly seemed less important to U.S. officials than ensuring a secure Asian military base from which the U.S. could deal with the new Chinese government and the increasingly hostile Soviets. The strategic geopolitical considerations gained even more importance once the Korean War began. In quick order, the Department of Defense placed several billion dollars in orders with Japanese industries, giving a strong economic stimulus to the country's economy, a U.S.–Japanese peace agreement was signed in April 1952, and the occupation was ended.

Out of these negotiations, a strange and unique relationship was created: Japan would be a U.S. satellite on foreign and defense policy matters in exchange for America's protection against foreign adversaries and the creation of a unequal economic arrangement between the two countries. In the succeeding years, each nation kept its pledge to the other, but for the U.S. there was a price: Japanese industry was given special access to the American market, even as American industry was kept out of Japan's.

After the peace agreement was concluded in 1952, the Japanese quickly cast away many of the edicts, laws, and regulations imposed by the occupation authorities. Among the first to go were U.S.–imposed antitrust laws. Cartels, subsidies, and protectionism were as central to the Japanese way as profits were to American capitalism.

Multiparty democracy was also discarded; Japan returned to its prewar tradition of one-party politics. Skilled bureaucrats-turned-politicians took control of Japan's postwar politics and government. But they were not just any bureaucrats. During the crucial period between 1957 and 1972, each of Japan's prime ministers had been a leader in Japan's wartime industrial production programs. Each knew industry intimately. Each was a nationalist, and each strongly supported the idea of state-directed development.

Nobusuke Kishi, prime minister between 1957 and 1960, played a key role in the colonization of Manchuria in the 1930s, then served as General Tojo's war production minister between 1941 and 1945. In 1943, he created and led the Munitions Ministry. Though jailed as a Class A war criminal during the American occupation, he was "rehabilitated" in 1952. This brilliant, well-educated, and cunning nationalist helped create the ruling Liberal Democratic Party in 1955 and remained a political force in Japan well into the 1970s.

Hayato Ikeda, who succeeded Kishi and served as prime minister until 1964, had been a Finance Ministry bureaucrat for twenty-three years, including the war years. In postwar Japan, he twice was minister of finance (1949–1952 and 1956–1957) and once was MITI minister (1959–1960).

Eisaku Sato, who led Japan from 1964 to 1972, was Kishi's brother. Sato was a senior official in the Ministry of Railways during the war and finance minister during his brother's administration. Kishi was his brother's political emissary both in Japan and elsewhere. President Nixon hosted Kishi in the White House in October 1971 to discuss a deal by which Japan cut its textile exports to the United States in exchange for the U.S. restoring Okinawa to Japanese control.

Unlike the United States, Britain, Germany, and other nations in the postwar era, Japan continued to operate its economy as it had during the war, still under the control of its wartime bureaucrats. Instead of producing military goods as they had during the war, MITI and Finance Ministry officials focused their efforts first on restoring Japan's industries and then on making them world-class competitors. In the 1960s, MITI focused on heavy and chemical industries, such as steel and dyes. Since the 1960s, MITI has concentrated on knowledge-intensive sectors, such as computers, advanced manufacturing, and pharmaceuticals.

The MITI bureaucrats succeeded brilliantly. By 1955, Japan's industrial output exceeded its 1944 wartime high. By 1960, production was 260 percent greater than in 1944. By 1972, when Sato left office, it was 850 percent greater. The world called it the "Japanese miracle," but it represented the results of the same systematic industrial planning that Japan had used to guide its economy during the war, a process the Japanese kept largely hidden from foreign view.

In *MITI and the Japanese Miracle,* Chalmers Johnson describes the Japanese way as a

> capitalist development state that combines private ownership of property with state goal setting. . . . It is based in part on an intentional blurring of the public and private.

The closest counterpart in the United States, Johnson claims, is the U.S. military-industrial complex, in which the government sets the goals and priorities, the companies remain privately owned and managed, and any profits are treated as private property, any successes as a national achievement. Japan's basic development strategy consisted of four elements. First, Japan concentrated its limited capital. Second, foreign firms were kept out so long as domestic firms were weak. Third, the government picked which industries to strengthen, when, and under what conditions. Finally, Japan set out to acquire the best technology in the world.

In the two decades after the occupation, Japan drove its high-growth economy by expanding home demand, which was filled by Japanese companies. Massive exports would come later; first, Japanese industries had to catch up and become world-class competitors—a transformation that was accomplished behind an impenetrable maze of protectionist barriers. To help Japan, experts, such as quality guru W. Edwards Deming, were hired to teach its corporations the secrets of U.S. industrial success, even as other Japanese scoured the world for its best technologies. U.S. inventors and corporations owned most of the patents and technologies that Japan coveted. In the 1950s, the Eisenhower administration actively encouraged, even forced, U.S. firms such as Motorola and GE to share their patents and knowledge with the Japanese. Often, the Japanese simply expropriated the patents they wanted, without the owners' knowledge and certainly without paying royalties.

Beginning in 1950 and continuing for almost another thirty years, MITI controlled the flow of technology into and out of Japan. Johnson writes that

> no technology entered the country without MITI's approval; no joint venture was ever agreed to without MITI's scrutiny and frequent alteration of the terms; no patent rights were ever bought without MITI's pressuring the seller to lower the royalties or to make other changes advantageous to Japanese industry as a whole; and no program for the importation of foreign technology was ever approved until MITI and its various advisory committees had agreed that the time was right and that the industry involved was scheduled for "nurturing."

MITI's control was total and its officials had no hesitation to use it, often giving foreign patent holders a Hobson's choice: "Either license your patents in Japan for almost nothing or MITI will keep you out of Japan's markets." Implicit was the threat that the Japanese would take the technology and use it without either getting a license or paying a royalty, leaving the patent holder with nothing. In the late 1950s, for instance, MITI officials told IBM to either license its basic patents on computer technology to Japanese companies at no more than a 5 percent royalty or face MITI opposition to all its Japanese operations. IBM capitulated, licensing its technology and subjecting itself to MITI's "administrative guidance" in the Japanese market. IBM was then the world's leader in computers. Using IBM's technology, Japanese companies entered the global computer industry.

It was extortion, pure and simple. Dozens of other leading U.S. corporations were shaken down in the same way by MITI, which led repeatedly to the creation of Japanese competitors that often destroyed their American beneficiaries.

Since most of the technology the Japanese took in that era was used in products made and sold in Japan, U.S. patent holders had few means of redress, other than the actions of their own government. But the complaints of American inventors were largely ignored by the U.S. government, because Japan supported U.S. foreign policies, sometimes at a high political price—Kishi was driven from office in 1960 for signing a U.S.–Japan security pact. Perhaps most important, Japan backed the U.S. in its war in Southeast Asia and its efforts to contain the Soviets. A succession of U.S. presidents judged Japan's foreign policy support and U.S. bases there too important to risk in a confrontation over an issue so trivial as the theft of a company's patent. The idea that Japanese companies might ever be able to destroy their U.S. competitors was considered simply preposterous.

What few Americans realized was the extent to which Japan was mining U.S. technology; often Japan's techniques were largely invisible to all but the victims. "Patent flooding" was a particularly successful, and largely imperceptible, means of stripping foreign patents from their owners. When a foreigner filed a desirable patent application with Japan's patent agency, administered by MITI, rival Japanese companies soon "flooded" that office with dozens, even hundreds, of nuisance patent requests, all of which were closely associated with the foreign application. Under Japanese patent procedures, the cost of litigating the validity of each nuisance patent can be between $100,000 and $250,000. When the foreign patent applicant protested, the Japanese companies offered a compromise: royalty-free cross-licensing, coupled with a nondisclosure agreement. Patent flooding, according to a U.S. General Accountability Office (GAO) survey, victimized one of every eight companies filing patent applications in Japan as recently as the early 1990s.

Imagine that you have invented something useful and unique, such as the bicycle, and sought a Japanese patent. After you file your application in Tokyo, a Japanese company suddenly files a patent application for the right pedal. A second requests a patent on the left pedal. A third asks for one on the latch that attaches the brake cables to the handle bar. A fourth seeks one for the left-hand screw used to attach the rear warning light, and so on. After all these are filed, representatives from these companies will appear with an offer to cross-license in Japan their pedals, latch, and left-hand screw technology if you will give them a worldwide, royalty-free license to use your patent. One real example the GAO cited was that of a producer of a breakthrough synthetic fiber that filed a patent application in Japan, but a major Japanese competitor then filed 150 trivial patents whose purpose was to limit the U.S. company's use of its own technology. Another electronics company firm got a patent on an innovation, and soon after a major Japanese company filed 200 patents associated with it. In both these examples, the U.S. company was offered a cross-license, which would have allowed the Japanese to use its breakthrough technology for free.

Regis McKenna, a venture capitalist and entrepreneur, estimates that in the twenty-eight years between 1950 and 1978, Japanese companies paid $9 billion for 32,000 technology licenses worth more than $1 trillion. That is less than a penny on the dollar. In many cases, patent flooding motivated many of these U.S. inventors and companies to sell out so cheaply.

In *Agents of Influence* (1990), I told the story of Fusion Systems, a small high-tech company in Bethesda, Maryland, that was victimized by a Japanese patent flooding attack. In 1990, Don Spero, the Fusion CEO, thought the matter was successfully concluded. It was not.

Spero, who earned his doctorate in physics from Columbia University, and another physicist created Fusion Systems in 1971. After three years of work in a one-room laboratory, Spero and his colleagues invented a commercial, high-powered microwave lamp capable of curing and drying industrial inks and coatings on plastic, metal, paper, glass, and other surfaces. Coors Beer, for example, employed Fusion's technology to put labels on its aluminum beer cans. (By 1989, the inventors had adapted the technology for use in the manufacture of semiconductor chips, which made it particularly valuable.)

In 1974, Fusion filed a patent application in Japan and licensed a Japanese distributor. Mitsubishi Electric, the giant electronics corporation, bought a Fusion lamp in the spring of 1977 and had it delivered to its R & D laboratory. That December, Mitsubishi filed three patents for high-powered microwave lamp technology. It also filed with the Japan Patent Office its opposition to the Fusion application. Fusion responded by filing its opposition to the Mitsubishi applications. Fusion was eventually granted patents on its technology. Meanwhile, Mitsubishi began filing patent applications in Japan, often on minor items associated with Fusion's technology. By 1989, Mitsubishi had submitted 283 patent applications, of which 27 were issued. By the mid-1980s, Fusion dominated the Japanese market, but Mitsubishi persisted.

In 1985, the two companies entered private negotiations. Mitsubishi demanded a worldwide, royalty-free license on Fusion's technology, plus cash and royalty payments for a cross-license on the Japanese technology. Don Spero offered to not oppose Mitsubishi's patent applications if the Japanese company agreed not to assert any patent violations by Fusion— each company would go its own way and compete. To avoid a costly legal battle, Spero even offered to sweeten his proposal with a $100,000 payment to Mitsubishi. The Japanese refused his offer.

Unable to reach an agreement with the Japanese company, Spero took the issue public, writing an article on patent flooding in the *Harvard Business Review*. He also brought the issue to Congress, where he attracted the attention of Senator John D. (Jay) Rockefeller (D.-W.Va.).

As a young man, Rockefeller had studied in Japan, and he remained interested in things Japanese. His Senate office is decorated with museum-quality Japanese prints.

In the late 1980s and early 1990s, Rockefeller held hearings on patent flooding, at which Spero testified. Working through a Washington lobbyist, Mitsubishi Electric planted negative questions for another senator to ask Spero. The senator was Robert Packwood (R.-Ore.). In subsequent Senate Ethics Committee hearings into Packwood's conduct, investigators discovered that the lobbyist who had planted the questions was also arranging a job for the senator's ex-wife, which would help Packwood reduce his alimony payments.

Despite the public attention Spero brought to the conflict, Mitsubishi was relentless in its efforts to get the Fusion technology. In 1992, Spero's partners removed him from his position as CEO. The new management and Mitsubishi soon settled their disagreement. Eventually, much of Fusion was split into parts and sold. A British company purchased Fusion's ultraviolet curing division for $121 million, and the Eaton Corporation acquired its semi-conductor manufacturing technology for $300 million. Although Spero's stock made him wealthy and he now directs the University of Maryland's Center for Entrepreneurship, he says getting rich was never his goal. As with so many creative people and inventors, he wanted to refine what he had invented and expand his company. But ultimately, it was too small to take on the government of Japan and a major Japanese corporation without the help of the U.S. government, which it did not get.

Because of the Fusion saga, Rockefeller became interested in how Japan's patent system really works. Many American companies having trouble protecting their patents in Japan were seeking his help and that of other senators. In response, Japanese officials generally explained that their patent system was complex but that most foreigners really were "not trying hard enough." Yet by the early 1990s, too many large, experienced U.S. companies were having too many problems in Japan for the issue to be one of "not trying hard enough."

In 1991, Rockefeller organized a petition, co-signed by Senator Lloyd Bentsen (D.-Tex.) and Senator Dennis De Concini (D.-Ariz.), for the GAO to review patent protections for U.S. inventions in Japan. The resulting study, *Intellectual Property Rights—U.S. Companies' Patent Experiences in Japan,* was published in 1993 and is available for downloading at the GAO's Web site. There has never been any other study of Japan's patent system as complete as this one.

The GAO examiners interviewed Japanese officials, U.S. patent attorneys, Japanese patent lawyers, and three hundred foreign corporate patent holders in Japan. Although the responding companies had hired the best legal talent in Japan and had done whatever the Japanese required, two-thirds reported having significant problems dealing with the patent system. By contrast, only 17 percent said they had similar problems in the United States. Only 25 percent reported having the same problems in Europe as they did in Japan. Clearly, Japan's patent system was different in its operations from both that of the United States and that of Europe.

The GAO observed that the Japanese system was also different in its purpose. The focus of the U.S. patent system, it said, was to protect individual patentees and provide them with exclusive rights to their inventions. By contrast, the focus of the Japanese patent system was to promote Japan's industrial development by disseminating technology. The difference is fundamental. In one system, the product of a person's mind belongs to the individual, who can make a bargain with society for exclusive use for a set period in exchange for disclosure. In the other, the nation has the first claim to the innovation, which it can disseminate and use for national development.

In stunning detail, the GAO study documented how Japan's patent system was at once a defensive, offensive, and strategic tool of national development. Japan uses patents to (1) exclude foreign goods, (2) examine the innards of proprietary foreign technology, and (3) strip patents from their foreign owners.

The GAO listed many of the tricks the Japan Patent Office used, such as delaying approval of foreign patents for years, limiting the scope of protection, allowing rivals to examine and comment on patent applications, and erecting unworkable enforcement mechanisms. In other words, Japan's patent system offered foreign inventors government-managed intimidation.

Since 1993, Japan has enacted several patent laws that have addressed some of the foreign concerns. Still, substantial differences between the U.S. and Japanese patent systems remain. In the U.S., the patent goes to the first-to-invent. In Japan, it goes to the first to file an application. In the United States, the Japanese language can be used to file an application. In Japan, an English-language application will be accepted, but a Japanese translation must be submitted within three months. Enforcement also differs. U.S. courts generally interpret patents broadly, while Japanese courts generally make narrow interpretations. Since the mid-1990s, the Japanese patent system has speeded up its processing time and eliminated pregrant reviews of applications by competing companies. Despite all this, the system remains a tool of national development, rather than an institution that protects the rights of individual inventors.

Patent flooding and patent office shenanigans are but a few of the means Japan uses to strip foreigners of their technology secrets. Much as Francis Cabot Lowell made off with the secret of England's power loom, Japanese spies have absconded with U.S. technologies. The difference between then and now is the direction, scale, and scope of the efforts. While Lowell operated alone, the Federal Bureau of Investigation reports that Japan operates one of the world's largest industrial espionage operations—far larger, more comprehensive, and more sophisticated than anything the Soviet Union had during the Cold War. Today, only China's efforts to acquire foreign technology through clandestine means are comparable.

Wall Street Journal reporter John J. Fialka traced Japan's technology espionage in his 1997 book *War by Other Means.* He reports that the system is "exceptionally efficient." When U.S. businesspeople visiting Japan enter their hotel rooms, for instance, they are probably unaware that their telephones are microphones that clearly pick up everything they might say, even when they are not on the phone. Most do not realize that agents regularly download the hard drives of computers in Japanese hotel rooms.

Japanese trading companies and governmental agencies in foreign nations regularly, even on a daily and hourly basis, send data and information back to Tokyo for analysis by the government. Japanese officials then take the bits and pieces and put them together. Much of that information comes from METI's global economic intelligence agency, the Japan External Trade Organization (JETRO), which has eighty offices in sixty countries, including seven in the United States. Its stated mission is to facilitate foreign economic relations with Japan. Its real goal is to collect economic intelligence for METI, including the identification of key foreign technologies.

For decades, Japan has obtained some of its most advanced knowledge about foreign technology and corporate strategies from some of the tens of thousands of researchers and graduate students who have worked in U.S. corporations, federal labs, and universities, and then returned home. Fialka reports that Japanese companies have repeatedly created front businesses near their technologically advanced foreign competitors, in order to hire these companies' key people and absorb their knowledge.

Japan also gains much from the strategic alliances it has created with U.S. companies. The National Science Foundation reports that in the period 1985–2000, U.S. and Japanese corporations created 820 such alliances in the fields of information technology, biotechnology, new materials, aerospace and defense, automotive, and chemicals, virtually all of which involved technology transfers to Japan. During the same period, U.S. companies signed 2,196 deals in those same six fields with European corporations. European companies had only 384 such arrangements with the Japanese. The disparity in these numbers raises some intriguing questions. Perhaps the Japanese did not think the Europeans had any technology they wanted. Or perhaps neither the Japanese nor the Europeans trusted each other sufficiently to share. Or maybe the Japanese had little the Europeans wanted. Regardless of which is true, Europe and Japan each has extended access to U.S. technology. Yet the numbers strongly suggest that both Europe and Japan seem reluctant to share technology with each other. The ultimate question is, Do European and Japanese CEOs know something that U.S. CEOs do not?

In recent years, Japanese and other foreign corporations have acquired the technologies they want by buying U.S. companies that possess it. Beginning in the late 1980s, as the Cold War was ending, the U.S. government allowed hundreds of such sales. Not only did the Japanese obtain the knowledge and patents, but their country also denied the same technology to its U.S. and other competitors—a complete lockup.

Washington's two-decade-long position on the foreign acquisition of key U.S. technologies and corporations is captured in the oft-quoted comment of Michael Boskin, chairman of the Council of Economic Advisers in the early 1990s. He said that he did not care whether the U.S. economy produced potato chips or computer chips. Richard Darman, then director of the Office of Management and Budget, went a step further. During the furor over Japan's dumping of semiconductors, he asked, "Why do we want a semiconductor industry? What's wrong with dumping? It is a gift to chip users because they get cheap chips. If our guys can't hack it, let them go."

In the face of such official indifference, other nations have taken control of, and often exported, many of America's best technologies in what are some of the world's most advanced industries. In the more than five years between January 1989 and May 1994, Japanese corporations bought more than 452 high-tech U.S. companies concentrated in those industries targeted by Japan's longer-term industrial policies. Of these acquisitions, 41 were in advanced materials, 30 in biotechnology, 120 in computers, 71 in advanced electronics, 55 in semiconductors, and 39 in semiconductor manufacturing equipment.

These U.S. companies were the beneficiaries of tens of billions of dollars of taxpayer-funded research. They held thousands of key U.S. and world patents, and their scientists, engineers, and workers possessed unique knowledge. Most of that knowledge, and virtually none of those people, went to Japan. Although the U.S. Treasury Department has responsibility for reviewing each of these acquisitions for its effect on U.S. economic and military security, it reviewed few and rejected none. In the early 1990s, the United States held the world lead in those industries. Now Japan does.

Ironically, the foresight and thoroughness of Japan's efforts to capture foreign technologies are well illustrated by one of its few technology acquisition programs to be discovered by the U.S. government and then go sour. This story begins in the years following World War II, when the United States helped Japan and Europe create cooperative research and development centers. Out of such work came companies such as Airbus, which now leads in the global production of passenger airplanes.

The idea behind such cooperation was that the cost of expensive R & D projects could be shared, thus allowing those nations to remain in the technology race. At the same time, such cooperative efforts were prohibited in the United States because they violated antitrust laws.

In 1985, Congress changed the antitrust law and helped create several U.S. research consortia, the best known of which is probably Sematech in Austin, Texas, formed to pursue semiconductor research. Congress also established another highly visible R & D consortium in Ann Arbor, Michigan—the National Center for Manufacturing Sciences (now called the Association for Manufacturing Technology). Starting with a $1 million grant from the National Machine Tool Builders Association and later with a $5 million annual federal grant authorized by President Ronald Reagan, this center grew into a $200-million-a-year research organization that U.S. corporations jointly funded with federal and state governments.

Japan's government and its industries responded to the new U.S. law by trying to "mine" all these new joint U.S. research programs through surrogates. In 1990, Edward Miller, president of the National Center for Manufacturing Sciences, learned that a Japanese government agency had contracted with a Michigan-based professional association to secure proprietary technical information from the academics advising the collaborative research projects on manufacturing.

Miller went to Deborah L. Wince-Smith, the newly appointed assistant secretary of commerce for technology policy. Wince-Smith, a dynamic and well-connected Washington insider, quickly arranged for the Bush administration to lodge a formal complaint with Japan that it was violating a bilateral science and technology agreement. Once confronted, the Tokyo government immediately stopped that particular technology acquisition program.

But Wince-Smith wanted something more. Under her leadership, the U.S. and the European Union, which was also experiencing similar technology "mining" by the Japanese, initiated negotiations to create a new treaty and new rules to guide international collaborative research on intelligent manufacturing systems. The U.S. and Europe invited Japan to participate, which it did, as did Australia, Canada, and Korea.

The protocol for the negotiations allowed a five-person team from each country—three from industry, one from academia, and one from government. Wince-Smith appointed Miller one of the three U.S. industry delegates; she also named him to be the U.S. representative on the executive committee guiding the negotiations. Over the next three years, the parties met twice in each participating region. The protocol also allowed the host to bring as many observers as it wished. By the very nature of the topic, their talks were obscure and certainly far from exciting. Few observers attended in other countries, but Japan was different.

Miller remembers his surprise when the negotiations shifted to Kyoto—Japan's ancient former capital, with its 1,600 temples, 250 shrines, and 60 elaborate gardens—which serves as a major conference center for the government. The surprise was not the beauty of the city but the substantial number of observers at the negotiations. The Japanese team had arranged for participants to conduct their talks in the middle of a large, bare auditorium where the negotiators sat at tables drawn into a six-sided configuration. Behind the Japanese negotiators, fifteen rows of tables were set up, one behind the other, with five chairs at each. The government had brought seventy-five observers. Most came from the METI. The back seats were for the junior staff, the second row for the second most junior and so on up to the first row. Eventually, the junior staffers will be in charge. They were there to watch and learn. They would become intimately familiar with the details of what would become an important agreement between Japan and its principal industrial competitors. If there were some future dispute over a provision in that agreement, in all likelihood the Japanese official could authoritatively declare that he had been at the original negotiations and the point meant whatever Japan then advocated. The observation by those future negotiators revealed the long-term view the Japanese take in such matters.

When the negotiations concluded in 1994 in Hawaii, Miller got another surprise that also displays the Japanese approach. On the night before the participating nations signed off on the new agreement on intelligent manufacturing systems, he received a private message from a major U.S. corporation that the agreement was subject to a special provision of Japanese law that would give Japan a unique advantage. As Miller soon learned, Japanese law requires the grant of a royalty-free patent license to the government whenever any research or development program that creates intellectual property is supported by one yen or more of Japan's public funds. Thus, any patents or copyrights flowing from a collaborative project with a Japanese company automatically are shared with the government, which can then license them to other Japanese corporations. To collaborate with one meant sharing the technology with all.

Removing or recrafting the Japanese law was impossible. Instead, Miller bargained for acceptance of a provision that allowed any nation or corporation to stop the involvement of any company that had taken Japanese funds, directly or indirectly, that would result in the Japanese government granting licenses to anyone other than the research participants. In short, representatives of other nations could blackball any Japanese corporation if it were going to share with its government any patents or copyrights created out of a joint project. The obligation fell on the Japanese participant to solve the problem.

Miller says that all the non-Japanese in those negotiations left quite impressed by how competent the Japanese are, how seamless the relationship is between their government and industries, and how dedicated both are to acquiring and developing the best technology in the world.

Four decades ago, U.S. leaders did not realize that Japan's old Munitions Ministry bureaucrats, then leading MITI and the Ministry of Finance, had quietly launched an undeclared industrial war with the United States and Europe. In the 1960s, the targets were textiles, steel, and consumer electronics. In the 1970s, they were automobiles, machine tools, and robotics. In the 1980s, they were computers, semiconductors, and advanced electronics. One by one, key U.S. industries were humbled. Even the largest U.S. corporations, such as General Motors, Chrysler, and Ford, had difficulty withstanding the assault.

For almost forty years, Japanese cartels, working with their government, humbled one U.S. industry after another. The Japanese strategy was almost always the same. First, MITI chose an industry for nurturing. Second, foreign technology was licensed or stolen. Third, a Japanese cartel was formed, which MITI guided. Fourth, the government provided special financial incentives, including grants and tax rebates, to help develop the industry. Fifth, the domestic Japanese market was mostly closed to foreign imports by a dense maze of protectionist measures. Sixth, prices for domestic sales were raised to provide a corporate subsidy that would enable Japanese companies to sell below cost in the target market (dumping). During the Japanese electronics cartel attack on the U.S. television makers, which began in the mid-1960s, five million sets a year were being sold in Japan annually. In 1977, only five hundred of these sets were imports. Japan protectionism was airtight. And finally, Japanese government and industry mounted a political and propaganda program in the target industry's homeland to divert attention and forestall any defensive actions by the victims. By the late 1980s, Japanese interests were spending more than $100 million annually in Washington, D.C., on lobbying and public relations, most of it directed to keeping Japan's market closed and allowing Japanese corporations to ravage their U.S. competitors in the American market.

For more than a half century, a succession of U.S. administrations quietly looked the other way as Japan and other nations, friend and foe alike, stole U.S.-owned technology, perhaps made a few minor changes, and then used it in their production processes or a later generation of goods. Now largely forgotten, many now defunct U.S. companies and industries fought back valiantly. The records of those fights, found in old lawsuits, court records, newspapers, congressional testimony, and books, are often all that remain of them. The records also reveal a U.S. government and American elites that were largely indifferent to those foreign attacks on U.S.-owned intellectual properties.

As the history of those fights makes clear, most of these U.S. industries did not expire because they failed to "try hard enough" or because they were incompetent or because they refused to defend themselves. Rather, they most often were taken down by acts that are forbidden under international trade agreements, U.S. law, and often the laws of the aggressor nations.

Of these conflicts, three are particularly important, and all involve Japan. The first concerns the U.S. loss of its machine tool industry. To an industrial society, machine tools are essential, for they are the machines that make the machines that make things. When attacked, U.S. leaders in that industry relied on their government and U.S. trade remedies. They chose poorly. Thirty years ago, the U.S. machine tool industry was the most innovative and productive in the world. Today, it is shattered.

A second example involves Zenith Corporation, once America's largest and most innovative manufacturer of radios and televisions. In the 1950s and 1960s, Zenith broke the RCA global patent monopoly. In the 1970s and 1980s, Zenith took on Japan's electronics cartel but lost, not because it lacked a good, competitive product but because the Japanese manufacturers had more clout in Washington than it did. Zenith's fight illustrates how intellectual property can be used as a tool of global monopoly. Most important, it shows the consequences when the U.S. government openly takes the side of foreign cartels against American companies and their workers.

The third example is robotics. U.S. companies invented robotics and led the world in its development. In the 1970s, however, U.S. companies and their government ignored the Japanese challenge and lost a vital industry of the future.

Often, a foreign government can get U.S. legal immunity for the misconduct of its industries by merely asking the American president for a favor. The U.S. machine tool industry is one victim of such a request.

In the early 1970s, America's machine tool industry was the global leader. Today, it is a shadow of its former self. The deciding event in this quick devolution of futures involved a company created by Fred Burg, a Czech immigrant who arrived in the United States in 1911, at the age of fifteen, and through hard work became a skilled machinist. In 1943, the forty-seven-year-old Burg moved to California and went to work as a machine tool operator by day and inventor by night and weekend. Soon he invented a tool-holding mechanism and went into business for himself. He then invented a turret drill, and after that advanced machine tools. Within a decade, Burg Tool, later renamed Burgmaster, became one of the world's premier machine tool companies—the classic story of an inventor who succeeded with superior innovations, strong patents, and hard work.

In 1965, Fred Burg, a successful and wealthy man, sold his company to Houdaille, a small East Coast conglomerate, and retired. The conglomerate then sold part of the company's technology to the Japanese for quick profits. The idea was simple but dangerous: get royalties from the Japanese manufacturers who were stealing U.S. machine tool technology to create a world-class industry of their own.

Throughout the 1950s and 1960s, the Japanese government tightly restricted investment in Japan by U.S. machine tool makers. Japan allowed some joint ventures, but only if Japan could get their most advanced technology, much as China is doing today. Simultaneously, the Japanese government encouraged Japan's machine tool makers to buy foreign machines, take them apart, reverse engineer their designs, and then produce knockoffs for the Japanese market. The Japanese government also provided massive financial subsidies to its tool industry.

Beginning in the late 1960s, most leading U.S. toolmakers, anxious to enter the rich Japanese market, but kept out by Japanese protectionism, struck co-production deals with their Japanese competitors. Warner & Swasey made a deal with Murata Machinery, Kearney & Trecker with Toshiba, Norton with Mitsubishi, and Houdaille with Yamazaki Machinery. In these deals, the U.S. companies were forced to share their technology and know-how with the Japanese.

While U.S. companies gained virtually no market share in Japan, the Japanese got the best technology in the world and soon installed it in machines that they exported back to the U.S. market. After mastering the U.S. technology, the Japanese added some improvements, claimed the improvements had nothing to do with the original licensing agreements, and stopped the flow of license payments to their U.S. partners.

Houdaille's technology allowed Yamazaki to rise to the top among Japanese toolmakers. The same technology allowed Yamazaki to attack its U.S. partner when, in 1976, Yamazaki introduced into the American market an advanced machine tool that Houdaille immediately recognized as a knockoff of one of its best products.

Houdaille went to the U.S. International Trade Commission with a complaint that Yamazaki had stolen its technology and demanded that the ITC bar Yamazaki machines from the U.S. market. Eventually the two companies made a private settlement in which they revoked their contract and Yamazaki paid Houdaille for access to certain of its patents.

By the early 1980s, Japanese companies were overwhelming the U.S. toolmakers and often using U.S. technologies to do it. Between 1976 and 1981, the Japanese share of the U.S. market soared from 4 percent to 50 percent. Under attack again, Houdaille went to Washington for help. In 1981, the company hired a prominent law firm, Covington & Burling, to prepare its case. What emerged was a well-documented, 700-page petition that traced the history of the Japanese government's subsidies, protectionism, and support for its machine tool makers, including the formation and guidance of an export cartel. All these acts are illegal in the United States.

The Houdaille petition eventually involved many of President Ronald Reagan's key offices—Treasury, State, Commerce, the U.S. Trade Representative, and the Council of Economic Advisers, among others. By April 1983, President Reagan's aides had forged a majority view on how to help the U.S. machine tool industry confront Japan's predatory attack. When the cabinet met with the president on April 22, 1983, to debate the issue, Reagan unexpectedly announced that he was going to reject Houdaille's petition.

Japanese diplomats had learned of the proposed decision before the cabinet meeting. Prime Minister Yasuhiro Nakasone then called President Reagan and asked for a personal favor: to reject the Houdaille petition. Reagan, who viewed Nakasone as a friend and Japan as a strategic ally against the Soviets, granted the favor.

Thus, in one phone call, Houdaille, and consequently the rest of the U.S. machine tool industry, lost the support and help of their own government, whereupon the Japanese manufacturers were free to flood the U.S. machine tool market, which they did.

Zenith's battle began almost simultaneously with the commercialization of radio in 1920—initially with an American patent cartel controlled by RCA.

Zenith was a classic start-up by two talented amateur radio operators. R. H. G. Matthews and Karl Hassel met during World War I as new navy recruits at the Great Lakes Training Station near Chicago. When the war ended, they created a Chicago-based company to manufacture and install radios. Their first laboratory and factory was Matthews's kitchen. Their first major venture was building a long-range receiver for the *Chicago Tribune* that enabled the newspaper to get dispatches directly from a long-range transmitter in France, thus giving the *Tribune* a twelve-hour lead on stories from the Versailles peace conference. To promote local sales of radio receivers, Matthews and Hassel built their own radio station, whose call letters were 9ZN, and provided programming. Their radio sets were sold under the trademark of "Z-Nith," later changed to "Zenith."

During World War I, German spies were caught broadcasting British shipping schedules to submarines off the New England shore. Thus, the U.S. Navy was put in charge of regulating all radio transmissions. After the war, Owen Young, CEO of General Electric Corporation, convinced the U.S. government that radio was such an important innovation that it should be put into the hands of a private American radio company. But which company? Westinghouse was interested. Marconi Wireless was as well. So was American Telephone & Telegraph. Each had something to contribute, and each held patents that could block the others. The solution Young engineered was to create a new company, the Radio Corporation of America, which would hold and share the patents of all the partners.

On October 17, 1919, the Radio Corporation of America was formed. Under the terms of incorporation, no more than 20 percent of the stock could ever be held by foreign interests, only U.S. citizens could be executives, and representatives from the navy were invited to attend all board meetings.

GE bought the stock of Marconi's American interests, including its patents. GE, AT&T, and Westinghouse put their radio patents into the newly formed RCA. In addition, RCA purchased the radio facilities and technology of United Fruit, which had its own private wireless network connecting its U.S. operations with its ships and Central American plantations, plus a patent on an important loop antenna. Altogether, RCA began business with 2,000 patents.

The new owners then secretly, and illegally, divided the radio and electric apparatus industry among themselves. AT&T got control of wire communications in the United States. RCA got control of radio and later television, receivers and tubes, licensing of such to others, broadcasting, and wireless communications for fees. GE and Westinghouse took control of all electric power, industrial, and railroad apparatus. The cartel effectively divided up the entire radio industry. In addition, Westinghouse would get 40 percent of RCA's manufacturing orders and GE 60 percent.

Just as thousands of Internet companies were created in the 1990s, hundreds of companies were created in the early 1920s to manufacture radio and broadcasting equipment. RCA quickly shut virtually all of them down, using its hold over the basic patents. Those few companies that survived did so because they already owned a license from Edwin Howard Armstrong, which Westinghouse purchased in 1920. Zenith had one of those licenses.

As Microsoft was attacked in the 1990s for its control over the operating systems of most computers, so RCA was attacked in the mid-1920s for its control over radio equipment. To avoid investigation by the U.S. Justice Department, RCA agreed to make its patents available to anyone for a fee of 7.5 percent of the value of the radio equipment it sold. The 7.5 percent, moreover, included the full value of the product, including such components as the wood cabinet. RCA considered it a risk-free business because it got paid whether the licensee made money or not. As part of the deal, the licensee also had to share its technology and patents with RCA, perpetuating the cartel's hold on the industry and guaranteeing its future license revenues, and the licensee had to agree never to sue RCA. RCA had a sweet deal by any measure.

Zenith was the first company to which RCA sold such a license. In 1920, Eugene McDonald, a lieutenant commander in the U.S. Navy during World War I, bought one of the first Zenith radios, became fascinated by the technology, and raised the capital needed by the new corporation. In 1927, he became Zenith's CEO and driving force. McDonald, a crusty individualist, believed in quality; he instituted a model quality control program that equals anything found anywhere today. He originated the Zenith slogan, "The quality goes in before the name goes on."

By the end of World War II, RCA's initial patents had expired and McDonald was tired of paying tribute to what he called RCA's "patent racket." He canceled RCA's license. Instead of waiting for RCA to respond with litigation, Zenith declared war on RCA, AT&T, Western Electric, GE, and Westinghouse, filing a federal lawsuit in Delaware District Court claiming that their patents had been pooled by an unlawful conspiracy and thus violated U.S. antitrust laws.

The Zenith-RCA patent war raged through the federal courts for more than a decade. By 1957, Zenith was able to sufficiently document that RCA and the other defendants were operating an anticompetitive enterprise. The proof was so conclusive that the U.S. Justice Department initiated a criminal prosecution case against RCA and opened related civil cases against GE, RCA, Philips of the Netherlands, and Westinghouse. RCA settled with Zenith, paying $10 million in cash and granting a five-year royalty-free license, worldwide, on all its patents.

A year later, a New York federal grand jury indicted RCA for criminal violations of the Sherman Antitrust Act. Philip Curtis, Zenith's longtime legal counsel and author of *The Fall of the U.S. Consumer Electronics Industry*, contends that David Sarnoff, RCA's CEO for four decades, was not personally indicted largely because of his wartime relationship with General Dwight Eisenhower, who was then president. Sarnoff, as an aide to Eisenhower, had brilliantly directed Allied communications during and after the D-day invasion.

RCA did not contest the charge. In October 1958, a federal judge fined the company $100,000, a pittance considering that the cartel had made billions of dollars of illegal profits over the thirty-eight years of its operation. No one went to jail.

In 1962, GE, Westinghouse, and Philips entered a consent agreement with the Justice Department in which they agreed to stop certain anticompetitive practices in the radio and television industry, such as restricting the export of their radio and television sets to Canada.

The breakup of RCA's patent cartel humiliated David Sarnoff, a proud man who had led RCA from its inception. The Zenith victory was Sarnoff's worst business defeat. He sought revenge.

Barely twenty-four months after the RCA settlement, lawyers from Hazeltine, a company that owned another radio and television patent pool, contacted Zenith, demanding a royalty payment on Hazeltine's five hundred radio and television patents. Zenith refused Hazeltine's demand, and in October 1959, Hazeltine filed suit against Zenith in Chicago's federal district court alleging patent infringement. Not surprisingly, Zenith countersued. During discovery, Zenith's lawyers learned that Hazeltine had a close, even clandestine, relationship with RCA. With that, the stalker became the stalked: Hazeltine became Zenith's target.

Philip Curtis claims that Zenith's lawyers always believed that Hazeltine was merely a surrogate for Sarnoff and RCA. Certainly, Hazeltine fought with an open checkbook; its lawyers battled with a punishing life-and-death fury. The case went to the Supreme Court twice and was not concluded until 1971, when again Zenith prevailed, winning $22 million in damages from Hazeltine.

What Zenith did not realize in the 1950s in the midst of the original patent war was that Sarnoff was creating an economic time bomb designed to destroy all of RCA's American radio and television competitors. RCA teamed up with the emerging Japanese electronic companies and helped them create a cartelized television industry, along the lines of what GE, Westinghouse, and RCA had done in 1919. As part of this package, RCA's engineers and technicians gave the Japanese companies all its cutting-edge technology, market information, and advanced production know-how and industrial skills. In exchange, the Japanese agreed to pay royalties to RCA on every television and radio set they sold. As a reward, Emperor Hirohito conferred on Sarnoff the Order of the Rising Sun, Japan's highest decoration for a foreigner.

Though the Zenith victory cost RCA its royalty income from U.S. manufacturers, Sarnoff's deal replaced that loss with income from Japan's radio and television cartel. Eventually, the Japanese cartel destroyed RCA's U.S. competitors, producing billions of dollars of royalties for RCA. When GE bought RCA in 1986, almost a quarter century later, the royalty income, largely from the Japanese manufacturers, was still more than $200 million per year.

Zenith fought the Japanese cartel just as aggressively as it had RCA and Hazeltine, but in this fight, the U.S. government did not remain neutral. It supported the Japanese manufacturers.

By the late 1950s, Commander McDonald no longer headed Zenith. His replacement, Joseph S. Wright, was an old-fashioned New Deal trustbuster who had headed the Federal Trade Commission's Antitrust Compliance Division in the 1940s. McDonald had hired Wright in 1951 and given him the job of busting the RCA cartel, which he had done luminously.

When Japanese competitors began to attack the U.S. consumer electronics industry in the mid-1960s, Wright repeatedly went to the U.S. government with evidence that the Japanese were violating U.S. laws on dumping and antitrust. The governments of Lyndon Johnson, Richard Nixon, Gerald Ford, and Jimmy Carter were not those of Franklin Roosevelt, Harry Truman, and Dwight Eisenhower. The later administrations not only ignored Zenith's requests, they actively opposed them. Always, the excuse was that Japan was a valuable ally in the fight against communism. Thus, the U.S. government refused to stop Japan's predatory actions in the U.S. radio and television markets.

Undaunted, Wright took matters into his own hands, just as he had against RCA; Zenith exercised its right to defend itself. In September 1974, the company filed a multibillion-dollar, triple-damage case against most members of the Japanese cartel doing business in the United States. According to Zenith, the Japanese scheme was simple. The government of Japan excluded all foreign televisions from its market, allowing Japanese manufacturers to charge $500 in Japan for the same set that sold in the United States for $300. The extra profits earned in Japan enabled Japanese companies to sell televisions for the cost of production or less in the U.S. market. The cartel's overall profits were between 10 and 15 percent, which meant that they could continue this illegal scheme indefinitely. Once the Japanese drove the U.S. manufacturers out of business, they could set their profit margins at whatever level they wished in a market they would dominate. It was an attack formula that the Japanese successfully repeated in dozens of other industries.

At great expense, Zenith hired investigators, translators, and outside counsel who went to Japan to document the case. Among evidence they uncovered was a report from Japan's Fair Trade Commission that provided detailed information on how the Japanese government had encouraged the formation of the television cartel and details on who was involved and how it operated. Zenith's investigators also uncovered documents that revealed price-fixing, kickbacks to U.S. retailers, predatory dumping, illegal rebates, and the filing of false information with U.S. Customs.

Zenith took all this information to the U.S. Justice Department, but federal officials were strangely uninterested. Later, Zenith learned that after the

Carter administration had come to power, it had concluded a secret agreement with the Japanese government to

a. limit the U.S. investigation of any predatory pricing by the Japanese cartel;

b. ignore monopolization charges against Japanese television manufacturers; and

c. inform the Japanese government quickly and privately of any significant findings arising from any U.S. investigations of the Zenith television case.

The Carter administration agreement with Japan gave Zenith two major challenges: It had to defend itself against a cartel organized and fully supported by the Japanese government. It also had to defend itself against the U.S. government, which was helping the Japanese cartel.

Finally, the Zenith case went to trial. The district court dismissed the case, saying that Zenith had insufficient evidence. With that, the case moved to the court of appeals which ruled unanimously that Zenith had proved what "amounted to sufficient evidence of the alleged conspiracy" to send the case to trial. Rather than go to trial, however, the Japanese manufacturers asked the U.S. Supreme Court to overturn the decision of the appeals court and thus end the case. In 1985, the Supreme Court agreed to make a review.

Amazingly, the U.S. Justice Department filed a "friend of the court" brief on behalf of the Japanese manufacturers. Among its arguments, the U.S. government told the Court that a finding against the Japanese cartel could harm U.S. foreign policy interests. The Justice Department's brief said that "the Governments of Australia, Canada, France, Japan, the Republic of Korea, Spain and the United Kingdom have formally advised the Department of State of their concerns about the potential impact of the court of appeals' decision."

The U.S. Supreme Court ruled 5–4 in favor of the Japanese. Writing for the majority, Justice Powell ignored all of the evidence cited by the court of appeals, including the fact that the Japanese had totally closed their market to imports and were subsidizing exports by allowing the Japanese manufacturers to charge twice as much in Japan as they did in the U.S. Instead, Powell based his decision on a theoretical analysis of the case presented in a University of Texas law review article written by Frank H. Easterbrook, a deputy U.S. solicitor general in the Carter administration. Easterbrook is a highly visible member of a group of laissez-faire academics that urges the judicial repeal of U.S. antitrust laws.

Displaying a complete lack of knowledge of Japan's business structure and operations, Justice Powell and four other justices accepted Easterbrook's arguments. Justice Powell wrote for the majority: "The predation-recoupment story . . . does not make sense, and we are left with the more plausible inference that the Japanese firms did not sell below cost in the first place. They were just engaged in hard competition."

With that, Zenith lost the right to show evidence to a U.S. jury that the Japanese cartel was indeed selling below cost. In addition, the Supreme Court established a new precedent for dismissing cases: plausibility. The courts can now ignore evidence and dismiss cases they think are implausible regardless of any evidence, and they define what is implausible.

The Reagan administration appointed Easterbrook to the Seventh Circuit Court of Appeals in Chicago, where he still sits. Later, Zenith attorneys learned that Easterbrook's paper had not been a "non-commissioned learned professional paper," as represented by the cartel's counsel to the Supreme Court. Rather, Easterbrook had been a paid consultant to the Japanese cartel on this case and had reviewed their materials. By the time Zenith learned this, the Supreme Court had ruled.

Zenith had done everything right—it was innovative, its patents were valid, its quality was the best in the industry, its customers were loyal, it defended its rights aggressively—but the actions of the Carter and Reagan administrations, plus the Supreme Court's decision, doomed the company. It also doomed the U.S. consumer electronics industry. In 1968, the U.S. had sixteen American-owned, independent television manufacturers. As of 1990, there was only one. In 1995, LG Electronics, the giant Korean conglomerate formerly known as Goldstar, took over Zenith.

Sarnoff retired from RCA in 1965. His successors, including his son, were unequal to the job. Two decades later, a greatly diminished RCA was sold to GE, which then sold the television and consumer products division to Thompson, a French company. The famous RCA labs, which for so long had led the world in communications research, were downsized, and the facilities were eventually taken over by Stanford Research Institute.

All that is left of RCA and Zenith is their famous names and trademarks. A French company owns the RCA trademark, and the Korean conglomerate owns Zenith's.

· · ·

Industrial robotics offers yet another example of how the U.S. government's indifference led to Japan's takeover of a key advanced technology industry that the United States pioneered. In 1968, the U.S. had a fifteen-year lead in research and an eight-year jump in production over any other nation. But by 1982, Japan had surpassed the U.S. in both the research and production of industrial robotics. Today, the U.S. has no robotics industry.

Japan's takeover of robotics is significant because robots are the heart of advanced manufacturing; they greatly increase quality and productivity, while lowering costs. Even three decades ago, U.S. industrial and political leaders understood that if America led the robotics revolution in manufacturing it would most likely dominate global production of machine tools, aircraft, cars, printing presses, computers, and other high-value items. In addition, they knew that those large corporations that first made use of robots in their factories would most likely gain the skills and knowledge needed to dominate the future production of such machines, which in itself would be a major new industry.

This example starts with a congressional hearing. On June 2, 1982, the U.S. Congress began two days of hearings on the robotics competition between Japan and the United States. The House Committee on Science and Technology, which conducted the hearings, invited leading experts and several high officials from the executive branch to testify. The first day was devoted to the global status of the industry. The second focused on U.S. efforts.

Despite the importance of the issue and the prominence of the witnesses, only one of the forty-one committee members attended. He was Congressman Albert Gore, Jr. (D.-Tenn.), a three-term member, who chaired both sessions. Had any of the other committee members been present, they would have learned that in 1967 Kawasaki Heavy Industries had bought Japan's first industrial robot from U.S.–based Unimation, licensed Unimation's technology in 1968, and then produced the first Japanese-made robot in 1969. They also would have learned that the Japanese government had in the late 1960s singled out robot development as a major strategic industry, which meant it got whatever aid was needed to ensure success. Finally, they would have learned that thirteen years after Japan's production of its first robot, Japanese corporations had 14,246 robotic machines on the job while U.S. companies had only 4,700, a three-to-one difference.

Paul H. Aron, the lead witness and executive vice president of Daiwa Securities America, told Gore and the handful of congressional staff who attended the session, "The Japanese lead is by no means so overwhelming." To buttress that conclusion, Aron described Japan's robotics strategy and described the Japanese government subsidies that the U.S. must match if it were to retake its lost lead.

First, he said that Japan's cost of capital was much lower than America's. The U.S. prime interest rate at that time was 16 percent; meanwhile, Japanese companies were borrowing money at 6 percent. Cheap capital, Aron explained, allowed Japanese manufacturers to invest in the internal development of robots and thus gain three to five years of production experience and make refinements before putting a fully debugged machine on the market. This in-house development also permitted many experienced manufacturing people to be involved in robot development. Aron noted that Hitachi alone had assigned five hundred employees to develop its robots, while Unimation, the U.S. leader, had only ninety research workers. Also, unlike in the United States, Japanese corporations, with their lifetime employment, had the full cooperation of labor. According to Aron, Japanese workers did not fear job loss. Instead, most saw automation as a means of improving both quality and productivity, which these companies pursue obsessively.

Equally significant, Aron noted, was that the Japanese government provided extensive financial and political incentives for its corporations to develop and use industrial robots. The government had reduced private investment costs by creating an organization that leased them robots at a sharp discount. In that early stage of robotics development, Japanese companies were improving the technology quickly. With government-subsidized leasing, they could replace obsolete machines at little cost, thereby keeping Japan's manufacturers in the forefront. For small- and medium-size corporations, the government provided low-interest loans for robot investments and also leased robots to small companies on the same terms it did to larger corporations.

Beyond this direct financial assistance, the government permitted companies to deduct 53 percent of each robot's cost from their taxes in the year of purchase and the balance over the next four years. It also subsidized corporate research on robotics and provided interest-free loans both for the development of new robot applications and for their worldwide marketing. Finally, METI scoured the world for every available piece of information it could find on robotics, which it then translated into Japanese. By 1982, Japan had translated every robotics patent issued in the United States and elsewhere in the world, and every article, speech, and any other bit of information that might help Japan's robot makers and users. Even two decades ago, Japan had the world's largest and most complete library on robotics, and it has been updating this library ever since.

The Japanese government largely financed the global acquisition of robotics patents and technology, the creation of Japan's robotics industry, and the deployment of those machines throughout Japan's economy. No similar commitment existed in the United States.

On June 23, 1982, the House Committee on Science and Technology held its second day of hearings. The witnesses were senior officials from the National Science Foundation (NSF), the National Bureau of Standards (NBS), the Department of Defense (DOD), and the National Aeronautics and Space Administration (NASA). They presented testimony on the current state of U.S. efforts. The testimony quickly revealed why the United States had lost its lead in robotics. First, the government was spending virtually nothing in the field. In fiscal year 1982, the NSF budgeted only $5 million for robotics research. The Bureau of Standards spent $2.3 million and NASA $2 million. Even the Department of Defense, whose budgets were rising to $300 billion a year, devoted less than $27 million to robotics research in 1982 and most of that was for weapons.

The testimony also revealed U.S. indifference. When Congressman Gore asked whether the Defense Department would consider creating a robotics center, the undersecretary for research and advanced technology responded bluntly, "Within DOD we have discussed establishing such a center for robotics but have not yet established one because we do not feel that robotics, per se, warrants it at this time."

In retrospect, it is clear that the U.S. government was clearly asleep at a critical moment. Japan's government and corporations were working together to capture a strategic global industry. So were the Germans. The U.S. robotics manufacturers stood alone. The result was predictable. The United Nations Economic Commission for Europe reports that as of 2003, Japan was the world's largest producer of robots and had 344,000 multipurpose machines in operation there. Germany was second largest, deploying 111,300 in 2003. Lacking its own robot industry, the U.S. imports robots, principally from Japan and Germany. As of 2003, the U.S. had 111,100 robots in operation, mainly in auto factories, many of which are Japanese- and German-owned.

As dramatic as the raw numbers are, they still do not capture how far behind other industrial nations the U.S. has fallen in robotics. More relevant is the measure of robot density, the ratio of robots to people employed in manufacturing. As of the year 2000, Japan had 308 operational robots for every 10,000 manufacturing workers. The United States had 58. Not only is U.S. manufacturing behind Japan's in the introduction of robots, it is also behind that of Spain (66), France (67), Finland (68), Sweden (91), Korea (128), and Germany (135).

Simply put, Japan took a U.S.–created technology and made the resulting industry its own. With robotics, Japanese companies cut their costs, increased their productivity, and improved their quality in a host of other industries, which then challenged their U.S. competitors. The result is akin to upright dominoes, stacked one against the other. When one falls, it touches another, which then tumbles, and so on down the line. But what are falling in this instance are entire U.S. industries, one after another.

Pirating the entire industry of another nation is not a simple, or quick, act. As the U.S. did with Great Britain in textiles two centuries ago, special institutional arrangements and cooperative public-private actions are required.

When the U.S. imposed a stiff tariff on British textile imports and refused to grant any patents for almost fifty years, it created a sanctuary in which the American textile industry could develop. Japan has done the same with the industries it has targeted. Foreign imports were and continue to be kept out of Japan's market, giving domestic companies a sanctuary in which they have time to develop. Japan's use of its patent system to strip foreign inventors of their technology is not that much different from U.S. policies two centuries ago that offered bounties to those who brought foreign technology to America, while refusing to honor foreign patents or issue patents to foreigners. If anything, the Japanese took a patent practice and refined it into an extractive technique that was largely invisible to anyone but the victims, who had no recourse, so long as their home governments were passive.

Most important, while the technologies stolen from Great Britain helped the U.S. to establish its textile industry, American companies and inventors were encouraged to improve on that which they had taken. Likewise, Japan has invested heavily and wisely in technology development since World War II. Initially, its motivation was to rebuild the war-torn economy. Then the task was acquisition and adaptation of technologies developed by others. But by the mid-1980s, Japan had become the technological equal of the United States and Europe. By then, it had licensed, extorted, or pirated so many U.S. and European technologies that the supply of new and desirable innovations was dwindling. In 1986, the Japan Development Bank acknowledged the problem in an understated way: "the importation of technologies from overseas to kindle further development, and the introduction of technology is becoming difficult."

Japan is now an advanced science and technological originator. This transition from a war-ruined nation whose manufactured goods were regarded as junk to a technological and manufacturing world leader was speeded by hard-nosed industrial policies and a host of government programs, including the following:

- The National Research and Development Program for large-scale projects in 1966, which has managed dozens of programs, such as building super-high-performance computers

- The national energy conservation programs, begun in the 1970s

- The Development Project of Basic Technologies, started in 1981

As Japan's government provided its companies financial incentives to develop and then export robots, similar incentives are provided in these other targeted industries. Unlike the U.S., the Japan does not openly share many of those technologies with other nations. Japanese corporations keep their most important techniques a trade secret. For all other technologies, they secure patents in the U.S. and elsewhere, and when the patents are infringed, they hire U.S. and European lawyers, who aggressively sue on their behalf.

Consequently, Japan now holds a monopolistic technological leadership in dozens of commodity and advanced industries. Eamonn Fingleton, a financial writer who has lived in Tokyo since 1985, reveals the extent of such U.S. dependency in his book *Blindside*.

Fingleton tells about epoxy cresol novolac resin, a vital ingredient in making most semiconductors. In 1993, a factory in a remote Japanese town exploded, destroying roughly 65 percent of the world's supply of this resin. Semiconductor prices doubled almost immediately. Worse, the United States soon learned that the Japanese also controlled the supply of resolving silica and the process used to mix it with the resin. Japanese corporations also control the world's supply of ceramic packaging, an alternative technology.

Fingleton estimates that such monopolistic leadership is a factor in almost one-third of Japan's exports. Japan effectively manages hundreds of U.S. industries by its oversight of key technologies. If Japan cuts the supply, the American economy slows down.

Fingleton distinguishes between two key forms of intellectual property involved in manufacturing, product concepts and manufacturing processes. He notes that though American consumers are more interested in the products, the manufacturing processes are a far more important factor in the economic competition between different countries. A U.S. company may be able to design an advanced portable computer, but few, if any, could manufacture it today. Fingleton uses the example of the liquid crystal display monitor. The Japanese have honed their manufacturing processes to the point where they can produce good LCD displays nine out of every ten tries. Such performance, he says, requires mastery of twelve different manufacturing processes, which in general are never patented. If Dell, Hewlett-Packard, or IBM tried to enter that business, only one out of ten coming off the line would be good, for they do not know the trade secrets associated with those manufacturing processes, and the Japanese will never tell them.

According to Fingleton, the Japanese have negotiated hundreds of deals with U.S. corporations by which they will do the design, software, and creative and marketing sides of the business and the Japanese will perform the advanced manufacturing. The Japanese have a name for all this: *kyosei,* or the *kyosei* movement.

In Japanese *kyosei* translates as "symbiosis" or "mutual prosperity." The more appropriate English translation is "dependence," because that is the result.

John J. Fialka concluded his study of technological and economic espionage with an observation about Francis Cabot Lowell:

> Lowell's world was Darwinian: you could keep what you could protect. It is still Darwinian when it comes to cross-border transactions, but Americans in the post–Cold War era feel they are protected in a snug, seamless, global cocoon of laws, customs, and rights. . . . The cocoon is hardly more than a fiction.

CHAPTER 6

CHINA RISING

For almost two decades, corporations from the United States, Europe, and Japan have been shifting their manufacturing facilities to China and other developing nations. More recently, they have begun moving their research and development activities as well. In the process of making these countries their manufacturing and research platforms, these corporations are stripping the developed world of significant parts of its innovative capacity—the intellectual and technical infrastructure needed to create the next great thing. Above all other factors, this capacity to innovate has been the heart of America's economic growth and national security for two centuries. Now it is at risk.

Of all nations, China is the largest recipient of this relocated investment and research. The issue is not whether China should develop or create its own innovative capacity—it should and it will. Rather, it is what the United States should do to stop China's flagrant theft of American-owned intellectual properties as it develops.

In China, demography, development, and political stability are in a spirited race. The China of 1919 had fewer than 500 million people. The China of 2005 has a population of more than 1.3 billion, who are crammed into a land area slightly larger than the United States. The Chinese economy must feed, clothe, and employ these people if they are not to revolt.

China's political leaders face a herculean challenge of creating jobs. The labor force as of mid-2004 exceeded 753 million workers: China has 100 million more workers than the combined populations of the United States, Mexico, Canada, Japan, and Germany. China's labor pool is expanding by almost 12 million workers annually, though its economy created only 6.9 million jobs in 2003—a shortfall that means almost one of every three newcomers to the labor force will not get a job or must displace someone who has one.

As of 2002, China's industries, which range from apparel to computers and pharmaceuticals, included 180,000 state-owned enterprises, most of which are inefficient. PricewaterhouseCoopers reports that these state enterprises consumed almost "80 percent of the nation's resources in 2002, but only produced around 40 percent of the industrial output." Between 1998 and 2001, the Chinese government laid off 25.5 million workers in those state-owned companies and predicted 2002 in that the number would quadruple over the next four years.

Half of China's laborers are still on the farm, doing work that could be performed faster, better, and more cheaply by machines. Even with literally tens of millions of workers engaged in agricultural work with hand tools, China still has vast unemployment. The 2004 CIA *World Factbook* reports that China has 80 to 120 million surplus migrant workers who are adrift between the cities and villages. Most are subsisting on part-time, low-wage work while looking for food, a place to sleep, and a full-time job. Urban unemployment may be as high as 25 million workers. Consequently, China is in a race to create enough new jobs for its people and hold down chaos as it shifts to more private ownership. The Chinese media report the demonstrations and strikes as moribund state enterprises close.

China needs jobs. To get those jobs, China needs foreign technology. To get the foreign technology, China needs foreign investment. To get the foreign investment, the Chinese government has introduced a host of national development initiatives. Each is built on a grand four-part, long-term development strategy.

Just like the United States and Japan before it, China is using all the usual means—licensing, theft, piracy, intimidation, spies, and cooperation—to get the technology it needs. China has also adopted a system of joint venture, an old and established tool for securing foreign intellectual property, and has elevated it to an art form. With joint ventures, China reduces its need to steal or expropriate foreign intellectual property because foreign corporations share it as a condition of doing business there. Though, to paraphrase an old quote of Lenin's, these capitalists may be preparing their own demise.

Second, China is creating a domestic capacity to innovate. At some point, China, like Japan, will have the West's best technologies and will then create its own. In this catch-up phase, China is persuading, luring, and sometimes forcing foreign corporations to locate their most advanced research and development facilities in China. To that end, China also has sent its best and brightest students to U.S. and European scientific centers. Many return home, where they are teaching others and producing large numbers of highly competent, dedicated Chinese scientists, engineers, and technicians, who are available for work in these research and development enterprises. China graduates from its universities three times more engineers annually than does the United States. As Western companies move their R & D operations to China to capitalize on this talent, they are also transferring their next generation of knowledge and innovations there and helping China become an independent innovative force.

Third, China is developing its capacity to import raw materials and export finished goods. COSCO, the Chinese state-owned shipping company, is now working with port authorities on both the west and east coasts of the United States to expand their capacity to handle far greater imports and exports with China. In 2002, for instance, COSCO opened a route to Boston. Within one year, the volume of goods shipped from the Boston port to Asia doubled, while the import volume from Asia to Boston increased fourfold. Equally significant, China has replaced the United States as the transport manager for the Panama Canal. The governments of Panama and China have had extensive negotiations on the construction of new locks for the canal, sufficient to carry the giant cargo ships that China envisions for the future. China is ensuring that it will be able to get the world's raw materials to its factories and its finished goods to world markets.

Finally, China will eventually try to control the principal retail outlets that market its products in other nations. China's growing monopoly on the manufacture of goods that foreign retailers sell provides the business advantage required in such negotiations and takeovers. Viewed from China's perspective, as the products it makes come to dominate U.S. and other markets, why should not the Chinese share in the profits made by Wal-Mart, Kmart, JCPenney, and other retailers that sell its goods, or even take them all if it can? This is the way capitalism works.

In making the delicate transition from the closed, Marxist China of Mao Zedong to the mixed economy that is emerging, Chinese leaders have made a marriage of convenience. The foreign investor puts up the capital, patents, copyrights, trademarks, know-how, and overseas distribution. In most circumstances, the local Chinese partner keeps half the equity in the new enterprise. Any improvements in technology and any new patents, trademarks, or copyrights developed in China by the joint venture belong to the new enterprise.

In exchange, China contributes an unlimited supply of low-wage, competent, compliant workers. The foreign corporations are allowed to serve their markets from Chinese-based factories that operate under the most limited public regulation of labor, production, pollution, and health and safety standards. Products from these ventures are often banned in China, leaving that market to state or locally owned enterprises. Foreign corporations also use local managers and engineers to operate their factories, teach the Chinese how to apply their technology, and follow the government's economic dictates. Through this, China gains know-how quickly.

This joint venture model of extracting technology from foreign sources is radically different from Japan's in the postwar period. The Japanese kept their market as a sanctuary for its own corporations. Only foreign corporations like IBM, which had a patent monopoly in a technology and political strength in the United States, were welcome, and even they were kept under local supervision.

With its joint venture model, the Chinese government has moved its industrial structure from the nineteenth to the twenty-first century in less than two decades. In the process, China is getting the knowledge and capacity it needs to become the world's manufacturing center. In 2002, economists at Lehman Brothers, the investment banking house, projected that China would have the world's second largest economy by 2030. But that projection will not be realized unless China can continue to (a) get the basic foreign technology, (b) create the capacity to develop proprietary technology domestically, and (c) control these core technologies worldwide.

For many U.S. manufacturers, China is an attractive proposition because it offers a virtually limitless supply of workers for low-paying, semiskilled manufacturing jobs. The average manufacturing wage in China in 2002 was approximately $800 a year, or one-fortieth that of a U.S. manufacturing worker. Unions do not exist, workers are grateful for a job, and the government will deal with dissident workers, often severely. Corporations can hire an unlimited number of Chinese workers for less than one-sixth the FICA insurance premiums they pay the U.S. government for American workers.

Not even Mexico can match that. Indeed, Mexico itself lost more than 218,000 jobs to China in the period 2001–2003, as 500 of that nation's 3,700 maquiladoras (factories on the U.S.–Mexico border) were shut down and the work moved overseas.

China offers more than an enormous pool of cheap labor for light manufacturing. It has a large pool of engineers and technicians available for more advanced work, many educated in the United States. The Chinese Academy of Engineering reports that as of the late 1990s China had more than 2.1 million trained engineers, including 600,000 senior-level people. This is a significant reservoir of technical talent. Most of these engineers are available at roughly 10 percent the salaries of their American, Japanese, or European counterparts.

The Motorola Corporation has been a pioneer in shifting its work, jobs, research, and development to China to take advantage of this vast pool of talent. In late 2002, Motorola announced its five-year China strategy and its "$10 billion plan" goals—$10 billion of investment, $10 billion of local outsourcing, and $10 billion of output in China by 2006. With this, Motorola is moving one-third of its worldwide research and development resources to China, where it has already established twenty-five regional and global R & D centers.

Microsoft has invested $130 million to establish three R & D centers in China, which it is constantly expanding. In 2002, the Chinese government identified thirty-five universities in which it would build software colleges. Microsoft also pledged $750 million over three years to help China strengthen its technological industries and to train Chinese producers of software and hardware. In September 2003, Microsoft agreed to help Chinese software companies expand overseas. IBM is also supplying money and expertise to help China develop its software industry. Microsoft realizes that China is determined to replace the U.S. software with a Chinese-produced Linux-based system. Although the U.S. company has not made a dime in China, it continues to invest there as a way to develop brand loyalty and find niche markets. And even as its software is being replaced, Microsoft continues to gain access to the some of the best software talent in the world.

General Electric, the ninth largest corporation in the world, plans to do at least $5 billion worth of annual production and sales in its China facilities by 2005. GE has also established, in Shanghai, one of its three major world-wide R & D centers. At the same time, it is shifting much of its advanced software, financial control, and medical technology research to India.

General Motors, the world's largest automaker, is helping China build a world-class automotive industry. GM has six joint ventures and two wholly owned foreign enterprises in China. In June 2004, GM announced it would increase its existing $1.5 billion investment in China by another $3 billion. This money will be used to build an "advanced prototype laboratory in China; a virtual reality design studio, a noise, vibration and harshness test lab; and a kinetics and compliance lab." GM says these new facilities will be the equal of any engineering and design center it has in the world. With this investment, GM will increase its capacity to produce vehicles from 530,000 units annually in 2004 to 1.3 million in 2007. With this commitment, GM is helping China develop the engineering expertise required to manufacture top-quality, low-cost automotive components. The company's other Chinese operations include Allison Transmission, Hughes Electronics, and the GM Electromotive Division. Soon GM will be able to supply a large portion of the parts it uses in the United States from China, and at substantial cost savings.

The scale of such foreign technology transfers to another country is unprecedented, far greater than what happened between the U.S. and Japan in the post–World War II era. The Chinese government reports that in 2001 alone, it approved 240,000 contracts for the foreign transfer of technology into China, up 23 percent from 2000. The Chinese put the value of these technology transfers at roughly $10 billion. In most cases, no money changed hands. The foreign company swapped technology and capital for equity in a local Chinese company, which was often newly created. As part of this package, the foreign firm often registered its technology with China's patent office. In 2001, there were more than 200,000 such registration applications, of which 114,000 were granted.

Like GM, GE, Motorola, and Microsoft, other U.S. and foreign investors are establishing joint R & D centers in China. In these facilities, the foreign companies and their Chinese partners will perform the advanced scientific, engineering, and design work that will produce the next generation of innovations and patents. The foreign company gets products and research at a fraction of the costs found in the United States, Europe, or Japan while China acquires sophisticated knowledge and moves up the technology ladder at warp speed, bypassing decades of developmental work.

In 2003, China's vice minister of commerce identified four hundred R & D centers that foreign firms had established in that nation. Since then, Japanese companies have announced the creation of several more such high-tech centers, which they will finance. The Chinese press reports that Motorola, Microsoft, and Nokia employ local staff in 80 percent of the engineering and managerial positions in these R & D centers. Other foreign investors are doing the same. Consequently, these R & D centers are a major means for China to secure advanced foreign technology while developing a domestic capacity to create future innovations.

In 2002 and 2003, China was the world's largest recipient of foreign investment, exceeding $50 billion in each of those years, according to China's Ministry of Foreign Trade and Economic Cooperation and the United Nations' *World Investment Report.* Almost half of that came from the United States. The U.S.-China Economic and Security Review Commission reports that between 73 and 90 percent of this investment goes into the building of new production and research facilities. By contrast, Dr. Charles McMillion of MBG Information Services states that almost 99 percent of foreign direct investment coming into the United States is used to buy existing assets or existing companies. The point is that $50 billion buys a great deal in China. As of 2002, China had attracted a total of $447 billion in foreign investment, almost all of which was used to construct new production facilities.

At the beginning of 2001, China had more than 363,000 foreign-funded enterprises. Its Ministry of Commerce approved more than 41,000 new foreign-invested firms in 2003, a jump of 20 percent over 2002. These investments have quickly transformed China from an isolated, technologically backward nation into a manufacturing platform from which many of the world's leading companies are serving their home and other markets. The Export-Import Bank of India reports that half of all China's exports worldwide now come from these foreign cooperative ventures, up from 9 percent a decade ago, and 90 percent of these exports are manufactured goods.

Strengthening China's military is one of that nation's top priorities. Acquiring foreign defense systems is a key component of that national goal.

In two recent books, *Red Dragon Rising* and *Year of the Rat,* national security analysts Edward Timperlake and William C. Triplett II document how the Chinese government stole some of this nation's most advanced military technologies and weapons systems from U.S. corporations and defense labs.

One of the most shocking examples concerns McDonnell Douglas Corporation's sale to China of advanced machine tools used for the manufacture of bombers and intercontinental missiles. In the early 1990s, McDonnell Douglas, facing a shortage of sales, shut down its military aircraft plant in Columbus, Ohio, where it had produced parts for the B-1 bomber and the Titan missile. A state-owned Chinese company proposed a $1 billion joint venture with McDonnell Douglas to produce passenger airplanes. As part of the deal, the Chinese wanted to buy the equipment in the closed Columbus facility, which included thirteen unique machine tools needed to manufacture advanced aircraft and missiles. In effect, the Chinese dangled a big contract as bait and the Americans took it completely.

For McDonnell Douglas to sell those machine tools, a license had to be issued by the U.S. Commerce Department. McDonnell Douglas received a transfer license in September 1994, took $5.4 million from the Chinese, and then helped its Chinese partner spirit the tools out of the country. Once the machines were in China, the joint proposal disappeared and the Chinese company diverted the machine tools to a military factory that produces Silkworm missiles. A chagrined McDonnell Douglas reported to the Commerce Department what had happened, but it was too late.

In October 1999, the state-owned Chinese company, McDonnell Douglas, and the American manager of this project were indicted for knowingly falsifying information on the license application. Subsequently, both companies were fined. The case against the project manager was dismissed because he had been indicted after the five-year statute of limitations had expired. Meanwhile, China got some of the world's most advanced machines, equipment that it needed to build military aircraft and missiles.

In a similar case, personnel from Hughes Electronics and Loral Space Systems gave the Chinese missile expertise and technology without obtaining the proper licenses from the U.S. government. This unauthorized transfer helped China produce missiles (civilian and military) that are more dependable and accurate than what they had or could develop in the near future.

In yet a third example, in 1995, the U.S. Treasury Department, which oversees foreign purchases of high-technology American companies, allowed the Chinese government to purchase Magnequench from the General Motors Corporation. Magnequench, which is located in Indianapolis, produces special magnets used in precision-guided munitions. In February 2003, Scott L. Wheeler reported in *Insight* magazine that the Chinese-owned company now holds the Department of Defense contract to produce the high-tech motors used in U.S. precision-guided smart bombs. Wheeler also confirmed that the Chinese were closing the Indianapolis plant and moving its machines, technology, and production to Tianjin, China, where its magnets will be used in China's long-range cruise missiles. Magnequench is the last U.S.-based producer of these magnets. Earlier, the Chinese bought the other two U.S. manufacturers of such magnets and moved their technology home. By these maneuvers, China gained an exotic technology it lacked and denied the U.S. military any domestic source of a vital weapon component. Consequently, the U.S. now depends on China for a key component it needs to build smart bombs.

As these examples suggest, much of this technology transfer is possible because of the laxity, naïveté, and greed of a handful of business leaders who have given Chinese intelligence agents and state enterprises extraordinary access to U.S. personnel and facilities. It also reflects incompetence on the part of key U.S. government officials, who were supposed to be watchdogs but failed to do their job. Triplett and Timperlake claim that there is also corruption: various American political leaders have received illegal contributions from Chinese sources and their U.S. supporters have gained special economic privileges in China. After the 1996 election, Congress held hearings on Chinese political contributions, but the investigation soon ended, largely because Chinese money had gone to both major political parties.

The most thorough and comprehensive study of China's theft of U.S. technology was performed under the auspices of the U.S. Congress. In January 1999, the House Select Committee on U.S. National Security and Military/Commercial Concerns with the People's Republic of China published a report that examined China's technology espionage. Released with unanimous concurrence by a bipartisan committee chaired by Congressman Christopher Cox (R.-Calif.), the full report remains classified. But the public portion is nothing less than an instruction manual on how to systematically steal vital U.S. commercial and military technologies. This part is frightening, and it remains available on the Internet.

The select committee reported that China has more than 3,000 companies operating in various guises in the United States; many of them are here to acquire advanced technologies for the Chinese military. Not only has the Chinese government stolen the designs of America's most modern nuclear warheads, it also has taken U.S. guidance technology currently used in a variety of missiles and aircraft, including the army's Tactical Missile System and the navy's F-14 and the air force's F-15, F-16, and F-117 fighter jets. The report also reveals that the Chinese have stolen electromagnetic weapons technology that could be used to destroy U.S. submarines.

Much of the technology China now seeks is of a dual-use nature, that is, it has both commercial and defense purposes. Among these are astronautics, information handling, lasers, automation, energy, and advanced materials such as specialized ceramics and metals used in weapons systems. The Cox report explains that one way the Chinese government evades U.S. export restrictions is to buy outdated equipment. In one example the Chinese bought a special machine tool, used in making complex military parts, that had cost the U.S. government $1 million to produce, but they paid only $25,000 for it at a liquidation sale of the bankrupt small defense contractor using it. The technology on the used machine, the report claims, could easily be made updated and made state of the art.

Despite China's invitation to foreign companies to come and invest, the Chinese government has reserved entire sectors of its economy for state-owned enterprises. Other sectors belong to China's private entrepreneurs. Foreign investors can participate in the rest on terms that China dictates.

China is using much of the profits from its U.S. trade surpluses to modernize and support its own state- and individually owned enterprises. To that end, the government sponsors projects to develop technical innovations these companies can use and finance the pilot production of new goods they can make and sell. This is a major subsidy for China's state-owned enterprises. The scale of this aid is enormous. In 2002, for instance, the Chinese government organized and sponsored 1,318 innovation projects and 1,288 new-product projects for those enterprises. Technology aid on such a scale strongly confirms that China intends to be a major global competitor in a host of products.

To procure some foreign technologies, the Chinese government will make some very untraditional arrangements through its corporations. One midwestern U.S. company, for example, with a high-technology product that could be used commercially to geoposition automobiles or militarily to target intercontinental missiles, took bids for an initial run of these products. A U.S. manufacturer offered to do the job for $250,000; a Chinese company bid $25,000 to carry out the same work. When the company was queried about its bid, it immediately lowered it to $15,000. When the technology owner hesitated, the Chinese bidder asked how much his U.S. competitor had bid, and when told, he offered to do the first batch for free, plus pay the patent owner $250,000. What the Chinese wanted was the technology, and this was a cheap way to get it. The U.S. company refused the offer.

China's five-year plans govern the nation's industrial policy and performance schedules. Among China's government-specified "pillar" industries are machinery, electronics, petrochemicals, automobiles, information technology, medicine, and chemicals. To support those industries, the Chinese government identifies which foreign investments it will "encourage," "permit," "restrict," or "ban." Also, the more than two hundred types of equipment that foreigners can import into China duty-free are those not yet produced there. As that machinery becomes available locally, investors can anticipate restrictions on what they can bring into China. Finally, the type of production permitted by foreign firms is likely to be limited to what can be exported for hard currency.

Most important, many of China's industrial policies are secret. A Communist dictatorship can change or ignore laws at will. It simply decides. This allows China's leaders to bargain with foreigners over the size and location of their investments, technology transfers, use of foreign intellectual property, training, equipment donations, and political matters, such as the foreign company's political support of China's policies in the investor's home country. As its technological sophistication has increased, China has come to demand the best its foreign partners have. The Chinese Academy of Sciences reports that as recently as 1997, only 13 percent of the foreign firms in China were using their parent corporation's most advanced technologies; however, by 2001, more than 50 percent were. That percentage is surely higher in 2005.

In June 2003, the Chinese government issued a draft of its auto industry policy. It requires that by 2010 half of all car sales in China must come from domestic companies that own 100 percent of the technology used to make the vehicle. Any foreign company with 10 percent or more of a Chinese automaker is required to share its technology with the domestic firm. China also expects U.S. auto part makers locating in China to export 40 percent of their sales by 2010. With this, U.S., European, and Japanese automakers are not only establishing a Chinese car industry, they are creating what will quickly become a technologically advanced global competitor. Soon China will be exporting cars just as the Japanese and Koreans have been doing. The U.S. Commerce Department predicts that Americans will import large numbers of cars built in China's low-cost labor market, beginning at the end of this decade. Already, China is exporting auto parts to America— $2.8 billion in 2003, up 100 percent from 2001. China's leaders are not hiding their long-term intentions; they are working to replace Detroit as the world's auto capital.

As a result, automakers are seeing the Chinese take their technology and become their rivals. The Yamaha Motor Corporation of Japan lost dominance in the motorcycle industry because Chinese manufacturers extensively infringed upon Yamaha's patents and copyrights. One Chinese manufacturer, Tianjin Gangtian, even produced and sold copies of Yamaha's motorcycles under the name Yamaha—an illegal practice anywhere.

General Motors learned in the summer of 2003 that Chery Automobile Company, a Chinese joint venture deal between Shanghai Automotive Industry Corporation (80 percent) and GM (20 percent), was introducing a subcompact called the QQ that looks identical to the Spark that GM manufactures in China for the domestic market. Congressman James Sensenbrenner Jr. (R.-Wis.), who returned from a trip to China in January 2004, reports that a door from GM's Spark perfectly fits the Chinese-made QQ. Apparently, all the other parts do as well.

GM's experience is not unique. Geely, China's largest automaker, used Toyota's distinctive logo on its Meiri sedan and in sales promotions, without permission. Even though Toyota had long supplied Geely with its engines, it sued. But in November 2003, a Chinese court ruled that the Toyota logo, which is used worldwide, is not recognized in China as a "distinctive brand." Toyota was then fined for court costs.

What is amazing about these revelations is not that the Chinese copied GM's design or purloined Toyota's logo. Rather, it is that despite GM's 20 percent equity in Chery and Toyota's long relationship with Geely, the Chinese companies did not hesitate to steal their partners' intellectual property. Equally amazing, these experiences will not keep GM and Toyota from expanding their investments in China. Both companies have made such an enormous commitment in China and have such large plans to serve both their domestic and Chinese markets that neither dares offend Bejing by protesting too loudly or seeking the aid of their home governments.

Such flagrant piracy raises four critical questions. First, if GM officials were unaware of the theft of an entire basic auto design, what less visible GM technologies are being used without their knowledge? Second, if the Chinese are unafraid to steal an entire auto design, what else are they willing to abscond with? Third, how much and just what must the Chinese steal before the U.S. automaker will protest? Finally, how many protests are needed to get the U.S. government to enforce treaties with China that prohibit its illegal taking of America's intellectual properties?

The answer is that just as China wants its own auto industry, it also wants its own electronics, semiconductor, pharmaceutical, biotechnological, petroleum, steel, machine tool, and software industries, to name a few. It will do whatever is required to create those industries, and it cares little whether foreign companies, investors, and governments are offended.

Just as the Chinese government established a "decree" on automobile production in 2003, it set one requiring the use of a China-specific wireless encryption standard for computers and communications equipment sold there after June 1, 2004. The China standard is incompatible with most computer and wireless products now made worldwide. The Chinese government has provided the software for its new standard to twenty-four Chinese companies but not to any foreign manufacturer. The decree requires that foreign producers must take one of those twenty-four as its partner, plus pay royalties to the government. With one of the world's largest computer markets and with more than 300 million digital mobile phones in use, China intends to dominate those industries worldwide by forcing foreign manufacturers to adopt its technical standards.

After China's announcement of its wireless decree, representatives of the U.S. and Chinese governments met in late April 2004. Afterward, they released a joint announcement that the Chinese would suspend its proposed implementation of a mandatory wireless encryption standard, while revising that standard and considering comments from foreign firms. China also agreed to technological neutrality on next-generation standards for mobile phones. Still, the episode clearly revealed China's intent. If this ploy fails, others will surely be devised. China's goal of market dominance remains.

To encourage foreign semiconductor companies to invest in China, the government has also imposed a 17 percent tax on imported semiconductors. Yet manufacturers pay only a 3 percent tax on semiconductors produced inside China. Such discrimination violates China's World Trade Organization (WTO) obligations to other nations. The United States has protested this tax both at the WTO and with the Chinese. China has agreed to slowly remove this tax. But the tax will be in place long enough to damage U.S. producers.

China is also developing its own computer software, even as it pirates that of Microsoft and other foreign companies. In September 2003, the Chinese, South Korean, and Japanese governments announced they were developing an open source alternative to Microsoft's Windows operating system, now used in most of the world. In 2004, Red Flag Software of China and Miracle Linux of Japan revealed a joint venture to produce such an operating system. According to the *San Jose Mercury News,* the Shanghai-based New Margin Venture Capital finances Red Flag and is controlled by "the son of former Chinese President Jiang Zemin, who heads China's military."

As these examples suggest, China's goal is technological self-reliance. George Washington and Alexander Hamilton would have understood perfectly. In large part, such a goal is motivated by economic considerations. But it also reflects China's security consciousness. Chinese officials fear that the code behind Windows allows the Central Intelligence Agency to invade their computers. Accordingly, they are moving aggressively to replace Microsoft as the principal source of software used in China's computers. Microsoft's American rivals are actively helping the Chinese. In March 2004, Hewlett-Packard, which sells almost 17 percent of the world's personal computers, announced plans to produce Linux-based machines in China and eleven other Asian nations. They will sell for $200 to $375 less than comparable Windows-equipped computers. Dell and Oracle also disclosed in March that they would offer Linux-based Oracle software on Dell machines. In November 2003, Sun Microsystems said that it was selling 200 million copies of its Linux-based Java Desktop System to the Chinese government for $100 a copy, roughly a third the price of Windows.

Inevitably, once China shifts from Windows to its own operating system, Hewlett-Packard, Dell, and other computer makers will begin offering American buyers inexpensive versions of their computers with the Chinese operating software. China's real goal is to control the world market for computer operating systems. Just as Microsoft's dominance has allowed it to enter related markets, China's will provide similar opportunities.

Chinese industries' dominant position in domestic markets will never require government intervention because Chinese consumers have a preference for "made in China." Already Motorola and Nokia, the two cellular telephone giants that helped establish China's mobile phone industry, are losing market share to local companies. Bloomberg News reports that the Ningbo Bird Company, the TCL Mobile Communications Company, and other Chinese phone firms have doubled the size of their market share between 2001 and early 2003, accounting for 35 percent of handset sales.

The Legend Group, another Chinese company, commanded 27 percent of the local computer market in early 2003 and is expanding. By contrast, Dell and IBM each had 5 percent and Hewlett-Packard 3 percent. Slek, La Fang, and other local Chinese shampoos are pushing Procter & Gamble out of that market, while local brands of razors, skin creams, and detergents are also taking over those markets from foreign investors.

As foreign companies become increasingly dependent on Chinese manufacturing for their worldwide production, they will come under correspondingly more pressure to make available and then share ownership of their foreign distribution systems. Eventually, just as the Japanese and Koreans did, Chinese companies will establish brand trademarks that become known worldwide, which they will sell through these joint distribution networks. Finally, the Chinese, just like the Japanese before them, will establish their own distribution networks. At some point, China will no longer need foreign corporations or their networks. The foreign (read U.S.) corporations can keep whatever part of the market they can hold on to. When dealing with foreigners, China's Marxist leaders operate under the rules of Darwinist capitalism.

U.S. corporate leaders are not the only ones transferring America's most advanced technology to China. The U.S. government and America's academic institutions are doing the same, perhaps on an even broader scale. The State Department reports:

> The large numbers of Chinese students, scholars, researchers and high-tech workers ubiquitously present throughout the U.S. academic and industrial research establishment collectively represent China's chief means of gathering information on scientific and technological development.

Student enrollment numbers back up the State Department's conclusion. The National Science Foundation reports that between 1985 and 2000, students from four Asian nations (China, Taiwan, India, and South Korea) earned 68,500 doctoral degrees in science and engineering from U.S. universities. More than 26,500 of those degrees went to students from China. The NSF also reports that many of these graduates are staying in the United States for postdoctoral, academic, or industrial work: 58 percent of those graduates had such plans in the early 1990s and 67 percent did by 2001.

One positive result is that the United States gets the benefits of thousands of talented scientists and engineers. The other is that China does too, as thousands of these graduates return home with the most advanced knowledge our nation can provide. In 2002, the NSF noted that while many of these younger scientists do remain in the United States for a while, there is evidence that older, more experienced Asian scientists and engineers are returning to their native countries, drawn in part by potential wealth and prestige, but also by a desire to help develop their home country. They are helping build the scientific and technological capacity of those nations, thereby diminishing the relative attractiveness of the United States as a destination nation for R & D activities.

The NSF analysis was prescient. The 2004 edition of *Science and Engineering Indicators* reveals that U.S.-sponsored R & D work outside the United States—an activity worth almost $20 billion in 2000—is increasingly being accomplished in fast-developing countries such as China. In 1994, majority-owned affiliates of U.S. companies did $70 million of R & D in China. In 2000, they did more than $500 million. By the end of this decade, they will carry out several billion dollars' worth of R & D in China, largely at the expense of R & D now done in the U.S. and Europe. Moreover, these reported values do not capture the full extent of the work, since Chinese scientist and engineers are paid a fraction—now roughly 10 percent—of what their U.S. counterparts receive.

Already, U.S. corporations have integrated much of their most advanced technologies into China's production system. An important measure of this shift of technology to China is the U.S.–China bilateral trade in advanced technology products (ATP). ATP is a special classification of goods used by the U.S. government. The list includes an ever-changing roster of hundreds of items, such as semiconductor manufacturing equipment. In 2002, the value of the ATP trade for the United States was almost $387 billion, or roughly one-fifth of all U.S. trade. For decades, the United States has dominated global ATP trade.

Beginning in 1995, however, China exported to the U.S. more advanced technology products than it imported. By 2001, China had an ATP trade surplus of more than $6.1 billion with the U.S. In 2002, that surplus rose to $11.8 billion, and in 2003 it exploded to $21 billion.

More important, the Chinese ATP trade surplus is concentrated in technologies that will shape the future, including biotechnology, optoelectronics, flexible manufacturing, advanced materials, nuclear technology, aerospace, and weapons. Increasingly, the U.S. depends on China to provide these goods. If there is any single indicator of what the U.S. manufacturing future holds, this ATP trade is it. China and Japan are well on the way to replacing the United States as the world's center of advanced manufacturing—one of the basic keys to national development.

With the recent construction of hundreds of major R & D centers, China is well on its way to developing its own proprietary and core technologies, a next step to dominating many global industries. If today's experiences are any guide, the Chinese government is unlikely to share its inventors' technology with the United States as generously as Washington and U.S. companies have shared theirs with China.

A technologically developed China using the talents of its people is far preferable to an underdeveloped nation with a billion people living on the edge of starvation. Paying a price to help in that process is something the United States has committed itself to doing. But there is a limit to the number of jobs and industries Americans can be expected to lose for China's benefit.

Today, China is basing much of its economic transition on the theft of U.S. intellectual property and then using it in beggar-thy-neighbor economic practices. Respect for private property is a foundation of capitalism and democracy. If the developed world fails to instill such basic principles in China and remains unwilling to enforce the contracts on property implicit in the trade agreements it has negotiated with the Chinese government, chaos and conflicts are inevitable.

When Japan ravaged certain U.S. industries, there was a natural limit created by Japan's relatively small population and limited geography. No such limits exist with China. Thus, China's respect for foreign intellectual property rights is a crucial test of whether free trade with a Communist government is possible.

Beyond the attraction of potentially high profits, most foreign corporations license their technology in China on the assumption that the Chinese government will protect their intellectual property. Yet China's system of protection is more about facilitating the theft of intellectual property than it is about protecting it for foreign owners.

The China Patent Office was not founded until 1980, largely because of the 1979 U.S.–China Agreement on Trade Relations. China's State Intellectual Property Office (SIPO) acknowledges in its official history that China created this function and organization for political reasons, namely, to avoid U.S. trade sanctions for pirating, to gain U.S. support for China's membership in the World Trade Organization, and to encourage foreign direct investment.

These are all practical reasons, but none reflects a strong desire by the Chinese to protect either domestic or foreign intellectual property rights. Also, the Chinese government acknowledges that the notion of private ownership and the exclusive use of an idea is alien to Chinese culture. Without question, it is an idea not appreciated by most Chinese.

Most of China's efforts to protect intellectual property are due to foreign pressure. Consequently, those actions are taken largely to give the impression of compliance. In the 1980s, China joined most of the world's intellectual property organizations, such as the Paris and Berne conventions. Beijing also enacted a trademark law in 1983, a patent law in 1985, and a copyright law in 1993. With its accession to the World Trade Organization, China agreed to establish an enforceable system of protections for foreign intellectual-property owners.

All these steps have been perfunctory. When pressured, the Chinese authorities have made many highly visible raids on video and music pirates—actions that seem geared to pacify foreign governments rather than to stamp out counterfeiting. The China Patent Office acknowledges that while Chinese officials have closed many illegal production lines, the counterfeiters simply move to Hong Kong, Macau, or elsewhere and then slip their fake goods back into China.

China's patent, trademark, and copyright systems, as designed and operated, cannot meet Western expectations of protection. The government hires few agents to accept and process applications, which leads to backlogs. It makes few judges available to hear intellectual property cases. It employs only a small number of government investigators to track down or even investigate complaints of piracy. Chinese law also prohibits the use of the subpoena to get the records of counterfeiters. Not being allowed to gather evidence is a major impediment to convicting a counterfeiter in any court.

The China Patent Office also lacks the personnel to make local investigations of piracy; consequently, it depends on grassroots organizations, where incompetence and corruption dominate. Finally, unlike in the United

States, the enforcement of intellectual property rights is state-centered. Although the Chinese government has permitted private action in the courts since 1997, it has neither encouraged nor helped foreign victims. The International AntiCounterfeiting Coalition (IACC) reports that in 2001, only 319 criminal cases involving intellectual property were initiated within China's judicial system. With billions of dollars of counterfeiting under way annually, foreigners have brought only a few dozen cases to court; most foreign businesspeople know that going to court is a waste of their time and money.

Attempts to use Chinese courts to protect intellectual property can produce some extraordinary results. The IACC documented one such outcome in a submission to the United States Trade Representative in February 2003. The owner of a successful footwear company and a well-known trademark made an agreement with a Hong Kong distributor to sell his brand in China and gave permission for special products to be made for the Chinese market alone. He executed a one-page trademark permission agreement with a Chinese manufacturer to confirm his authorization of the production and the deal. Soon after, copies of the branded shoes appeared in China and throughout the world. The brand owner then canceled the deal with the Hong Kong distributor and the Chinese manufacturer.

Subsequently, the trademark owner learned that the Chinese manufacturer had registered his single-page contract with the China Trademark Office. The Chinese manufacturer continued to deluge the world with the popular shoe, paying the real owner nothing. The owner sued in Shenzhen. Among the defendants was a large local department store that was selling the pirated shoes. It immediately settled. The Chinese manufacturer took the position that the contract allowed him to produce the shoe in unlimited quantities and to distribute it worldwide without payment of royalties or fees of any nature to the trademark owner.

The brand owner submitted evidence that the only authority given the manufacturer was a purchase order, which China tightly regulates, and that he had canceled it. After a hearing, the Shenzhen court ruled in favor of the local manufacturer, holding that the counterfeiter had a license "to make, sell, and distribute the trademark owner's product, virtually without restriction as to style, type, territory, price, quality, or any other controls." The court did not require that any royalty or fee payments be made to the real owner. Because of the court's action, the Chinese authorities are now prohibited from seizing any of these pirated shoes until a higher court rules on the appeal, a process that may consume years. Meanwhile, the pirate manufacturer prospers.

As this story suggests, despite China's admission to the World Trade Organization and its enactment of legislation to enforce its intellectual property laws, it remains a counterfeiter's paradise. Chinese authorities secure virtually no convictions against native counterfeiters. China does not enforce its laws against China-based exporters of counterfeit goods. It does not even impose its laws on counterfeit sales inside China.

In December 2003, the U.S. Trade Representative issued a detailed report on China's compliance with the obligations it accepted as part of joining the World Trade Organization. The USTR said that China was in serious violation of its obligations to protect the rights of owners of U.S. patent, copyright, trademark, and other intellectual properties. Counterfeiting was rampant. China had taken few actions to establish a functioning judicial system. Its investigations of intellectual property violations were perfunctory.

The International Intellectual Property Alliance's 2004 report estimates that China's rate of piracy for motion pictures is 95 percent. For records and music, it is 90 percent. For entertainment software it is 96 percent, and for books it is 40 percent.

The copyright-based industries are only part of the story. The International AntiCounterfeiting Coalition's 2003 report on piracy identified a broad range of other products manufactured in China and marketed domestically and worldwide, including the following:

- Pharmaceuticals

- Electronics, such as televisions, microphones, and amplifiers

- Office machines and accessories

- Shampoos, toothpaste, soaps, and detergents

- Perfume and skin care and other cosmetic products

- Razors

- Auto parts, including windshields, brake pads, and filters

- Tools, such as electric drills

- Cigarettes

- Apparel

- Shoes

- Baggage

- Film and batteries

- Motorbikes

- Mobile phones

- Food and beverages

- Computers and peripherals

- Home appliances

- Toys

- Knapsacks

- Branded vision care products

In each of these areas, Chinese manufacturers copy a well-known, trademarked good and pass it off as the real thing, an illegal activity that violates another company's intellectual property rights.

Again, under intense U.S. and European pressure, in 1996 Beijing enacted a trademark protection law for well-known brands and a provision for registering such trademarks. In the three years following passage of that legislation, the China Trademark Office registered 153 trademarks, all from Chinese companies. In those same three years, the office did not validate even one foreign trademark.

In January 1999, the trademark office circulated a request to its regional and local offices requesting them to nominate foreign-related registered trademarks of no more than ten enterprises. Subsequently, the trademark office registered 130 foreign-related marks as well as another 43 Chinese marks.

During this process, the China Trademark Office refused to publish its list of registered well-known trademarks, keeping it as an internal document. However, it distributed the list to local administrations for industry and commerce (AICs) so officials would know which marks the government considered as perhaps deserving enforcement resources.

Pepsi-Cola, which entered China's market in the mid-1970s, is one foreign victim. Pepsi has several registered trademarks in China. Beginning in 1991, a local Chinese company seriously infringed upon Pepsi's logo. Even though Pepsi supposedly got some relief from the State Intellectual Property Office in 1996, the local enforcement agencies proved powerless. When the local AIC issued an order embargoing the infringing goods, the Chinese company merely transferred them elsewhere. When the AIC tried to enter the infringing company's site, thugs attacked the government officials. Though attacking public officials is illegal, nothing happened to the infringer. Meanwhile, the pirate kept selling his product with the Pepsi trademarks on the bottle.

Chinese counterfeiters continue to produce and export in volume. The economic effects of this state-ignored crime affect more than just producers from wealthy nations. The European Union, which includes both rich and poor nations, reports that of the 50 million counterfeit and pirated goods it interdicted in the first half of 2003, 15 percent were made in China.

Counterfeit goods from China have ravaged major portions of Mexico's manufacturing sector. The *New York Times* reports that Chinese counterfeiters have hit Mexico's textile, shoe, and garment producers particularly hard. A decade ago, the Mexican government imposed duties of as much as 1,100 percent to protect those domestic industries. Nevertheless, almost 58 percent of the clothes in Mexico are counterfeit goods from China, many of them bearing well-known trademarks. Their import is largely aided by local corruption and falsified documents. President Vicente Fox cleaned up Mexico's customs service, replacing 80 percent of the professional employees and most of the forty-eight port directors in an effort to reduce corruption.

Even with a tenfold increase in Mexico's Customs Administration budget, the introduction of new technology, and more employees who are honest, 30 percent of contraband clothing from China still gets through Mexican customs with well-placed bribes. Still, that is down from 60 percent two years ago. This Chinese contraband costs the Mexican government its tariff revenue and thousands of Mexican workers their jobs.

China's protections for intellectual property look like a Potemkin village. The Chinese government has joined various global intellectual property organizations, including the WTO, largely to deflect foreign pressures. The national bureaucracies created to protect intellectual property are struggling to put into place the forms, regulations, and institutional mechanisms that real systems have.

In China, local officials have great power and often little connection with national authority. Many are corrupt, and most are ideologically driven to promote China's interests. In their view, why should a local official take jobs away from neighbors, friends, family, and constituents and give them to an unknown foreign corporation whose operations may be elsewhere, maybe not even in China?

Now that China has taken in so much foreign technology and manufacturing capacity, the Communist Party is moving to insinuate itself into the Chinese workforce. The *Financial Times* reports that the party is "zealously pursuing a programme to have at least one party member in private sector enterprises with 50 or more employees, and to establish a committee in companies with over 100." Many Westerners forget that China is run by a single-party dictatorship, "bent on colonizing every branch of society." If the party is to retain firm control of the country, it ultimately must be able to exert oversight over the private companies that operate there. The party membership of Chinese middle managers and workers is part of that effort. The great irony is that many Western companies that moved to China to escape unions may eventually find themselves in much the same position as those Europeans in the 1930s who foresaw the coming of World War II and relocated to what they thought were safe havens, such as Guadalcanal.

As for private enforcement of intellectual property rights, the very idea of patents, copyrights, trademarks, and trade secrets is as novel to China as ideas of constitutional rights and civil law. China is an old civilization. To graft the U.S. system of intellectual property rights onto China's ancient political culture may be as difficult and odd a task as trying to graft a grapevine onto a mature oak tree.

Professor William P. Alford of Harvard Law School captures the essence of the problem in *To Steal a Book Is an Elegant Offense*. He writes:

> A system of state determination of which ideas may or may not be disseminated is fundamentally incompatible with one of strong intellectual property rights in which individuals have the authority to determine how expressions of their ideas may be used and ready access to private legal remedies to vindicate such rights.

China's culture, of course, can change, but its political leaders acceptance of foreign notions of intellectual property laws, individual civil rights, and private legal remedies as a central part of its political tradition is not likely to happen soon, if ever. To expect the Chinese public to forgo pirated products simply because some foreigner owns the exclusive use of an invention, trademark, or copyright is to risk disappointment, at least in the near future.

If China's economy evolves as did Japan's, the Chinese may become interested in intellectual property protection when they develop proprietary technologies that they want to secure in other nations. Until then, foreign intellectual-property owners must regard China as the great threat to their property that it is.

The great challenge of global piracy, whether by nations, corporations, gangs, or individuals, is how to enforce intellectual property laws. In the U.S., that responsibility resides with the owner of the intellectual property, and adequate ways and means have been provided for private action. The most challenging problem is how to stop the piracy of U.S. intellectual property in other nations where such ways and means do not exist.

PART III

NATIONAL AND GLOBAL ENFORCEMENT

AUTHOR'S NOTE

By the late 1970s, the piracy of U.S. intellectual properties had become a major issue for both U.S. inventors and U.S. companies. Thus, a number of remedial efforts were initiated to deal with the problem. They came to fruition between 1993 and 1999, making historic changes to U.S. and global intellectual property (IP) protections. The story is divided into four parts, though several individuals are involved in each.

The first concerns the evolution of IP enforcement in the United States. The first patent and copyright laws gave IP owners rights, which they defended through private actions in the courts. A century after the first patent and copyright laws were enacted, the federal government criminalized some IP theft and provided for federal pursuit of thieves, fines, and imprisonment.

Because IP rights are defined and enforced nation by nation, private lawsuits are unable to deal with those IP infringements occurring in nations that lack either IP laws or a functioning judicial system. Chapter 8 tells the story of how a small, elite group of corporate executives masterminded the creation of a new global regime of IP protections inside the World Trade Organization.

Even as major international corporations and the governments of Japan and Europe were trying to strengthen global IP protections in the developing world at the WTO, they were also trying to weaken U.S. patent laws in a way that put individual inventors at a disadvantage. Chapter 9 tells that story.

The digital revolution, as embodied in the Internet, threatened the protections provided to copyrighted works. Chapter 10 tells how Congress imposed controversial limits on the Internet in order to help copyright owners reassert control of their property. It also explains why and how copyright terms were extended in 1998 by twenty years, explains the consequences, and reviews a proposal to speed copyrighted materials into the public domain while protecting the rights of IP owners.

CHAPTER 7

EVOLVING ENFORCEMENT

In the early 1980s, Japan Inc. launched a major assault on the U.S. computer and semiconductor industries. Many American companies wilted as Japanese firms began selling chips at below their production cost. Others went to the U.S. government for political help.

One American corporation, however, approached Japan's threat quite differently. Texas Instruments, the high-tech, Dallas-based company, launched a counterattack. TI, as it is commonly known, has a rich storehouse of patents. Before the 1980s, it rather passively used those patents as bargaining devices to get into other markets, such as Japan's, or to ease the exchange of technology with other companies.

But in 1985, TI changed its tactics from patent bargaining to patent litigation. In *The Patent Wars,* Fred Warshofsky describes how Melvin Sharp, an engineer and lawyer who headed the corporate patent division, put together a team of fifteen patent attorneys and fifteen engineers and reverse engineered the suspect foreign products to determine if they violated any TI patents. They found dozens of infringements. Without any warning or notice, TI sued nine Japanese and Korean violators in the federal district court in Dallas, Texas. The TI tactic was "sue first, talk later." Eight of the nine defendants quickly settled. Eventually, the ninth followed. Each took five-year licenses. Subsequently, the TI patent protection strategy created a flow of royalty income for the company. The resulting royalties, generated between 1986 and 1990, produced $1 billion in income for TI. After the five-year period lapsed, the licenses were renewed and the royalty rates increased. Since 1985, TI has collected billions of dollars of royalty income from its patent licenses.

The lesson taught by the TI campaign of aggressive litigation is that a patent is more than a document to hang on a wall or a trading card to exchange for the use of someone else's technology. Rather, a patent can be a major source of revenue, plus the means to mount an offensive against predatory commercial attacks. The message TI sent was simple: "Don't mess with Texas Instruments."

Melvin Sharp became a living legend, and other companies followed the TI example. Honeywell, for instance, successfully sued Minolta for infringement of its auto-focus camera technology. In 1992, it won $96 million in damages. Subsequently, Honeywell licensed its technology to Minolta for an additional $30 million. Ten other Japanese camera makers paid Honeywell $175 million to settle the lawsuits against them for infringing the same patents. Gregory Aharonian, a writer and expert on intellectual property issues, has posted on his Web site three hundred prominent patent and copyright lawsuits where the plaintiff won or negotiated a settlement against an infringer. The awards ranged from $71,000 to $2.5 billion. In the period 1993–2002, seventy-two plaintiffs won individual awards of more than $100 million each. Stealing ideas can be expensive in the United States. The larger point, of course, is that U.S. intellectual property owners can enforce their copyrights, patents, trademarks, and trade secrets in U.S. courts. Protecting those rights in other nations is more problematic.

Intellectual property rights are worthless unless they can be defended. From the enactment of the first U.S. patent and copyright acts in 1790 until now, that responsibility has resided primarily with IP owners and their lawyers rather than with the government. To that end, the U.S. provides a functioning judiciary system where private action can take place. The presumption is that those with the most at stake will initiate actions where appropriate and defend their rights most aggressively. The risk with government-led defenses is that they depend on political decisions by political appointees inside an administration that may change direction because of an election, or the job may fall to agencies that lack the expertise, motivation, or resources.

When George Washington and the first U.S. Congress created the first patent and copyright laws in 1790, they considered court-ordered civil sanctions sufficient to deter infringers. History has demonstrated, however, that there are circumstances where federal action is necessary. Over the past two centuries, intellectual property theft has proven so rewarding that Congress has progressively increased the penalties for it. Congress has also expanded the list of creations covered under U.S. intellectual property laws, mirroring the changing nature of innovation. Most important, Congress has repeatedly steered intellectual property disputes into the federal courts, thereby elevating the issues to matters of national concern. For patent cases, the federal courts were established as the only judicial forum. For copyright infringement, plaintiffs could seek relief in either federal or state courts, as several states had their own copyright laws. This dual system existed until 1976, when Congress effectively made most copyright violation a federal offense. With the passage of the Lanham Act in 1946, Congress expanded intellectual property protections to include trademarks. Since most states also provide trademark protections, owners are able to seek remedies against infringement in both federal and state courts.

In 1909, Congress first decided that civil sanctions were insufficient to stop some brazen copyright infringers, so criminal prosecutions were authorized as an additional deterrent. In 1992, Congress broadened the law, making copyright infringement a felony offense under federal law "if at least ten infringing copies of *any type of copyrighted work* with a value of $2,500 or more are made or distributed in a 180-day period."

The Justice Department defines a trade secret as "any formula, pattern, device or compilation of information used in a business to obtain an advantage over competitors who do not know or use it." Trade secrets, regardless of their nature, have long presented a special protection problem for their owners, namely, keeping others from discovering the secret. They also have posed problems for the courts in that many prosecutors have long disagreed as to whether a trade secret is really an intellectual property. But the best-known company in America is based on a syrup formula that remains a long-held secret of great value. The Coca-Cola formula has been kept a trade secret since its creation in 1886, more than a century ago. A lone copy of the formula reportedly exists in the vault of an Atlanta bank, where it is also reportedly unavailable to anyone except by a formal vote of the company's board of directors. The formula is considered so valuable that in 1919 the one copy was given as collateral to Guaranty Trust Bank in New York for a $1 million loan. According to Frederick Allen *(Secret Formula),* when in 1977 the government of India ordered Coca-Cola to share the formula with local distributors, the company spent $2 million to grind up all its glass containers and then withdrew from a market that purchased 900 million bottles of its product annually.

Federal law did not explicitly prohibit the theft of trade secrets, such as the Coca-Cola formula, until 1996. Federal convictions for such a crime were possible, but only under statutes that prohibited the violation of a fiduciary or confidential relationship. Even then, many prosecutors disagreed as to whether a trade secret was a form of property. But the Economic Espionage Act of 1996 made the theft of trade secrets a federal crime regardless of who benefits.

Unlike copyrights, trademarks, and trade secrets, patent infringement is not a criminal act under federal law. However, federal law does make it a felony "to make, forge, counterfeit, or otherwise alter letters patent, or to pass or publish same knowing them to have been forged." In other words, representing a fake document as a genuine patent certificate is a felony. Unauthorized replication or use of the innovation that the patent protects is not a felony offense.

America is a litigious society. Whether this is so because we have almost one million practicing lawyers or we have one million practicing lawyers because it is so remains an enigma. Regardless of the reason, most U.S. intellectual-property owners rely on their own attorneys, not their government, to defend their rights. Foreign corporations fully understand this difference. Former U.S. patent commissioner Bruce Lehman notes that foreigners "are particularly freaked by [patent] litigation." The reason is clear: U.S. courts are far more difficult to subvert than U.S. politicians.

In the United States, private lawsuits to defend patents, copyrights, trademarks, trade secrets, masks, and plant varieties are potent because the federal courts, where they are mostly heard, are strong judicial bodies with great power. The strength of the courts is the judges, whose qualifications are reviewed and approved by the U.S. Senate. For more than two centuries, America's federal judges have been mostly capable, often brilliant, and uncompromisingly honest.

To further ensure fairness, the courts have a strong appellate system, which allows an impartial and competent review of lower court decisions by panels of other judges. To provide knowledgeable review of complex patent and trademark cases, Congress created the U.S. Court of Appeals for the Federal Circuit, which is located in Washington, D.C. Created in 1982, this court hears all appeals on patent and trademark cases.

Before 1982, any appeal of a trial court decision on patent infringement went to one of the eleven federal circuit courts of appeal. Because few appellate judges had expertise in such matters, the results could differ sharply among the eleven courts. In the decade before the creation of the Court of Appeals for the Federal Circuit, the Fifth Circuit Court in New Orleans ruled in favor of patent holders in more than 80 percent of the cases it considered. By contrast, the Eighth Circuit Court in Minneapolis did not uphold the validity of a single patent during that same period.

The judges at the U.S. Court of Appeals for the Federal Circuit become knowledgeable in intellectual property matters. One lawyer who practices before that court notes, "Almost to a person, they are unusually bright, conscientious, and industrious. Most of them are even polite." Before the creation of this new court, the eleven (now twelve) appeals courts upheld only 40 percent of U.S. patents in litigation; in the ten years afterward, the new federal circuit court upheld roughly two-thirds, revealing the new court's propatent position.

Equally important, the U.S. legal system provides the strong supporting infrastructure that effective private litigation requires. As of 2003, the United States had more than 21,000 attorneys and agents certified to practice before the Patent and Trademark Office. Although an inventor can file an application independently, the patent office urges the use of patent attorneys or patent agents. An agent is someone who does not hold a law degree but does have a technical degree and has passed a rigorous examination by the patent office. These certified patent attorneys and agents help ensure that strong patents are filed.

America's strong intellectual property laws and equally strong judicial system are hazards for counterfeiters, pirates, and infringers. The statistics of private patent suits illustrate why. Alexander I. Poltorak and Paul J. Lerner, in *Essentials of Intellectual Property*, estimate that only 1.1 percent of all patents are ever litigated. This low percentage is a positive reflection on the Patent and Trademark Office, suggesting that its examinations are thorough and the patents it issues are strong.

Of that one percent that are litigated, almost 76 percent are settled before going to trial, generally after an expenditure of $1 million or more by each side. Only 4 percent of all suits filed eventually do go to trial. The other 20 percent are either withdrawn or dismissed.

Of cases where a patent's validity is challenged, Poltorak and Lerner report that court decisions uphold 67 percent. When infringement is litigated, patent owners win 66 percent of their cases. These are very good odds for patent holders and very bad ones for pirates, counterfeiters, or infringers—at least in the United States.

In addition to the federal court system and a strong body of intellectual property laws, there is another means U.S. IP holders have to keep infringing goods out of the United States. Under section 337 of the Tariff Act of 1930, the U.S. International Trade Commission is empowered to investigate allegations of patent, copyright, and trademark infringements of imported goods, as well as the misappropriation of trade secrets. The commission is an independent, quasi-judicial federal agency that analyzes the effects of imports on the economy and directs actions against unfair trade practices, such as intellectual property infringement.

If an IP holder thinks that its rights are being infringed upon by unauthorized imports, it can file a formal complaint with the commission. If the commission votes to investigate, it appoints an administrative law judge to preside over the proceedings and make an initial decision. Hearings are held, and eventually the commission makes a decision or a settlement is reached. Between the mid-1970s and January 2004, the commission heard 505 cases involving alleged violations on items that ranged from integrated circuit chipsets to rodent bail stations (a better mousetrap). When the commission finds there has been an infringement of a valid and enforceable U.S. patent, copyright, trade secret, or trademark, it orders the Customs Service to exclude the good from entry into the United States.

Cisco Systems' quick legal victory over Huawei Technologies in early 2003 illustrates how intellectual-property owners can defend their rights in a functioning judicial system.

California-based Cisco is a worldwide leader in the creation and manufacturing of computer networking products. It is one of the leading builders of the Internet. Huawei is China's largest maker of network and telecommunications equipment. A multibillion-dollar corporation, it does business worldwide and had a subsidiary corporation in Plano, Texas, named FutureWei.

In January 2003, Cisco filed a complaint against Huawei and its U.S. subsidiary in the federal district court in Marshall, Texas, alleging that the Chinese corporation was selling "clone" Cisco routers and switches as its own and doing so worldwide. Such equipment is the backbone of the Internet. Cisco also claimed that Huawei had copied and sold its copyrighted operating software as its own.

Cisco's explanation of Huawei's actions reads like a manual on how to steal someone else's patents and copyrights. The software used by the Chinese company was almost exactly like Cisco's, though Cisco had never shared its codes with the Chinese company. Huawei's software even had the same errors as Cisco's. Cisco charged that the routers and switches sold by Huawei violated at least five of its patents.

Another count in the suit was that Huawei had copied Cisco's operating manual and sold it as its own. Cisco's complaint included six pages of examples. One revealed that Huawei had copied entire paragraphs from the Cisco manual almost word for word, including illustrations.

Two months after filing its initial complaint, Cisco submitted two damning declarations. One was from a Cisco engineer whom Huawei had tried to recruit for its Texas subsidiary. According to the engineer, the Chinese company wanted him to bring Cisco's proprietary and confidential information with him so it could be copied. More explosive, a former human resources manager at FutureWei said in his sworn affidavit that corporate executives had "twice given him the task of locating and hiring Cisco employees who had worked on projects that FutureWei hoped to mimic."

Huawei responded by filing a countersuit against Cisco claiming that its action was part of a campaign of misinformation and that the U.S. corporation was improperly using its patents and copyrights to fend off competition.

In October 2003, the *New York Times* reported that Cisco and Huawei had reached a settlement. Huawei agreed to stop selling the disputed products. It also said it would modify its routers and switches so they did not violate Cisco's patents. Independent experts would be hired to check compliance. With this suit, Cisco stopped Huawei from taking its technology and using it in the U.S. and European markets. Huawei could not afford to lose in a U.S. court, because it would have faced massive damage awards. In China, it is unlikely that Cisco would have prevailed with its case; in the United States, it got a resolution in less than five months.

One of the important features of America's judicial system is that a small company or an individual inventor or author with a good lawyer has equal standing with even the largest corporate infringer. Even the absence of resources is not a legal barrier in many cases. Some lawyers and their firms operate on a contingency basis. They are paid a certain portion of the proceeds if they win and nothing if they lose. The richer the accused infringer, the more attractive the case is to most contingency lawyers. A classic example of small inventors and their contingency lawyers prevailing over giant corporations is that of GoVideo.

The story begins in 1953 at the Ampex Corporation, a high-tech California company, when its engineers invented video recording. By the mid-1980s, Ampex was out of the VCR business and Japanese companies totally controlled the industry. Then, just when the Japanese victory seemed complete, two Arizona-based inventors devised a way to make a dual-deck VCR that allowed users to make high-quality copies of video recordings or tape live programs while watching another television show or another tape on the other deck. Unlike single-deck Japanese VCRs, the GoVideo machine was simple to operate: put the programmed VCR in one deck, put a blank in the other deck, and punch the red "record" button. Even better, the GoVideo clock was just as easy to program—a feature most other VCR makers found impossible to make user-friendly.

GoVideo was the creation of two Scottsdale, Arizona, entrepreneurs, R. Terren (Terry) Dunlap and Richard Lang. In the early 1980s, Dunlap, then a struggling lawyer in his early thirties, bankrolled the company by borrowing $5,000 from each of his twelve credit cards. Originally, that capital financed a mobile video production truck that went to events, such as weddings and conferences, and videotaped them—thus the name GoVideo. The company's profits came from producing and selling duplicate tapes of those events.

After struggling to make high-quality duplicates by coupling two single-deck VCRs, Dunlap saw an advantage for a device with two videotape mechanisms operating from a common switch panel, all within one housing. The major problem with daisy-chaining two single-deck VCRs was that the quality of duplicates deteriorated from one recording to another, largely because of unsynchronized electronics between the two machines. Dunlap took the new design to a consulting engineer, who built a prototype of a videocassette recorder and taping system in which two decks were combined within a single housing with electronics that synchronized the decks. The result was a machine that could produce duplicates as good as the original. In September 1984, Dunlap and Lang filed for a basic utility patent on the dual-deck VCR at both the U.S. and the Japanese patent offices.

The inventors' next step was to find a manufacturer. Dunlap tried to locate U.S. companies that would produce his machine, only to learn that American VCR makers had been shut out of the business in the 1970s. Even Zenith, one of the few remaining U.S.–owned television manufacturers, relied upon a Japanese company to produce its VCRs. Dunlap then turned to Japanese producers. Nippon Electronic Corporation (NEC) seemed anxious to make the machine. In January 1985, Dunlap went to Tokyo, where he settled what he thought were the final details with company executives. After he returned home, however, NEC suddenly terminated the negotiations. When Dunlap called, NEC executives refused to give an explanation. While NEC and other Japanese VCR manufacturers were eager to produce an unlimited number of single-deck VCR machines for anyone and were already shipping dual-deck audiocassette recorders, they refused to build a dual-deck VCR for GoVideo or sell parts to anyone who would.

The reasons for this became clear in late April 1985. The Electronics Industry Association of Japan (EIAJ) announced that all Japanese VCR manufacturers had joined a "voluntary restraint agreement" to neither manufacture dual-deck VCR machines nor sell component parts to others. Korean VCR makers, who were dependent upon Japanese licenses, had been forced to join the agreement.

The Japanese shut the door on GoVideo for two basic reasons. First, the cartel did not want any new competitors. Second, the companies that had the capability to manufacture the dual-deck VCR had just barely survived the infamous Betamax case brought by the motion picture industry over the selling of single-deck VCRs. In a 5–4 ruling, the U.S. Supreme Court had held that consumers could videotape television shows for their own use. Jack Valenti, who led the Motion Picture Association of America (MPAA), threatened that if the Japanese produced a dual-deck VCR that enabled Americans to copy rented movies, his industry would lobby Congress to impose a royalty on each videotape and VCR sold in America.

Hollywood and the Japanese VCR makers made a deal. The Japanese would not make a dual-deck VCR and the MPAA would not lobby Congress for a royalty on all blank VCR tapes. Dunlap had articles from newspapers and trade journals that quoted officials' description of the restraint agreement. In one article about GoVideo's search for a manufacturer, a Valenti aide said, "Realistically, who are they gonna get? The Japanese have kept their word about not making dual-deck units so far, and there's no reason to believe they're going to change their minds because of some little company from Arizona."

There was, of course, a reason for all those involved with this agreement, whether in Hollywood or Japan, to change their minds: America's antitrust laws make such a deal illegal. Proving a monopoly conspiracy is tough. The conspirators hide what they do, and when sued they hire the best, most obstructionist defense lawyers money can buy. Proving a monopoly conspiracy is possible, however. It often takes millions of dollars in legal fees and years to conclude, but it is possible.

Dunlap went to Joseph M. Alioto Jr. and Daniel Schulman. They are among a handful of antitrust lawyers in America who represent the victims in private antitrust lawsuits. Unlike most attorneys, who are paid by the hour, Alioto and Schulman often work on a contingency basis: they take as their compensation a percentage of what they recover for their clients. In antitrust suits, the law automatically triples the amount of any proven damages. In a case such as GoVideo's, the damages could be in the hundreds of millions of dollars.

Alioto and Schulman are a formidable team. Schulman, a Harvard Law School graduate and legal scholar who lives in Minnesota, does the analysis, prepares the detailed briefs, and manages the paper. Alioto, a skilled trial lawyer, politician, and son of the former mayor of San Francisco, performs most of the trial presentation. They jointly carry out the investigations. Together, they have won some of the largest antitrust judgments in U.S. history.

The first action of the two lawyers was to solidify GoVideo's patent position. Consequently, in May 1987 Dunlap and Lang filed several improvements to their first patent application. On August 30, 1988, the U.S. Patent and Trademark Office awarded them a wide-ranging patent on a dual-deck videocassette recorder and taping system, which the inventors then assigned to GoVideo. Now GoVideo owned the exclusive right to produce dual-deck video machines in the U.S. But they still had to find a manufacturer.

Alioto and Schulman advised GoVideo to use what seemed at the time an unusual tactic to get cooperation from an unwilling manufacturer. They went to court in Phoenix, where GoVideo was located, and sued every Japanese and Korean VCR maker for their participation in an anticompetitive conspiracy to thwart GoVideo's production of dual-deck machines. Among their evidence were Japan's voluntary restraint agreement and statements from the MPAA. Subsequently, the MPAA and its member Hollywood studios were added as defendants. Valenti was quoted as noting the ease with which the dual-deck VCR could duplicate rental movies.

Dunlap reacted: "We had to remove their red herring, so I met with the MPAA lawyers and struck a deal." Dual-deck VCRs would include an anti-copy chip to prevent duplication of "copy-protected" rentals. This removed the Hollywood threat as an excuse for the Japanese manufacturers. (A few months after the litigation with the Japanese was completed, GoVideo would remove the chip and rely on the "fair use" provisions of copyright law to keep the MPAA at bay.)

Early in the lawsuit, the U.S. attorneys for the Japanese defendants asked the district court to dismiss the GoVideo case because their clients designed and manufactured all of their VCRs outside the U.S. and therefore were outside the scope of U.S. antitrust law. The district court ruled in favor of the defendants and dismissed the GoVideo case.

However, on appeal, the Ninth Circuit Court of Appeals decided in GoVideo's favor, ruling that since the Japanese were marketing their products in the United States they were subject to U.S. laws. This precedent meant that for purposes of antitrust laws, the Japanese were to be treated the same as any group of U.S. companies engaged in collusive economic tactics. If GoVideo won, it also had the legal right to collect from the Japanese corporations' U.S. operations. The appeals court's decision sent the case back to district court. The district court allowed the GoVideo lawyers to do discovery and take depositions in Japan, including that of Akio Morita, co-founder of Sony.

Eventually, Alioto and Schulman met their counterparts from the twenty-seven Japanese and Korean defendant companies. Many wanted to settle the suit quickly in exchange for a cash payment. The GoVideo lawyers desired both the cash and a manufacturer. Samsung, the giant Korean company, hinted that it would produce GoVideo's machine, but only if Toshiba, from which it held VCR licenses, would agree. Alioto and Schulman then asked Toshiba's attorney if that company was prohibiting Samsung from entering a manufacturing agreement with GoVideo. If Toshiba said yes, GoVideo would assuredly win its case. Not surprisingly, Toshiba said no and then paid GoVideo a nominal sum to exit the antitrust lawsuit. Through this, Alioto and Schulman got a manufacturer—Samsung, which was released from the case.

By the time the Phoenix court was ready to hear the GoVideo case in 1991, all but three of the Japanese defendants had settled. As a result, the company received almost $12 million of badly needed capital. A part went to the attorneys, some went to other legal expenses, and the balance was used for product development. During the intervening years between the first filing and the trial, Dunlap and Lang filed for additional patents, broadening their claims and their hold on their invention.

The trial took almost two months in the summer of 1991. The remaining defendants were Matsushita, JVC, and Sony. Alioto presented witnesses and documents discovered in Japan, and then described the creation and operation of the Japanese television cartel. He then showed how that cartel had illegally seized an entire industry through dumping, market-sharing arrangements, cross-licensing of patents, and violations of U.S. customs laws.

The American attorneys for the Japanese presented their clients as doing business in a manner that would befit any U.S. company. They denied all accusations about the formation of a cartel or any predatory activities. They also derided the dual-deck VCR as a "rich man's toy," something with so limited a market that no Japanese manufacturer would ever be interested in producing it. When the case was presented to the jury, the jurors took less than an hour to reach a decision. Their unanimous verdict was that the Japanese were innocent of any conspiracy.

Following the trial, several jurors agreed to interviews. None believed that Japanese businesses operated any differently from American companies. All had had good experiences with Japanese products. The jury forewoman told Dunlap's wife that she was sorry but she just did not see evidence of a conspiracy. A couple of jurors believed that the GoVideo complaints were nothing but an attempt to get rich quickly at the expense of the Japanese. The jurors found implausible the idea that a government and its companies would actually work together to take over another nation's industry or that Japanese consumers and workers would tolerate high prices and limited choices in their own market to help their companies gain overseas market share.

Two months after GoVideo lost its case, Sharp announced that it would produce dual-deck VCRs for the Japanese and other world markets. Other Japanese and Korean VCR makers quickly followed. Apparently, the machines were not "rich men's toys" after all.

Although the Japanese VCR makers got to market quicker than GoVideo, which introduced its machines, made by Samsung, in early 1992, they were afraid to sell them in the United States because GoVideo had a patent on the invention and was obviously willing to sue. Though the Japanese had won the antitrust case, they did not want a rematch on a patent infringement suit.

The protection provided by GoVideo's patents allowed the company to prosper. For almost five years, the only dual-deck machines available in the U.S. market came from GoVideo. Eventually, the company licensed its technology and was able to collect a royalty on every dual-deck VCR machine sold in the United States. Between 1992 and 2002, dual-deck VCRs manufactured and sold under the GoVideo license produced retail revenues in excess of a half billion dollars.

The GoVideo experience is precisely what the authors of the Constitution intended. Two inventors made a useful innovation. In exchange for sharing their knowledge with the public, they got exclusive rights for a set period to make and sell their products. In the process, they formed a company, provided the public a useful product, and created value for their shareholders.

Terry Dunlap acknowledges that the GoVideo experience greatly changed his life. For one thing, he became wealthy and now invests in start-up companies. In the mid-1990s, Dunlap left GoVideo and began another company, Duraswitch, which produces magnetically coupled electronic switches. Most recently, he has headed Ultra-Scan Corporation, which makes optical fingerprint scanners.

With each company, Dunlap developed a patent-based business plan. First he looks for pioneering technologies that can be protected with an intellectual property strategy. Then he surrounds it, as he says,

> like the layers of an onion with technical improvements, business process ideas, continuation in part patents, manufacturing process and business method patents, trade secrets, copyrights, and trademarks. Some of these patents can be narrow, some broad, some have many claims, some have few. The more diverse layers to the IP "onion" the more difficult and expensive it is to competitors to lay claim to, dispute, penetrate or challenge your inventions.

He hires at least two outside patent law firms to review all the company's patent applications and look for better ways to describe the claims. He assigns an in-house patent lawyer and engineer to try to reverse engineer the company's patents, find any backdoor approaches, and then close them with new patent filings. Dunlap also takes the offense with his patents: he publishes his patent numbers on the back of his business card, on letterheads, brochures, spec sheets, and Web sites. He makes sure everyone knows his technology has intellectual property protections that he will aggressively defend. Finally, he is always willing to license his technology at a reasonable rate. For most companies, he says, it is preferable to license at a fair price rather than deny access and thus encourage others to steal your ideas. Dunlap sums up his approach: "Your IP capital is like owning a pile of gold; it needs to be watched after, protected and nurtured just as you do your business capital funds or capital equipment."

Fortunately, the United States is not alone in its respect for intellectual property rights. A handful of other nations also have strong judicial systems where patent, copyright, trade secret, and trademark owners can successfully defend their rights against foreign infringers through private lawsuits. Not surprisingly, Britain, which provided the original model for U.S. patent and copyright laws, is one of those countries.

An ongoing trademark dispute illustrates how well-functioning and compatible judicial systems can help IP owners protect their works. This particular case involves a group of English musicians first known as the Quarrymen and then as Johnny and the Moondogs. Johnny, the founder and leader of the band, admired the work of the American musician Buddy Holly and his band, the Crickets. Johnny was amused that Holly had named his band after an insect and decided to do the same, renaming the Moondogs the Beetles and then the Beatles—"beat" being a musical term. Johnny, of course, was John Lennon. In 1968, the Beatles, by then world famous, created their own music company and gave it what seemed an iconoclastic name: the Apple Corps.

Fast-forward a decade to when two American geniuses—Steve Jobs and Steve Wozniak—are working in a garage inventing a personal computer. Jobs admired the Beatles' music and named his new company Apple Computer. Almost overnight, Apple succeeded, producing annual sales of almost $130 million by its fourth year. Still, the Beatles owned the "Apple" trademark. In the early 1980s, an agreement was reached: the Beatles would stay out of the computer business and Apple would stay out of the music business.

Fast-forward to the early 1990s. Apple Computer was very much into music. The surviving former members of the Beatles and John Lennon's heirs sued Apple Computer in England for $250 million for breach of the trademark agreement. Eventually, a settlement was reached in which Apple Computer paid the Beatles $26.4 million.

Fast-forward again to 2003. Apple Computer opens its iTunes Music Store and begins distributing songs online for a fee. Apple Corps, owned by

Sir Paul McCartney, Ringo Starr, Lennon's widow, and George Harrison's estate, sue to enforce their earlier agreements and for damages resulting from breach of contract.

This case is instructive. The offended party, the Beatles, did not seek their government's help but instead the services of their lawyers. They took private action. They could sue an American corporation in England with confidence that both legal systems were competent and honest. Also, the parties settled out of court twice. There was no trial. In political cultures where private legal rights are meaningful, parties can make reasonable estimates of their success in court and most often reach agreement without a trial.

Because American judges and jurors understand the concepts of patents, copyrights, trade secrets, and trademarks, private litigation is an effective defense against infringement in the United States and a handful of other countries, such as those of Europe. The problem faced by intellectual-property owners is that each nation establishes its own laws and the judicial processes by which such rights are defended. The differences between countries are vast. Equally significant, many of the developing nations, such as India, China, and Brazil, have large counterfeit and pirate industries and weak intellectual property protections. They serve as sanctuaries for government-defended intellectual property gangs. Two experiences illustrate just how vulnerable most U.S. companies are when attacked by state-sheltered criminals.

The first example concerns Milliken & Company, the largest private textile company in the United States. Founded in 1865, Milliken is a family-owned textile and specialty chemical business with sixty manufacturing locations throughout the United States, Asia, Europe, and South America. In 1989, the U.S. Department of Commerce awarded Milliken the Malcolm Baldrige National Quality Award. It has received similar awards in Europe. Milliken is one of the world's leaders in the production of patterned carpets, a highly specialized business. It employs forty full-time professional textile designers who create unique patterns; these are applied to carpets with proprietary technologies that produce ink-jet patterns of up to 400 dots per inch. Milliken holds copyrights on the patterns and patents on the processes.

For sales purposes, Milliken groups the various patterns into collections, puts the collections into catalogs, and then sells these goods to upscale hotels, designers, homes, and businesses throughout the world.

In 1999, Milliken's Beijing-based sales representative bid on a contract to supply carpet for the Beijing Radisson Hotel. After extensive consultation, the hotel selected the Milliken design. At the last minute, however, Haima, a Chinese corporation, offered to install the hotel's carpet, with a counterfeited Milliken design, for a lower price, and was awarded the contract. Subsequently, Haima was chosen to lay its carpet, with the Milliken designs, in five other Chinese hotels.

Haima's piracy and counterfeiting were not the result of some accident by a small company with unsophisticated management that is unaccustomed to the ways of global business. Haima is the largest woven-carpet manufacturer in Asia. In 1990s, it formed China's first carpet research institute. In 1997 and 1998, it built a computerized design and development center. Haima exports to the United States and Europe, and its literature and Web site even claim that its carpets are now used in the White House, Number 10 Downing Street, and Japan's Imperial Palace.

After losing the Beijing contract, Milliken personnel obtained a copy of Haima's 1999 carpet catalog. It featured sixteen copyrighted Milliken designs. The images Haima used were perfect duplicates of those in the Milliken catalogs.

In February 2001, Milliken lawyers filed a complaint with China's state copyright office, claiming infringement. The national office sent the complaint to the regional office, which, eight months later, issued a report and an injunction ordering Haima to stop distributing catalogs and producing carpet using Milliken designs. Then the regional office sent the file back to the national copyright office to review the regional office's ruling and injunction. The result is legal Kabuki, Chinese style.

Haima stopped nothing. In May 2002, the carpet maker distributed its new carpet design collection catalog at the Las Vegas Hospitality Design Expo. The new catalog contained thirty-two copyrighted Milliken designs— twice as many as the 1999 catalog.

The significance of all this, of course, is that in Las Vegas Haima was violating Milliken's copyrights in the United States. In October 2002, Milliken sued Haima in the U.S. Circuit Court of Appeals, seeking damages. Haima did not contest the lawsuit. In May 2003, the federal court awarded Milliken a default judgment of $4 million plus attorneys' fees and costs.

The Milliken example illustrates the power of a copyright in a nation where the laws are real and enforcement is possible. China's copyright laws are placebos that give the illusion of legal protection. Timothy Monahan,

Milliken's lawyer, said, "If that Haima carpet in the White House uses our copyrighted designs, we look forward to ripping it out." Milliken lawyers checked. The White House had no Haima carpet installed. Haima's advertising was as false as its designs.

Although Milliken has been able to keep the Haima counterfeits out of the U.S. market, the Chinese company sells its designs throughout Asia. And since Haima is not established in the United States, Milliken must collect its $4 million judgment from it in China, which it is unable to do. In dealing with infringements of American-owned intellectual properties in other nations, particularly Asian countries, U.S. protections end at the U.S. border.

Milliken's experience is not unique. Super Vision, a small company incorporated in 1989 and located in Orlando, Florida, is a world leader in the production of fiber-optic cables used for displays and signs. Among its dozens of completed projects are the Coca-Cola and AT&T signs on New York's Times Square, the 1,100-foot-tall spire at the Arts Centre in Melbourne, Australia, the Euro Disney Light Parade in Paris, and the Universal City-Walk in Orlando. Brett Kingstone, the company founder and CEO, has advanced the technology to the point that his fiber-optic cables are brighter than neon, almost equal in cost, and require only a third of the electricity. Unlike neon tubes, which usually break if dropped, Super Vision's cable can be run over by a tractor-trailer without damage. Not surprisingly, Kingstone is trying to replace neon with fiber optics as the lighting of choice for signs and displays. "Worldwide, neon sales were close to $30 billion last year," Kingstone says. "When people start understanding the huge commodity that neon is worldwide for signage and lighting, they'll realize what a huge opportunity fiber optics provides." Samson Mong Wu, a Hong Kong–based entrepreneur, fully understood that opportunity, stole the American company's technology, and became a fierce competitor.

Wu entered the picture in 1994 when his company, Optic-Tech International Corporation, became Super Vision's exclusive distributor in Asia, an arrangement that eventually collapsed because of Optic-Tech's low sales. What Kingstone did not know is that Wu and his family ran a major counterfeit operation out of Hong Kong.

After Kingstone took back Wu's distributor rights, Wu bribed a couple of Super Vision's key employees to steal the company's customer lists, vendor lists, chemical formulas, blueprints, and diagrams of the plastic fiber-optic cable-manufacturing process. Wu also had his agents take a key piece of manufacturing equipment, an optic bench that is used to align the light in the fiber-optic cable.

In 1998, Wu began to counterfeit Super Vision's product. By midyear, Super Vision's Asia sales had dropped by 50 percent. The company's European distributors were soon reporting that someone was selling the same product at half price there, including items Kingstone knew were being developed by the Florida-based company but had not yet been released. Also, Super Vision's inventory of fiber cables began to shrink, machinery disappeared, and unexplained glitches developed in its production operations. Kingstone knew he was under attack, but he did not know the source.

Then two of the American thieves fell out with each other. The loser gave Kingstone documentary evidence of a conspiracy that connected Wu with bribery, shell corporations used for money laundering, numerous bank transfers, and operations on four continents. Kingstone also caught two of Wu's hired thugs who were intimidating warehouse employees after work and stealing supplies. Kingstone, who is a martial arts expert, took the two into his office, locked the door, and emerged two hours later with two handwritten confessions—though some of his office furniture was destroyed in the process.

With evidence in hand, Kingstone went to the FBI for help. Soon federal agents were listening to the telephone calls of Super Vision's former R & D director, who was recorded bragging about the $1.4 million bribe Wu had paid him. Kingstone also learned that Wu had used stolen information to apply for a U.S. patent on one of Super Vision's innovations. In November 1999, Super Vision sued Wu, members of his family, his companies, and the former R & D director in Orlando's Circuit Court for the Ninth Judicial Circuit. Wu, who had established a Florida office and warehouse, immediately wired more than $28.5 million of his money out of the United States. He also filed for bankruptcy, which gave him time to ship his inventory of fiber-optic cable and the stolen equipment to Shanghai, where he continued to operate. Super Vision got an injunction ordering Wu to stop his foreign sales operations, which he ignored.

After the 9/11 terrorist attacks in 2001, the FBI agents assigned to the case were transferred to the war on terrorism, leaving Super Vision to its own devices against a criminal enterprise operating out of China. Kingstone says that he and the other corporate executives were so discouraged that they considered dropping the case. Instead, he hired a private investigator, who traveled to Shanghai in the guise of a investor from Dubai wanting to buy fiber-optic displays for a new shopping center. The investigator met with Super Vision's former R & D director, now living in China, and one of Wu's sons-in-law. Without their knowledge, the two men's sales pitch was secretly videotaped. The detective also got pictures of custom-built equipment stolen in Florida. Once the trial judge saw the tape, he sent the defendants to trial with liability stipulated—that is, the purpose of the trial was to determine how much they owed. The Chinese defendants exercised their Fifth Amendment right not to testify, which, their defense counsel wryly noted, "significantly limited defense options."

On September 22, 2002, a Florida jury awarded Super Vision $33.1 million in compensatory and punitive damages, plus another $8.1 for civil theft— $42.1 million altogether. By then, however, all the Wu assets were outside the United States. The trial judge also ordered that Wu, his companies, and his employees assign Super Vision the patent they had obtained with the stolen information. Though the U.S. company now holds that patent, it has been unable to collect one penny of its civil judgment.

With a court verdict in hand, Kingstone went to the U.S. attorney in Florida with a request that the defendants be indicted for criminal acts. He was rebuffed with the excuse that the office had insufficient resources to take the case. Kingstone then asked a senior Commerce Department official to encourage the Justice Department to examine the Florida court documents and bring a criminal case. He got sympathy but no action. On February 25, 2004, Congressman Ric Keller (R.-Fla.), a member of the House Judiciary Committee, wrote the undersecretary of commerce for international trade and the attorney general of the United States, asking that they review the case and take action. As of September 2004, neither agency had acted on that request. Wu continues to operate out of China, selling fiber-optic displays throughout Asia. Reflecting on the case, Brett Kingstone asks three questions:

- Why does our government allow foreign interests to steal our technology with relative impunity?

- Why, when the few companies that have the resources try to challenge these actions, do our laws offer more protection for the criminals than for the victims?

- Why does the United States allow these overseas predators to ignore U.S. civil convictions and jury verdicts and continue plundering our national interests?

Super Vision's experience reflects a contemporary reality: America's inventors and those who own copyrights, trademarks, and trade secrets have ample protections inside the United States through the federal courts. But they largely stand alone when foreign criminals, operating overseas— particularly in the developing nations—steal their intellectual property. And this situation exists despite the fact that the U.S. government has the full legal authority to help stop such foreign theft of its citizens' intellectual properties.

Overall, the "American system" of enforcement—relying on private actions initiated and financed by IP owners—worked well until the later decades of the twentieth century. It still works well when the offenders operate inside the United States. But globalization of the world's economy provides pirates and counterfeiters with foreign sanctuaries, allowing other governments and their corporations to steal vital U.S. intellectual property with ease and impunity.

In 1996, the director of the FBI reported that twenty-three nations were actively engaged in economic espionage activities against the United States. The *Special 301* annual reports issued by the Office of the United States Trade Representative identify several dozen others engaged in similar activities outside the United States. Consequently, Congress in 1996 gave the FBI greater authority to fight such crime.

In the mid-1990s, the U.S. also successfully led global negotiations that put stiff intellectual property provisions into the trade pacts administered by the World Trade Organization (WTO), which is discussed in the next chapter. The WTO agreement, called the Trade Related Intellectual Property System (TRIPS), obligates all 147 WTO member governments to enact strong intellectual property laws, operate effective judicial procedures, and crack down on pirates and counterfeiters in their countries.

To bring cohesion to federal efforts, the U.S. Congress in 1999 enacted legislation that established the National Intellectual Property Law Enforcement Coordination Council, to which it assigned the job of "coordinating the U.S.'s domestic and international intellectual property enforcement activities." The council consists of six federal agencies, with the Copyright Office as an adviser. The six are:

- the Office of the United States Trade Representative

- the Department of Commerce

- the Department of Homeland Security

- the Department of Justice

- the Department of State

- the Patent and Trademark Office

The council is co-chaired by representatives from the Justice Department and the Patent and Trademark Office. Each year, the six agencies submit to the president and Congress a report of the actions each has taken to enforce U.S. intellectual property laws. The picture of their work that emerges from these reports is one similar to the nation's counterterrorism efforts before the 9/11 terrorist attacks: officials are aware of the problem, limited resources are devoted to it, and there is little coordination among the responsible agencies. Consider the following: the Office of the USTR, which has only 202 staff members, has six people devoted to intellectual property matters. One is a litigation expert assigned to Geneva to focus on China. The others are involved with the intellectual property provisions of various trade agreements under negotiation and the preparation of the annual *Special 301 Report* about other nations' intellectual property practices. This office is also responsible for initiating cases at the WTO against other nations for violations of trade-related intellectual property agreements. Since June 2000, the USTR has not filed a single intellectual property case at the WTO.

The Commerce Department monitors the actions of other nations and assists the USTR to prepare the *Special 301 Report.* It also conducts training programs on intellectual property matters, advises U.S. companies on IP-related issues in other nations, and consults with other governments to help solve the problems confronted by U.S. businesses, such as Super Vision.

The State Department's enforcement role is limited to monitoring trade agreements and putting pressure on foreign governments to fulfill their treaty obligations. It also provides training in intellectual property issues for foreign law enforcement officials.

The Patent and Trademark Office provides policy advice to the executive branch, assists the USTR in negotiating the intellectual property provisions of trade agreements, and helps the USTR prepare its annual *Special 301 Report.* It also supplements the efforts of the State Department and the USTR in training foreign officials in intellectual property matters. It does not enforce U.S. agreements.

The U.S. Copyright Office provides expert guidance to other agencies that are negotiating intellectual property agreements, assistance to other governments in developing their copyright laws, and training services for both domestic and foreign officials who administer and enforce copyright laws. It does not enforce U.S. agreements either.

The Department of Homeland Security operates the Customs Service, which both excludes infringing products identified by the International Trade Commission and seizes counterfeit goods. Out of more than $671 billion of imported goods that came into the United States in the first half of FY2004, Customs seized counterfeit goods with a total value of only $64 million. Clearly, that agency's focus and resources are devoted to other priorities.

The Department of Justice investigates and prosecutes criminal cases involving "the piracy of copyrighted works, trademark counterfeiting and theft of trade secrets." In 2001, Justice strengthened the ability of the U.S. attorney's offices to enforce federal IP laws by putting specialized prosecutors and support staff in ten U.S. attorney's offices around the nation. Their primary focus is on prosecuting high-tech crimes, including intellectual property piracy and counterfeiting. These teams are called CHIP (computer hacking and intellectual property) units.

Justice also has a team of thirty-five lawyers in its Criminal Division's Computer Crime and Intellectual Property Section, which deals exclusively with computer and intellectual property crimes. They supplement the work of the ninety-four U.S. attorney's offices. The Justice Department has several ongoing investigations at any given time, and each year it secures a few high-profile convictions, largely related to piracy of software, music CDs, and movies, or to Internet crimes. The victims or their trade associations bring many of these crimes to the government. Since 9/11, almost all of the agents assigned to the FBI's economic espionage section have been reassigned to the war on terrorism.

The caseloads, conviction, and imprisonment records of the Justice Department for intellectual property crimes reveal in startling detail the lack of national attention and resources devoted to IP theft. In fiscal year 2004, the U.S. government filed only ten cases against persons knowingly trafficking in counterfeit CDs and movies. It filed fifty-four cases for criminal infringement of copyrights, one case for trafficking in recordings or videos of live musical performances, and forty-six cases for trafficking in counterfeit goods or services. The total for the year was 101 cases. Of the 107 cases that reached a conclusion, 122 defendants either pleaded guilty or were found guilty by a jury. Only sixty people were sent to prison. Of those sent to prison, forty received sentences of one to twenty-four months. Only four were sentenced to more than five years.

In FY2004, the U.S. filed no IP cases at the WTO for the fourth straight year, captured $60 million in counterfeit goods at the border, filed 101 federal cases against pirates and counterfeiters, and sent sixty defendants to prison, most for a short term (see table on page 219).

These efforts are so limited that they hardly qualify as token measures. Though the federal government estimates that piracy, counterfeiting, and intellectual property theft cost the U.S. $200 billion or more annually, it leaves American inventors, artists, publishers, authors, and other intellectual property owners defenseless against domestic thieves and especially against well-organized predators operating from within national sanctuaries such as China, Taiwan, and India.

The fact that the federal government is doing so little is not a reflection on agency administrators, prosecutors, or civil servants. Rather, a succession of presidents and congressional leaders from both parties has failed to appreciate the nature of this global crime wave or to understand how the resulting losses are undermining U.S. invention and innovation. Nor do they seem to realize how ineffective the old defenses—private action and import exclusion—are outside the United States, particularly with those nations that have no functioning judiciary system or that refuse to honor their treaty obligations to create one. While our public leaders have enacted laws that created powerful, and sufficient, legal tools to deal with this crime wave, they have failed to provide the commensurate resources, leadership, and oversight.

On November 24, 2004, the day before Thanksgiving, Congress enacted the Consolidated Appropriations Act, 2005. Tucked away in that 3,600-page piece of legislation was a little noticed provision that creates what the media calls an "Intellectual Property Czar," which is shorthand for the official title: Coordinator for International Intellectual Property Enforcement, The National Intellectual Property Law Enforcement Coordination Council. Congress gave this "czar," who will be appointed by the President, and the Council a mandate to develop a strategy for protecting American intellectual property overseas and to coordinate and oversee implementation of that strategy by the various federal agencies. Even as Congress took this first

INTELLECTUAL PROPERTY REPORT
UNITED STATES DEPARTMENT OF JUSTICE
FY 2001–2004
(All Districts—All Statutes)

	FY 01	FY 02	FY 03	FY 04
REFERRALS AND CASES:				
Number of Investigative Matters Received:	191	169	229	269
Number of Defendants:	283	289	333	334
Number of Cases Filed:	84	78	100	101
Number of Defendants:	121	149	165	141
Number of Cases Resolved/Terminated:	81	82	65	107
Number of Defendants:	106	135	119	137
DISPOSITION OF DEFENDANTS IN CONCLUDED CASES:				
Number of Defendants Who Pleaded Guilty:	83	103	87	114
Number of Defendants Who Were Tried and Found Guilty:	3	3	5	8
Number of Defendants Against Whom Charges Were Dismissed:	17	26	22	8
Number of Defendants Acquitted:	0	0	3	1
Other Terminated Defendants:	3	3	2	6
PRISON SENTENCING FOR CONVICTED DEFENDANTS (# represents defendants):				
No Imprisonment:	46	58	50	62
1 to 12 Months Imprisonment:	23	25	18	26
13 to 24 Months:	8	14	13	14
25 to 36 Months:	3	5	1	9
37 to 60 Months:	2	4	9	7
61 + Months:	4	0	1	4

Source: *FY 2004 Performance and Accountability Report,* "Intellectual Property," United States Department of Justice, Washington, D.C., Appendix C, January 2005, p. c-4.

Title 18, United States Code:
• Section 2318—Offense: Knowingly trafficking in a counterfeit label affixed or designated to be affixed to a phono record or a copy of a motion picture or audiovisual work.
• Section 2319—Offense: Willful infringement of a copyright for purposes of commercial advantage or private financial gain, or through large-scale, unlawful reproduction or distribution of a protected work regardless of where there was a profit motive. Online Infringement: where the infringer advertised or publicized the infringing work on the Internet or made the work available on the Internet for download, reproduction, performance or distribution by other persons.
• Section 2319A—Offense: Without the consent of the performer, knowingly and for the purposes of commercial advantage or private financial gain, fixing the sounds or sound and images of a live musical performance, reproducing copies of such a performance from an authorized fixation; transmitting the sounds or sounds and images to the public, or distributing, renting, selling, or trafficking (or attempting the preceding) in any copy or an authorized fixation.
• Section 2320—Offense: Intentionally trafficking or attempting to traffic in goods or services and knowingly using a counterfeit mark on or in connection with such goods and services.

step to create a coherent U.S. IP protection strategy, they effectively undercut the effort by providing only $2 million of funding to deal with a crime that costs the U.S. more than $200 billion annually. The same piece of legislation provided the FBI with $5 million to counter economic espionage in the U.S., which is also inadequate. At best, these two gestures say that the Bush administration and Congress recognize the problem of IP theft, but they are not yet prepared to deal with it seriously.

CHAPTER 8

A GLOBAL SOLUTION

Thirty-five years ago, American companies technologically dominated their competitors everywhere. In 1968, the French author Jean-Jacques Servan-Schreiber captured the fear such power created among nations in his best-selling book *The American Challenge*. He saw a national economic colossus so aggressively competitive and so technologically advanced that by the 1980s its corporations in Europe would be the third most powerful industrial force on Earth. He foresaw a nation so economically far-ranging that it would hold a monopoly of power, dominating the world in every basic area: culture, politics, technology, the military, and economics. He thought that only a few nations could stave off U.S. domination and only in a few niche industries.

But even as Servan-Schreiber was writing his book, America's power was weakening. Other nations had absolutely no intention of tolerating U.S. dominance. The key to resistance was their own national development. Even in 1968, foreign corporations and their governments were actively stealing the U.S. technologies they needed for their domestic growth. That thievery became so rampant in the 1970s and early 1980s that it threatened the very future of many American industries.

Consequently, the gamble U.S. corporations took whenever they invested to develop a new medicine, computer processor, or some other advanced technology was whether they could get back their money, plus a competitive profit, before pirated versions took over the global market. Corporations were in an economic race with pirates, many of which were operating with at least the tacit approval and protection of their home governments.

The International Trade Commission (ITC) reports that by 1986, piracy cost U.S. IP owners between $43 billion and $61 billion annually. The principal technologies the thieves targeted were those with the greatest promise of creating more and better U.S. jobs: pharmaceuticals, chemicals, computer software, semiconductors, motion pictures, sound recordings, and books, among dozens of others.

Developing nations had few, if any, legal obligations to protect foreigners' IP rights. Argentina, Brazil, Chile, Egypt, India, Indonesia, Mexico, China, Saudi Arabia, Thailand, and Turkey, for instance, did not grant patents on pharmaceuticals. Brazil, Egypt, India, Indonesia, and Saudi Arabia provided no patent protections for chemical products.

The United States had no legal means of stopping such thievery outside its borders. Domestically, the U. S. could ban the import of goods that violated an American patent, copyright, trademark, or trade secret. Internationally, however, the U.S. government lacked the authority to take retaliatory actions against nations that harbored pirate operations. The issue was so insignificant to U.S. policy makers that no federal agency even monitored foreign IP violations until 1988.

And while there were international organizations devoted to intellectual property matters, such as the World Intellectual Property Organization (WIPO), they were powerless. Their function was to provide a forum for negotiating IP treaties among nations, not to enforce agreements.

If the problems of pirating and counterfeiting were to be addressed, the victims had to put the issue on the public agenda. The obstacles they faced were formidable. The most significant is that no forum for action existed. WIPO was a United Nations organization that operated on a one-nation, one-vote basis. Ultimately, the developing countries controlled the organization, and their objective was to gain the free use of the developed world's intellectual properties, not protect the rights of their owners.

Also, U.S. policy makers did not understand the issue. For almost two centuries, intellectual property matters had been relegated to the policy sidelines. In the 1970s and 1980s, the combined membership of the U.S. House and Senate included perhaps five or ten individuals who could be considered experts in intellectual property matters.

Any new arrangement would require acceptance by the developing nations, many of which were profiting from pirating and counterfeiting. Some significant incentives would be required if these countries were to place themselves voluntarily under some new form of global regulation. Finally, any new global arrangement would require the concurrence of Japan and the advanced technological nations of Europe, many of whose companies were also being victimized.

Before a new global intellectual property regime could be established, all of these obstacles had to be overcome. But who could provide the vision and leadership for such an effort? In the late 1970s and early 1980s, Congress knew too little, and the president faced other, more pressing problems. Action required that U.S. industry could develop a vision, embody it in a concrete proposal, convince governments around the world to accept it, and then push its solution through Congress. Such a course, moreover, would require a level of organization that would take a lot of effort and money over a long period of time.

In the late 1970s, two corporate leaders stepped forth to provide leadership and resources: John Opel of IBM and Edmund T. Pratt Jr. of Pfizer. These two men were the driving force behind the creation of a new global regime, TRIPS—the Trade Related Intellectual Property System. What they did is a little-known but extraordinary story.

Opel was the perfect "IBM man"—white shirt, dark tie, dark suit, close-cut hair, no beard, no mustache, shined lace-up black shoes, with an MBA from the University of Chicago. Opel began in 1949 as a sales representative in Jefferson City, Missouri, and ended in 1993 as the chairman of the IBM board's executive committee; advancing IBM's interests was Opel's career.

Pratt was part of the "Greatest Generation" that Tom Brokaw described in his book of the same title. Born in 1927, he served in the navy in the last days of World War II. After the war, he quickly earned a BS degree in electrical engineering from Duke University and then an MBA from Wharton. As had Opel, Pratt joined IBM immediately after graduation. Taking military leave to serve in the navy during the Korean War, Pratt returned to IBM and eventually became the comptroller of its World Trade Corporation, a position he held from 1958 to 1962. Then he joined the Kennedy administration as assistant secretary of the army for financial management. In 1964, Pratt became Pfizer's comtroller. Eventually, he was appointed chairman and chief executive officer, a job he held for twenty years. During those two decades, Pratt tripled the portion of Pfizer's corporate revenues devoted to research, while increasing corporate revenues by more than 700 percent, leading a company that *Fortune* magazine twice selected as the most admired in the

United States. In 1999, he donated $35 million to Duke University to support its engineering school.

Opel and Pratt were among the few corporate CEOs of that era who understood that the world's economy was shifting to a new knowledge-based foundation. While most of IBM's revenues came from selling and leasing advanced computers, much derived from royalty payments and licenses on its technology. IBM wanted minimal patent protections and for the Berne convention to recognize copyrighted software. Pfizer, then a 130-year-old company, was rapidly taking a leading role in global pharmaceutical research. In Brazil, Argentina, and India, among dozens of other nations, however, its U.S. patents were not honored, allowing local companies to pirate virtually all of Pfizer's products. Opel and Pratt understood that to succeed in the future global marketplace, U.S. companies had to have worldwide protections for their prime assets: the ideas and technology embodied in their patents, copyrights, trademarks, and trade secrets.

In a speech before a Washington, D.C., business group, Pratt quoted political philosopher Michael Novak on the role that intellectual properties exert on development:

> What is distinctive about the capitalist economy is the original dis-covery that the primary cause of economic development is the mind. The cause of wealth is invention, detection, enterprise.

When Opel and Pratt first began to work on international trade and property rights issues in the late 1970s, they encountered a federal establish-ment consumed with such matters as hostages in Iran and negotiations between the executive and congressional branches over legislation needed to ratify the Tokyo Round trade agreement. Virtually no official was con-cerned about foreign violations of U.S. intellectual property rights.

While Opel and Pratt found indifference in Washington, they experi-enced outright hostility in Geneva at the World Intellectual Property Organization (WIPO), then the principal global organization dealing with patent and copyright issues. In the 1970s and 1980s, WIPO was a battle-ground between the industrially developed north and the developing south. The industrial nations wanted protections for their intellectual goods; the developing countries hoped for easy, no-cost access to the technology of companies such as IBM and Pfizer. Because WIPO operated on a one-nation, one-vote basis, developing countries dominated the organization's agenda. The developed nations had the technology and no incentive to share. Stalemate was the result.

Even more incapacitating, the developing nations refused to even discuss giving WIPO or any other global body the power to impose intellectual property rules on nations or enforce agreements. Consequently, WIPO was reduced to a debating society located close to a lovely lake, good hotels, and superior restaurants.

Gradually, Opel and Pratt concluded that they needed another forum. They decided to try something never before accomplished: to persuade the governments of the world to include intellectual property issues in the multilateral global trade talks that were ongoing under the auspices of the General Agreement on Tariffs and Trade (GATT). Most nations supported trade negotiations, and if intellectual property were considered as trade, then many possibilities for action would exist.

The two CEOs wanted all the other nations to adopt the U.S. system of IP protections—the toughest system in the world. Had the two men not been two of America's most distinguished and powerful business leaders, they would have been ignored as delusional. Viewed from the outside, the real power and influence of large corporations, such as IBM and Pfizer, are largely concealed but substantial. In the late 1970s and early 1980s, Opel and Pratt also enjoyed a advantage in Washington, D.C.: both were members of an exclusive committee that advises the president of the United States on trade matters—the Advisory Committee on Trade Policy and Negotiations, generally known as ACTPN. By statute, membership on this committee is limited to forty-five people. ACTPN members have top-secret intelligence clearances and personal access to the United States Trade Representative. Most important, they usually have access to the president.

Pratt was appointed to ACTPN by President Carter and was promoted to chairman by President Reagan. In the early 1980s, Pratt created an eight-person intellectual property subcommittee and arranged for Opel to become its chairman.

Beginning in the early 1980s, Pfizer and IBM inundated Washington with accounts of pirated goods and the resulting costs to U.S. companies and workers. They commissioned studies. They engaged allied business groups. They organized congressional hearings, and they courted the media. Pfizer and IBM were particularly effective because they brought their various networks to bear. For example, Pfizer's general counsel, Lou Clemente, chaired the Intellectual Property Committee of the Council for International Business. Dr. Gerald Laubach, Pfizer's president, was a board member of the Pharmaceutical Manufacturers Association, which strongly supported Pratt's efforts.

Laubach was also a member of the Business–Higher Education Forum, a little-known group of forty corporate leaders and forty university presidents. Forum members formed task forces that studied business-education issues, met twice annually for three-day discussions, and then issued reports. Among the members were the presidents of Harvard, Stanford, MIT, and the University of Chicago. The CEOs included those of Ford, TRW, Rockwell International, Motorola, and AT&T.

In the spring of 1983, the forum issued a report, *America's Competitiveness Challenge.* The CEOs and academics then met with congressional leaders and President Reagan, to whom they recommended the creation of a group to study and make recommendations on U.S. competitiveness. Soon after that meeting, Reagan appointed the Commission on Industrial Competitiveness. John A. Young, CEO of Hewlett-Packard, was appointed its chair. In 1984, that commission issued its final report, which included several recommendations on reforming global intellectual property protections.

Even as the Young commission was completing its work in 1984, the eight major U.S. copyright-based trade associations banded together and created the International Intellectual Property Alliance (IIPA). Its mission was to get the U.S. government to apply direct pressure to individual nations that tolerated copyright theft from their members. While Opel and Pratt were working on a multilateral approach, IIPA urged Washington to take unilateral actions against nations that refused to provide IP protections. Consequently, Congress amended trade law to make violators of IP rights eligible for U.S. trade retaliation. With that, Congress gave the Reagan administration a license to hunt down global IP pirates and a powerful weapon with which to punish uncooperative countries.

To demonstrate the United States' seriousness, Washington opened highly visible bilateral negotiations with South Korea in late 1985. The objective was made clear: either South Korea stopped its pirating practices or the United States would halt imports of that country's footwear, tires, and electronics. The list of grievances was long. South Korea, for instance, protected only those pharmaceutical trademarks that were licensed to Korean firms under joint ventures. Korean patents on chemicals and medicines applied only to the production process, not to the product itself. Thus, by using different processes, Korean companies were manufacturing U.S.–invented medicines and paying no royalties to the real owners. Korean publishers were printing books without permission, paying no royalties to U.S. authors and publishers. And Korean pirates were duplicating movies, music, and art without any regard for copyrights.

Initially, the Koreans argued that they were far too underdeveloped and small a market to harm U.S. intellectual-property owners, but the U.S. negotiators rejected that defense. Then the Koreans stalled—while continuing to tolerate piracy. Their parliament enacted laws that appeared to address the issues but did not. By 1988, U.S. officials had grown impatient. They announced that the United States was making a five-month study of what had been done. If there were no improvements, America would ban imports of many Korean products.

When faced with a real threat, the Koreans corrected the problem. The Seoul government assigned police and legal staffs to catch, fine, and imprison pirates. It enforced anticounterfeit legislation, and it educated its people about intellectual property. Soon the pirating of books and videos dropped dramatically and abuses of U.S. IP rights began to disappear. The demonstration of resolve worked. Many nations came to understand that they must either address IP issues seriously or they, too, would soon be in the same type of one-on-one negotiations with the United States. Nonetheless, many countries, such as India, Thailand, and Argentina, continued their old ways. A showdown was inevitable.

By 1985, Congress, the Reagan administration, and Washington's policy-making community were ready to place intellectual property on the U.S. trade negotiating agenda. Before the United States could take such an unorthodox step, particularly given the position of developing nations, American trade negotiators needed a smart legal and political strategy on how to deal with other nations, plus strong corporate support. In 1984, Opel commissioned IBM consultant Jacques Gorlin, an economist with a PhD in economics from Johns Hopkins University, to prepare a white paper on the next steps, including a legal justification for including intellectual property issues in a global trade treaty.

In March 1986, Pratt and Opel announced the formation of the Intellectual Property Committee (IPC). The founding members were IBM, Pfizer, Merck, Johnson & Johnson, Bristol-Myers, Hewlett-Packard, General Motors, General Electric, DuPont, Monsanto, and CBS. Later, FMC, Warner, and Rockwell International joined. Before 1983, Gorlin had been an aide in the U.S. Senate, the Treasury Department, the State Department, and the U.S. Agency for International Development. Having worked with Opel and IBM, he knew the issues, their evolution, and their political implications intimately. Gorlin's ideas, insights, contacts, and skills have greatly shaped

IPC's work and its success for nearly two decades. IPC commissioned Gorlin to prepare a draft of the provisions that the United States should advocate for inclusion in any new global agreement.

While the trade talks provided a vehicle for creating a new global system of IP protections, a unifying theme was also needed. The idea, the logic, and the explanation were self-contained in three words, "intellectual property rights." As Peter Drahos and John Braithwaite, two Australian scholars, note: "Property is a key institution, perhaps the key institution, of social and political morality. Western traditions of constitutionalism and the natural rights of persons have been deeply influenced by the desires and instincts of groups and individuals to protect their property rights." To the extent that ownership of patents, copyrights, trademarks, and trade secrets is viewed as being in that tradition, a powerful case exists for equally powerful protections of these properties.

By itself, the United States could not get intellectual property rights onto the agenda of the forthcoming global trade negotiations. U.S. trade officials needed European and Japanese support. IBM, Pfizer, and the other IPC members, of course, had substantial business interests in both Europe and Japan. In addition, they were well acquainted with many of their counterparts at foreign companies. Soon Gorlin was traveling regularly to Europe and Tokyo to meet with various business groups to work out IPC's strategy. They had six months to get European and Japanese support and then put together an agenda the governments that supported the IPC could present at the forthcoming September 1986 GATT meeting in Uruguay, where decisions about the global round of trade negotiations would be made.

First the IPC sought European support, which was quickly obtained. Then Japanese backing was secured. Despite their differences on many other issues, U.S., European, and Japanese corporations found themselves agreeing on the need for strong global intellectual property protections. All believed that pirates from developing countries were victimizing them.

In these business-to-business negotiations, the IPC represented its thirteen corporate members. UNICE, the Union of Industrial and Employers' Confederations of Europe, was the official voice of businesses and industries from twenty-two European nations. The Keidanren, whose membership includes all major Japanese companies and industry associations, represented Japanese business. This corporate trio—IPC, UNICE, and the Keidanren—decided on a three-step process. First, they would agree among themselves what provisions they wanted in a new global IP regime. Second, each participant would help persuade its government to adopt the unified corporate agenda. Finally, the U.S., Japanese, and European governments would put the IP issue on the GATT negotiating agenda and eventually use any new global trade agreement as the vehicle to impose these new rules on all trading nations.

On September 20, 1986, at the GATT Ministerial Declaration in Punta del Este, Uruguay, the ministers announced the beginning of negotiations to develop a new multilateral framework of principles, rules, and applications for intellectual property. In the end, the ministers gave the trade negotiators a virtual blank check to create a new structure and extend the rules to include all countries.

U.S. negotiators then turned their attention to other aspects of those trade talks, allowing the U.S., Japanese, and European corporations to find agreement on new intellectual property rules. Pratt played a particularly important role. By then, he was chairman of the Business Roundtable, composed of almost two hundred CEOs from America's top corporations. Thus, the influence of the IPC went far beyond its thirteen member companies. In effect, it was representing the much larger business community, much as the Keidanren was for Japanese business and UNICE was for that of Europe.

With this declaration, the strongest, richest, most powerful corporations in Europe, Japan, and the United States set about negotiating a global agreement on intellectual property. The Gorlin paper was the starting point. European corporations were facing the same piracy problems as those of the United States. Consequently, John Beton, chair of the UNICE Working Group, rewrote almost half the Gorlin paper. Working in private and meeting in Europe, Tokyo, and the United States, the businesspeople concluded an agreement within eighteen months. Throughout the negotiations, the IPC was adamant that the system must have strong protections similar to those found in the United States.

In June 1988, the three groups jointly released their ninety-eight-page report, *Basic Framework of GATT Provisions on Intellectual Property*. The USTR immediately distributed a hundred copies throughout the executive branch and to Congress. The IPC and the USTR briefed key members and staff at the House and Senate Judiciary Committees, which are responsible for intellectual property legislation. They also briefed the House Ways and Means Committee and the Senate Finance Committee, which are responsible for trade law.

The U.S., Japanese, and European governments adopted the corporate IP agenda in its entirety. They agreed to establish through the forthcoming global trade agreement a new worldwide intellectual property regime that would incorporate preexisting conventions, including the following:

1. Paris Convention for the Protection of Industrial Property (1967)

2. Berne Convention for the Protection of Literary and Artistic Works (1971)

3. International Convention for the Protection of Performers, Producers of Phonograms, and Broadcasting Organizations

4. Rome Convention (1961) for the Protection of Performers, Producers of Phonograms, and Broadcasting Organizations

5. Washington Treaty on Intellectual Property in Respect of Integrated Circuits (1989)

Beyond defining goals and calling for a major new global intellectual property regime, the *Basic Framework* report presents the precise language that was used in the final text of the treaty. Peter Drahos and John Braithwaite interviewed dozens of people involved with the creation of TRIPS. They write: "Fewer than 50 individuals had managed to globalize a set of regulatory norms for the conduct of all those doing business or aspiring to do business in the information age." It was an extraordinary coup by an elite group of corporate leaders. They imposed U.S. IP standards on the world.

Predictably, the *Basic Framework* quickly came under intense censure. The leading critics came from Argentina, Brazil, Cuba, Egypt, India, Nicaragua, Nigeria, Peru, Tanzania, and Yugoslavia. Presaging the long fight that was to come, India wanted to exclude pharmaceutical products, food, and chemicals from patent protection altogether, shorten the term of such protections, and permit mandatory licensing of patents under preferential terms set by national governments.

To break the political will of those critic nations, the Reagan and Bush administrations unilaterally imposed sanctions for continuing violations of U.S. patents, copyrights, trademarks, and other IP protections. India, Thailand, South Korea, Mexico, Brazil, and others quickly came to understand that opposition to TRIPS carried a stiff price.

Simultaneously, a reward was offered for those who cooperated. By shifting negotiations on intellectual property from WIPO, which could offer

no incentives, to GATT, which could, deals could be arranged. Trade diplomats call the technique "linkage-bargain" negotiations. Others call it simply
"quid pro quo." Regardless of the name, the United States, the European participants, and Japan agreed that if their IP agenda were adopted, they would
eliminate all their quotas on textile and apparel imports.

Lest the significance of the U.S. offer be overlooked, textiles and apparel
was then America's largest manufacturing sector. Nonetheless, U.S. trade
negotiators offered up the entire industry and all of its jobs, if the developing nations would adopt U.S.–style intellectual property laws. More than
1.6 million U.S. jobs and thousands of companies would be traded away to
get TRIPS. It was an extraordinary proposal.

Textile and apparel trade has traditionally been one of the hardest-fought
issues in global negotiations. Developing nations usually have an abundant
supply of cheap labor that can be trained to produce apparel. Once clothing manufacture commences, the textile mills often migrate to where the
apparel makers are located. And where the textile mills are, the supplier
industries are also found—machinery, chemicals, fiber, specialized packaging, finance, and transport. It is an industrial package. Since developing
nations often generate much of their foreign currency through the export
of apparel, opening the U.S., European, and Japanese markets to them was a
very, very big incentive to adopt TRIPS.

Despite these sticks and carrots, the GATT trade talks faltered in 2000,
not because of TRIPS or the developing nations' opposition but because the
United States, Japan, and Europe could not concur on new terms for agricultural trade. However, the parties had agreed that they would agree on all
issues or on no issues. Failing to come to agreement on agricultural trade,
the major trading nations in December 1990 put the GATT talks into hiber-
nation, where they remained for another two years.

With the GATT talks closed, the U.S. trade negotiators turned their
attention to Mexico and Canada. The idea was simple: if the United States
couldn't realize a global trade arrangement, it would create its own regional
trading bloc, composed initially of Canada and Mexico and then including
the rest of Latin America. Thus, the North American Free Trade Agreement
(NAFTA) was negotiated.

As part of that proposed agreement, Pratt and the IPC persuaded President George H. W. Bush to include their basic framework for intellectual
property. Under U.S. pressure, Mexico and Canada agreed. After a bitter
political fight, Congress ratified NAFTA in 1993. The United States realized

two victories. First, Mexico and Canada adopted the strict U.S. system of IP protections. Second, NAFTA created a precedent that would be applied in all subsequent bilateral or regional trade deals. Henceforth, IP rights would also be trade rights.

Once Congress ratified NAFTA in November 1993, the Clinton administration used that political momentum to conclude the renewed GATT negotiations in Geneva less than six weeks later. The IPC, UNICE, and Keidanren recommendations were adopted virtually in their entirety. Gorlin claims that they got 95 percent of all they desired. The other 5 percent was the provision on the timing for the implementation. Developed nations had one year to adopt their TRIPS obligations, developing nations were given five years, and the least developed countries got eleven years. Thus, TRIPS came fully into force on January 1, 2005, for WTO member nations. WTO members have had plenty of time to meet their TRIPS obligations, though most have not.

The 1994 TRIPS agreement is the most significant intellectual property accord of the twentieth century. It covers four broad areas. First, TRIPS defines the basic principles of how international intellectual property agreements will be applied. The main principle is national treatment—that is, governments will deal with foreigners and their own citizens equally. A corollary is called "most-favored nation"—that is, all WTO members will be treated equally. If the U.S. gives a trade concession to Mexico, it must also be willing to grant the same concession to Chile, Brazil, and all other member nations. This mandate prohibits discrimination.

Second, TRIPS ensures that adequate standards of protection are provided by all participating nations. To this end, TRIPS strengthened the provisions of the principal international agreements that existed before it was created, including the Paris Convention for the Protection of Industrial Property, which includes patents and industrial designs—setting new and higher standards. For copyrights, TRIPS included computer programs and databases. It expanded international copyright rules to include rental rights, thus taking pirates on directly. TRIPS also gave performers the right to prevent the unauthorized recording and use of their live performances for fifty years. With that, the WTO took on bootleggers.

TRIPS gave international protection for trademarks, defining what is eligible and the minimum rights nations must provide. When place-derived names, such as "tequila," "scotch," and "champagne," are used to identify a product, TRIPS provides special protections for those products as well.

Industrial designs are protected by TRIPS for a minimum of ten years and patents for at least twenty years. Nations must provide patents for both products and production processes, though they may exclude diagnostic and therapeutic techniques, surgical methods, plants, animals, and biological processes for the production of plants or animals. Plant varieties, however, have TRIPS patent protections. A process patent extends to the product directly created by the process. The TRIPS agreement allows governments to issue a patent holder's competitor a compulsory license for a patented product or process, but only under strict and defined conditions. Governments are also permitted to intercede if patent holders enter noncompetition licenses but are required to consult with other governments when considering such a step. Integrated circuit layout designs are protected for a minimum of ten years under TRIPS. Governments are required to take all necessary steps to protect undisclosed information and trade secrets of commercial value. Most important, part 2 of TRIPS defines minimal standards. If any party to TRIPS wants higher standards and longer terms of protection for the intellectual properties, it can have them.

The third part of TRIPS is enforcement. The pact requires all signatory governments to enact laws that ensure the enforcement of this arrangement and to provide penalties that are sufficient to deter future violations. TRIPS enforcement requirements are defined in detail, including rules for getting evidence, provisional measures, injunctions, damages, and other penalties. Under TRIPS, governments must provide courts that can review administrative decisions and order the disposal of counterfeit goods. Governments are also required to make willful trademark counterfeiting and copyright piracy criminal offenses, punishable with jail sentences, and to prevent the import of counterfeit and pirated goods.

The fourth part of TRIPS is its dispute settlement procedures. If any nation thinks that any other nation is violating TRIPS provisions, it can take its case to the WTO, where a three-person panel will hear the complaint. The loser in that situation can file an appeal at the WTO and be heard by a new appeal panel. Its decision is final. If a defendant nation loses the case, it must change its laws and practices or pay damages to the plaintiff nation. Those damages may be paid in cash, or the winning plaintiff may impose tariffs on a list of the defendant's imports sufficient to collect an amount set by the TRIPS dispute panel. Unlike WIPO, WTO can impose costly penalties on nations that fail to uphold their IP agreements.

The WTO dispute settlement procedure is a powerful tool, though it is highly undemocratic and secretive. If the U.S. believes, for instance, that China is not fulfilling its TRIPS obligations to provide protections against piracy in China, it can take a case to the WTO. And if the U.S. can prove that this piracy is costing its authors, artists, inventors, and other IP owners $2 billion per year, it can ask for annual compensation so long as the theft and institutional unresponsiveness continue. Moreover, the U.S. does not need China's permission or help to collect the money. Under the WTO, the U.S. can impose a small tariff on every good imported from China and then distribute those funds to U.S. victims. Or it can levy large tariffs on a few Chinese imports. All that is required is political will and lawyers who can prove that the victims' claim is justified.

A decade has passed since the world's trading nations created the WTO and the TRIPS agreement. In that period, the United States has kept its part of the deal with developing nations: it has eliminated quotas on the imports of foreign-made apparel and textiles. As a result, producers from developing nations, particularly China, have largely pushed U.S. apparel makers out of their own market. The price is enormous. In 1986, the U.S. had 1.6 million people employed in these industries. By the middle of 2004, they employed barely 600,000 American workers, a loss of more than one million U.S. jobs. Imported apparel now fills more than 96 percent of the U.S. market. The resulting loss of production is approximately $65 billion annually. The human cost to these workers, their communities, and their states is immeasurable. The cost in lost tax revenues to the state and local governments is massive. The Labor Department estimates that only two-thirds of displaced manufacturing workers find replacement jobs, and most of these pay less than the job they lost. The others remain unemployed or drop out of the workforce.

Another cost of TRIPS is intangible. By joining the WTO, the United States agreed that it could no longer apply unilateral sanctions against other nations for any form of trade violation, as the Reagan administration had done with Korea. Ironically, Mickey Kantor, the United States trade representative during the concluding negotiations of this pact, did not realize that he was agreeing to such a concession. When confronted in private conversations or in congressional hearings, Kantor repeatedly asserted that the WTO dispute settlement provisions did not prevent unilateral U.S. actions. Kantor was sincere in his statements. He was just wrong. Thus, the United States signed away its right to act unilaterally against other nations in intellectual property disputes. Consequently, we must now take any complaint about other nations' violations of their TRIPS obligations to the WTO for resolution.

Strangely, the United States, which fought so hard and paid so much to put TRIPS into place, is not using these protections. Between the creation of TRIPS in 1995 and June 2000, the U.S. took only eleven intellectual property cases to the WTO. It won or settled ten of those. The first administration of George W. Bush did not file a single IP case with the WTO. Overall, the Bush administration filed only twelve cases with the WTO during its first four years in office. Six of those dealt with foreign impediments to U.S. agricultural exports—beef, rice, genetically enhanced foods, corn, wheat, cheeses, dairy products, and apples. The seventh case opposed the European Union's provisional safeguards on the import of U.S.-made steel. The eighth dealt with China's imposition of discriminatory taxes on imported semi-conductors. The rest deal with manufactured goods.

It is not as though the WTO's quasi-judicial mechanism is overloaded with cases. Between January 13, 1995, when Singapore filed the first WTO case against Malaysia for prohibiting imports of polyethylene and poly-propylene, and January 1, 2005, the WTO has taken only 324 cases, or fewer than three a month. In the entire year of 2004, the WTO received only twenty-one new cases from its 148 member nations.

In contrast, U.S. district court judges handle an average of four hundred cases each year. The median time from filing to disposition for federal civil cases is nine months. The number of appeals handled annually by each three-judge federal appeal panel is roughly 1,000 cases. The median time from notice of appeal to final disposition is less than eleven months. Overall, U.S. federal district court judges handled 341,000 civil and criminal cases in 2001, while the U.S. courts of appeals handled 57,000. U.S. federal judges are diligent.

At this level of inactivity, the entire WTO dispute settlement mechanism, including that for resolving TRIPS disputes, is little more than a dead-letter box. Worse, the United States has agreed not to fill that void with unilateral actions against other nations, as was done in the 1980s during the Reagan administration. The result is paralysis—something unimagined when the U.S. was creating TRIPS.

For all these reasons, including the strange reluctance of officials to enforce the agreement, Washington has gained little from TRIPS. Dozens of nations that have signed the TRIPS agreement are not honoring their commitments, either in spirit or in law.

The Office of the United States Trade Representative documents these violations annually in its *Special 301 Report*. The 2003 report identified fifty nations as massively violating U.S. intellectual property rights. That list did not include China, the greatest pirate of them all. China is in a special category. Eleven of the fifty countries are on a priority watch list for their lack of protections, including Brazil, India, Russia, Taiwan, the Philippines, and Poland. All these nation ratified the same WTO agreement, and all are refusing to honor their commitments.

Equally troubling, the administration of George W. Bush may have secretly exempted some nations from their TRIPS obligations. As often happens in diplomacy, a fog exists around this. In December 2001, during the WTO's meeting in Doha, Qatar, developing nations pressured the USTR to "clarify" language in the TRIPS agreement in a way that would have loosened regulations. Those nations threatened not to participate in the new global trade talks unless they got their "clarification." What they sought was authority to expropriate foreign pharmaceutical patents to fight diseases that they designated as critical.

Jacques Gorlin, the IPC expert, asserts that the USTR did not make any concessions at the Doha meeting. In an affidavit dated May 28, 2002, Gorlin stated that the WTO Doha Ministerial Declaration on TRIPS and Public Health did not "repudiate, rescind, or contradict the basic objective of TRIPS Agreement." He further concluded: "Accordingly, the obligation found in TRIPS Article 7 that signatory countries meet the TRIPS objective regarding the need for a balance between the interests of intellectual property producers and users remains in force."

Most developing nations, particularly those in Africa, believe that the United States did make such a waiver in exchange for their support of the Doha Round negotiations. Perhaps there were private understandings; perhaps not. Certainly, secret side agreements in such negotiations are common. Generally, even congressional oversight committees are kept in the dark about such arrangements.

What is clear is that the WTO operates on a one-nation, one-vote basis, just as WIPO does, and the developing nations have most of the votes. While a consensus is the usual basis for WTO decisions, the WTO charter does not require it as GATT does. Moreover, the developing nations are seeking to expand their list of exclusions in other intellectual property areas. As some nations now want waivers on patents that produce medicines, others are likely to seek them for software, entertainment, and virtually any other creation protected by patents, copyrights, trademarks, trade secrets, and other forms of IP.

The great risk now is that U.S. negotiators will yield and concede Americans' intellectual property rights in order to gain foreign support for other policy and trade objectives. In short, IP rights are likely to become the "textile and apparel" bargaining chip in future trade and foreign policy pacts. Ultimately, such a course would greatly diminish U.S. IP rights, as it has destroyed the U.S. textile and apparel industry.

As always, the ultimate issue is balance: how do we protect the rights of creators, expand the base of knowledge, and avoid the trap of monopolists, while serving the needs of society? Congress tried to answer that question in the late 1990s.

CHAPTER 9

THE PATENT BATTLE

The grainy picture shows nine men bunched tightly together, all raising their champagne glasses to the camera. Eight are Japanese. All of them have grimaced smiles. The ninth man is a tiny American. He is so obviously happy that the *Wall Street Journal*'s caption under the picture asks, "Why is this man smiling?"

The American is Jerome Lemelson, the most prolific U.S. inventor since Thomas Edison. The men surrounding him are executives from Japan's leading automobile companies. Lemelson is smiling because the executives have just paid him $100 million to license his robotics patents, something they never wanted to do but had to do because of U.S. laws.

Unknown to Lemelson, much of the publicity he was then receiving was not the result of his inventions but part of a much larger campaign to weaken the U.S. patent protections of independent inventors. Lemelson was the designated villain in a concocted public morality play.

Jerome Lemelson, who died in 1997, was a quiet, soft-spoken engineer, and a genius. Unlike most inventors who either work for others or transform their innovations into goods or services, Lemelson dedicated himself to pure invention and then licensed his ideas to others. His creations range from bar-code scanners, automated warehouses, fax machines, pothole repair machines, robots, crying baby dolls, and propeller beanies to the audiocassette drive mechanism in the Sony Walkman. In his last days, he invented new ways for scientists to analyze tissue from the human body—a desperate but unsuccessful effort to help save his own life from cancer.

While many of Lemelson's inventions were toys, such as the Hot Wheels line of cars, others were pioneering advances. In his work on machine vision, Lemelson filed his first patent in 1954, which included a detailed 150-page application. His creation—which first linked cameras, computers, and production machines—was so advanced that it involved dozens of inventions, all contained in that one application. It is as though Edison, who received hundreds of patents for his inventions involving electricity, had put all of them into one patent application.

In 1956, the U.S. Patent and Trademark Office divided Lemelson's application into seven parts, thereby forcing him, over his objections, to seek seven separate patents. Then, in 1973, the patent office made him split the patent into a different seven-way division. Eventually, the patent office decided that even those seven patents were so pioneering that they really represented twenty separate inventions and more than six hundred claims.

The patent office issued Lemelson the first of his many machine vision patents in 1963. That patent revealed to the world the basic contents of Lemelson's invention. The last of the subdivided patents was issued thirty-one years later. From 1954, the year of his first filing, until then, Lemelson received only thirty months of continuance time to respond to inquiries by the patent office. The ultimate result was patents on bar-code scanning, flexible manufacturing, and robots that could see, innovations now used in industry around the world.

Lemelson's most challenging problem was collecting royalties from those who used his patents. Some companies, such as IBM, willingly paid to license his computer patents. Others employed Lemelson's ideas, such as Mattel in its Hot Wheels toy, but stoutly refused to pay him anything. In those instances, Lemelson sued.

Often, bringing a lawsuits was the only way he could collect. The $100 million Japanese payment is one example. In 1989, Lemelson asked twelve Japanese automakers to pay royalties for their use of his machine vision patents. As often happens, the Japanese dragged out the negotiations for more than two years. In 1992, Lemelson stopped negotiating; he sued Toyota, Nissan, Mazda, and Honda for patent infringement. In thirty days, these four Japanese auto companies and eight others settled. For the Japanese, the deal was a bargain. After all, Lemelson's patents were valid, the Japanese were doing business inside the U.S. and were subject to American laws, and U.S. courts could have forced the automakers to pay billions of dollars for their patent infringements. Ultimately, they got a bargain.

The Japanese settlement, according to the *Wall Street Journal*, set a precedent for several European automakers, which then also paid Lemelson to use his machine vision patents. U.S. automakers initially refused to pay for a similar license, and Lemelson sued them. They, too, eventually settled.

Lemelson's corporate critics charged that he, as the inventor, had deliberately made additional filings to Patent Office examinations, thereby keeping his patent "submerged" until a corporation did something that violated one of his claims, at which time he would "surface" the patent. Japanese companies invented a clever name for this: "submarine patents," implying that Lemelson was lying in wait for a sneak attack. His critics also alleged that he was only the most successful of many independent inventors victimizing unsuspecting corporations with submarine patents. The U.S. media repeated these claims widely.

In the process, the press ignored important facts about the accusation. Among the most important is that the patent office awarded Lemelson more than five hundred patents, a major proof of his ideas' uniqueness. Also, he repeatedly prevailed in federal courts against infringers. And the patent office's records document that its delays, not Lemelson's, consumed most of the time between his applications and its issuance of a patent. Finally, the basic machine vision patent was hardly hidden: it was fully available to the public from 1963 onward at the U.S. Patent Office, where anyone could get a copy.

The charge also ignores another ugly reality in modern corporate life: big companies regularly steal one anothers' patented technology. In the 1980s, Hitachi paid IBM hundreds of millions of dollars after the FBI caught it illegally using that corporation's software. In 1997, General Electric was forced to compensate the Fonar Corporation, a company created by Dr. Raymond V. Damadian, the discoverer of magnetic resonance, $128.7 million for infringement of Fonar's cancer detection patent. In 2003, Boeing was banned from certain air force contracts because it was caught stealing Lockheed's technology.

The problem for Hitachi, GE, and Boeing is that they were caught. Clearly, each of these companies understood the risks before it committed the theft and each decided the rewards were worth it. It is not unlike the risk assessment a burglar makes before entering a building. But unlike common criminals, such corporations have the capacity to change the statutes they violate. Weakening intellectual property laws, therefore, reduces the risks of "taking" the patents and copyrights of others.

For at least the past century, Congress has modified U.S. intellectual property statutes through a process where the interested parties first come to an agreement among themselves on what the changes will be. They then give Congress legislative language that it is expected to convert into law. In effect, the legislators rubber-stamp and enact legislation drafted by the concerned parties.

In the 1990s, U.S., Japanese, and European corporations attempted to alter American patent law to their advantage at the expense of independent inventors. Those big corporations never tried to reach a consensus of interests with independent inventors. It was a major political blunder. The resulting fight provides a rare insight into how patent laws are crafted and enacted, plus the longer-term goals of these transnational organizations.

Jerome Lemelson never quite understood the dishonesty behind the campaign against him. However, the corporate political operatives did. The issue was never about Lemelson or submarine patents. In the corporate campaign to weaken U.S. patent laws, Lemelson was merely a scapegoat being used to represent independent inventors as greedy, unprincipled, little people trying to take advantage of corporations. What Lemelson understood clearly, however, is that creators such as himself are a natural enemy of the status quo, large corporations, and state-owned enterprises.

"Innovation is a hostile act as it threatens the status quo and those who benefit from it," says Paul Heckel, president of Intellectual Property Creators, an independent inventors' group. That threat, Heckel claims, explains the difference between the U.S. patent system and those of Japan and Europe. Those systems were developed to minimize the threats to entrenched interests, while the American system was created after the Revolution, when the entrenched interests—that is, the British—had been overthrown and those in power had little but the future of a nation to develop.

The American experience suggests that an independent inventor can devastate an entrenched interest almost overnight. A brilliant scientist, for instance, can develop a new drug based on biotechnology that quickly replaces medicines made by traditional means and create a multibillion-dollar rival corporation named Amgen. Two geniuses operating out of a garage can invent the Apple computer and soon wipe out the typewriter industry. Another genius, working out of his living room and assembling computers, can invent a business model that enables his tiny company, Dell Computer, to overtake IBM as the world's largest computer maker. A college student can write a thesis that outlines a new way to create a spoke-and-hub overnight distribution system that is faster and more reliable than the U.S. Postal Service and then use that thesis to get funding and create Federal Express.

Such innovation is the heart of what economist Joseph Schumpeter called "creative destruction." For most large corporations, creative persons working independently are their worst nightmare. Not surprisingly, many U.S. corporations have long sought to weaken patent protections for independent inventors. Repeatedly, they have been able to persuade several administrations (those of Lyndon Johnson, George H. W. Bush, and Bill Clinton) to appoint patent reform commissions composed largely of themselves, the entrenched interests, and their representatives. And these blue ribbon groups repeatedly offer the same solutions:

- Cut the term of a patent.

- Permit public inspection of a patent application before the Patent Office decides whether to issue a patent.

- Permit third parties, from outside the government, to participate in the Patent Office's review of an application, both before and after it is issued.

- Establish prior users' rights—that is, provide some legal means by which infringers can use a patented innovation royalty-free if they can prove they were doing something vaguely similar before the patent was issued.

- Issue a patent to the first-to-file, rather than to the first-to-invent.

- Take the U.S. Patent Office out of the Commerce Department and make it a private corporation, governed by a private board.

Each of these recommendations—"the old corporate favorites"—is significant. Cutting the patent term would mean that large institutions would get quicker, royalty-free access to the innovations of others. From the first Patent Act until the Lincoln administration, the U.S. patent term was fourteen years. From the Lincoln to the Clinton administrations, it was seventeen years. Under NAFTA, Congress changed the patent term to twenty years from the date of filing or seventeen years from the date of granting, whichever period is longer.

The minimum patent term set by TRIPS as part of the World Trade Organization treaty is twenty years from filing, but any nation can set a higher standard, as was done with the NAFTA treaty. The Clinton administration persuaded Congress to adopt the TRIPS minimum—twenty years from filing.

The difference between the period set under NAFTA and the minimum under TRIPS can create a important loss of protections for the inventor. If the inventor gets the TRIPS minimum and if the patent office takes twelve years to issue a patent, which is common for pioneering inventions such as lasers and machine vision, then the inventor realizes only eight years of protection. Had the TRIPS minimum been U.S. law in the second half of the twentieth century, Lemelson would have had only one year of protection, as it took the patent office nineteen years to issue his first patent on machine vision.

But if U.S. law says the inventor gets protection for either seventeen years *or* the TRIPS minimum of twenty years, the inventor is not penalized if the patent office takes nineteen years to do its work. The inventor would receive seventeen years of protection from the date the patent was granted.

Secrecy has been a key ingredient in the U.S. patent system. For more than two hundred years, the patent office kept secret the details of an inventor's application until a decision was made. If the patent was rejected, the materials were still concealed and the inventor could rework his application or use the creation as a trade secret.

The Japanese and European systems are different. They publish the patent application after eighteen months regardless of whether a patent was issued or not. The publication of the details of an application at eighteen months, when the patent office may take five or six years to complete its assessment, gives established corporations a jump start on developing a competing set of technologies. It doesn't matter that the independent inventor may have the future right to sue those who pirate the idea: the cost of litigation may be too high. Today, an average patent suit can cost more than $1 million and take several years. If the patent thief comes from Japan, India, Brazil, China, or another nation where the judicial process is slow and tightly controlled, there may be no relief at all.

Japan long allowed third parties to participate in its patent office's pregrant review process. Japan's government lobbied the U.S. to adopt this procedure. This review allows competitors to learn the details of someone else's inventions, delays the grant of a patent, and gives opponents time to line up and make their best objections against claims allowed by the patent examiner. In the 1980s, Genentech faced twenty-eight pregrant oppositions in Japan to its application for a patent on the tissue plasminogen activator and the process to produce it. Genentech sued one opponent and won; then it had to take on the remaining twenty-seven, one by one. Often, foreign inventors were given a choice: provide a license to a large Japanese corporation or spend years in court.

A similar ploy is to allow third-party participation in the reexamination of a patent after it is issued. In the 1980s, Congress enacted legislation authorizing the U.S. Patent and Trademark Office (USPTO) to reexamine patents it had issued. Tight rules were established. Between 1981 and late 1993, the USPTO issued 2,096 reexamination certificates. Only 304 patents were invalidated. During that same period, the patent office granted 1.1 million patents. The invalidation rate was roughly 0.00027 of one percent of patents issued. This is remarkable testimony to the competence of the USPTO examiners, who are the most talented patent experts in the world.

With such an extraordinarily low rate of invalidations, why did Japanese and U.S. corporate interests desire a looser reexamination process? Again, the answer is simple: the laxer the review process, the easier it is to threaten patent holders with reexamination if they refuse to grant a low-royalty license. It is commercial extortion.

A "prior-user right" is a slick way to neutralize a patent. The idea is to allow anyone using an innovation similar to that covered by the patent to pay no royalties to the owner if it can be proven their innovation was in use before the patent was issued. Of course, the independent inventor has to discover such violations and then sue. This gives deep-pocket corporations a defense in court, allowing them to claim a prior-user right and then violate with impunity the patents of those unable to pay the high legal fees required to challenge it.

America has always used the first-to-invent principle. The idea is that the inventor should get the patent, not the person who may steal an idea and win the dash to the patent office.

The recommendation that the patent office be removed from the Commerce Department, out from under the oversight of Congress, and made into a private corporation is the ultimate power grab. This would be like privatizing the federal court system. The decisions of a patent examiner are quasi-judicial in nature. The examiners decide between inventors as to who was first to invent and whether an idea is unique enough to merit a patent.

Sometimes, the patent examiner's decision decides the fate of entire industries, individual companies, and millions of workers. Often, the issuance of a patent is the equivalent of handing someone a lottery ticket worth hundreds of millions of dollars, or more. Outsourcing the work of the Patent and Trademark Office to a private corporation would ultimately put decisions into the hands of those whose interests are threatened by innovation.

The most recent attempt to restructure U.S. patent laws to the disadvantage of individual inventors and small companies began during the administration of President George H. W. Bush (1989–1993). The same U.S. corporate interests that were also attempting to create TRIPS in Geneva led this effort in Washington. While their global agenda was to harmonize the IP laws and procedures of the developing world and bring them up to the U.S. standard, their domestic goal was to harmonize the U.S. patent standard down to Europe's level.

The initial vehicle for these proposed patent changes was the Advisory Committee on Patent Law Reform, a blue ribbon group created in 1990 by President Bush's secretary of commerce, Robert Mosbacher. The committee was composed largely of corporate CEOs and lawyers, including Edmund T. Pratt Jr., the Pfizer CEO who also headed the IPC and ACTPN. Small companies, independent inventors, and consumer groups were notably absent.

In August 1992, the committee's final report was issued. It was largely a rehash of President Johnson's 1966 Presidential Commission on the Patent System. The committee urged adoption of all the old corporate favorites, including a first-to-file system, the European patent term, and the publication of patents at twenty-four months.

After Bill Clinton became president in 1992, opponents of the Mosbacher committee's recommendations were relieved, thinking the threat was gone. They could not have been more mistaken. The Clinton administration adopted the Bush administration's patent reform agenda virtually intact and pursued it with far greater vigor than had its predecessor.

The first public indication of the Clinton administration's intentions was revealed in a *New York Times* report from Tokyo dated January 24, 1994. The article revealed that the U.S. patent commissioner had come to Tokyo and signed an agreement with the government of Japan that committed the U.S. to change its patent term from seventeen years from the issuance of a patent to twenty years from the filing of a patent application. The story went on to say this was part of a larger, joint U.S.–Japan effort to control the "submarine patents" problem.

Beverly Selby, a trade expert who had been a senior policy analyst in the Reagan White House, saw the article and took it to her boss, Congresswoman Helen Delich Bentley (R.-Md.). Bentley immediately began organizing a campaign to cancel the Tokyo agreement.

A maverick Republican from Baltimore, Bentley had worked as a journalist with the *Baltimore Sun* for almost twenty-five years, eventually becoming the paper's maritime editor. In 1969, President Nixon appointed her to the Federal Maritime Commission, and in 1982, Baltimore voters elected her to the U.S. House of Representatives. Bentley opposed the Mosbacher committee's recommendations because she was convinced they worked against U.S. inventors. Now the Clinton team was moving fast and audaciously to implement them.

The point man for the Clinton administration in the U.S.–Japan patent negotiations was Bruce A. Lehman, assistant secretary of commerce and the U.S. commissioner of patents and trademarks. His career is the classic example of Washington's revolving door. For nine years, Lehman had worked at the House Judiciary Committee, where he was one of the principal legal advisers to Congress on IP issues. In the early 1980s, he left public service and became a partner at Swindler Berlin, an influential Washington law firm, where he quickly became one of the capital's best-paid IP lobbyists.

More important to many Republican members, Lehman was a Democratic activist who reported to Secretary of Commerce Ronald Brown. Like Lehman, Brown was an IP expert, having been chief counsel for the Senate Judiciary Committee, which oversees patent and copyright matters. Later, as chairman of the Democratic National Committee, he brilliantly rebuilt the party and helped take the presidency away from the Republicans. Most infuriating to Bentley and others, Brown had long been one of Japan's main lobbyists in Washington.

Now Brown's subordinate, Lehman, had signed an agreement with the Japanese promising that Congress would, by June 1, 1994, enact legislation giving the Japanese government what its American representatives had long lobbied for in Washington: a cut in the U.S. patent term for U.S. inventors.

Even administration supporters were troubled by the Lehman promise, for it was so obviously one-sided. In exchange for committing the United States to shortening its term of patent protection, all Lehman got in return was a Japanese promise to accept U.S. patent applications in English, with a Japanese translation to follow in two months—a trivial concession.

Despite the uproar over the first U.S.–Japan agreement, seven months later, on August 16, 1994, Brown and Lehman seemed to lose their otherwise well honed power of political judgment. Lehman concluded an even more one-sided patent deal with Japan, and Brown signed it. It committed the Clinton administration, by January 1, 1996, to make U.S. patent applications—including drawings, specifications, claims, and bibliographic information—available to the public eighteen months after the inventor filed the papers, regardless of whether a patent has been granted or not. In exchange, Japan agreed to allow challenges to its patents to take place only after the grant of a patent, and it promised to accelerate patent examinations—steps Japan should have taken without any U.S. compensation.

Finally, the agreement Brown signed promised to "expand the opportunity for third parties to participate in any examiner interview and to submit written comments on the patent owner's response to any action in the patent under reexamination." With this, any third party, including Japanese corporations, could effectively be a participant in the quasi-judicial process by which the U.S. Patent and Trademark Office reexamines a patent.

Instead of transforming the Japanese patent system into one like America's, Brown and Lehman proposed to make the U.S. system into one like Japan's. In the process, they unwittingly launched a five-year patent war between the the Clinton administration and a large portion of the U.S. Congress.

In 1994, Democrats controlled both the Senate and the House. Japanese negotiators, therefore, believed Brown and Lehman could get Congress to ratify their agreements easily. Brown and Lehman thought the same and sent Congress draft legislation to implement their agreements with the Japanese government.

However, the political climate in 1994 was too bitter. Many Democrats opposed the Lehman proposals, and a hard-core group of conservative Republicans who backed Bentley would never support any legislation being pushed by Brown and Lehman, even if it were beneficial.

In the Senate, passage was largely ensured because patent legislation came under the control of Senator Dennis DeConcini (D.-Ariz.). DeConcini was not running for reelection in 1994, and many observers anticipated that once in private practice he would become one of Washington's most influential intellectual-property lobbyists—helping those who had once lobbied him. They were correct. However, in March 1994, he was still in the Senate, where he was pushing the patent commissioner to quickly implement the Japanese agreements. DeConcini was powerful. Opponents knew that if the House ratified these twin deals, he would zip them through the Senate. If these deals were to be killed, it had to be done in the House, and to accomplish the task Bentley needed help.

Enter Dana Rohrabacher (R.-Calif.). For seven years, Rohrabacher was a special assistant to President Reagan and one of his senior speechwriters. During the last year of Reagan's second term, Rohrabacher returned home to Orange County, California, stood for Congress, and won. His constituents have returned him to Washington ever since.

Neither Rohrabacher nor Bentley was on the House Judiciary Committee, which oversees U.S. IP laws. Like Bentley, Rohrabacher is an iconoclast who largely goes his own way in Congress, generally supporting the GOP leadership but sometimes opposing it. By 2004, Rohrabacher chaired the House Subcommittee on Space and Aeronautics and was a member of the House Science Committee's research subcommittee, which oversees U.S. science policy. In 1994, however, he held a minority view in the minority party. His influence lay in his single vote and his ability to persuade his colleagues.

The idea of weakening intellectual property protections for inventors struck Rohrabacher as a basic threat to the United States. He became a man possessed. He made saving the traditional protections of the U.S. patent his cause. Cato the Elder could not have been more determined to destroy Carthage than Rohrabacher was to stop the Clinton administration and, after 1994, a GOP-controlled Congress from weakening the U.S. patent system.

After studying the TRIPS agreement and the U.S.–Japan bilateral agreements, Rohrabacher was incensed that Lehman and Brown had agreed with Japan to make the TRIPS minimum term the U.S. maximum. Bentley and Rohrabacher took up the challenge of explaining this complex technicality to members, one by one. They also composed a joint letter to the president, urging him to delete those provisions in his forthcoming GATT treaty implementing legislation. Seventeen members, mostly Republicans, co-signed their letter.

The letter was significant because it revealed that Bentley and Rohra-bacher might be able to generate enough GOP opposition in the House to block ratification of the GATT treaty, which would be considered later in 1994. The Clinton administration responded with a request for a joint House-Senate hearing. In reality, the administration wanted a highly visible debate on patents, such as the one between Vice President Al Gore and Ross Perot during the 1993 fight over ratification of NAFTA. This showdown would feature Rohrabacher and Lehman. The administration thought that its patent commissioner, an intellectual property expert and articulate advocate, could easily best the congressman from Orange County.

The administration got its debate on August 12, 1994, and with it a big surprise. While most congressional hearings are sparsely attended, this one was standing room only. Rohrabacher tore into the proposed twenty-year patent term as a "total sellout, a surrender . . . to an unholy alliance between big business and Japanese interests that are trying to weaken our intellectual property protection. We can be in full compliance with GATT," he said, "by changing U.S. patent law so the patent term is seventeen years from grant, or twenty years from filing. WHICHEVER IS LONGER." He then provided detailed documentation about how this could be done.

Lehman enthusiastically explained, "TRIPS is the emerging international standard." He also described how the delays in issuing U.S. patents would generate political pressure on Congress to provide the patent office more resources—certainly an eccentric point to make before a congressional committee that would be the target of such pressure. Finally, Lehman said, the TRIPS minimum term had been adopted as a means of eliminating "submarine patents"—the administration's bogeyman.

Rohrabacher prevailed. Any possibility that the Clinton administration could get any stand-alone patent legislation enacted in 1994 evaporated at that hearing. The only parts of the U.S.–Japan deal that could be implemented would have to be hidden in another piece of legislation. Legislation to ratify the GATT treaty provided an opportunity for such legislative sleight of hand. Under a special rule called "fast track," Congress was obligated to vote on the bill ratifying the trade treaty in 1994. Under fast track, no amendments could be made, debate would be limited, the vote would be up or down, and no Senate filibuster was permitted.

While the GATT treaty could not be amended, the legislation that ratified it could include extraneous items. This allowed President Clinton to "buy" votes from members with pork projects and favors. But to keep the price reasonable and forestall a political firestorm, the president also had to keep his deals secret. The approach he used was to get the congressional leadership to deny most members of Congress access to the 4,000-page proposed legislation. Thus, most members were expected to vote without reading the bill under consideration.

Lori Wallach, director of Public Citizen's Global Trade Watch and an opponent of the legislation, obtained a copy of the draft legislation several days before the scheduled vote. She had dozens of copies made and distributed. The opponents and media soon discovered dozens of shabby political deals costing taxpayers billions of dollars, most of which had nothing to do with the Uruguay Round trade agreement.

Of all these deals, the federal grant of three special cellular telephone licenses at a substantial discount was the most controversial, particularly after the *Wall Street Journal* revealed that the Washington Post Company was one of the recipients. The other two were a prominent Wall Street firm and the company that owns the *Atlanta Constitution.*

While the *Washington Post*'s editorials were urging immediate congressional passage of the GATT-implementing legislation, the paper did not reveal the Washington Post Company's financial stake in the bill's passage. What galled Republican House members was that the *Post* had long scourged them for such hypocrisies. Bentley taunted her GOP colleagues with a simple question: "Are you going to vote for or against a $200 million federal gift for the *Washington Post*?"

Under the fast-track rules by which Congress considers trade legislation, members could not remove the *Post*'s deal, or any other, from the administration's bill. They could be canceled only if Congress rejected the entire piece of legislation that ratified the new global trade treaty. This would force the president to resubmit his ratification legislation in 1995 without any fast-track rules and thus, most likely, stripped of any political pork. In early October 1994, a majority of the GOP caucus decided they would rather reject the trade treaty altogether than give anything to the *Washington Post*.

But the Clinton administration convinced House and Senate leaders to reschedule the vote to a lame-duck session after the 1994 elections. If Congress voted before the end of December 1994, the legislation could be considered under the fast-track rule, with all the pork deals attached. Equally important, by shifting the vote until after the 1994 midterm elections, members would not have to face voters for another two years.

But something extraordinary happened in that election: American voters switched control of both houses of Congress from the Democrats to the Republicans. When members returned to Washington after the election, Newt Gingrich, the soon-to-be Speaker of the House, warned senior Republican House members that this bill was going to be ratified during the lame-duck session and those who opposed it would not be considered for major committee positions in 1995. Most of the Republicans fell into line, though Bentley, Rohrabacher, and a handful of others did not. On November 29, 1994, the bill passed in the House on a roll call vote of 288 for and 146 against. The Senate ratified the treaty soon after by a vote of 76 to 24. On December 8, 1994, the president signed the legislation into law.

Most of the parties in this intellectual property debate won something major. The companies that wanted a new global minimum standard had TRIPS. Brown and Lehman got their twenty-year TRIPS maximum patent term. Opponents of the bill kept out of the legislation other harmonization proposals, such as first-to-file, the eighteenth-month publication rule, and third-party reviews. The Washington Post Company got its FCC license discount.

In early 1995, the administration quickly moved to get the balance of its intellectual property proposals enacted into law. Simultaneously, Rohrabacher set out to defeat the administration's proposals and roll back the twenty-year-patent provision. In retrospect, it is apparent that the real fight on patents had just begun.

At any moment in Washington, dozens of issues, such as patent law change, are under consideration. Most lobbyists and elected officials participate out of self-interest. Sometimes an activist comes along with a different motivation.

Steven Shore became involved in this patent fight in August 1994 when he visited Washington and met Helen Bentley. From friends, he had learned of the proposed patent changes and wished to hear more from her. What Shore found out changed his life—literally.

Shore, a successful executive from Los Angeles, is a copyright expert, largely because of his investments in the music and recording industries. As much as anything, Shore's visit to Bentley's office was a search for a political issue he could use to run for Congress. "In that meeting," Beverly Selby, Representative Bentley's adviser on trade, recalls, "I told him that 'we are fighting a spiritual battle for the soul of America, and if we lose the patent issue we will be a third-rate economic power.' "

Subsequently, Selby arranged for Shore to meet with others, both inside and outside Congress. Shore says that what he found was appalling: few members or their staffs understood the role intellectual property played in the economy. To most, he says, the proposed changes in the patent system were just another set of political issues.

Shore had found his issue: organizing inventors to defend the patent system. Within sixty days of meeting with Selby, he had created the Alliance for American Innovation. Unlike most groups that attempt to influence national policy through nonprofit lobbying fronts, the alliance was organized as a private company, which allowed it to operate in semisecrecy just as foreign governments and major U.S. corporations do. Shore put $1 million of his own funds into the alliance to pay start-up costs. By December 1994, he had rented office space in downtown Washington, hired lobbyists, and moved to a new home outside Washington. His race for Congress was forgotten.

Shore offered Beverly Selby the position of executive director of the alliance; she accepted the job after the 1994 elections. Using Selby's extensive network of inventors and inventors' groups, the alliance soon represented most of the major U.S. inventor groups as well as dozens of prominent inventors.

One of Shore's important allies was Ronald J. Riley, a Michigan-based engineer and consultant who holds several patents. Riley became president of the alliance's advisory board. Riley created a Web site that in the late 1990s was for inventors what the *Drudge Report* was for political junkies, a way of keeping current on important IP issues (www.inventored.org).

When the 104th Congress convened in January 1995, Bentley had left to run for governor of Maryland. Dana Rohrabacher assumed her role as opposition leader to the patent harmonization proposals. He was joined in that fight by dozens of other members, the most active of whom were Marcy Kaptur (D.-Ohio) and Duncan Hunter (R.-Calif.); they co-chaired the bipartisan Congressional Fair Trade Caucus and led the House opposition to ratification of the NAFTA and GATT deals.

On January 4, 1995, Rohrabacher moved quickly. He introduced legislation that would give inventors either a twenty-year patent term from the time they filed an application or seventeen years of protection after the patent was issued, whichever was longer. The proposal was legal under

TRIPS. Rohrabacher, Kaptur, and Hunter quickly got 217 co-sponsors on the bill, which gave them almost a majority in the House. With this, they could procedurally force the bill onto the floor for a quick vote. However, the House Republican and Democratic leadership convinced eleven co-sponsors to withdraw their support, thereby forcing the bill into normal legislative procedures. Then the bill was sent to the House Judiciary Committee, which killed it with a bipartisan vote.

The Judiciary Committee's rejection of Rohrabacher's bill revealed that those on the key authorizing committee supported the twenty-year patent term and the other Clinton harmonization proposals. Rohrabacher's only real alternative was to implement a "siege politics" strategy—that is, to demonize the administration's proposals and stall them long enough to force a political compromise.

In 1995, events worked in Rohrabacher's favor. The congressional Republicans, heady with their new power, closed down much of the federal government in December of that year, which inconvenienced and infuriated much of the American public and perpetuated a long-running budget fight between the executive and legislative branches that consumed everyone's political energies. Then, on April 3, 1996, Commerce Secretary Ron Brown and many on his staff died in an airplane crash in the Balkans. With that, the administration, the Commerce Department, and the patent office lost their best Capitol Hill lobbyist.

Finally, the newsletter *FDA Week* reported on April 5, 1996, that Bruce Lehman had agreed to provide the Chinese patent office with the entire U.S. patent database on magnetic tapes, as well as data on certain unapproved future patent filings. *FDA Week* quoted an unnamed patent official: "We have offered to provide [the Chinese] the entire collection of U.S. patent documentation, covering more than 160 years of patents, in digital form."

Lehman, according to the report, also offered to furnish English translations of portions of French and German patent documents in U.S. possession. The official explanation for Lehman's actions was that he was trying to make it easier for the Chinese patent office to search previously patented materials and thus give that country no excuse for infringing on U.S. patents. A growing chorus of Lehman critics claimed that this was just another Clinton administration giveaway to the Chinese government. Lehman's proposed transfer of patent information to China ended any possibility that the administration could get its patent legislation enacted in 1996. China got the tapes. Rohrabacher's siege continued.

Baiting opponents is a tactic as old as politics. Lehman's opponents seemed to enjoy infuriating the patent commissioner. As they hoped, Lehman usually responded. In one interview with the *San Jose Mercury News,* he characterized his critics as "on the lunatic fringe."

The paper quoted him.

Steven Shore responded by organizing a joint letter to Congress from twenty-seven U.S. Nobel Prize winners, thereby cleverly refuting Lehman's "lunatic fringe" slur. Among the signatories were ten economists, including Milton Friedman, Paul Samuelson, James Tobin, Robert Solow, Franco Modigliani, and Herbert A. Simon. This may have been the only time these scholars had ever agreed on any economic issue. In mid-September 1977, the Nobel laureates held a news conference in Cambridge, Massachusetts, at which they agreed that the administration's bill would damage America's independent inventors and "thereby discourage the flow of new inventions that have contributed so much to America's superior performance in the advancement of science and technology."

The Nobel laureates also pointed out that the draft legislation's prior-use provision (which gave companies the free use of someone else's patent if it could be proven that the idea had been used before the patent was issued) would increase industries' reliance on trade secrets, which can be kept hidden forever. This would reduce the incentive for inventors to rely on limited-life patents, which are published, and would thus diminish general knowledge—just the opposite of what the Founding Fathers intended when they established the patent system.

On October 17, 1997, the *New York Times* published an editorial opposing the administration's patent legislation, calling it "misguided" and "mischievous." The editorial highlighted as particularly harmful to U.S. inventors the provision that would require publication of an application at eighteen months even if no patent had been issued, and the prior-use proposal. The *Times* also urged the Senate to take testimony from the laureates before it proceeded further. Shore tried repeatedly to arrange for their appearance before the Senate, but the Senate Judiciary Committee refused their offer.

In yet another political blunder, Lehman alienated most of his patent examiners. Federal civil servants normally refrain from making known their views on policy or political matters, but not this time. A large portion of Lehman's own workforce opposed the administration proposals because many feared the ultimate goal was to politicize their work on behalf of global corporate interests.

To add even more fuel to the fire, Ross Perot, presidential candidate for the Reform Party in 1996, made protection of America's patents, copyrights, trademarks, and other intellectual property rights one of his major campaign issues and the subject of his infomercials. Though patent law issues are hardly the stuff of normal presidential campaigns, Perot explained this obscure, technical topic to millions of people, just as he had done in 1992 with the federal budget deficit. In 1998, Shore arranged for Perot to speak to more than a thousand patent examiners, who took time off from work to hear the speech. Perot saluted them for their patriotism and dedication.

When the 105th Congress convened in January 1997, the administration moved quickly to get its patent legislation enacted. With unusual congressional dispatch, the House Judiciary Committee reported out the administration's bill and sent it forward for accelerated consideration by the entire House of Representatives.

On the morning of April 17, House Republicans and Democrats met in their separate caucuses to discuss the day's activities, including the debate on the patent legislation. Howard Coble (R.-N.C.) made the patent case to the Republicans. Dana Rohrabacher, Duncan Hunter, and Tom Campbell (R.-Calif.) announced their opposition.

Rohrabacher attacked the bill as a foreign-inspired attempt to steal U.S. technology. Hunter, a populist conservative from San Diego, cited it as a threat to small business and independent inventors. Campbell, a PhD economist and Harvard-trained lawyer who represented technology-rich Silicon Valley, pointed out the technical flaws in the bill. Most members left the meeting confused.

At the Democratic caucus that same morning, the bill got little attention. John Conyers (D.-Mich.), the ranking Democrat on the House Judiciary Committee, distributed a brief summary of the proposed legislation. Marcy Kaptur, a fierce advocate of U.S. domestic development, raised the only objections, explaining how this bill would harm independent inventors and small companies, but the leaders cut her comments short so the caucus could recess.

That afternoon, the sponsors of the bill proceeded in the way in which complicated legislation is usually considered on the House floor: that is, they moved to get a quick victory before any opposition could be mounted. To kill or modify the administration's legislation, the opponents had to raise serious doubts about its origins, details, and consequences. Their challenge was to take a highly technical piece of legislation and reduce it to bumpersticker political terms that other members could easily understand.

When the bill was considered, the sponsors made three basic arguments. First, they argued that the legislation would harmonize the U.S. patent system so it would be like those of Japan and Europe. The opponents rebutted: "The U.S. has more innovation than the rest of the world combined. Why should we change a system that has worked so well for us for so long, just so we could treat our inventors and patents the same way as other countries do?"

Second, the advocates argued that early publication of U.S. patent applications was necessary to end "submarine patents." The opponents pointed out that Bruce Lehman had testified earlier before Congress that between 1971 and 1993, only 627 patent applications out of 2.3 million could be classified and not published, and at least a third of those had been U.S. government military secrets. In the late 1970s, the patent office had established a system to prevent submarine patents, and not one had been issued since then. The opponents asked, "Why should we radically change the total U.S. Patent System to address a tiny problem the Patent Office solved a decade ago?"

Finally, the advocates argued that the proposed patent changes were beneficial for U.S. business and for our trading partners. The opponents responded: "Certainly, big corporations and other nations want an advance peek at what U.S. inventors are doing, but why should we in Congress allow them to have it?"

Finally, Rohrabacher introduced substitute legislation. After an hour's debate, the House voted on the Rohrabacher bill, which lost 227 to 178, with 28 not voting. The next round would be a week later, when the House considered the administration's bill.

In that week, both sides furiously lobbied individual members, most of whom still had little understanding of, or even interest in, this legislation. When the debate began on April 23, the Rohrabacher group introduced three amendments to the administration's bill. Tom Campbell introduced an amendment that would have eliminated the provision that allowed anyone using a technology before it was patented to continue using it free of charge. The Campbell amendment was defeated. Then Duncan Hunter moved that "all examination and search duties for the grant of United States letters of patent are sovereign functions which shall be performed within the United States by United States citizens who are employees of the United States Government." The Hunter amendment, a tough one for Republicans to vote against, was also defeated.

The killer proposal, however, was Marcy Kaptur's. Late in the debate, she offered an amendment that exempted from the legislation all individual inventors and any firm classified by the U.S. Patent and Trademark Office as a small business—that is, a firm with 500 or fewer employees. Kaptur argued: "Big business may need the provisions of the administration's bill, but inventors, entrepreneurs and small companies would be harmed."

Lehman and congressional sponsors of the bill were furious—Kaptur's amendment effectively demolished their legislation. Giving big corporations and foreign nations an advance look at the patent applications of inventors and small companies was one of its principal purposes. More critically, the vote was a test of whether members would put the interests of big corporations over those of small businesses. To raise the political stakes, Kaptur demanded a roll call so every member's vote would be on the record. Her amendment passed by more than thirty votes—a resounding victory.

Then a vote was taken on the amended administration bill. But no member on either side of the issue wanted to be on record supporting the legislation as it now stood. Everyone in the House knew what to do: the bill was passed, as amended, by voice vote. Rohrabacher, Kaptur, Hunter, and Campbell had totally upended the administration's legislative strategy.

At this point, a White House intern named Monica Lewinsky became instantly famous, and Washington skidded into impeachment politics. Despite Bruce Lehman's best efforts, Steven Shore, the Alliance for American Innovation, and their Senate allies, such as Kit Bond (R.-Mo.), were able to divert and postpone action in the Senate for the balance of the 105th Congress.

By the time of the 106th Congress, which convened in January 1999, the administration and congressional sponsors of the patent legislation were ready to compromise. Rohrabacher's siege had succeeded. What emerged was the American Inventors Protection Act of 1999 (November 29, 1999).

The first big concession was that the patent office was not taken out of the U.S. government and privatized: it remains part of the Department of Commerce. That alone was worth the entire fight for inventors.

The legislation also extended the expiration date of a patent when the patent office fails to act within a set schedule, if it does not issue the patent within three years, or if the application is delayed by the introduction of secrecy orders or delays caused by appeals. This was a big victory for those who had fought the Brown-Lehman pact with Japan.

For applicants who do not intend to file for a patent abroad, the legislation required the patent office to keep their applications secret. Independent inventors were big winners.

The Japanese demand for outside pregrant examination of U.S. patent applications was rejected. The legislation established some new rules for reexamination: if a challenger chooses to use the patent office's reexamination process, the challenger automatically forfeits the right to go to court later if it loses. This was a draw. A prior-use standard was established, but only under certain specified conditions. It was a loss for independent inventors.

Finally, and perhaps most important, the legislation kept America's historic first-to-invent system. The true inventor gets the patent, not the person who gets to the patent office first. This also was a big win for independent inventors.

In other words, the siege and fight resulted in a victory for Rohrabacher, Bentley, Kaptur, Hunter, Campbell, Shore, Selby, the Nobel laureates, the Patent Examiners Association, the various inventors groups, and all the others who had fought so hard to preserve the U.S. patent system's strong protections. Most of all, it was a victory for America's independent inventors.

After the 1999 American Inventors Protection Act was signed into law, most of the independent inventors thought the fight was over. The alliance broke up. Shore returned to California. Although Ronald Riley continued to post materials on his Web site, no organization stepped in to fill the vacuum left in Washington. But the advocates for the Lehman legislation remained in place, well funded by U.S. and foreign transnational corporations. They are still working to complete, bit by bit, their long-term agenda of privatizing the patent and trade function, removing it from congressional oversight, and changing America's first-to-invent rules to Europe's and Japan's first-to-file system.

No political battle in Washington is ever over.

Fast-forward to February 9, 2004. On that date, each member of the House of Representatives received a letter signed by Marcy Kaptur and Duncan Hunter. Later in the week, it said, the House would be considering a bill, the

U.S. Patent and Trademark Fee Modernization Act, which contained an obscure provision that permitted the outsourcing of the patent office's search function to private persons or groups, including foreign companies and citizens. Before a patent is issued, the patent office searches other patents to see if there is any conflict. For more than two centuries, employees of the patent office have done this work in complete secrecy. Kaptur and Hunter pointed out that this legislation would remove the Patent and Trademark Office from congressional oversight.

The Kaptur-Hunter letter caused a quiet firestorm among House leaders. The bill was pulled from the week's schedule. Frank Wolf (R.-Va.), chairman of the House appropriations subcommittee that has jurisdiction over the patent office, strongly opposed the provision that removed congressional oversight. He went to the House leadership and arranged for that language to be stripped from the bill, thereby assuring Congress its right to review the patent office's budget, plans, and work.

On March 3, 2004, the House of Representatives considered an amended bill that retained Congress's right of oversight. The legislation also dedicated to the Patent and Trademark Office all the application fees that it collected, thereby providing enough money to hire an additional 2,900 patent examiners. This new staff could help speed patent examinations, which now take an average of 26.7 months. The bill also contained a modified outsourcing provision, allowing research and examination work to be contracted to U.S. companies and the work to be done by U.S. citizens.

Kaptur took the floor in opposition. She noted what a change this outsourcing represented to two centuries of tradition and the threat it created for the security of patent applications. Kaptur pointed out that under U.S. law if a Japanese, French, Italian, or Chinese corporation establishes itself inside the U.S., it is by definition an American company. She also queried the bill's sponsors: "If there are additional staff that will be working directly for the U.S. Patent and Trademark Office, then why does this bill permit commercial operations to do the review process?"

Their response was "It will speed up the process." The real answer was that outsourcing the patent review function is step one in outsourcing the entire patent process—the privatizing of the Patent and Trademark Office as proposed by Bruce Lehman in 1995 and still supported by virtually every large business lobby in Washington, as well as the governments of Japan and Europe.

Unlike in 1997, Kaptur was the only member who went to the floor of the

House of Representatives and argued against the new bill's outsourcing provision. The bill was adopted by a vote of 379 to 28. Then it was sent to the Senate, where it was rubber-stamped by the Senate Judiciary Committee. During the rush of the 2004 elections, the Senate did not have time to consider the bill. But it is likely to brought back for consideration in the 109th Congress.

On August 2, 2004, the U.S. Patent and Trademark Office (USPTO) announced that "anyone with Internet access anywhere in the world can use USPTO's Web site to track the status of a public patent application as its moves from publication to final disposition, and review documents in the official application file, including all decisions made by patent examiners and their reasons for making them." Patent applications will be published eighteen months after they are filed. The USPTO announced that it expected 300,000 application files to be put up on the Net annually.

For almost two centuries, the patent office treated an inventor's application with the utmost secrecy, knowing that competitors and pirates would like nothing better than to get an advanced peek at an innovation before it had patent protection. Now, any counterfeiter, pirate, intellectual property thief, or competitor can. The ultimate responsibility for this global release of vital U.S. secrets can be traced directly to the U.S. Congress. In the 1999 Patent Act, it forced the patent office, which takes almost twenty-seven months on average to make a patent determination, to publish at eighteen months the details of patent applications that seek global protection. The big losers are America's independent inventors and small entrepreneurial companies.

Fortunately, no political battle in Washington is ever over.

CHAPTER 10

THE COPYRIGHT WARS

The elegance of the U.S. Constitution's "authors and inventors clause" is reflected in the flexibility it gives Congress to adjust U.S. intellectual property laws to meet new and changing circumstances. And Congress has repeatedly used that authority, though sometimes not well.

The great danger inherent in this constitutional provision is that the "rights" it confers are undefined; the task of defining them is left to Congress, which thereby renders them less than absolute, for both creators and consumers of copyrighted works. Instead, those rights are "situational"; they vary over time in response to circumstances and congressional action.

In the latter part of the twentieth century, the rapid creation of new technologies and globalization, coupled with special interest politics, have challenged Congress's ability to assure adequate IP protections, even for long-protected works, and to set a reasonable balance between the interests of copyright owners and users.

Xerox's introduction of the first commercial photocopy machine in 1959 created one of these technology-based challenges. Suddenly, duplicates of copyrighted materials could be easily and inexpensively produced without the permission of the owners. In 1976, Congress responded by creating an exception to copyright holders' right of "exclusive use" by enacting a law that allowed library photocopying, without permission, for purposes of scholarship, preservation, and interlibrary loan. The same 1976 Copyright Act also defined what was "fair use" of copyright materials—permitting such works to be used, again without the owners' permission, for purposes of criticism, commentary, news reporting, teaching, scholarship, and research.

Congress then specified four factors the courts were to consider in any test of its fair-use provision: (1) the purpose of the use, (2) the nature of the copyrighted material, (3) the portion used in relation to the whole of the copyrighted work, and (4) the effect on the market for the protected piece.

After Congress revised the copyright laws in 1976, educational institutions and publishing companies negotiated guidelines on how photocopied materials would be used in classrooms and for other learning purposes. A number of high-profile court decisions further defined those fair-use standards. In one case, the courts ruled that a consortium of public schools could not tape privately owned educational programs broadcast over public television and then distribute copies (*Encyclopaedia Britannica Educational Corp. v. Crooks*, 1983). In another case, the federal courts ruled that unauthorized quoting for publication from unpublished materials was not fair use (*Salinger v. Random House*, 1987).

Even as an IP détente on photocopying was being established, the growing use of home videocassette recorders (VCRs) provoked a conflict over who would control the content those machines were duplicating. By the late 1970s, millions of people were copying movies and programs shown on their home televisions for reuse at their discretion. In November 1976, Universal Studios and the Walt Disney Company sued the leading Japanese VCR maker, Sony; some video retail stores; and a handful of other VCR manufacturers for violating their copyrights with such recording. The studios also sought damages, which could have run into the billions of dollars, and an injunction against the sale and distribution of VCR machines.

In 1979, a federal district court ruled that home taping of television programs was legal. A three-judge panel from the Ninth Circuit Court of Appeals then reversed that decision, concluding that home VCR recording constituted copyright infringement. The next step for both sides was the Supreme Court, which took the case in 1983. Both sides—the VCR manufacturers and their allies in the American video rental industry, and the Hollywood studios—were uncertain how the Court would rule. Because the stakes were so high and the district court's decision so fateful, both sides lobbied Congress for a political solution. To lead their fight, the Japanese electronics industry retained Ronald Brown of the Patton, Boggs & Blow law firm in Washington, D.C. The Hollywood team hired Bruce Lehman, then one of Washington's top IP lobbyists and a partner at the law firm of Swindler Berlin.

The studios wanted legislation granting them a royalty payment on the sale of every VCR and on the rental of every video. The manufacturers sought a law that exempted home VCR recording from copyright infringement. To no one's surprise, President Reagan sided with Hollywood and his friends in the industry.

The Court's decision was handed down in January 1984: by a 5–4 margin, it reversed the appellate court ruling, making the home copying of videos and the sale of VCR machines legal. Disappointed with the Court's action, the movie studios tried to rush its royalty legislation through Congress, anticipating that Reagan would sign it. But members refused to tax VCR users for Hollywood's benefit.

In retrospect, it is clear that Hollywood was lucky to lose. Far from destroying the studios, the new technology created an entirely new market, allowing them to earn literally billions of dollars in rentals and sales. Still, old fears die slowly, and Hollywood interests continued to seek a means to stop the free copying of their products.

Those fears became nightmares with the advent of the "digital revolution" in the late 1980s and early 1990s. As the Congressional Budget Office (CBO) noted in *Copyright Issues in Digital Media* (August 2004): "The digitization of creative content poses a more serious challenge to copyright law than did earlier episodes of technological advance." Why? Because digital technologies, including the Internet, greatly expand the ways that pirate copyright-protected works can be duplicated, while lowering the costs.

By 2004, for less than $1,000, anyone could own a high-speed computer, printer, and scanner that would enable the almost instant duplication, input, manipulation, and storage of information that the Internet can transmit as digital copies, indistinguishable from the originals, to anyone in the world, from anywhere in the world, for virtually zero cost. One copy of a digital work can be perfectly duplicated endlessly.

The promise of these digital tools is that they allow billions of people throughout the world to exchange ideas and information freely and immediately, hopefully empowering each of them to expand the use of knowledge in ways never even imagined before. The menace is that these same tools can be used to evade copyright restrictions and thus extinguish, or at least diminish, incentives for creativity. Conversely, these same technologies, as the CBO notes, "provide copyright owners with growing capacity to either restrict or charge for subsequent uses of their creative tools."

The great copyright issue of our time, therefore, is how to deploy these new digital technologies in a way that balances the interests of both owners and consumers in a political environment where the IP rights of neither are absolute or permanent.

The future of the digital revolution may be less than what is technologically possible, perhaps far less. In *The Future of Ideas: The Fate of the Commons in a Connected World,* Lawrence Lessig, a copyright expert, attributes such a diminished future to efforts by the world's major corporate copyright-based industries to tightly control what the Internet can distribute. The conflict he paints is one between a system designed to disseminate knowledge as freely as possible and an established order that has long controlled such distribution but is now threatened by the new technologies.

The vital component in this clash is the Internet, which Lessig describes as nothing more than a group of computer networks, each composed of millions of computers around the world, mostly connected by telephone lines that are generally privately owned. In essence, the Net is a simple system because the intelligence resides in the individual computers at the ends of those telephone lines. The Internet merely moves information from one computer to another. Unlike prior information distribution networks, such as radio, recording, or publishing, where the distributors were few in number and the content they shared could be controlled, tens of millions of Net users are potential distributors, making control of what they dispense correspondingly difficult.

Originally, the Internet had no controls over the content that could be sent from one computer to another. To the Net, it made no difference if the package of information sent over the wires was an e-mail, a picture, a speech, a chemical formula, pornography, literature, or a grandmother's favorite cookie recipe. In an information-hungry world, the Internet was almost too good to be true. It facilitated the transfer of vast amounts of information between large numbers of people at little cost.

But a problem quickly emerged. The Internet, with its absence of control over what was moving over the wires, threatened the rights of copyright owners, whose works were being made available widely and freely.

For companies that had previously controlled the distribution of their copyrighted works, the Internet was a frightening threat whose use had to be regulated. Digital tools provided the technical means to reimpose their control, but these companies lacked the legal authority to use those tools. Thus, Congress was pressed to define IP rights in a way that could be used to impose controls on the Internet. This is the story of what happened.

Hollywood personalities and studios were among presidential candidate Bill Clinton's main supporters in the 1992 election. Pirates were ripping off their movies and recordings in the United States and around the world and making a fortune doing so. Clinton promised he would help the studios stop such theft. In February 1993, after being in office fewer than thirty days, the new president formed the Information Infrastructure Task Force (IITF), a truly dreadful name for an organization composed of all federal agencies that are involved in communications. The IITF's mission was to define a U.S. vision for the emerging digital world.

Clinton chose Ronald Brown, his first secretary of commerce, to lead this task force. He also picked Bruce Lehman, now the commissioner of patents and trademarks, to lead the working group on intellectual property. Thus, two of Washington's formerly top patent and copyright lobbyists were now in charge of U.S. intellectual property policy.

Brown appointed a private advisory committee, composed of thirty-six people. Of these, twenty-five were from the media business, each of whom had a direct private interest in whatever policy emerged. Consumer interests were essentially unrepresented.

Eighteen months later, on July 7, 1994, Lehman's Working Group on Intellectual Property Rights issued a preliminary draft of its report, known as the "Green Paper" because of its green cover. Hollywood got everything it wanted, and more.

The draft report recommended that Congress expand the reach of copyright law in a way that would allow content providers, such as moviemakers, to charge for virtually any use of their copyrighted material. The report also recommended that telephone and Internet providers be responsible for monitoring what flowed over the Internet to their customers. Finally, it sharply limited the fair-use standard, which had long permitted authors, libraries, teachers, and others to use some portions of a copyrighted work for education, illustrative, and documentation purposes without having to pay.

If any means existed for copyright holders to license a work and collect royalties, it would be made legal. Existing fair-use provisions would become largely meaningless. The report also advocated a ban on devices or software that decoded the "latches" (cyberlocks) on copyrighted products, put there by manufacturers to prevent unauthorized duplication. The proposed law even prohibited purchasers from making a backup copy of a commercially produced CD, software, or DVD solely for their own protection in case of accident or loss. In *Digital Copyright,* Wayne State University Law School professor Jessica Litman summed up the Green Paper as a brash attempt by copyright owners to "colonize cyberspace."

In an attempt to take the edge off the criticism which quickly came, Brown and Lehman took their report on the road to explain it. This was a mistake because it actually increased the opposition: the more interested parties learned, the more intense opposition to the report became.

In September 1995, Brown and Lehman released the final report of the working group. It was called the White Paper, because the jacket was white. Although the color of the cover had been changed, most of the controversial recommendations remained. With that, the fight moved to Congress.

What Lehman and Brown brought Congress was not a consensus position but a bitter disagreement between powerful interests that could not resolve their conflict. The Clinton administration was proposing an enormous expansion of copyright coverage, one that would wall off from the public major portions of the Internet, the most promising new communications technology created since the telephone. To critics, the proposals were unbalanced, favoring commercial interests over the public good and even the advancement of knowledge.

Opposition quickly emerged. Some of the first and most important opponents came from professors of many leading U.S. law schools. In the fall of 1995, Peter Jaszi, a law professor at American University in Washington, organized a roundtable discussion of library associations and other legal scholars. Subsequently, they reviewed Lehman's White Paper and explored the possibility of organizing a coalition to oppose the legislation. Out of that meeting, the Digital Future Coalition, a lobby group, was formed. Soon its membership included more than forty libraries and educational, archivist, and public interest associations, including the Home Recording Rights Coalition, which had helped defeat the Hollywood studios in the VCR battle a decade earlier.

The Digital Future Coalition had three strengths. First, the Home Recording Rights Coalition was a skilled lobbying organization with local membership composed of store owners in nearly every congressional district. Second, the proposed legislation would make telephone and Internet companies assume the role of cybercops, in effect making them responsible for policing the actions of their customers, an awesome potential liability by any measure. Third, and most important, the coalition had several articulate law professors as advisers. In addition to Jaszi, this legal talent included

Lawrence Lessig, now a professor of law at Stanford, Jessica Litman, and Pamela Samuelson of the University of California.

These scholars and others wrote law journal articles, op-ed pieces, and magazine stories, gave speeches, and prepared congressional testimony that clearly explained the issues and dangers of the Lehman bill. Because of these academics' work, which was widely distributed, no member of Congress could truly claim a lack of understanding about this complex legislation.

Among the earliest and most effective articles inspired by the White Paper were those by Samuelson, who has a joint appointment to the University of California's law school and its School of Information Management and Systems. In 1997, the MacArthur Foundation awarded her a "genius grant."

In articles and speeches, Samuelson deconstructed the Lehman proposals and predicted their consequences. One of her most influential pieces was "The Copyright Grab," published in *Wired* in January 1996. She summarized Lehman's agenda as follows:

1. Give copyright owners control of copyrighted works in digital form, including even temporary copies in the random-access memory on someone's computer.

2. Give copyright owners control of distribution by defining the sending of digital works via the Net as transmission of copies to the public.

3. Eliminate fair-use rights whenever copyright owners might license a use—and they can license virtually every use.

4. Eliminate "first sale" rights for digital goods by treating forwarding as a violation of reproduction and distribution rights.

5. Attach copyright management information to digital works, allowing the tracking of every use made of all digital products.

6. Protect digital works technologically and make illegal any attempt to bypass that protection.

7. Make Internet service providers impose pay-per-use rules and report copyright crime to authorities.

8. Teach the new copyright rules to children in elementary and secondary schools.

Samuelson then suggested that Lehman's second goal, after getting this bill into U.S. law, was to impose its provisions worldwide through a treaty at the World Intellectual Property Organization, not unlike what the United States had just done with TRIPS at the World Trade Organization.

The White Paper, as well as the legislation introduced by Lehman, seemed reasonable enough when viewed in tiny parts. Certainly, it was well written and argued. Unlike the Green Paper, however, it claimed that existing copyright laws covered almost all its recommendations; all Congress needed to do was make some minor clarifying, cleanup amendments.

Samuelson and the other scholars, however, showed that part of the copyright industry was trying to use the legislation to tilt the balance away from advancing knowledge and toward making more money for them. This included putting much of the Internet under private control—their control.

In February 1996, the House Subcommittee on Courts, the Internet, and Intellectual Property held hearings on the proposed legislation, an initial step in enacting a new law. In April, the administration's efforts to convert the White Paper's recommendations into law stalled after Secretary Brown's death. Lehman could not pull the opposing interests together.

Lehman's fair-use standards particularly disturbed library associations. Traditionally, libraries have been able to photocopy books or other printed publications and make them available to individuals, while also preserving the actual books for future users. A long-established legal principle called the "first sale doctrine" permits copyright owners to control only the first sale of their work, not subsequent sales of that specific copy of a book or publication. This doctrine undergirds America's public library system; thus, someone who legally buys or receives a book can sell it to someone else, such as another reader or a used bookstore, without the copyright holder's permission.

Under Lehman's proposal, however, the right to dispose of, pass on, or distribute some digital works did not include the right to make copies, even though all electronic distribution first requires the computer to make a copy. Libraries would be required to obtain the permission of the copyright owners before making a digital copy, which essentially means they would be licensing works and creating pay-for-view libraries. At best, the White Paper did not set clear guidelines for fair-use duplication. At worst, it eliminated fair use. Samuelson's premise was dead on: whether intentionally or not, Lehman was engineering a "copyright grab" for the copyright-based industries.

Throughout this battle, Lehman's background as a lobbyist for copyright-based corporations overshadowed his reputation as an intellectual property expert. Articles describing the legislation would typically note his past work and relationships, inferring that he was still doing the bidding of his former clients.

Such criticism ignored how Washington's revolving-door culture works. While writing a book on lobbying, I interviewed Harry McPherson on this subject. Over McPherson's long career, he had been President Johnson's White House counsel and an important adviser to President Clinton as well as other major political figures of our time. McPherson is also one of Washington's quieter but more effective lawyer-lobbyists. He observed: "Most lobbyists are not born with a position on catalytic converters. In developing the argument for their client's position, they often convince themselves of its truth." His point is that lobbyists tend to seduce themselves into believing what their clients pay them to say.

All evidence suggests that Lehman strongly believed in what he advocated. He was a true believer, skilled in the ways of Washington and obsessed with implementing his legislative agenda.

Lehman was unable to get his White Paper legislation approved by either the House or Senate in 1996. Key congressional leaders told him they would never enact his legislation as drafted. Their message was simple: do not come back until you have a consensus bill approved by the major interests.

Lehman was undeterred. He had figured out how to make an end run around his opponents. He would convert his draft legislation into language that could be incorporated into a new international copyright treaty at the forthcoming WIPO meeting in Geneva. Once a majority of the other nations were won over, Lehman intended to submit the resulting treaty to Congress for ratification with an up-or-down vote. He would do in Geneva, through a treaty, what he could not do with stand-alone legislation in Congress.

Lehman moved quickly, since the WIPO conference was scheduled to convene in Geneva on December 2, 1996. He posted a notice and request for public comments in the *Federal Register* in mid-October, allowing five weeks for responses. In the notice, Lehman announced that the United States would attempt to establish three new international agreements at the WIPO conference. One would strengthen global protections for sound recordings and recordings of live performances. The second would enhance safeguards for copyrights in the digital world. The third would create new protections to secure databases against the destruction of their commercial value.

Lehman's notice in the *Federal Register* created a political firestorm. Opponents of the White Paper recommendations began to understand his strategy, and they mounted a counterattack. The proposed database treaty attracted the most controversy. It also drew a particularly formidable opponent: James Love, director of the Consumer Project on Technology, an organization created by consumer advocate Ralph Nader in 1995. Love, who holds degrees from Harvard's Kennedy School of Government and Princeton's Woodrow Wilson School of Public and International Affairs, had long worked to get developing nations better and less expensive access to medicines. In the 1990s, he also became involved in a variety of public policy disputes surrounding electronic commerce. It was this involvement that brought him to the database issue.

The legal niceties of such a proposed treaty don't normally raise politicians' blood pressure. Love, however, found a way to attract the interest of the politicians. He published several papers describing how Lehman's treaty would change the way private vendors controlled and distributed statistics currently in the public domain. Stock prices, weather data, train schedules, and data from AIDS research, he wrote, would be only part of the information that vendors would control. A private company would be able to take formerly public data and charge a toll for each use.

If this weren't alarming enough, Love argued that the treaty would also cover sports statistics. It would allow major-league baseball owners, the National Football League, the National Hockey League, and other sports organizations to tightly control statistics and their distribution. Team owners could create a pay-for-view world for fans who now got their statistics free. Of course, few doubted that the owners would try to wring a few more dollars out of fans if Congress gave them the means. Any politician could understand how unpopular this would be with both voters and the media.

The concern, however, went far beyond sports statistics. Lehman's request for comments in the *Federal Register* brought many sharply worded responses in opposition. James H. Billington, librarian of Congress, wrote Laura D'Andrea Tyson, assistant to the president for economic policy, that while the Copyright Office, which is part of the Library of Congress, had assisted Lehman in his prior work, information concerning the proposed database treaty had not been available until September 1996, and Congress had not yet debated it. Billington urged that the United States not make this treaty a part of the WIPO agreement.

Michael F. DiMario, head of the Government Printing Office, wrote Lehman that if the printing of such government publications as the *Congressional Record* were placed in private hands, as many Republicans in Congress were then urging, private contractors would then own congressional databases, including transcripts of sessions, legislation, hearings, reports, and related documents. DiMario pointed out that the database treaty would give private-sector contractors, operating at the taxpayers' expense, control of government-generated information and drastically reduce free public access to that information.

Dun and Bradstreet also wrote Lehman a letter of opposition to the database treaty, as did publisher Michael Bloomberg, another important database provider. The presidents of the National Academy of Sciences, the National Academy of Engineering, and the Institute of Engineering sent a joint letter of opposition arguing that the White Paper represented a threat to the distribution of data among scientists and researchers.

This opposition, however, deterred neither President Clinton, who had just won reelection in 1996, nor his patent commissioner, who let his critics have their say and then went to Geneva to put his White Paper into the global copyright treaty. His U.S. opponents joined him there.

Geneva has roughly the same population as Omaha or Tulsa, about 400,000. It is both an ancient and a modern city; more than a third of its population is composed of foreigners from more than two hundred nations. Most of them are involved with the many international organizations headquartered there—the World Health Organization, the World Trade Organization, the Red Cross, and the WIPO, among others—making Geneva a diplomatic central point. Geneva provides the infrastructure diplomats and lobbyists need to do their jobs, though at a very high price. Some companies spent as much as $30,000 per lobbyist during the three-week WIPO conference.

The issues in the WIPO meeting were divided among working groups, and decisions were made by vote; each member nation has one vote. As in Congress, delegates tried to influence one another, formed coalitions, and made deals. With a majority vote, a proposal at WIPO could be killed or enacted.

Those opposing the Lehman proposals in Geneva included Love, the forty-two-member Digital Future Coalition, the Home Recording Rights Coalition, and librarian associations. Lobbyists for the copyright industries were also there in full force, including the software, music, and movie industries, supporting Lehman.

The American opponents to Lehman's treaty kept daily vote counts on the various proposals. Their big harvest was from the many small and developing nations at the conference. Asian delegates, for instance, feared that a ban on digital decoding devices might apply to the computers Asia manufactured for export to the United States and Europe. African representatives opposed protections that benefited copyright holders from advanced industrial nations—a traditional developing-world stance. Back in the United States, Lehman's opponents were bombarding President Clinton with letters and e-mails, urging that he withdraw the treaty proposals. One letter's signatories included Steve Case of America Online and the heads of BellSouth, CompuServe, MCI, PSI, NYNEX, Prodigy, and UUNet Technologies.

Three days after the opposing telecommunication letter arrived at the White House, the president received a message from the CEOs of IBM, Microsoft, and the movie companies supporting Lehman's position, pledging their aid for the administration's proposals in Congress.

Ultimately, the WIPO negotiations degenerated into an endurance match. The first thing delegates dropped was the proposed treaty on databases—the opposition was simply too great, both in Geneva and in Washington. On the last evening, however, the delegates still had not settled the issue of whether to make the telephone companies and Internet providers responsible for monitoring copyright infringements; finally, they also removed that provision from the treaty.

The delegates also diluted the Lehman proposal outlawing the manufacture or use of devices that could get around encryption of copyrighted digital works. Under article 11 of the final treaty, member nations were obligated only to provide "adequate legal protection and effective legal remedies against circumventions" not authorized by the copyright owners or by law. In other words, WIPO made illegal the act of pirating but not the technology used. Under the provisions, legal purchasers of CDs, DVDs, or software could still make personal copies, if that did not violate the license agreements and if they could successfully get around the disc's internal software that prevented copying—the cyberlock.

A little after midnight on the last day, negotiations were completed and the delegates approved two treaties. The accord on performances and phonograms gave individuals the exclusive rights to broadcast their performances to the public. The compact also granted them the right to control their work for broadcast, recording, reproduction, distribution, and rental, and the right to be paid when anyone uses copyrighted computer programs as literary works. It permitted authors of literary and artistic works to authorize the communication of their works to the public by wire or wireless means. Copyrights thus entered the digital age. The treaties set the minimum duration of WIPO protection at fifty years; however, member nations were empowered to provide protections in their home countries for longer periods if they desired.

Whatever provisions Lehman lost in Geneva, he still had a chance to restore them back in Washington, because new implementing legislation was required to enact the WIPO treaty.

Working privately, the principal U.S. corporate interests affected by the WIPO treaty reached their own agreement on what the eventual legislation would contain. The telephone companies, Internet service providers, and computer makers would get legal immunity for what was transmitted over the Net. In exchange, they agreed to remove any offending content once notified by the copyright owner. Thus, the movie, music, and other copyright industries received control over their works distributed through wire or wireless means.

Lehman reintroduced his White Paper proposal on circumvention devices as part of the legislation implementing the WIPO treaty. His proposal went much further than required by WIPO, completely banning the manufacture, distribution, or use of circumvention devices and setting stiff penalties for violations. He also introduced his database proposals.

Representative Rick Boucher (D.-Va.) led the opposition against Lehman's proposals. Boucher, a lawyer and expert on intellectual property, wrote the 1992 legislation that allowed the first commercial traffic on the Internet. In 1996, he also formed the Congressional Internet Caucus, which he chaired. Despite Boucher's knowledge and opposition, Lehman and his Hollywood backers prevailed and Congress passed the legislation, including the provision banning circumvention devices but excluding the database proposal. Thus, even if you own a recording or piece of software, it is illegal to break any cyberlocks it may contain, even to make a personal backup copy.

The principal factor in Lehman's victory was the telephone and Internet companies. Now they had their deal and were no longer responsible for what ran over their wires. With that decided, these corporations moved to the political sidelines and the fight became one between the copyright interests and the librarian associations, an unequal match for sure: the librarians lost.

On October 25, 1998, Lehman announced his resignation. Three days later, in a White House ceremony with Lehman standing in the background, President Clinton signed the Digital Millennium Copyright Act of 1998 and praised his patent commissioner for his efforts.

After leaving the patent office, Lehman formed the International Intellectual Property Institute (IIPI), a Washington-based think tank devoted to educating developing nations on how tougher intellectual property laws would help their economic growth. The founding contributors included Microsoft, IBM, Merck, Schering-Plough, Ford, the Business Software Alliance, the Biotechnology Industry Organization, and Bacardi.

In 2001, Congress directed the patent office to provide Lehman's institute not less than $1 million "to promote sustainable development in developing countries and to protect business interests by assisting in the establishment of intellectual property legal frameworks." The IIPI's Web site reports that 93 percent of its funding now comes from the U.S. government and 3 percent from WIPO, where Lehman is a member of the director general's policy advisory committee. In June 2004, the Washington law firm of Akin Gump Strauss Hauer & Feld announced that Lehman had joined it as senior counsel in Washington to advise clients on "all aspects" of intellectual property law.

Lehman's exit from the public spotlight was opportune, for he barely escaped being caught in the middle of two contentious political battles involving copyright legislation enacted during his public tenure. The first concerned the Digital Millennium Copyright Act. The fight was triggered by an eighteen-year-old dropout from Boston's Northeastern University named Shawn Fanning, who wrote a piece of software, distributed for free, that allowed Internet users to swap music stored on one another's computers.

Napster, a corporate name based on Fanning's nickname (because of the nappy hair under his ever-present baseball cap), was one of the fastest successes in U.S. business history and went far beyond the management capacities of its founders. Napster was an instant threat to the music industry. On December 7, 1999, the Recording Industry Association of America (RIAA) sued Napster for damages amounting to $100,000 for each song copied. The suit was the first big test of Lehman's Digital Millennium Copyright Act. By then, millions of people were using their Internet connections to download tens of millions of songs, with not a penny of royalties going to the artists or music companies who owned the copyrights.

In July 2000, the RIAA persuaded a federal judge to issue a preliminary injunction and order Napster to close down. At this point, Napster claimed to have 38 million users. If it was guilty of copyright violations, so too were its 38 million users. And if the swapping of music were eventually penalized with damages of $100,000 per song, as the lawsuit sought, the RIAA case represented one of the potentially largest monetary awards in U.S. history.

Various "white knight" rescuers attempted to devise a business solution that could transform Napster into a fee-based subscription company that would pay royalties to artists and recording companies whenever their music was downloaded. But a workable deal was never struck. Napster went bankrupt in the fall of 2002, and its assets, including the company name, were sold at auction. By then, millions of music buyers were disgusted with the recording companies, which many people perceived as greedy and grasping.

A more appropriate description for those executives would be "unimaginative." The new copyright law gave them every legal advantage against Napster; yet they were unable to devise a new formula or a business model for selling their music to Napster's 38 million potential customers.

Ironically, a successful new business model did appear, not from the music industry but from a computer company. In April 2003, Steve Jobs, CEO of Apple Computer, introduced a new Internet service, the iTunes Music Store. It allows customers to download individual songs for 99 cents or complete albums for $9.99. No subscription is needed, and customers pay only for the music they download. In its first year of operation, more than 70 million songs were downloaded. The purchased songs can be sorted into personalized playlists. The Apple download license allows the songs to be played on five computers at any one time, and the buyer can burn seven copies of a playlist. Individual songs can be legally copied onto an unlimited number of CDs for personal use.

Time magazine named the iTunes Music Store one of the "coolest inventions of 2003" and congratulated Apple for "converting millions of music pirates into credit-card-wielding music buyers." Several other companies quickly followed Apple's lead and now offer their own equipment and music lists.

Even though the Digital Millennium Copyright Act was tightly written, making illegal any unauthorized exchanges of copyrighted material, millions of Americans continue to violate that law. In September 2003, the recording industry filed lawsuits against 261 people, including a twelve-year-old New York girl living in public housing, for illegally sharing music over the Internet. Suing a young girl living in poverty, and then taking her family's money, was a clear signal that no one was immune to prosecution by the music industry. Subsequently, hundreds of other suits have been filed.

The objective of these lawsuits is threefold: (1) to educate file sharers that they are breaking the law; (2) to make illegal song swapping so risky that most people will not do it; and (3) to encourage people who download songs over the Internet to use legal vendors, such as Apple and Sony. The RIAA believes its strategy is working. On March 23, 2004, it released the results of a poll conducted by Peter D. Hart Research Associates that revealed that 63 percent of the U.S. public believes it is illegal to "make music from the computer available for others to download for free over the Internet." Hart also reported that a majority of the American public (56 percent) is "supportive and understanding" of the recording industry's lawsuits against "those who are illegally sharing music over the Internet."

While the Napster saga dominated the attention of millions of Internet users between 1999 and 2003, a less visible, but equally significant, copyright war was being fought in Congress and the courts. It concerned the Sonny Bono Copyright Term Extension Act of 1998, which President Clinton signed into law one week after Lehman's resignation as patent commissioner.

Sonny Bono was a showman, entrepreneur, and popular member of Congress who died in a January 1998 skiing accident. Congressional leaders honored his memory by attaching his name to legislation that would extend a copyright's duration for an additional twenty years. A more appropriate name for the legislation would have been the Disney Corporation Copyright Protection Act because Disney's copyrights on Mickey Mouse would have expired in 2003 and those on Goofy, Pluto, and Donald Duck would have lapsed in 2009. Without those copyrights, Disney would have lost its exclusive right to market literally thousands of products based on these cartoon characters. Other copyright holders, such as the Gershwin Trusts, holders of the copyrights on the music of George and Ira Gershwin, faced the same loss of control and royalties on older works. Rather than allow their valuable properties to enter the public domain, these copyright holders and others arranged a legislative fix: they persuaded President Clinton and the Congress to extend the duration of copyright protection—the eleventh incremental extension between 1962 and 1998.

If legislation were named for political tactics, this bill would be called the Stealth Copyright Extension Act, because its sponsors sneaked the legislation through Congress. The bill's managers arranged for the draft legislation to arrive on both floors the same day, October 7, 1998. That morning, the Senate Judiciary Committee discharged the bill by unanimous consent (everyone agreed and no vote was recorded) and sent it to the floor, where it was quickly passed by voice vote. The entire process on the floor of the Senate took fewer than thirty minutes.

Then the Senate sent the bill to the House, where it was officially received at 4:34 p.m. At 10:02 that same evening, House members suspended the rules by a voice vote. At 10:24 p.m.—only twenty-two minutes later—the bill was approved by another voice vote and sent to the president for his signature. No one objected and no one asked for a recorded roll call vote in either the Senate or the House. Twenty days later, the president signed the legislation, making it Public Law No. 105-298.

The Congressional Research Service estimates that this twenty-year copyright extension will cost consumers approximately $330 million in additional royalties on works from the twenty-year period 1922–1941, whose copyrights would otherwise have expired.

With the Bono Act, Congress threw aside any pretense that the "limited time" it sets for exclusive use by copyright holders has any connection whatsoever with providing creative incentives for authors or artists. The act was passed for one purpose: to reward a handful of powerful political supporters and political interests whose old copyrights are still commercially viable. One wag suggested that Congress just extend the copyright term to perpetuity and save Disney and others the expense of hiring more lobbyists in 2017.

For many legal scholars and public interest groups, Congress and the copyright industry crossed an invisible line by radically altering copyright law's balance in favor of commerce at the expense of the public domain. Their anger was transformed into a constitutional challenge to Congress's power to extend the term of an existing copyright. The point person in this case was Lawrence Lessig, a widely recognized expert on constitutional law, technology, and cyberspace.

In January 1999, Lessig filed a lawsuit on behalf of Eric Eldred, a noncommercial Internet publisher, challenging the twenty-year copyright extension. He made two basic arguments: that the extension violated the Constitution's "limited time" requirement in the "authors and inventors clause" and that it violated the First Amendment's freedom of speech provisions.

The lower courts dismissed the case, but the Supreme Court agreed to review their decision. A group of lawyers whose practices regularly brought them before the Court assisted Lessig in preparing his case. In addition, friend-of-the-court briefs supporting the petition were filed by five constitutional law professors, seventeen distinguished economists (including several Nobel Prize winners), fifty-three intellectual property–law professors, fifteen library associations, the National Writers Union, the Organization of American Historians, and the Eagle Forum, among others.

Supporters of the Bono Act also filed friend-of-the-court briefs, among them the Directors Guild of America, the Symphonic and Concert Composers, the Motion Picture Association of America, and the Recording Artists Coalition, plus a group of House Judiciary Committee members and the Songwriters Guild.

The Supreme Court heard arguments on October 9, 2002, and issued its ruling on January 15, 2003. Writing for the 7–2 majority, Justice Ruth Bader Ginsburg announced that Congress had acted constitutionally when it had extended the copyright term of both existing and future works.

The Court's decision was an impressive victory for the copyright industry, making another constitutional challenge unlikely, at least in the near future, if not for several decades. In the meantime, the industry could return to Congress for another term extension.

Lessig responded to his Supreme Court defeat by writing a critically well received book, *Free Culture,* which delves into the history of the case and the issues and then reviews his arguments. He concludes that he argued constitutional issues to the justices, when he should have made a political argument about the social costs of the Bono Act. Whether or not a different argument would have made any difference, the social cost argument is powerful. It begins with the economic fact that most copyrighted works have a limited commercial life—only a tiny portion of books, articles, records, or movies produce any royalties two or more years after they are introduced. Only 2 percent of the works whose copyrights were extended by the Sonny Bono Act (those released between 1923 and 1943) still have any commercial value, according to Lessig.

Jason Schultz, a staff attorney at the Electronic Frontier Foundation, a nonprofit civil liberties organization based in San Francisco, has also calculated the economic life of copyrighted books and movies. For books, the measure is the number kept in print for sale over time. For films, it is the number available for rent or sale. For the twenty-year period affected by the Copyright Extension Act of 1976 (1927–1946), Schultz found that of the 187,280 titles published over those two decades, only 4,267 were still available from publishers in 2002. Thus, by Schultz's count, only 2.3 percent of those works are still commercially available.

Schultz reports that 36,386 movies were released during that twenty-year period, the "golden age" of films, but as of 2002, only 13 were in theaters, 871 were available on DVD, and 2,480 were on VHS. From that era, he calculates, only 6.8 percent remain commercially available.

In other words, more than 93 percent of the movies released and almost 98 percent of the books published in the twenty-year period 1927–1946 are past their economic life, unable to produce rents for their owners; they are languishing, mostly unused, on library shelves or in storage bins, often with their very existence unknown. Under existing copyright laws, they cannot be digitalized or used without the permission of the owners, a daunting condition, since that ownership is often unclear and the risk of violating copyrights is high and can be expensive.

This "great lockup" of most old copyrighted materials exists because the economic rewards from extending those few that are still commercial can be significant. The song "Happy Birthday to You," for instance, produces $2 million a year in royalties. The song was copyrighted in 1935. Absent the term extensions provided in the 1976 and 1998 copyright acts, it would have entered the public domain in 1991. Because of the extensions, however, the copyright on "Happy Birthday to You" runs until the year 2030. Approximately half of the $2 million royalties the song earns annually go to the AOL Time Warner media conglomerate, the world's largest music publisher.

If people are still singing "Happy Birthday to You" in 2029, executives at AOL Time Warner, or its successor company, will surely mount, or join, a lobbying campaign to get another copyright term extension. Indeed, given the high probability of political success, the company would be failing its stockholders if it didn't make an attempt.

The political point is this: the copyright extension laws of 1831, 1909, 1976, and 1998 were predictable responses by Congress to the demands of a handful of copyright owners. If a fifth major term extension is likely and constitutional—and it is both—the two most practical means to move commercially dormant materials under copyright into the public domain are through voluntary agreement by copyright owners and through new legislation.

To encourage voluntary action, in 2001 Lessig and others created a nonprofit organization called Creative Commons that helps copyright owners offer some of their rights to others in a flexible manner. Initiated at the Harvard Law School's Berkman Center and now housed and staffed at Stanford Law School, Creative Commons has devised eleven licenses that copyright holders can apply to their materials to give them wider use. One allows others to use copyrighted works as long as credit is given. Another permits the use of materials, but only for noncommercial purposes. Nine other variants also exist.

While Creative Commons offers a laboratory for demonstrating what is possible, only new legislation can break the grip copyright laws hold on the vast bulk of noncommercial works, particularly older materials. Following the 2003 Supreme Court decision, Lessig and a group of his colleagues developed a legislative proposal to that end. In June 2003, it was converted into draft legislation and introduced by Representative Zoe Lofgren (D.-Calif.). The short title is the Public Domain Enhancement Act. It requires the Register of Copyrights to charge $1 "for maintaining in force the copyright in any published U.S. work."

Lofgren's bill had twelve co-sponsors in the House but none in the Senate. The draft legislation was referred to the House Judiciary Committee, where it was shelved. As currently structured, the Public Domain Enhancement Act has not proven appealing to members of Congress. The proposed legislation does contain provisions that any new law should include. It shortens the original patent term. It allows extensions at ten-year intervals. It makes registering for an extension easy and inexpensive.

The bill's principal flaw is that it offers nothing to the owners of those relatively few valuable copyrights that will move into the public domain after 2020. If the treasury of materials now needlessly held captive by existing copyright law is to be freed into the public domain without violating the rights of copyright owners, bolder legislation is required.

Public domain advocates, working closely with the copyright industries, might forge what could be called the "great copyright deal." The goal would be to (a) provide incentives for creativity, (b) quickly move copyrighted works into the public domain after their commercial life is ended, and (c) facilitate longer terms (even forever) for those rare works with an extended economic life. Ideally, the legislation would contain the following elements:

280

- Copyrights would be granted for a short period, perhaps the fourteen-year term set by Congress in 1790.

- Copyrights could be extended thereafter in ten-year blocks if registered with the Copyright Office by their owner.

- Copyright owners who failed to register their work when the original copyright expired would have a grace period of some time, such as two years, to make their first filing, with a shorter grace period, such as one year, after each subsequent tenth-year registration.

- Copyright owners could register their works in ten-year blocks for as long as they wished, even in perpetuity.

- Copyright owners would have the exclusive right to decide whether to register their works for an extension.

- When the original copyright term, or the extended term, expires, and after the end of the grace period, the work would enter the public domain, becoming freely available for use by anyone.

This proposal offers the copyright industries something they want but are unlikely ever to gain on their own: an extended copyright on works that have a long commercial life. Absent this, owners must continue buying incremental term extensions from Congress.

One argument for such an arrangement is that it would treat copyrights like trademarks. If Nike can own its trademarked "swoosh" forever, then the Disney Corporation should be able to own its Mickey Mouse copyright just as long. Trademarks can be renewed forever in ten-year increments, if the owner cares to do so. If not renewed, they enter the public domain.

Politically, this is a simple solution. The copyright industries get long-term exclusive use without having to finance another major lobbying campaign. Public domain advocates are spared another expensive battle they are virtually sure to lose. Creative people have a copyright they can renew as long as they wish, and they are assured that their work, when it is no longer commercially viable or when they no longer want copyright protection, will enter the public domain. Most important, the public would gain speedier access to a large body of knowledge now kept on the shelf by copyright laws that do nothing for the copyright owners or for potential users.

Much of the knowledge created in the twentieth century exists on printed pages, wax discs, plastic tapes, and nitrate films that are slowly rotting away.

These works, the knowledge they contain, and the culture they record are available to only a handful of people, most of whom are academics or those few with access to America's premier archives.

Now, for the first time in history, we have the technological capacity to save all those works in digital form at a tiny cost and, through the Internet, easily put them at the fingertips of everyone, anywhere in the world. With that, the contributions of hundreds of thousands of authors, artists, inventors, public figures, educators, engineers, doctors, lawyers, architects, and others, now at risk of being lost, would forever be available for use.

These works are kept from public use, not for any intended national purpose but as an unintended consequence of copyright law extensions. Technically and politically, copyright laws can be modified in a way that protects works that have a long commercial life, while speeding into the public domain works that do not.

Whoever unties or cuts this Gordian knot will earn a place in history for liberating a century of knowledge for the benefit of people everywhere. It would be an accomplishment equal in importance to sending the first American to the moon.

EPILOGUE

I n early 1938, Europe was moving toward war, and President Franklin Roosevelt realized that when it came, America would be involved. To help the nation prepare itself, the president asked Congress to create a joint congressional–executive branch committee—made up of members from both houses and several federal agencies—for the purpose of investigating monopolies and concentrations in U.S. industry and recommending legislation to rectify the situation. If the challenges of war were to be met, the president believed, changes in the existing structure of business and its relationship to government would be necessary.

The Temporary National Economic Committee operated from the summer of 1938 until December 31, 1941. It examined monopoly and concentration of economic power. Its most important report, issued in the spring of 1941, revealed numerous cartel arrangements, dozens of which involved Nazi Germany, that were crippling America's ability to arm itself. In 1938, Roosevelt knew much of what the committee would eventually discover, but others had to be educated. Also, in 1938, a strong isolationist movement existed in the U.S., and the German government was financing a propaganda effort to keep the U.S. unguarded. To put a spotlight on Germany's U.S.–based propaganda efforts, Roosevelt persuaded Congress to enact the Foreign Agents Registration Act of 1938, which required lobbyists and promoters working for foreign interests to register with the Justice Department and identify their clients.

Roosevelt did not wait for the committee's report: he began his campaign against the cartels in 1938. His instrument was Yale Law School professor

Thurman Arnold, whom the president appointed assistant attorney general for antitrust. Born in Wyoming in 1891, Arnold entered Princeton at age sixteen, graduated Phi Beta Kappa in 1911, and earned a law degree from Harvard in 1914. At various times, he was a sheep rancher, mayor of Laramie, professor at the Yale Law School, federal appellate judge, and founder of a major Washington, D.C., law firm—Arnold and Porter. The historian Kenneth S. Davis describes Arnold as flamboyant, irreverent, and assertive. He enjoyed legal combat, was indifferent to criticism, and was not hesitant to use coercive power. He believed that monopolists should be imprisoned, a view frightening to many corporate CEOs of that era.

When Arnold arrived at the Justice Department in 1938, he found an Antitrust Division that had effectively been closed for two decades. Presidents Wilson, Harding, Coolidge, and Hoover were not active trustbusters. Neither was Roosevelt during the first five years of his administration, but now war was imminent and cartels posed a threat. Arnold was asked how he could possibly do his job since the Antitrust Division had only forty-eight attorneys. His answer was that he would hire all the lawyers and investigators that he needed and together they would enforce the U.S. laws. With the president's strong support, Congress gave Arnold the budget he wanted. Within twenty-four months, he had a staff of more than three hundred lawyers, including the best, brightest, and most vigorous young graduates from the leading law schools, plus a handful of experienced antitrust specialists. With great energy and publicity, Arnold and his team prosecuted 230 companies for monopoly practices and filed dozens of criminal indictments against corporate executives. No violator was immune. Most important, they discovered and broke German control over vital parts of U.S. industry and provided fodder for spectacular Senate hearings chaired by Senator Harry Truman.

The threat created by the global theft of intellectual property occurring today is parallel in many ways to the situation in 1938. Then, the cartels, the most important of which were German-controlled, were secretly imposing limits on what U.S. companies could do and were thus deliberately weakening America's capacity to arm and defend itself. Now, foreign governments are requiring the transfer of U.S.–owned technologies to their local companies as a condition of access to their markets, a requirement that both weakens the U.S. economy and national security. Then, as now, the crimes were largely invisible and enforcement of existing laws was almost nonexistent. And then, as now, the foreign governments and corporations that were stealing ideas and U.S. intellectual properties hired U.S.-based propagandists to minimize the problem and confuse the issues.

Unlike in 1938, however, important studies have been completed on the state of the U.S. scientific and technological base. We know the nation is in scientific and technological decline, though the real causes are perhaps not fully understood. In early 2003, the President's Council of Advisers on Science and Technology undertook a study on the condition of the U.S. "innovation ecosystems"—that is, America's infrastructure of basic research, precompetitive improvement, design, prototyping, and product development.

Released in January 2004, the report concluded that with manufacturing leaving the United States, the nation now runs the risk of losing much of its innovation infrastructure. The advisers explained that the relationship between manufacturing and its "ecosystem" is dynamic. Each benefits from proximity to the other, allowing new ideas to be tested, reviewed, and discussed with what the council termed "those working on the ground."

The consequences are potentially historic. Science, technology, and innovation have been the basic engine of America's economic expansion and national security for almost two hundred years. Now that engine is faltering, and a number of other major reports confirm it. The National Science Foundation reported in May 2004 that while the U.S. still leads in science and engineering, uncertainties complicate the outlook for the future. Increasingly, the NSF reports, the U.S. is relying on foreign scientists and engineers, here and abroad, to fill key jobs, largely because the proportion of young Americans earning science and engineering degrees is falling, dropping from third in the world in 1990 to seventeenth in 2004. U.S.-based authors' output of scientific articles has remained flat since 1992. The NSF also notes that China and Korea are producing a growing share of the world's high-tech exports (30 percent in 2003), an area once dominated by U.S. companies.

A collective of fourteen groups associated with academia and business announced in April 2004 the formation of the Task Force on the Future of American Innovation. The group cited the reason for its creation as the "serious risk that the American discovery stream will be reduced to a trickle with a negative impact on innovation in the U.S." The task force says that despite the importance of science, research, and innovation to the nation, funding for such efforts both in constant dollars and as a share of GDP has declined by 37 percent since the early 1970s.

Strikingly, the massive theft of U.S.–owned intellectual properties as a contributing cause to America's technological decline has been almost totally overlooked in these reports. The President's Council of Advisers on Science and Technology recommends, but with no explanation, "that the Administration and the USTR work with the WTO to implement an expedited dispute resolution process to deal with Intellectual Property (IP) violations and denial of market access."

The implication is that the WTO is not acting speedily enough on U.S. filings. But the issue is not the pace with which the WTO resolves intellectual property disputes, it is that the United States has not brought a single intellectual property case to the WTO since June 2000—not one. The larger issue is that the U.S. government devotes virtually no resources to deterring, catching, and punishing those foreign-based pirates who are stealing our ideas and intellectual properties.

In political, diplomatic, business, and academic circles, the stealing of ideas is an unpleasant topic, often ignored, particularly when the identity, mores, and motivations of the alleged thief are part of that discussion. Certainly, this is the American experience of many decades. The United States has had such a treasure trove of scientific advances and technologies that its political and business leaders have been willing to overlook the theft of even the most important discoveries, inventions, and applications in order to avoid unpleasant confrontations.

But now global intellectual property theft is so widespread that it threatens America's technological preeminence, its economic well-being, and its national security. Fortunately, the global treaties, international mechanisms, and domestic laws needed to stop this crime wave already exist. The financial resources required to hire more customs inspectors, more investigators at the Food and Drug Administration, more FBI agents, and more federal prosecutors are trivial, particularly compared to the cost and consequences of the crime. America also has many capable people who could lead this fight, educate the public about the issue, and secure widespread public support, much as Thurmond Arnold and his team did more than six decades ago.

What is missing is the will of U.S. political leaders to confront those who are stealing U.S.-owned intellectual properties and with them the future of the American people. Until that will is developed, the United States will remain in economic, scientific, and technological decline. The tragedy is that this decline need not be.

ACKNOWLEDGMENTS

A book's acknowledgments section is one of the many small pleasures that reading provides. Most authors realize how much their work depends on the efforts of others. Certainly, I do. It is always interesting to see how and to whom they express their gratitude.

Hot Property would not have been written without the support of four people. Kay Casey, my wife, re-ordered our work and leisure so that I would have the time and solitude needed to research and write, and she patiently tolerated my inevitable obsession with the subject. Jerome Lemelson, who tutored me on the role that intellectual property protections exert in the innovation process, convinced me to do the book and his foundation provided the initial funding to do my research. He is missed. Ashbel Green, my editor, supported the project from its inception, conceived the title less than five minutes after I began my pitch for the book and provided wonderful insights and suggestions as it took shape. Roger Milliken granted the funding that sustained my work on this project and he maintained a much-appreciated inquiring interest in the subject.

Several other people contributed greatly. Luba Ostashevsky, Ashbel Green's editorial assistant, made insightful recommendations as the book was being written, and she kept the mechanics of the process moving in a most orderly way. Susanna Sturgis did a brilliant job of copyediting the manuscript. Larry Klayman managed the Freedom of Information requests that got me access to so many otherwise unavailable sources.

One of the many disadvantages of a friendship with an author is that you might be asked to read an initial draft and offer candid comments—a burdensome task at best. Edward and Helen Miller, Susan and Martin Tolchin, Steve Clemons, Roger Fontaine, and Eamonn Fingleton each suffered that fate. With grace, they carefully read various editions of the manuscript and shared their observations with me. John Davis, a neighbor and friend, who thought of himself as a retired editor, kindly located his red pencil and offered many insights that greatly improved the book.

Richard McCormack provided endless examples (www.manufacturingnews .com).

Sam and Wanda Snead found us a quiet place to work and Berkeley Hobson skillfully translated the many reference works I used into useful notes.

Dozens of other people have generously given me their time and suggestions. Many remain in positions where they prefer anonymity. I will thank them privately.

Throughout this book, I highlight books, reports and articles that I found particularly interesting and informative. For those who wish to know more, they are an appropriate starting point.

To all these friends and colleagues, thank you.

Washington, Virginia
January 2005

NOTES

INTRODUCTION: MY FAKE ROLEX

4   These sales are: Terminology is basic in the discussion of any issue. Not surprisingly, certain words and phrases associated with a discussion of patents, copyrights, trademarks, and trade secrets may seem vague or appear to represent a foregone conclusion. Richard M. Stallman has captured several of what he calls "loaded" words in an essay in *Free Software, Free Society: The Selected Essays of Richard M. Stallman,* published by the Free Software Foundation, Boston, Mass. He writes that the term "intellectual property" contains a "hidden assumption" that equates patents, copyrights, trademarks, and trade secrets with "our ideas of physical property." He also objects to the term "piracy" being used in connection with copyrights because it implies that illegal copying is "ethically equivalent to attacking ships on the high seas, kidnapping and murdering the people on them." Instead of "protection," he thinks it more correct to explain that a "copyright has a long term" or "copyright restrictions last a very long time." His essay contains several other terms that, he thinks, cause confusion. I found Stallman's piece useful. It is on the Internet, and I recommend it to those interested in this topic.

Noting his objections, and those of others who hold a similar view, I have generally used the more commonly employed definitions of "intellectual property," "pirates," "counterfeiting," and "bootlegging." The U.S. Department of Justice presents these definitions in its manual *Federal Prosecution of Violations of Intellectual Property Rights,* chapter 1, "The Protection of Intellectual Property—An Overview," U.S Justice Department, 1997, footnote 2, p. 2:

> The terms "bootlegging," "piracy," and "counterfeiting" are similar but not synonymous. "Bootlegging" generally refers to the unauthorized recording and distribution of musical performances. "Piracy" involves the unauthorized reproduction of an existing copyrighted work or distribution of an infringing copy. However, the original packaging or graphics

of the genuine merchandise are not copied. "Counterfeiting," by contrast, occurs when an infringer not only reproduces and distributes infringing merchandise, but also copies the genuine packaging of the product. In such cases, the counterfeiter is attempting to pass off his or her products as legitimate goods produced by the original manufacturer.

The Justice Department uses this manual to educate federal prosecutors and agents on intellectual property rights. The Justice Department defines patents, copyrights, trademarks, and trade secrets as "intellectual property." The department views its job as helping this nation's intellectual-property owners to "protect" their legal rights against those who would "bootleg," "pirate," "counterfeit," or "steal" their patents, copyrights, trademarks, or trade secrets.

5   Consider this: the Chinese government: Craig S. Smith, "Tale of Piracy: How the Chinese Stole the Grinch," *New York Times,* December 12, 2000.

5   Yet, throughout China: "2003 China Piracy Fact Sheet," *MPA Worldwide Market Research,* December 2003, p. 2. Much of the digital piracy in China is done on video compact discs (VCDs), a format akin to DVDs' though its quality is inferior. However, VCD machines are much less inexpensive to make than DVD-only players.

5   To get a copy: "2003 China Piracy Fact Sheet," *MPA Worldwide Market Research,* December 2003, p. 2; Chris Buckley, "Helped by Technology, Piracy of DVDs Runs Rampant in China," *New York Times,* August 18, 2003.

5   Pirated copies of: Claude Brodesser, "Meeting Raul: On the Trail of the Copycats," *Vlife,* December 2003, p. 69. Brodesser went to downtown Los Angeles, where he found pirate distributors selling DVDs of movies. He found pirates selling movies that had not yet been released, including *Master and Commander* and *Looney Tunes: Back in Action.* In late October 2003, U.S. commerce secretary Dan Evans went to China to discuss that nation's lack of enforcement on pirating and counterfeiting. Michael A. Lev, foreign correspondent for the *Chicago Tribune,* reported that Evans could walk into Broad Luck, a chain of state-owned stores, "controlled by a government-run studio that operates under the Ministry of Culture," and pay $1 for a DVD copy of Quentin Tarantino's movie *Kill Bill: Vol. 1.* "U.S. Prods China to Crack Down on Counterfeit Goods; Even State-owned Shops Sell Bootlegs," *Chicago Tribune,* October 29, 2003.

5   The country's knockoff vendors: Smith, "Tale of Piracy."

5   In Pakistan, illegally duplicated: "IIPA 2004 'Special 301,' Recommendations to USTR" (Washington, D.C.: International Intellectual Property Alliance, February 13, 2004), p. 1.

5   In Russia, music thieves: Ibid.

5   In China and Vietnam: International Planning and Research Corporation, "Piracy Study" (Washington, D.C.: Business Software Alliance, June 2003), pp. 7–8.

5   In Eastern Europe: Ibid.

5   Only days after it was introduced: Pete Engardio and Dexter Roberts, "Microsoft's Long March," *Business Week,* June 24, 1996, international edition.

5   A decade later: Kristi Heim, "Microsoft Hopes for Return on Costly Investment in China," *San Jose Mercury News,* March 16, 2004.

5   Three out of four Italian producers: International Chamber of Commerce Commercial Crimes Services, "Fakes Threaten Fabric of Italian Society," news archives 2000, December 11, 2000.

5   Also, more than 80 percent: Ibid.

6   For instance, anyone who flies: National Safety Council, "What Are the Odds of Dying?" Ithaca, IL, Figures were calculated from data presented on pages 1 and 2.

6   The Federal Aviation Administration (FAA) reports: William L. Maynard and Paul D. Moak, *Repaired and Reconditioned Products in the Aviation Industry* (Houston: Beirne, Maynard & Parsons, LLP, 1997), p. 1.

6   And while the FAA is responsible: Report on Aviation Safety, "Part VII, Aircraft Parts: 'Bogus' or 'Unapproved,' "Association of the Bar of the City of New York Aeronautics Committee, *Aviation Today,* June 1998, p. 2.

6   It enables counterfeiters: Ibid.

6   In its 1996 study: Willy Stern, "Warning! Bogus Parts Have Turned Up in Commercial Jets. Where's the FAA?," *Business Week,* June 10, 1996. Stern cites the FAA for the 26 million parts installed on airplanes each year. He also notes that the FAA did an internal audit of its own repair facilities, which revealed that 2 percent of the parts in its bins were bogus. He also notes that the FAA "says the sample in its audit was too small to extrapolate the prevalence of counterfeit parts."

6   Strandflex: NASA Office of Inspector General, "NASA Contractor Pleads Guilty," news release (Washington, D.C., June 4, 2001).

6   Airline cable connects: John Sullivan, "FAA Lagged in Its Response to a Warning," *New York Times,* June 17, 2000. In January 1999, a former employee of Strandflex went to federal prosecutors with the allegation that the company was not testing the cable it was selling to airlines and the U.S. government. Federal investigators soon confirmed the story and informed the Department of Defense. However, the FAA did not inform the airlines. When John Sullivan learned of the story in May of that year, the FAA quickly posted a notice.

6   When tested by the U.S. Air Force: Letter to Kenneth Mead, inspector general, U.S. Department of Transportation, Washington, D.C., from Representatives Peter A. DeFazio (D.-Ore.) and William O. Lipinski (R.-Ill.), House Aviation Subcommittee, U.S. House of Representatives (Committee Print, June 30, 2000).

6   Air force investigators: "Causing False Claims," Defense Criminal Investigative Service, Office of the Inspector General, U.S. Department of Defense, *Crime Awareness Newsletter,* vol. 03-02, May 2002, pp. 4–5.

6   The plane was grounded: Ibid.

6   Southwest Airlines found: John Sullivan, "F.A.A. Is Faulted over Its Warning

on Airline Cables," *New York Times,* August 14, 2000. On December 5, 2002, David Waddell, the former manager of the Strandflex plant where the cable was produced, was sentenced in U.S. District Court in Syracuse, New York, to one year's probation, including six months of home confinement. Strandflex was ordered to pay a criminal fine of $500,000 and restitution of $100,000. The company also paid $1 million to settle the civil complaint filed by the former employee. (See Office of Inspector General, U.S. Department of Transportation, "Former Plant Manager Sentenced for False Claims About Aircraft Control Cable, news release, December 5, 2002.)

6   Or consider the case: Office of the Inspector General, U.S. Department of Transportation, "Firm, Vice-President Plead Guilty in Substandard Aircraft Parts Case," news release, July 7, 1999.

6   "flight-critical": Ibid.

6   But Air-Pro falsified: Ibid.

7   Finally, investigators discovered: Ibid. The U.S. District Court in Miami fined John Wilson, vice president of Air-Pro, $2,000 and put him on probation for eighteen months. Air-Pro agreed to pay a fine of $200,000 and pay for approximately $138,000 of replacement hoses. James Harris, the quality control manager for the company, was fined $1,500, given three hundred hours of community service, and put on probation for two years.

7   Or consider West Coast Aluminum Heat Treating Co.: U.S. Department of Transportation, "Firm, Principals Convicted for Failure to Properly Temper Critical Aircraft Parts," news release, March 3, 1999.

7   In April 2001, the FAA: Federal Aviation Administration, "Unapproved Parts Notification," news release, April 12, 2001; U.S. Department of Transportation, "Processor of Key Aircraft Parts Indicted, Fraudulent Quality Control Alleged," news release, May 26, 1998. A U.S. District Court judge in Los Angeles fined the company $1.6 million. Company president June Fitch was fined $70,000 and put on probation for three years. Vice president Eugene Fitch was sentenced to fifty-five months in federal prison. (See U.S. Department of Transportation, "Firm, Principals Convicted for Failure to Properly Temper Critical Aircraft Parts," news release, March 3, 1999.)

8   worldwide, mosquitoes infect: Jeremy Laurance, "WHO Failures Led to Hundreds of Thousands Dying from Malaria, Say Medical Experts," *Independent. co.uk,* April 8, 2004 (www.news.independent.co.uk); "Malaria," International Federation of Pharmaceutical Manufacturers Associations, 2004, p. 1, www. ifpma.org/health/health-malaria.aspx.

8   One reason for these deaths: "Combating Counterfeit Drugs," news release, U.S. Food and Drug Administration, Rockville, Md., February 2004, p. 6.

8   The International Federation of Pharmaceutical Manufacturers Associations: Harvey Bale, "South Africa; Health Talks Should Look at Fake Drugs," African News Service, Africa News, August 28, 2002, www.africanews.com. Harvey Bale is president of the International Federation of Pharmaceutical Manufacturers Associations. World Health Organization, "Essential Drugs and

Medicines Policy: Counterfeit Medicines," Geneva, 2004. In this list of frequently asked questions, Eshetu Wondemagegnehu of the World Health
Organization explains why the WHO can provide only limited information
about the nature of global counterfeiting. He says, "Only less than 5% of the
191 WHO Member States report to WHO cases of counterfeit drugs detected.
Most Member States are reluctant to report detected cases."

8   Tijuana, for instance: "Implementation of Policies Concerning Personal
Importation of Prescription Drugs at the Mexico–U.S. Border," committee
correspondence, House Committee on Energy and Commerce, U.S. Con-
gress, Washington, D.C., March 14, 2001. See also "Continuing Concerns over
Imported Pharmaceuticals," statement of James C. Greenwood, chairman
Subcommittee on Oversight and Investigation, Committee on Energy and
Commerce, Hearing, June 7, 2001.

8   In contrast: Ibid.

8   Whether these people really are trained: "Shopping for Pharmaceuticals," *San
Diego Union Tribune*, April 10, 2004.

8   Roughly a fifth of these stores: Ibid.

8   The threat to those: "Continuing Concerns over Imported Pharmaceuticals," testimony of James Christina, formerly special agent with the United
States Secret Service in charge of suppression of counterfeiting U.S. currency in Latin America, now head of global corporate security for Novartis
International. Subcommittee on Oversight and Investigations, Committee
on Energy and Commerce, U.S. House of Representatives, Washington, D.C.,
July 7, 2001.

9   The Texas study found that: Office of Public Affairs, University of Texas, "UT
Austin Pharmacist Issues Warning About Drugs from Abroad," news release,
Austin, July 9, 2001.

9   Of the 1,900 packages: "Continuing Concerns over Imported Pharmaceuticals," testimony of William Hubbard, associate commissioner, Food and Drug
Administration, before Subcommittee on Oversight and Investigations, Committee on Energy and Commerce, U.S. House of Representatives, Washington, D.C., June 7, 2001.

9   The study's principal conclusion: Ibid.

9   "Overwhelmed customs workers": Gilbert M. Gaul and Mary Pat Flaherty,
"U.S. Prescription Drug System Under Attack: Multibillion-dollar Shadow
Market Is Growing Stronger," *Washington Post*, part 1 of 5, October 19, 2003.

9   "Not all medicines": Partnership for Safe Medicines, "Foreign Drugs: Back-
ground," www.safemedicines.org/safety/foreign-bkgd.html (accessed 2003).
California Pharmacists Association, "Health Experts Warn About Growing
Danger of Counterfeit Drugs," Los Angeles, April 8, 2004.

9   More alarming, Canada's: California Pharmacists Association, "Health
Experts Warn."

10   Federal officials are unable: See previously cited testimony, June 7, 2001,
House Energy and Commerce Committee.

10 Most important: U.S. Food and Drug Administration, "New FDA Initiative to Combat Counterfeit Drugs," news release, Washington, D.C., July 2004.

10 By contrast, half or more: Interpol, "The Impact and Scale of Counterfeiting," fact sheet, August 20, 2004.

10 In contrast, three primary wholesalers: "New FDA Initiative to Combat Counterfeit Drugs."

10 The FDA requires that all: FDA, "Counterfeit Formulas," *FDA Consumer Magazine,* June 1996. "Infant Formula Basics," KeepKidsHealthy.com, August 2004, www.keepkidshealthy.com/nutrition/infant_formula_basics.html.

10 In 1999, FDA agents arrested: "Counterfeiting Couple Pays High Price for Baby Formula Fraud," *FDA Consumer Magazine,* November–December 2000.

10 According to the FDA: Food and Drug Administration, "FDA Warns About Infant Formula Fraudulently Labeled as Nutramigen in South California," news release. United States Attorney, Central District of California, "Fugitive Who Sold Counterfeit Baby Formula Sentenced to 44 Months Imprisonment," news release, December 16, 2002.

11 In May 2004, the Xinhua News Agency: "China Faces Fake Baby Milk Scandal," FoodQualityNews.com, April 23, 2004; "Arrests in Fake Baby Formula Case," CBS News, Beijing, May 10, 2004.

12 Music piracy is so rampant: International Federation of the Phonographic Industry (IFPI), "Piracy Threatens Future of Music Industry in Mexico," news release, Mexico City, May 17, 2001.

12 The European Union: The European Commission, "Counterfeiting and Piracy: Munich Hearing Endorses Need for EU Action," Brussels, March 3, 1999.

12 The sale of knockoff vehicle spare parts: European Commission, "Report on Responses to the European Commission Green Paper on Counterfeiting and Piracy," June 1999, p. 15.

12 One of every five firms: Commission of the European Communities, "Combating Counterfeiting and Piracy in the Single Market," a green paper, Brussels, 1998.

12 The Federal Bureau of Investigation: FBI, "Intellectual Property Crimes: About the Financial Institution Fraud Unit," Washington, D.C., April 11, 2004. The estimate used by the FBI is attributed to the International Anti-Counterfeiting Coalition estimate of 1997. This estimate does not include losses due to the theft from the rich U.S. treasure of patents.

12 The European Commission (EC): European Commission, "Report on Response," p. 15.

12 The EC also calculates: Ibid., p. 4.

12 If that estimate is correct: World Trade Organization, "Stronger than Expected Growth Spurs Modest Trade," Geneva, Switzerland, p. 4, table 2.

12 Between 1990 and 1999: European Commission, "Report on Responses," p. 4.

14 This is the only place: When I began the project that ultimately resulted in this book, one of the people I interviewed was Robert Galvin, former CEO of

Motorola, one of the world's foremost technology-based companies. He pointed out that the "authors and inventors" clause is the only place that the word "right" is found in the U.S. Constitution and shared a speech where he had made that point, illustrating how much the Founding Fathers had valued patents and copyrights.

14 This twenty-seven-word clause: Trademark protections are based on the interstate commerce provisions of the Constitution.

14 Lawrence J. Siskind: "Protect This," memo, Lawrence K. Siskind, Harvey Siskind Jacobs LLP, San Francisco.

15 Patents also are given: U.S. Patent and Trademark Office, "General Information Concerning Patents," www.uspto.gov/web/offices/pae/doc/general/whatis. htm (accessed April 11, 2004). The following definitions for a patent, copyright, trademark, or service mark are provided online by the U.S. Patent and Trademark Office. The definition of a trade secret is from the Online Ethics Center for Engineering and Science at Case Western Reserve University.

WHAT IS A PATENT?

A patent for an invention is the grant of a property right to the inventor, issued by the United States Patent and Trademark Office. Generally, the term of a new patent is twenty years from the date on which the application for the patent was filed in the United States or, in special cases, from the date an earlier related application was filed, subject to the payment of maintenance fees. U.S. patent grants are effective only within the United States, U.S. territories, and U.S. possessions. Under certain circumstances, patent term extensions or adjustments may be available. The right conferred by the patent grant is, in the language of the statute and of the grant itself, "the right to exclude others from making, using, offering for sale, or selling" the invention in the United States or "importing" the invention into the United States. What is granted is not the right to make, use, offer for sale, sell, or import, but the right to exclude others from making, using, offering for sale, selling, or importing the invention. Once a patent is issued, the patentee must enforce the patent without aid of the USPTO.

 There are three types of patents:

- Utility patents may be granted to anyone who invents or discovers any new and useful process, machine, article of manufacture, or compositions of matters, or any new useful improvement thereof;
- Design patents may be granted to anyone who invents a new, original, and ornamental design for an article of manufacture; and
- Plant patents may be granted to anyone who invents or discovers and asexually reproduces any distinct and new variety of plant.

WHAT IS A COPYRIGHT?

Copyright is a form of protection provided to the authors of "original works of authorship" including literary, dramatic, musical, artistic, and certain other intellectual works, both published and unpublished. The 1976 Copyright Act generally gives the owner of copyright the exclusive right to reproduce the copyrighted work, to prepare derivative works, to distribute copies or phonorecords of the copyrighted work, to perform the copyrighted work publicly, or to display the copyrighted work publicly. The copyright protects the form of expression rather than the subject matter of the writing. For example, a description of a machine could be copyrighted, but this would only prevent others from copying the description; it would not prevent others from writing a description of their own or from making and using the machine. The Copyright Office of the Library of Congress registers copyrights.

WHAT IS A TRADEMARK OR SERVICE MARK?

A trademark is a word, name, symbol, or device that is used in trade with goods to indicate the source of the goods and to distinguish them from the goods of others. A service mark is the same as a trademark except that it identifies and distinguishes the source of a service rather than a product. The terms "trademark" and "mark" are commonly used to refer to both trademarks and service marks.

Trademark rights may be used to prevent others from using a confusingly similar mark, but not to prevent others from making the same goods or from selling the same goods or services under a clearly different mark. Trademarks, which are used in interstate or foreign commerce, may be registered with the USPTO.

WHAT IS A TRADE SECRET?

A device, method, or formula that gives one an advantage over the competition and which must therefore be kept secret if it is to be of special value. It is legal to use reverse engineering to learn a competitor's trade secret. "Know-how" concerning research procedures may function as something like a trade secret.

15 For works made for hire: U.S. Copyright Office, *Copyright Basics*, (Washington, D.C.: GPO, 2004), p. 9.

15 In many instances, the FBI: FBI, "Intellectual Property Crimes," p. 1.

16 In India, writing: Martha Ann Overland, "Publishers Battle Pirates in India with Little Success," *Chronicle of Higher Education*, April 2, 2004.

19 Americans, who make up: U.S. Patent and Trademark Office, *The Technology Assessment and Forecast (TAF) Special Report, All Patents, All Types, January 1977–December 2001*, Washington, D.C., April 2002, p. A1-1; Intellectual Property Creators, "IPC Study Shows 90% of World's Major Invention Done in

the United States, Only 10% Percent Abroad," Los Altos, California, May 5, 2001. The TAF report identifies all patents issued of all types for the twenty-five-year period 1977–2001. Of the 2,548,929 patents granted, more than 58 percent went to U.S. corporations and 14 percent went to U.S. individuals. Most major innovations are patented in the United States, the world's largest market.

The Intellectual Property Creators is a nonprofit organization of independent inventors. Three of its five founding board members have been inducted into the National Inventors Hall of Fame. The Hall of Fame inducts members from around the world; twenty-four of its inductees were born in a nation other than the United States, and twelve still reside outside the United States. The only relevant criterion for nomination to the Hall of Fame is that the individual hold a U.S. patent, which all with a major invention do. The IPC analyzed these inductees' work history and found that ninety-one had done their work in the United States. The IPC concludes: "The only reasonable interpretation of the results is that some aspect of the culture, laws, and/or institutions of the United States strongly encourages inventors and the development of inventions through mass manufacturing and mass distribution."

Although the precise percentage of the world's major innovations created by those working in the United States is unknown, the portion of patents issued to U.S. residents out of all U.S. patents issued over this twenty-five-year period appears to be a conservative estimate.

CHAPTER 1: THE GOLDEN COVENANT

23 Manhattan's 30,000 citizens: "Inauguration of First President," *Brooklyn Daily Eagle*, April 2004, www.angelfire.com.

23 Soon after 10:30 a.m.: New York's City Hall was refurbished under the direction of Pierre L'Enfant. His work so impressed George Washington that he hired the French army major to design and build what became our nation's capital, Washington, D.C. (See Philip Ernest Schoenberg, "The First Inauguration," [www.presidentialexpert.com/stories7.htm].)

23 Before the Revolutionary War: Smithsonian, "George Washington, a National Treasure," exhibition, National Portrait Gallery, April 11, 2004.

23 Yet the new president's: Ibid.

23 Washington's overture was widely noted: Stefan Lorant, *The Presidency* (New York: Harper & Row Publishers, 1951), pp. 29–30.

23 In the first year: Barbara Tuchman, *The First Salute* (New York: Alfred A. Knopf, 1988), p. 7.

24 At the battle of Bunker Hill: Ibid.

24 In a letter dated: James Madison Center, "George Washington Writes from Valley Forge," letter from George Washington to the Continental Congress, December 23, 1777, James Madison University, Harrisonburg, Va.

24 Instead, the mother country restricted: Tuchman, *First Salute*, p. 7.

24 Thus, the U.S. economy: Ibid.

24 He bought 80,000: H. W. Brands, *The First American* (New York: Doubleday, 2000), pp. 522–538.

24 St. Eustatius, a Dutch island: Tuchman, *The First Salute*, p. 15.

25 As the historian Doran S. Ben-Atar: Doron S. Ben-Atar, *Trade Secrets* (New Haven: Yale University Press, 2004), pp. 156–158.

25 At almost the same time: Alexander Hamilton, *Report on Manufactures*, Congress of the United States, Washington, D.C., December 5, 1791, p. 1.

26 In his report, Hamilton: Ibid., p. 16.

26 By the late 1700s: "Origins," in *Patent History*, Patent Office of the United Kingdom, April 2004.

26 In exchange, the foreign glassmaker: Thomson and Derwent, "The History of Patents," Derwent Information, www.thomsonderwent.com/patins/patent faqs/history.html (accessed April 2004).

26 It gave a fourteen-year monopoly: "Tudors and Stuarts," in *Patent History*, p. 1.

27 Likewise, the colonists: Paul Goldstein, *Copyright's Highway: The Law and Lore of Copyright from Gutenberg to the Celestial Jukebox* (New York: Hill and Wang, 1994), p. 51.

27 Under that act: William F. Patry, "England and the Statute of Anne," in *Copyright Law and Practice* (Washington, D.C.: Bureau of National Affairs, 2000).

27 After independence: Ibid. Pennsylvania and Maryland enacted patent laws, but they were conditional on all the other colonies doing the same before their laws took effect. The Pennsylvania and Maryland state laws never took effect. Instead, the U.S. adopted the Patent Act of 1790, which provided uniform federal protections.

27 The concept was so fundamental: Mary E. Webster, ed., *The Federalist Papers in Modern Language* (Bellevue, Wash.: Merril Press), pp. 175–176.

27 When the "authors and inventors clause": The Avalon Project: Madison Debates, "The Debates in the Federal Convention of 1787 (Reported by James Madison: September 5)," special project, Yale Law School, April 12, 2004.

27 In his first State of the Union message: Kenneth W. Dobyns, "The First U.S. Patent Statute," in *A History of the United States Patent Office: The Patent Office Pony* (Sergeant Kirklands, August 1997), pp. 1–8, www.myoutbox.net.

27 Congress acted quickly: Goldstein, *Copyright's Highway*, p. 52.

28 The total cost: Dobyns, *History of the U.S. Patent Office*, pp. 1–8.

28 He urged Congress: E. C. Walterscheid, "Thomas Jefferson and the Patent Act of 1793," in *Essays in History*, Corcoran Department of History, University of Virginia, volume 40 (1998), Letter, Jefferson to Robert R. Livingstone (February 4, 1791) p. 10, www.etext.virginia.edu/journals/EH/EH40/walter40.html.

28 In 1792 Jefferson: Ibid., p. 10.

28 The board abhorred: Ibid., pp. 7–8.

28 The courts were assigned: Ibid., chap. 6, p. 1.

29 Between 1793 and 1836: U.S. Patent and Trademark Office, *U.S. Patent Activity: Calendar Years 1790–2001* (Washington, D.C.: USPTO, 2002).

29 In the end, the most: Patent Act of 1793, chap. 11, sec 1., 1 *Stat.* 318–323 (February 21, 1793).

29 In 1800, the law: Public Knowledge, "An Intellectual Property Timeline," www.publicknowledge.org/content/references/timeline.

29 They also had to work: Ibid.

29 In 1836, Congress finally: *Patent Act of 1836*, chap. 357, 5 *Stat.* 117, sec. 6 (July 4, 1836).

29 Subjects of the king: Ibid., sec. 9.

30 In such locales as Edinburgh: Adam Hart-Davis, "Richard Arkwright, Cotton King," On Line Science and Technology, www.exnet.com/1995/10/10/science/science.html. In 1771, Richard Arkwright, a former hairdresser and wig maker, built the world's first automated spinning mill in Nottingham, England. Before his invention, six spinners were needed to keep one weaver busy. Then a spinner took a sliver of cotton and teased it into a long, thin sliver of material that was then stretched and twisted into a strong thread. The process required skilled workers and their production was limited. By contrast, Arkwright's machine could spin 128 threads at the same time. Over the next twenty years, he built more mills; he hired adults to weave and their children to feed the automated spinning machines. At his death in 1792, Richard Arkwright was worth today's equivalent of roughly $300 million.

30 The secrets of this technology: John J. Fialka, *War by Other Means: Economic Espionage in America* (New York: W. W. Norton and Company, 1997), pp. ix–xiv.

30 But the nation: Ibid.

31 His bags were searched: Ibid.

31 Soon the Boston Manufacturing Company: Kenton Beerman, "The Beginning of a Revolution: Waltham and the Boston Manufacturing Company," *Concord Review*, January 3, 1997, pp. 1–9. Note: In 1818, BMC had two mills producing a total of 250,000 yards of fabric annually, which translates to 142 miles of cloth. Lowell and his brother-in-law, Patrick Tracy Jackson, also created the first U.S. stock company. They sold 100 shares of stock for $1,000 each. The $100,000 of capital was enormous at a time when "large" companies usually had no more than $10,000. This capital allowed the Boston Manufacturing Company to weather economic downturns, while continuing to expand.

31 In 1816, Webster: Robert Remini, *Daniel Webster: The Man and His Time* (New York: W. W. Norton and Company, 1997), pp. 138–139.

32 It was Webster and Calhoun's: Ibid., pp. 199–200. Webster's relationship with the Boston Manufacturing Company, later renamed the Boston Associates, deepened after he successfully secured tariff legislation. In 1821, the associates permitted Webster to buy four shares in the Merrimack Manufacturing Company at $1,000 per share. For the next quarter century, the associates contributed generously to Webster's campaigns, and he, in turn, helped them with legislation and legal matters in Washington.

32   Apparently, Lowell's health: "Francis Cabot Lowell (1775–1817)," *A Classification of American Wealth,* www.raken.com/american_wealth/index.asp.

32   Slater's first mill: Woonsocket, "Samuel Slater: Child Labor," www.woonsocket.org/childlabor.html.

32   The company, moreover: Beerman, "Beginning of a Revolution," pp. 6–10.

32   And most did not wish: Ibid.

33   Also, the patent went: Patent Act of 1836.

33   In 1842, the system: Ladas and Parry, "A Brief History of the Patent Law of the United States," available at www.ladas.com/Patents/USPatentHistory.html.

34   For example: The Public Broadcasting System, "The American Experience, Technology Timeline: 1752–1990," www.pbs.org/wgbh/amex/telephone/timeline/timeline_text.html.

34   In 1832, Samuel Morse: Dobyns, *A History of the United States Patent Office,* pp. 1–3.

35   Morse filed his patent: "Samuel F. B. Morse, Obituary," *New York Times,* April 3, 1872.

35   The message, chosen: Dobyns, *A History of the United States Patent Office;* "Samuel F. B. Morse," Lemelson-MIT Program: Inventor of the Week Archive, http://web.mit.edu/invent/iow, p. 1.

35   Within ten years: "Samuel F. B. Morse," p. 1.

35   By October 1861, the west: "Pony Express Information," Pony Express Museum, St. Joseph, Mo., April 17, 2004.

35   Among the more than 13,000: Victorian Station, "The Great Exhibition at the Crystal Palace," www.victorianstation.com/palace.html.

36   As James McPherson writes: James M. McPherson, *Battle Cry of Freedom: The Civil War Era* (New York: Oxford University Press, 1988), pp. 17–21.

36   "even counting the slaves": Ibid., pp. 20–21.

36   As one British observer noted: McPherson, *Battle Cry of Freedom,* pp. 17–21.

36   Samuel Colt, for instance: Ellsworth S. Grant, "Samuel Colt (1814–1862)," Connecticut's Heritage Gateway, www.ctheritage.org/encyclopedia/topicalsurveys/colt.htm.

36   Charles Goodyear worked: Dobyns, *A History of the United States Patent Office.*

37   Samuel Morse was literally: Reader's Digest Association, "Charles Goodyear and the Strange Story of Rubber" (Pleasantville, N.Y., 1957), www.goodyear.com/corporate/strange.html.

37   In those four war years: Dobyns, *A History of the United States Patent Office.* The Confederate States opened a patent office in Richmond, Virginia, in August 1861. Rufus Randolph Rhodes, a former U.S. patent examiner and member of the board of appeals, headed the office. Interestingly, soon after the Texas revolution, the new Republic of Texas established its own patent office. Kenneth W. Dobyns observes, "There is something about the American people that demands a patent system."

37   Throughout the Civil War: Inventors Museum, "Abraham Lincoln," www.inventorsmuseum.org.

37 Lincoln also extended: "Patents and Trademarks, The History of American Technology," www.bryant.edu/~history/index.html.

38 Since the Civil War: Ibid.

38 In 1870, the requirement: Ibid.

38 As the name suggests, trademarks: University of Texas Library, Austin, "What Is a Trademark?," pamphlet, p. 1, www.lib.uTexas.edu/engin/trademark/tm.html.

38 Ceramics from ancient Greece: Ibid., "Prehistory to the Fall of the Roman Empire," p. 1.

38 The 1870 act created: "Patents and Trademarks."

38 The Constitution allows: Ibid.

38 In 1881, Congress responded: "History (Trademarks)," International Trademark Association, www.inta.org/about/history.html.

39 In 1946, Congress passed the Lanham Act: Ibid., "The History of American Technology."

39 In 1930, the Plant Patent Act: Ibid.

39 That view changed: Daniel Tysver, "The History of Software Patents," Bitlaw, www.bitlaw.com/software-patent/history.html.

39 Before the 1981 decision: "Software Patents: IBM's Role in History," IPC Intellectual Property Creators, www.ipccreators.org.

39 Absent software patents: Ibid.

39 However, after the Supreme Court: Ibid.

39 In the calendar year 2003: IBM, "Innovation: IBM Tops U.S. Patent List for Eleventh Year and Sets Record," news release, January 2004, at www.ibm.com/news/us/2004/01/21_01.html.

39 In this period, 1993–2003: Ibid.

39 IBM over those eleven years: Ibid.

40 IBM makes more than $1 billion: IBM, "IBM Tops U.S. Patent List for Eighth Consecutive Year," news release, January 2001, www.ibm.com/.

40 Noah Webster, a young schoolmaster: Richard and Patricia Kahn, "A Brief History of Epidemic and Pestilential Diseases by 'That Pestilential Writer,' Noah Webster," Penobscot Bay Medical Center, Rockport, Maine, www.icml.org.

40 Webster, whose father: Ibid.

40 Webster's ambitious response: Ibid.

40 The spelling book was known: "A Short Summary of Noah Webster's Life," www.ctsatcu.cdu.

41 By the time of the Constitutional Convention: Kahn, "A Brief History of Epidemic and Pestilential Diseases."

41 The state laws in Maryland: William F. Patry, "The Colonies and Copyright," *Copyright Law and Practice,* Washington, D.C.: Bureau of National Affairs, 1994.

41 The royalties from: Among the lesser-known contributions of Noah Webster are his writings on public health. In 1799, he wrote a two-volume, 712-page work on epidemics and diseases such as yellow fever. It was a world standard

for almost a century. See the previously cited paper by Richard and Patricia Kahn, which is available on the Web, for a fuller description of his work in this field.

41 As with Britain's law: *The Copyright Act of 1790*. Library of Congress of the United States.

41 Ironically, the first copyright: "Fun Facts," the *Princeton Review*, www.princetonreview.com.

41 While the Copyright Act: David G. Post, "Some Thoughts on the Political Economy of Intellectual Property: A Brief Look at the International Copyright Relations of the United States" (paper, prepared for the National Bureau of Asian Research Conference on Intellectual Property, Chongqing, China, available from Temple University Law School, Cyberspace Law Institute, September 1998).

41 In the early nineteenth century: Ibid.

42 Pirated copies of Dickens's: William P. Alford, *To Steal a Book Is an Elegant Offense: Intellectual Property Law in Chinese Civilization* (Stanford, Calif.: Stanford University Press, 1995), p. 130.

42 Dickens lobbied his American: Philip V. Allingham, "Dickens 1842 Reading Tour: Launching the Copyright Question in Tempestuous Seas," The Victorian Web, www.victorianweb.org/authors/dickens/pva/pva75.html.

42 Trollope ridiculed the argument: Anthony Trollope, *An Autobiography*, etextlibrary, University of Adelaide Library, University of Adelaide, South Australia, chap. 17, p. 3.

42 His argument was that: Post, "Some Thoughts on the Political Economy of Intellectual Property."

42 Eventually, pirated copies: "Harriet Beecher Stowe," Sunshine for Women (2001), www.pinn.net/~sunshine/whm2001/stowe.html.

42 Stowe received not a penny: James Parton, "International Copyright," *Atlantic Monthly*, October 1867, available online at www.theatlantic.com.

43 According to Fred Kaplan: Fred Kaplan, *The Singular Mark Twain* (New York: Doubleday, 2003), p. 283.

43 In 1876, Toronto publisher: Philip V. Allingham, "Nineteenth-Century British and American Copyright Law," The Victorian Web, www.victorianweb.org/authors/dickens/pva/pva74.html.

43 Though the trip was a burden: Ibid.

43 Congress confined: Ibid.

43 This "manufacturing clause": Alford, *To Steal a Book Is an Elegant Offense*, p. 130.

43 In the more than two hundred years: "A Brief History and Overview of the United States Copyright Office," circular 1a, U.S. Patent and Trademark Office, at www.loc.gov/copyright/docs/circ1a.html.

44 Again Congress acted: Ibid.

44 Another bill extended: Ibid.

45 Nobel Prize winner: Peter S. Menell, *Intellectual Property: General Theories,*

Berkeley Center for Law and Technology, monograph, University of California at Berkeley, p. 6, www.encyclo.findlaw.com/1600book.pdf.

45   Edward Dennison of: Ibid.

CHAPTER 2: THE AMERICAN SYSTEM

46   In 1859, Abraham Lincoln: Abraham Lincoln, "Lecture on Discoveries and Inventions," *Abraham Lincoln Online: Speeches and Writings*, http://showcase.netins.net/web/creative/lincoln/speeches/discoveries.htm.

46   Finally, patents secured: Ibid.

48   And he adapted milling: Benjamin A. Gorman, "Discover Eli Whitney," pamphlets, Yale–New Haven Teachers Institute. Gorman notes that although Whitney was a major inventor and entrepreneur, Christopher Phloem of Sweden was producing clock gears in the early eighteenth century. Thomas Jefferson described the idea in a letter to John Jay in August 1785 about Honoré Blanc's machine production of gauged parts that were used in muskets. Eight months before Whitney made his first delivery of muskets to the U.S. government, Blanc discussed the ideas of interchangeability and mass production with Jefferson, a friend and admirer. As to milling machines, Gorman notes that Simeon North was producing five hundred pistols using milling machines in 1799. North's shop was only twenty miles from Whitney's.

48   He was Mark Twain's model: "Jere W. Clark: An Introduction," in *Full Circle: The Moral Force of Unified Science*, ed. Edward Haskell (New York: Gordon and Breach, 1972), p. 1.

48   During the Revolutionary War: Dobyns, *History of the United States Patent Office*, chap. 6.

48   He prepared himself: Constance M. Green, *Eli Whitney and the Birth of American Technology* (New York: Harper & Row, 1956), pp. 29–30.

48   Whitney paid for: Ibid., p. 36.

48   Miller graciously invited him: Ibid., pp. 38–39.

48   Worse, in the middle of the night: Ibid., p. 40.

48   Once they arrived, Whitney: Ibid.; "Smallpox: A Great and Terrible Scourge," National Institutes of Health, Rockville, Md., at www.nlm.nib.gov/exhibition.small pox/sp.variolation.html.

49   She found him: "Smallpox," National Institutes of Health.

49   Whitney, a poor sailor: Green, *Eli Whitney and the Birth of American Technology*, pp. 40–41.

49   Whitney's biographer, Constance Green: Ibid., p. 42.

49   To the delight: Bruce Chadwick, *George Washington's War* (Naperville, Ill.: Sourcebooks, 2004), p. 365. Though generally portrayed as a remote and silent figure, Washington loved to dance and was a great favorite of society ladies of that era. Chadwick reports that Washington forced his officers to subscribe to

several dances while in winter camp. The events built esprit among the officers and their wives. Chadwick notes that while he was a planter, Washington often held dances that lasted until dawn. George and Martha Washington viewed Kitty Greene as a daughter. Nathanael Greene was not only one of Washington's most competent generals; he was one of the most trusted. When Washington fell ill at Valley Forge, Chadwick writes, he called together his senior officers in his bedroom and informed them that should he die or become incapable of action, he had appointed Greene to serve as commander until the Continental Congress decided who should lead.

49 During the war, Nathanael Greene: After Greene's death and with the political support of George Washington, Congress did reimburse General Greene's estate for his expenditures of personal funds for the uniforms and other necessities of war that he had purchased for his troops.

50 Moreover, removing the seeds: Holland Thompson, "Eli Whitney's Letter to His Father, September 11, 1793," in *The Age of Invention: Eli Whitney and the Cotton Gin* (New Haven, Conn.: Yale University Press, 1921), pp. 38–40.

50 Consequently, textiles: Thompson, *The Age of Invention,* pp. 32–35.

50 Whitney, who had never: Dobyns, *History of the United States Patent Office,* chap. 6.

50 Whitney would produce: Denison Olmsted, *Memoir of Eli Whitney, Esq.* (1846; repr., New York: Arno Press, 1972), pp. 15–16. The agreement was executed between Phineas Miller and Whitney on May 27, 1793. They immediately began business as Miller & Whitney.

51 Whitney's hand-cranked cotton: "Eli Whitney: Cotton Gin," Lemelson-MIT Program: Inventor of the Week, http://web.mit.edu/invent/iow/whitney.html.

51 Then another roller: Dobyns, *A History of the United States Patent Office.* Various accounts say that Whitney perfected the machine alone. Others suggest that Whitney was stymied by the accumulation of fiber on the discs but that Kitty Greene solved the problem by taking a broom and whisking them aside, showing him how to resolve the last major problem in producing a complete cotton gin.

51 Most important, the machine: "Eli Whitney's Story," Lemelson Center for the Study of Invention and Innovation, National Museum of American History, Smithsonian Institution, Washington, 1998, http://invention.smithsonian.org/centerpieces/whole_cloth/u2ei/u2materials/eiPac1.html.

51 Jefferson, a Virginia: Green, *Eli Whitney and the Birth of American Technology,* p. 58.

51 In February 1974: "Eli Whitney, Hall of Fame Inventor's Profile," National Inventors Hall of Fame, www.invent.org/hall_of_fame/152.html.

51 Less than a month: Dobyns, *History of the United States Patent Office,* chap. 6.

51 The gin allowed: "Eli Whitney's Story."

52 In conclusion, he asked: Thompson, *The Age of Invention.*

52 Regardless of which: Green, *Eli Whitney and the Birth of American Technology,* p. 75.

52 The young entrepreneurs: Thompson, "Commercializing the Cotton Gin," in *The Age of Invention.*

52 The price of cotton land: Green, *Eli Whitney and the Birth of American Technology,* p. 93.

52 By 1845, the U.S.: Thompson, "The Cotton Gin's Effect on the Cotton Industry," in Thompson, *The Age of Invention.*

52 In the 1920s, the U.S.: Ibid.

53 In Georgia, the inventors: Ibid.

53 Despite such victories: Green, *Eli Whitney and the Birth of American Technology,* pp. 88–89.

53 Denison Olmsted writes: Denison Olmsted, *Memoir of Eli Whitney, Esq.,* (New Haven, Conn.: Durrie & Peck, 1846), pp. 26–32, www.law.du.edu.

53 He coined a maxim: "Inventor of the Week Archive: Eli Whitney," Lemelson-MIT Program, August 2000, http://web.mit.edu/invent/iow/whitney.html.

54 Miller married Catharine: Andrew Koransky, "Brief Timeline of History on Cumberland Island," www.koransky.com.

54 In 1799, to pay: Ibid.

54 According to the curator: "Guide to the Eli Whitney Papers," Manuscript Group Number 554, Yale University Library, Manuscripts and Archives, August 1996, p. 4.

54 In the caring tradition: Ibid.

54 An outraged American: "XYZ Affair," *The Columbia Encyclopedia,* 6th ed., www.bartleby.com/65/xy/xyzaffai.html.

55 In three years of operation: Green, *Eli Whitney and the Birth of American Technology,* p. 101.

55 Though he had no arms factory: Gorman, "Discover Eli Whitney."

55 The contract was issued: Ibid.

55 Elizur Goodrich, a participant: Green, *Eli Whitney and the Birth of American Technology,* p. 127.

55 The historian Merritt Roe Smith: David Lindsay, "Eastman and Mass Production," www.pbs.org/wgbh/amex/eastman/peopleevents/pande11.html.

55 And he probably did: Vernon W. Ruttan, *Military Procurement and Technology Development,* chap. 2, Hubert H. Humphrey Institute of Public Affairs, University of Minnesota, www.unm.edu/faculty/vruttan.

56 His total profit: Gorman, "Discover Eli Whitney."

56 On the morning of: Alexander Graham Bell, "Improvement in Telegraphy," United States Patent Office, dated January 20, 1876, filed February 14, 1876.

57 Two hours later: "Elisha Gray," *The American Experience,* Public Broadcasting System, www.pbs.org/wgbh/amex/telephone/peopleevents/pande02.html; Herbert N. Casson, "Holding the Business," in *The History of the Telephone* (Chicago: A. C. McClurg & Co., 1910). Casson reports that the patent logbook records Bell's patent application as the fifth entry of that day and Gray's caveat as the thirty-ninth. He also points out there is a vast difference between a patent and a caveat. A patent application announces a perfected invention. A

caveat is an announcement that someone thinks that he or she is about to invent something; it has lesser rights than a patent.

57 Three weeks later: "Significant Scots: Alexander Graham Bell," *Electric Scotland,* www.electricscotland.com/history/other/alexander_bell.htm.

57 Born in Scotland, he came: Casson, *History of the Telephone,* p. 2.

57 Eliza Symonds Bell, his mother: "Alexander Graham Bell," www.alexander-graham-bell.org.

57 She was also deaf: "A Family Affair," More About Bell, www.pbs.org.

57 Bell left Scotland: Ibid.

58 While recovering, Bell taught: "Significant Scots," *Electric Scotland.*

58 In 1871, now in good health: "Clarke School, Historical Information," Clarke School, www.clarkeschool.org/history.html.

58 He helped Cambridge: Casson, *The History of the Telephone,* p. 4.

58 In 1871, he persuaded: "Clarke School, Historical Information."

58 More important to: Gardiner G. Hubbard, "Proposed Changes in the Telegraphic System," *North American Review* 117, no. 240 (July 1873): 80–108, www.cdl.library.cornell.edu. Hubbard was an advocate of public services and viewed telegraph services as one of the most important. The battle to nationalize the telegraph companies obviously shaped his views on how public utilities should price and manage their services. While building what became AT&T, Hubbard constantly advocated low rates, standard equipment, and universal access. This 1873 article on the dangers to a republic and a free press created by concentrated media control remains as fresh now as it was when it was written.

60 Hubbard organized a trust: Robert C. Ward, "The Chaos of Convergence," (dissertation, Virginia Polytechnic Institute and State University, Blacksburg, Va., 1997), www.scholar.lib.vt.edu/theses/available/etd-0698-91234/unrestricted/etd.pdf, p. 123.

60 Bell lived with the Sanders family: Casson, *History of the Telephone,* p. 9.

60 On their wedding day: "Alexander Graham Bell," www.alexander-graham-bell.org.

60 The exposition was: "The Centennial Exhibition of 1876," www.park.org.

60 The exhibits from all over the world: W. D. Howells, "A Sennight of the Centennial," *Atlantic Monthly* (July 1876): 92–107, www.cdl.library.cornell.edu.

60 The telephone exhibit: Dee Brown, *The Year of the Century: 1876* (New York: Charles Scribner's Sons, 1966), p. 133.

61 He started to trot: Casson, *The History of the Telephone,* p. 7.

61 Afterward, the emperor: Ibid.

61 As one observer noted: "Welcome to the Telephony Museum," www.telephonymuseum.com.

62 Immediately, many newspapers: Casson, *The History of the Telephone,* p. 9.

62 A year after the exposition: Burton J. Hendrick, "The Telephone, America's Most Poetical Achievement," in *The Age of Big Business,* 1921, www.classicbook.info/books/the-age-of-big-business-a-chronicle-of-the-captains-of-industry/chapter-04-page-01.html.

62 Almost eighteen months: Ward, "Chaos of Convergence," p. 123.

62 Orton rejected the offer: Casson, *The History of the Telephone,* p. 11.

62 With the telephone, people could: Ruth Schwartz Cowan, *A Social History of American Technology* (New York: Oxford University Press, 1997), pp. 160–161.

62 That man turned out: Casson, *The History of the Telephone,* pp. 12–13.

62 To attract even more: Robert C. Ward, "The Chaos of Convergence" pp. 124–126.

63 By 1879, the Bell Telephone Company: Ibid.

63 He recruited Chauncey Smith: Casson, *History of the Telephone,* pp. 20–21.

63 The other was with Jay Gould: Maury Klein, *The Life and Legend of Jay Gould* (Baltimore: Johns Hopkins University Press, 1986), p. 197.

63 Forbes concluded a deal: Ward, "Chaos of Convergence," pp. 124–126.

64 Most important, Western Union: Casson, *History of the Telephone,* p. 16.

64 By 1920, the first year: Hendrick, *The Telephone.*

64 Today, almost 95 percent: U.S. Census Bureau, "Selected Communications Media: 1920 to 2001," in *Statistical Abstract of the United States* (Washington, D.C.: U.S. Department of Commerce, 2003), table HS-42.

64 Bell won every case: Casson, *The History of the Telephone,* pp. 20–21.

65 "It was a Gibraltar": Ibid.

66 Between 1869 and 1931: "Thomas Edison's Patents," Rutgers University, www.edison.rutgers.edu/patents.htm.

66 In addition, he was awarded: Ibid.

66 Among his creations: "Thomas Edison Patent List," National Park Service, www.nps.gov/edis/edisonia/Table1_1.html.

66 Despite his creativity: Neil Baldwin, *Edison, Inventing the Century* (Chicago: Hyperion, 1995), p. 411.

67 In 1868, the twenty-year-old: "Thomas Edison Patent List," National Park Service, www.nps.gov/edis/edisonia/Table1_1html.

67 Edison's first money: Thompson, *Age of Invention,* p. 208.

67 In 1870, under contract: Klein, *Life and Legend of Jay Gould,* pp. 197–201.

67 In 1870, under contract: Frank Lewis Dyer and Thomas Commerford Martin, "Automatic, Duplex and Quadruplex Telegraphy," chap. 8 in *Edison, His Life and Inventions,* Electric Text Center, University of Virginia Library, www.wylie.lib.virginia.edu.8086.

68 Yet the money-desperate: Ibid.

68 In an argument with George Harrington: Klein, *Life and Legend of Jay Gould,* p. 198.

68 Then, in exchange for: L. J. Davis, *Fleet Fire* (New York: Arcade Publishing, 2003), pp. 180–181.

68 Orton wanted Edison's patent: Klein, *Life and Legend of Jay Gould,* p. 198.

68 Edison made three offers: Ibid.

68 Meanwhile, Edison was paying: Ibid.

68 He also took: Ibid., p. 200.

69 Edison accepted: Davis, *Fleet Fire,* p. 184.

69 In 1906, the court appointed: Dyer and Martin, *Edison, His Life and Inventions.*

69 The log of that telegraph litigation: "Telegraph Litigation," Edison National Historic Site, Rutgers University, www.edison.rutgers.edu/.

69 Among the dozens: "Edison Companies and Business Associates, 1899–1910, and Edison Companies, 1879–1886," Rutgers University, www.edison.rutgers.edu.

70 Indeed, Morgan's house: Baldwin, *Edison, Inventing the Century,* p. 138.

71 One measure of Edison's: "Electric Light and Power," in *Edison's 424 Patents,* www.edison.rutgers.edu.

71 Direct current, used by: Davis, *Fleet Fire,* p. 236.

71 Tesla, who stood: Jill Jonnes, *Empires of Light: Edison, Tesla, Westinghouse, and the Race to Electrify the World* (New York: Random House, 2003), pp. 87–116.

71 Tesla offered Westinghouse: Marc J. Seifer, *Wizard: The Life and Times of Nikola Tesla,* pp. 51–72.

72 Edison attempted to secure: Richard Moran, *Executioner's Current: Thomas Edison, George Westinghouse, and the Invention of the Electric Chair* (New York: Alfred A. Knopf, 2002), pp. 53–54.

72 Instead, he administered: Ibid. pp. 98–100.

72 Westinghouse responded to: Ibid., pp. 158–159.

72 Villard, a naturalized citizen: Davis, *Fleet Fire,* pp. 273–275.

73 Thomson-Houston under Charles Coffin: Jonnes, *Empires of Light,* pp. 240–241.

73 The two companies: Davis, *Fleet Fire,* pp. 274–275.

73 He devoted years: Ibid.

73 He devised a way: Baldwin, *Edison, Inventing the Century,* pp. 238–239.

73 As with his foray: "Edison's Cement Patents," Rutgers University www.edison.rutgers.edu.

73 Neil Baldwin writes: Baldwin, *Edison, Inventing the Century,* pp. 298-299.

73 In the movie business: "Edison's Motion Pictures Patents," Rutgers University, www.edison.rutgers.edu/filmpats.htm.

74 Thus it was that Auguste: "Continued Legal Battles," Rutgers University, www.edison.rutgers.edu.

74 The method: "The Rise of Competition," Rutgers University, www.edison.rutgers.edu.

74 In a 1907 decision: "A Shorter Chronology of Edison's Life," www.edison.rutgers.edu/brfchron.htm.

74 Thus, in 1907, he organized: "The Motion Pictures Patents Company," Rutgers University, www.edison.rutgers.edu.

74 Using his monopoly power: Ibid.

74 In 1917, the U.S. Supreme Court: "A Shorter Chronology of Edison's Life," www.edison.rutgers.edu.

74 A year later, Edison sold: Ibid.

75 With that, the Edison family: Baldwin, *Edison, Inventing the Century,* p. 411.

75 The first such patent: USPTO, "U.S. Patent and Trademark Office Celebrates Valentine's Day" Washington, D.C., February 13, 2002, www.uspto.gov/web/otties/com/speeches/02-12.htm.

75 In 1957, Edison Industries: Baldwin, *Edison, Inventing the Century,* pp. 411–416.

75 Fittingly, that company's: Scott Rexinger, the president of the Toastmaster Division, was famous for going to friends' homes, heading straight for their kitchen, and throwing out the back door any toaster other than a Toastmaster. Whenever this happened, a messenger would arrive very early the next morning with a top-of-the-line Toastmaster and a note from Rexinger explaining that he could not stand the embarrassment of knowing that his friend was starting the day with toast made on anything less than the world's best toaster.

75 The filament used: Alan Rexinger in discussion with the author, December 2003, Washington, Virginia.

CHAPTER 3: A WORLD OF PIRATES

77 The damage was: "Lynn Brown," Wobblers Anonymous, 2004, www.wobblers.com.

77 She is also lucky: Vestibular Disorders Association, "Gentamincin Ototoxicity Makes Prime Time," quarterly newsletter, Summer 2000.

77 CBS News reports: CBS, "Counterfeit Drugs: Rx for Danger," January 31, 2002, www.cbsnews.com/stories/2002/01/31/health/main326515.shtml.

77 Flavine acquired these: CBS, "Counterfeit Drugs"; Patricia L. Maher, Deputy Assistant Attorney General, Civil Division, U.S. Department of Justice, "Counterfeit Bulk Drugs," statement at hearings before the Subcommittee on Oversight and Investigations of the Committee on Commerce, U.S. House of Representatives, June and October 2000.

77 Eventually, a deal was: "Counterfeit Bulk Drugs," statement of Patricia L. Maher.

78 In May 2003, the FDA: "List of Firms and Pharmaceuticals to Be Automatically Detained," U.S. Food and Drug Administration, announcement 66-40, February 13, 2002.

78 Samuel Johnson said: "In Praise of the Real Thing," *Economist,* May 17, 2003.

79 Not surprisingly, Colombian: Naomi Aoki, "U.S. Health Officials View Spate of Recent Cases as Evidence of Rising Trend," *Boston Globe,* May 29, 2002.

79 Of the 76 defendants: "Performance Report," U.S. Department of Justice, Washington, D.C., April 2001.

79 By contrast, in 2001: Ibid.

79 As for the size of the market: FBI, "Intellectual Property Crimes," Washington, D.C., April 11, 2004. The estimate used by the FBI is attributed to the International AntiCounterfeiting Coalition calculation of 1997. This estimate does

not include losses due to the theft from the rich treasury of U.S. patents. When patent theft is also considered, the actual damages are likely to be double or triple the 1997 estimates.

80 In March 2003, the FDA discovered: FDA, "FDA Warns of Contaminated, Fake Procrit," WebMDHealth, March 11, 2003, http://my.webmd.com/content/article/62/71524.htm?lastselectedguid={5FE84E90-BC77-4056-A91C9531713 CA348}.

80 The pharmaceutical maker: "Drug Alert: Serono Learns of Another Fake Batch of Its AIDS Drug," WebMDHealth, http://my.webmd.com/NR/internal. asp?GUID={D2974B05-5507-48C9-B19F-D606EB489C3A}.

80 In February 2002, the FDA warned: Food and Drug Administration, "FDA Warning: PC SPES, SPES (BotanicLab)," announcement, Washington, D.C., February 2002.

80 A company representative: Guy Gugliotta, "FDA Warns of Potent Drugs Found in Two Herbal Products," *Washington Post,* February 9, 2002.

80 Often, these drugs: Food and Drug Administration, "FDA's Counterfeit Drug Task Force Interim Report," U.S. Department of Health and Human Services, Washington, D.C., October 2003.

80 No one really knows: World Health Organization, "Counterfeit and Substandard Drugs: Answers for Frequently Asked Questions," June 4, 2004, www.who.int/medicines/organization/qsm/activities/qualityassurance/cft/counterfeit_faq.htm.

80 The problem, Bale says: "Health Talks Should Look at Fake Drugs," African News Service, August 28, 2002.

81 They divided them: WHO, "Counterfeit and Substandard Drugs."

81 During Niger's 1995 meningitis: World Health Organization, "Revised Drug Strategy," presentation in Geneva, www.who.int; WHO, "Substandard and Counterfeit Medicines," fact sheet, November 2003.

81 In Latin America: "Health Talks Should Look at Fake Drugs," African News Service.

81 In Pakistan: European Federation of Pharmaceutical Industries and Associations, "Counterfeit Medicines," 2004, www.efpia.org/2_indust/counterfeit drugs.pdf.

82 In Africa, an estimated: The Global Fund, "Malaria—Facts & Figures," 2003, www.theglobalfund.org/en/in_action/events/africamalariaday/2004/malaria/.

82 More than 71 percent: Ibid.

82 The WHO claims that prompt: WHO, "Substandard and Counterfeit Medicines."

82 The WHO reports that between: WHO, "What Is Malaria?," "Malaria in Africa," and "Children and Malaria," Roll Back Malaria Project, 2004.

82 The infection rate: United Nations, Statistical Division, "Malaria Prevalence, Notified Cases per 100,000 Population, 1988–2002," in *Millennium Indicators.*

82 In Botswana and Angola: Ibid.

82   The WHO reports: WHO, "Substandard and Counterfeit Medicines."

82   The others have varying: WHO, "Counterfeit and Substandard Drugs: Answers for Frequently Asked Questions."

82   The FDA, in its 2002 Performance Plan: FDA, "Performance Plan: 2002," U.S. Food and Drug Administration, Washington, D.C., December 2000, p. 7.

83   However, that agency lacks: Committee on Energy and Commerce, "Statement of Representative James C. Greenwood," hearing on Continuing Concerns over Imported Pharmaceuticals, U.S. House of Representatives, Washington, D.C., June 7, 2001.

83   Much of this Mexican: Ibid.

83   In 2000, the FDA had only: Committee on Commerce and Energy, "Statement of Congressman Richard Burr (R-NC)," hearing on Counterfeit Bulk Drugs, U.S. House of Representatives, June 8, 2000.

83   More troubling, the FDA reports: Committee on Commerce and Energy, "Statement of Congressman John D. Dingell (D-MI)," hearing on Counterfeit Bulk Drugs, U.S. House of Representatives, June 8, 2000.

83   A bulk quantity: Committee on Commerce and Energy "Statement of Congressman Fred Upton (R-MI)," hearing on Counterfeit Bulk Drugs, U.S. House of Representatives, June 8, 2000.

84   In August 2003, the WTO: World Trade Organization, *Decision Removes Final Patent Obstacle to Cheap Drug Imports,* report, August 30, 2003.

84   Finally, countries making: World Trade Organization, "TRIPS and Public Health," 2004, www.wto.org/english/tratop_e/trips_e/paper_develop_w296_e .htm.

85   More discouraging, almost all: "WHO Essential Medicines Library," mednet3.who.int/.

85   In Argentina: Pan American Health Organization, "Average Prices of a One-Year Treatment with Antiretrovirals in Countries of Latin America and the Caribbean," 2003.

86   Its duties then were: Customs and Border Protection, "Fraud Investigations: Fact Sheet," U.S. Department of Homeland Security, 2004.

86   In 2002, its staff: Customs and Border Protection, "Customs Statistics and Accomplishments," news release, U.S. Department of Homeland Security, May 5, 2003.

86   The Federal Bureau of Investigation: Office of the United States Trade Representative, *2004 Special 301 Report,* Washington, D.C.

87   Brazil, for example: Ibid., p. 15.

87   Taiwan's criminal organizations: Chris Cockel, "Taiwan Almost Certain to Remain on U.S. Piracy Blacklist," *China Post,* March 26, 2003.

87   Movie and game pirating: Office of the United States Trade Representative, International Intellectual Property Alliance, *USTR 2004 'Special 301' Decisions on Intellectual Property,* Washington, D.C., 2004.

88   Cranston, which was founded: "Cranston Print Works," www.cpw.com/ history.htm. In late 2001, George Shuster gave me one of the neckties that I

describe. It is attractive, and whenever I wear it I generally get questions about where I purchased it.

88   George Shuster, CEO: "Pirates and the U.S. Textile Industry," Reuters, May 30, 2004, www.reuters.com.

88   If they are right: Ibid.

89   Thus, proving pattern: George Shuster, interview with the author, June 10, 2004.

89   The portion of the U.S. market: International Trademark Association, *Estimation of the Impact of Trademark Counterfeiting and Infringement on Worldwide Sales of Apparel and Footwear* (New York City, 1998), p. 1.

89   Another measure of the threat: "FY 2002 and FY 2003 Top IPR Commodities Seized," U.S. Customs and Border Protection and U.S. Immigration and Customs Enforcement, U.S. Customs and Border Protection, L.A. Strategic Trade Center, December 2, 2003.

89   Today, China and Hong Kong: National Labor Committee, "Riding the Asian Tiger," www.nlcnet.org/China/riding.htm.

90   In the four-year period: U.S. General Accounting Office, "U.S. Customs and Border Protection Faces Challenges in Addressing Illegal Textile Transshipment" (GAO-04-345), Washington, D.C., January 2004, pp. 12–18.

90   Despite such successes: Joanna Ramey, "GAO Report Critical of Customs," January 29, 2004, p. 11, www.wwd.com/content/article.cfm?ID=%25%22%2DH%2ERET%20%0A&mag=wwd03.

90   As long ago as 1992: American Textile Manufacturers Institute, "U.S. Customs Reports on Transshipment Activity," special report, Washington, D.C., 2003.

90   In 1994, Customs reported: Ibid.

92   According to the International: Stephen E. Siwek, *Copyright Industries in the U.S. Economy: The 2002 Report*, Economists Incorporated, International Intellectual Property Alliance, Washington, D.C., 2002, p. 3.

92   Stephen E. Siwek, a principal: Ibid., p. 1.

93   While the U.S. economy: Ibid.

93   The Motion Picture Association of America: "International Copyright Piracy: Links to Organized Crime and Terrorism," statement of Jack Valenti before the Subcommittee on Courts, the Internet, and Intellectual Property, Committee on Judiciary, U.S. House of Representatives, Washington, D.C., March 13, 2003.

93   Equally significant, the MPAA: Bob Sullivan, "Hollywood Gets Tough on Copying," MSNBC, July 12, 2003.

93   In the U.S. alone: "Software Piracy Fact Sheet," Business Software Alliance, 2004, www.bsa.org/customcf/popuphitbox.cfm?ReturnURL=/resources/loader.cfm?url=/commonspot/security/getfile.cfm&PageID=1292.

94   He warned that: "International Copyright Piracy," statement of Jack Valenti.

94   The rate ranged: International Planning and Research Corporation, "2001 U.S. Software, State Piracy Study," 2002.

94   One contained 174,000 pirated: "International Copyright Piracy," statement of Jack Valenti.

94 In November 2001, a task force: Microsoft Corporation, "Largest Counterfeit Software Seizure in U.S. History: Law Enforcement Breaks Highly Organized Counterfeit Software Supply Chain," news release, Redmond, Wash., November 16, 2001.

95 Although the raid broke: Microsoft Corporation, "What Is Piracy—Internet Piracy," www.msn.com/piracy/basics/what/ip.asp.

96 In 2000, the trade: Motion Picture Association of America, "Anti-Piracy," www.mpaa.org/anti-piracy/content.htm.

96 In 2002, it seized: "International Copyright Piracy," statement of Jack Valenti.

96 The *Chronicle of*: Burton Bollag, "Don't Steal This Book," *Chronicle of Higher Education*, April 2, 2004.

97 In 2003, U.S. publishers: Ibid.

97 Publishers report that: Ibid.

97 The *Chronicle* of *Higher Education*: Ibid.

98 For many centuries: Authorship Collaborative Program, "Neem Seed," Case Western University, home.cwru.edu; Foodnet, "Neem," www.foodnet.cgiar.org.

98 But more than eighty other: "Biopiracy-Friendly Laws Worry Neem Battle Winner," *Asia Times*, May 27, 2000.

98 Over the centuries, Indians: Ibid.

98 The Indian government: N. K. Dubey, Rajesh Kumar, and Pramila Tripathi, "Global Promotion of Herbal Medicine: India's Opportunity," *Current Science* 86, no. 1 (January 2004): 10.

98 Rice Tec, Inc.: Diverse Women, "GMO's: The Failed Promise," *Bija*, no. 29, (Navdanya, December 2002), available online at www.diversewomen.org/pdf_files/bija2002.pdf.

98 A Colorado firm: Lori Wallach and Patrick Woodall, *Whose Trade Organization?* (New York: New Press, 2004), pp. 205–207.

99 The United Nations Convention: Janis Kelly, "Hague Meeting Targets Biopiracy," *The Scientist* (April 24, 2002), www.biomedcentral.com.

CHAPTER 4: THE GERMAN METHOD

103 By early 1915, only a third: Robert K. Massie, *Castles of Steel* (New York: Random House, 2003), p. 507.

103 When the war began: Thomas R. Howell, "Dumping: Still a Problem in International Law," in *International Friction and Cooperation in High-Technology Development and Trade* (Washington, D.C.: Dewey Ballantine LLP Trade Group Publications, National Academy Press, 1997), pp. 10–14.

103 The U.S. also relied on: Kathryn Steen, "Patents, Patriotism, and 'Skilled in the Art': USA v. the Chemical Foundation, Inc., 1923–1926," *Isis*, (March 2001): 96.

104 Limited amounts of novocaine: Victor Lefebure, *The Riddle of the Rhine: Chemical Strategy in Peace and War*, with a preface by Marshal Foch and an introduction by Field Marshal Sir Henry Wilson, Chief of the Imperial General Staff (New York: Chemical Foundation, 1922), chap. 10, Gutenberg e-text.

104 The squat, wide-beamed: Captain Paul Koenig, *Voyage of the Deutschland* (1916; repr. Honolulu: University Press of the Pacific, 2000), pp. 1–5.

104 At midnight on August 2: Ibid.; "Deutschland U-155," Ron's Submarine Covers, www.users.skynet.be/RonSubCovers.

105 Germany preferred patents: Peter Hayes, *Industry and Ideology: IG Farben in the Nazi Era* (New York: Cambridge University Press, 1987), p. 3.

106 What he did not know: Simon Garfield, *Mauve* (New York: W. W. Norton & Company), pp. 5–13.

106 The medal recognized: "Perkin Medal," Society of Chemical Industry, 2004, www.soci.org/SCI/awards/awardsbook/award.jsp?awardID=AW31.

106 In 1856, the seventeen-year-old: John Cornwell, *Hitler's Scientists: Science, War, and the Devil's Pact* (New York: Viking Books, 2003), p. 42.

106 In 1841, Hofmann discovered: Garfield, *Mauve*, pp. 23–33.

106 Since the demand for: Ibid.

106 Harvard professor Robert Burns Woodward: Nobel Foundation, "Robert B. Woodward—Biography," Nobel e-Museum, 2004, www.nobel.se/chemistry/laureates/1965/woodward-bio.html.

106 Working there the Easter weekend: Garfield, *Mauve*, p. 35.

107 Perkin named his dye: "Purple Passion: The Synthesis of Mauve," chem.brown.edu/chem33/labs-2003/purplepassion.pdf/.

107 An ounce of Perkin's dye: Susan Bryant, "More Colors to Dye For," *A Thimblefull*, January 2002, www.thestatusthimble.com/Nwsltr/NwsLtr200201.pdf.

107 Perkin's father: Garfield, *Mauve*, pp. 51–52.

107 Perkin and his family: "Purple Passion: The Synthesis of Mauve."

107 Thereafter, pale violet: Pat Bowley, "Tinctorial Matters: On the Dying of Yarn," *Knitting Now*, newsletter, winter 1999–2000.

107 Then, only months later: Ibid. Also see "Purple Passion: The Synthesis of Mauve."

108 The wedding was perhaps: Jerrold M. Packard, *Victoria's Daughters* (New York: St. Martin's, 1998), pp. 65–67. "Vicky" was Queen Victoria's favorite child and Prince Albert's devoted *student*. The marriage to the future ruler of Germany was a political and social event of enormous significance. Packard tells a story that describes both the significance of the wedding and Queen Victoria's sense of majesty. The German government wanted the marriage to take place in Berlin. When the queen learned of this, her response was "The assumption of its being too much for a Prince Royal of Prussia to come over to marry the Princess Royal of Great Britain IN England is too absurd, to say the least . . . Whatever may be the usual practice of Prussian Princes, it is not every day that one marries the eldest daughter of the Queen of England. The question must therefore be considered as settled and closed." The happy couple were married in England.

108 One after another: Bowley, "Tinctorial Matters"; Bryant, "More Colors to Dye For."

108 In 1858, the French: Garfield, *Mauve*, pp. 61–62.

109 Among the most famous: Ibid., pp. 84–85.

109 Tired of business: Ibid., p. 109.

109 In 1863, for instance: Richard Sasuly, *IG Farben* (New York: Bone & Gaer, 1947), pp. 24–27.

109 BASF began with: Ibid., p. 25.

109 By 1900, six German companies: Ibid. See also Joseph Borkin, *The Crime and Punishment of IG Farben* (New York: Free Press, 1978), pp. 4–5.

110 By 1900, German dye companies: Ibid., pp. 27–29.

110 In the late 1860s: German Embassy, "Milestones in History," pamphlet (Washington, D.C., 2004).

110 Under Bismarck, and after: Federal Research Division of the Library of Congress, Country Studies Program, *Germany,* report, Washington, D.C., 1995.

110 Within thirty years: Howell, *International Friction and Cooperation,* p. 30.

110 It established a discriminatory: Hayes, *Industry and Ideology,* p. 2.

110 After an economic depression: Federal Research Division of the Library of Congress, *Germany,* chapters on "Political Parties and the Economy."

110 In 1897, the *Kaiser Wilhelm der Grosse: Ships of the World: A Historical Encyclopedia* (Boston/New York: Houghton Mifflin, 1997), s.v. "*Kaiser Wilhelm der Grosse.*"

111 The first Atlantic liner: Ibid. See also "*SS Kaiser Wilhelm Der Grosse,*" www.marconicalling.com/html/index.html.

111 Most important, Germany: Library of Congress Country Studies Program, *Germany,* "Patterns of Development."

111 As a group, German banks: Library of Congress Country Studies Program, *Germany,* "Banking and Its Role in the Economy."

111 In 1900, for instance, Germany: Library of Congress Country Studies Program, *Germany,* "History."

111 In 1919: Sasuly, *IG Farben,* pp. 23–30.

112 "Duisberg failed to mention": Sasuly, *IG Farben,* pp. 23–24.

113 Most important, the factories: Victor LeFebure, *Riddle of the Rhine,* Gutenberg e-text. LeFebure was a distinguished British military officer who saw the World War I gas attacks. He subsequently described dye factories as arsenals, since the same machinery used to produce dyes could easily be transformed to produce poison gases.

113 Between 1911 and 1948: Professor William E. Seidelman, "Science and Inhumanity, The Kaiser-Wilhelm/Max Planck Society," University of Toronto, St. Michael's Hospital, www.baycrest.org/PDFs/science.pdf.

114 U.S. universities had few: John M. Barry, *The Great Influenza* (New York: Viking Books, 2004), pp. 34–35.

114 Systematic medical research: Ibid. Fortunately, U.S. scientists and doctors were fast learners. John Hopkins Medical School led the way then.

114 Thus, between 1870 and 1914: Ibid., p. 43.

114 The most important measure: The Nobel Prize Internet Archive, www.almaz.com/nobel/.

114 In 1931, Bosch: Cornwell, *Hitler's Scientists,* pp. 38–60; Borkin, *Crime and Punishment of IG Farben,* pp. 11–30.

115 An investigative team: Borkin, *Crime and Punishment of IG Farben,* p. 155.

116 In the early twentieth century: Ibid.

116 By 1916, domestic competition: Sasuly, *IG Farben*, pp. 25–31.

116 Before World War I: Ibid., p. 37.

117 In 1913, only one remained: Lefebure, *Riddle on the Rhine*.

117 After the United States: Ibid.

117 He pointed out that: Garfield, *Mauve*, p. 84.

118 As Simon Garfield notes: Ibid., p. 148.

118 Between 1891 and 1895: Ibid., p. 150.

118 The British government: Ibid., p. 154.

118 In 1919, the U.S. Alien: Lefebure, *Riddle on the Rhine*.

119 The driller showed: Don Whitehead, *The Dow Story: History of the Dow Chemical Company* (New York: McGraw-Hill Book Company, 1968), p. 20.

119 The brine waste: Ibid.

120 Firefighters were barely able: Ibid., p. 35.

120 One of those was: E. N. Brandt, *Growth Company: Dow Chemical's First Century* (East Lansing: Michigan State University Press, 1996), pp. 10–11.

120 Another professor was: Ibid.

120 The bleach "pool": Brandt, *Growth Company*, pp. 44–45.

121 But although Dow Chemical: Whitehead, *Dow Story*, pp. 53–55.

122 He then lectured: Burton W. Folsom Jr., *Empire Builders: How Michigan Entrepreneurs Helped Make America Great* (Traverse City, Mich.: Rhodes and Easton, 1998), pp. 95–96.

122 He issued Dow: Brandt, *Growth Company*, p. 45.

122 Within days, a New York: Whitehead, *Dow Story*, p. 56.

122 In early 1905: Brandt, *Growth Company*, pp. 44–48.

122 This left 12 cents: Ibid.

123 He also learned from: Ibid.

124 Dow countered: Whitehead, *Dow Story*, p. 69.

124 In 1909, prices began: Ibid.

126 But Bosch would not: Borkin, *Crime and Punishment of IG Farben*, pp. 38–39.

126 When the German press: Ibid.

126 Soon the four German: Ibid.

127 Thus, America developed: Kathryn Steen, "Patents, Patriotism, and 'Skilled in the Art': USA v. the Chemical Foundation, Inc., 1923–1926," *Isis*, 92 (March 2001): 91–122. This is a fascinating look at how President Woodrow Wilson, a free trader by inclination, put into place an industrial policy designed to ensure that the United States had an organic chemical industry. After Wilson left office, a furious lawsuit challenged the legitimacy of what he had done. Professor Kathryn Steen of Drexel University tells that story in her extended article.

127 Alcoa threatened Dow: Sasuly, *IG Farben*, pp. 172–173.

128 Foolishly and inexplicably: Whitehead, *Dow Story*, pp. 168-170; Dow Chemical, "Dow Chemical, A Brief History," 2004, www.geo.msu.edu.

128 Historian E. N. Brandt: Brandt, *Growth Company*, pp. 247–251.

128 After taking testimony: Report of the Senate Special Committee Investigating the National Defense Program, March 13, 1944, as cited in Brandt, *Growth Company*, p. 251.

128 Still, it took time: Whitehead, *Dow Story*, pp. 168–170.

129 At its creation: Borkin, *Crime and Punishment of IG Farben*, pp. 43–44.

129 After General Motors: Robert Franklin Maddox, *The War Within World War II: The United States and International Cartels* (Westport, Conn.: Praeger, 2001), pp. 39–40.

129 It produced all: Hayes, *Industry and Ideology*, p. 17.

129 The two companies: Borkin, *Crime and Punishment of IG Farben*, pp. 43–45.

129 Ultimately, it had 500: Maddox, *War Within World War II*, pp. 38–40.

130 Among those partners: Ibid.

130 "This means," Howard wrote: Borkin, *Crime and Punishment of IG Farben*, pp. 45–52.

131 In addition, Farben: Ibid.

131 Under the terms: Ibid.

131 Once Adolf Hitler: Borkin, *Crime and Punishment of IG Farben*, pp. 76–95.

131 Consequently, the U.S.: Ibid.

131 The Justice Department agreed: Ibid.

132 DuPont's position was: Ibid., p. 77.

132 As a result, the Luftwaffe: Ibid.

132 When Hitler took power: Maddox, *War Within World War II*, pp. 59–69.

132 Thus, the U.S. entered: Ibid.

132 In the early days: Ibid., pp. 38–40.

133 As soon as U.S. authorities: Ibid., pp. 67–70.

133 Under German pressure: Sasuly, *IG Farben*, pp. 172–174.

133 Similarly, the Remington Arms Company: Ibid.

133 Aluminum, and atabrine: Ibid., p. 177.

133 The principal transfer: Jean Medawar and David Pyke, *Hitler's Gift: The True Story of the Scientists Expelled by the Nazi Regime* (New York: Arcade Publishing, 2001).

134 In *The Crime and Punishment of IG Farben*: Borkin, *Crime and Punishment of IG Farben*, pp. 56–57.

134 Within a year, almost: Medawar and Pyke, *Hitler's Gift*, p. 10.

134 Altogether, Medawar and Pyke: Ibid., p. 29.

134 In a stunning departure: Ibid.

134 Of the twenty-seven German scholars: Ibid., appendix 1, pp. 241–242.

135 They developed stereo: Cornwell, *Hitler's Scientists*.

135 Among these were 8,000: Michael White, "Alien Property Custodian Patents," October 3, 2002, http://piug.derwent.co.uk/archive/piug/piug-2002/1092.html.

136 U.S. Army officials: Howard Watson Ambrustger, *Treason's Peace: German Dyes and American Dupes* (New York: Beechhurst Press, 1947), p. 395.

136 Farben's main office in Frankfurt: "I.G. Farben Building," May 5, 2004, www.angelfire.com.

136 Not one was found: Borkin, *Crime and Punishment of IG Farben*, pp. 135–156.

137 On April 1, 1978, BASF: Ibid., p. 220.

137 The price was: Paul A. Schons, "German Contributions to Your Health," St. Paul, Minn.: Germanic-American Institute, October 2001.

137 In 2004, another French: Company information provided by Hoover's Online, www.hoovers.com.

CHAPTER 5: JAPAN'S WAY

138 In 1943, that control: Chalmers Johnson, *MITI and the Japanese Miracle* (Stanford, Calif: Stanford University Press, 1982), pp. 155–197.

139 Consequently, the occupation: Karel van Wolferen, *The Enigma of Japanese Power* (New York: Alfred A. Knopf, 1989), pp. 389–390.

139 Thus the same: Ibid.

139 The single most important step: Ibid.

139 If it complied: Ibid., p. 394.

140 Black markets thrived: "Post War Japan," http://web3.woodbury.edu/faculty/dcremer/courses/japan/Postwar%20Japan.ppt.

140 In quick order: Ibid.

140 After the peace agreement: Johnson, *MITI and the Japanese Miracle*, p. 225.

140 Nobusuke Kishi: Infoplease Library, "Nobusuke Kishi," biography, www.infoplease.com.

141 In postwar Japan: Encyclopedia.com, s.v. "Hayato Ikeda," www.encyclopedia.com/html/i/ikeda-h1a.asp.

141 Kishi was his brother's: Nobel e-museum, "Eisake Sato," biography, www.nobel.se/peace/laureates/1974/sato-gio.html.

141 President Nixon hosted: Nixon Presidential Materials Staff, White House Tapes Release: Complete Conversations Arranged by Reference Cassette Number Conversation 281-1, October 21, 1971, www.ssa.gov/history/Nixon/Complete%20Conversation%20Report%20—%20By%20Reference%20Cassette%20Number.pdf.

141 The world called it: Johnson, *MITI and the Japanese Miracle*, pp. 4–5, table 1.

141 "capitalist development state": Author interview by telephone with Chalmers Johnson, November 16, 2004.

142 "no technology entered": Ibid., p. 17.

143 IBM capitulated: Ibid,. pp. 246–247.

143 Patent flooding, according: United States General Accounting Office, *Intellectual Property Rights: U.S. Companies' Patent Experiences in Japan* (GAO/GGD-93-126), July 1993, pp. 22–23.

144 In both these examples, the U.S.: Ibid.

144 Regis McKenna, a venture: Pat Choate, *Agents of Influence: How Japan Manipulates America's Political and Economic System* (New York: Alfred A. Knopf, 1990), p. 127.

144 In *Agents of Influence:* Ibid., pp. 126–131.

144 By 1989, the inventors: Ibid.

145 By the mid-1980s: Krista McQuade and Benjamin Gomes-Cassares, "Fusion Systems Corporation in Japan," case study, Harvard Business School, rev. December 15, 1993.

145 The senator was Robert Packwood: Skip Kaltenheuser, "Packwood's Subtler Touch," Intellectual Property Creators, June 2003, www.ipcreators.org/issues/packwood/packkalt.htm

145 A British company purchased: "Fusion Systems Corporation," *Washington Post,* April 28, 1997; Robert H. Smith School of Business, University of Maryland, "Donald M. Spero Appointed Director of Dingman Center for Entrepreneurship," news release.

147 In the other, the nation: 6AO/66D-93-126, p. 7.

147 *Wall Street Journal* reporter: John J. Fialka, *War by Other Means: Economic Espionage in America* (New York: W. W. Norton, 1997), pp. 3–17.

148 Much of that information: Japan External Trade Organization, "Overseas Offices," www.jetro.go.jp.

148 European companies: NSF, "Science and Engineering Indicators—2002," "International Strategic Technology Alliances," appendix, table 4-39.

149 He said that he: Joseph Stiglitz, "Public Policy for a Knowledge Economy" (paper presented at the Center for Economic Policy Research, London, January 27, 1999).

149 During the furor over: Carl M. Cannon, "Letter from Washington: The Bill Comes Due," *Forbes,* September 10, 2001.

149 Of these acquisitions: Linda Spencer, "Foreign Acquisitions of U.S. High Technology Companies—October 1988 to December 1993," report, Economic Strategy Institute, Washington, D.C., 1994.

150 In 1990, Edward Miller: Author interview with Edward Miller, Washington, D.C., December 2003.

152 In 1977, only five hundred: Choate, *Agents of Influence,* pp. 77–105.

154 The deciding event: Max Holland, *When the Machine Stopped: A Cautionary Tale from Industrial America* (Cambridge, Mass.: Harvard Business School Press, 1989), pp. 7–10.

154 Warner & Swasey made a deal: Ibid., pp. 127–128; MachineTools.com, "Murata Machinery, LTD."

155 Eventually the two companies: Holland, *When the Machine Stopped,* pp. 142–143.

155 Between 1976 and 1981: Roderick Seeman, "U.S. Government Rejects Machine Tool Petition," *Japan Law Letter,* June 1983.

156 Reagan, who viewed: Clyde H. Farnsworth, "U.S. Heeded Nakasone Plea in Air-Cargo Dispute," *New York Times,* May 8, 1986.

156 Their radio sets: Philip J. Curtis, *The Fall of the U.S. Consumer Electronics Industry* (Westport, Conn.: Quorum Books, 1994), pp. 24–25.

156 The solution Young engineered: Tom Lewis, *Empire of the Air: The Men Who Made Radio* (New York: HarperCollins Publishers, 1991), pp. 141–159.

156 Under the terms of incorporation: Ibid.

157 Altogether, RCA began: Ibid.

157 In addition, Westinghouse would: Ibid.

157 Zenith had one: Curtis, *Fall of the U.S. Consumer Electronics Industry,* p. 26.

157 As part of the deal: Ibid., p. 33.

158 He originated the Zenith slogan: Ibid., p. 27.

158 Instead of waiting for RCA: Ibid., pp. 33–74.

158 RCA settled with Zenith: Ibid., p. 98.

159 With that, the stalker became: Ibid., pp. 103–109.

159 The case went to the Supreme Court: Ibid., pp. 104–106.

159 As a reward: Ibid., p. 108.

159 When GE bought RCA: Ibid., p. 226.

160 The cartel's overall profits: Ibid., p. 204.

160 Zenith's investigators also uncovered: Choate, *Agents of Influence,* pp. 64–105.

160 Later, Zenith learned: Ibid.

161 The Justice Department's brief: Ibid., p. 102.

162 By the time Zenith learned: Curtis, *Fall of the U.S. Consumer Electronics Indus-try,* pp. 208–210.

162 In 1968, the U.S.: Ibid., p. 128.

162 As of 1990, there was: Choate, *Agents of Influence,* p. 78. Taylor White, LLC, a contract manufacturer that assembles television components for Samsung and Philips Electronics, producing televisions sets sold under their labels. In June 2004, the International Trade Commission found that Chinese produc-ers were dumping similar sets in the U.S. market.

163 Industrial robotics: *Robotics,* hearings before the Subcommittee on Inves-tigations and Oversight of the Committee on Science and Technology, U.S. House of Representatives, Ninety-seventh Congress, 2nd session, June 2 and 23, 1982.

163 In 1968, the U.S. had: *Robotics,* ibid., statement of Paul H. Aron, Executive Vice President, Daiwa Securities, America, Inc., p. 9

163 But by 1982, Japan had: Ibid.

163 The second focused: Ibid.

163 Finally, they would: Ibid.

164 Even two decades ago: Ibid.

165 When Congressman Gore asked: Ibid., p. 365.

165 The United Nations: United Nations Economic Commission for Europe, "Robot Production/Use," press release, ECE/STAT/03/P01.

165 Not only is U.S.: Ibid., figure 4.

166 In 1986, the Japan: Kenko Hoshi, Chief Economist, Japan Development Bank, *Financial Assistance to Foster Technological Innovation: The Case of Japan,* report, Tokyo, 1986, p. 1.

167 This transition from: Ibid.

167 Eamonn Fingleton, a financial: Eamonn Fingleton, *Blindside* (Boston and New York: Houghton Mifflin, 1995).

167 Japanese corporations also control: Ibid., pp. 66–67.

167 Fingleton estimates that such: Ibid.
168 If Dell, Hewlett-Packard, or IBM tried: Author interview with Eamonn Fingleton, Washington, D.C., April 22, 2004.
168 The Japanese have a name: Fingleton, *Blindside*, p. 46.
168 "Lowell's world was Darwinian": Fialka, *War by Other Means*. p. 14.

CHAPTER 6: CHINA RISING

169 The China of 2005: *The World Factbook*, "China," U.S. Central Intelligence Agency, May 2004.
169 The labor force: Ibid.
169 China has 100 million: Ibid.
170 China's labor pool: Ibid.; "China: 6.92 Million New Jobs Created in 2003," *Asian Labour News*, June 1, 2004.
170 PricewaterhouseCoopers reports that: Allan Zhang, "China's State Enterprises: Riding the Wave, Part 1," *Business*, April 2003.
170 Between 1998 and 2001, the government: Zhao Miaomiao and Wen Chihua, "Holes in China's Social Safety Net Leave Workers Reeling," *Panos-China*, September 9, 2002.
170 The 2004 CIA *World Factbook* reports: *World Factbook*, s.v. "China."
171 China graduates from its: John Schmid, "China Engineers Its Next Great Leap," *Milwaukee Journal Sentinel*, December 30, 2003.
171 Within one year: "COSCO Praised for Effort to Closer U.S.–Asia Trade Ties," *People's Daily*, April 2, 2003.
172 The foreign corporations: Johnson, *MITI and the Japanese Miracle*, pp. 245-246.
172 In 2002, economists: Alastair Newton and Robert Subbaraman, "China: Gigantic Possibilities, Present Realities," Lehman Brothers, Global Economics, January 21, 2002.
172 The average manufacturing wage: *World Development Indicators*, "Wages and Productivity" (Washington, D.C.: World Bank, 2004).
173 Indeed, Mexico itself lost: "Mexico Loses Jobs to China," NewsMax.Com, September 9, 2003, www.newsmax.com/archives/articles/2003/9/8/140300 .shtml.
173 The Chinese Academy: Zhu Guangya, "Engineering in China," *The Bridge* 28, no. 2 (National Academy of Engineering, 1998), www.nae.edu.
173 In late 2002, Motorola: Motorola Corporation, "Motorola China Announces Five-Year Strategy," June 2002.
173 With this, Motorola: "Transnationals Locate More R&D Centers in China," *ChinaWe*, March 21, 2003, http://asset.chinawe.com:8080/html/news/2003321122454. html.
173 Microsoft has invested: Ibid.
173 In 2002, the Chinese government: Kristi Heim, "Software Schools Evolve to Help Students Compete," *San Jose Mercury News*, March 17, 2004.

173 Microsoft also pledged: Sonya Rabbitte, "Ballmer in a China Shop: Microsoft Invests $750 million," Silicon.com, June 28, 2002, http://hardware.silicon.com/desktops/0,39024645,11034238,00.htm.

173 General Electric, the ninth: General Electric Corporation, "GE China," press release and annual report, 2003.

174 GE has also established: "Transnationals Locate More R & D Centers in China," ChinaWe.

174 This money will: General Motors Corporation, "General Motors Continues Rapid Expansion in China," news release, June 7, 2004, www.gm.com.

174 With this investment, GM: Ibid.

174 The Chinese government reports: "Over 200,000 Patent Applications in 2001," People's Daily, March 1, 2002.

174 The Chinese put: Ibid.

174 In 2001, there were more: Ibid.

175 In 2003, China's: "China an Ideal Place of R & D: Commerce Official," People's Daily, September 10, 2003.

175 The Chinese press reports: "Transnationals Locate More R&D Centers in China," People's Daily, March 19, 2003, http://english.people.com.cn/200303/19/eng20030319_113567.shtml.

175 In 2002 and 2003: United Nations, "Asia and the Pacific: Sources of FDI Finance in Select Economies, 1999–2002," in World Investment Report 2003 New York, 2003, annex table A.ll.1.

175 Almost half of that: Charles W. McMillion, "China's Very Rapid Economic, Industrial and Technological Emergence," U.S.–China Commission, MBG Information Services, 2002.

175 The U.S.–China Economic and Security: Ibid.

175 By contrast, Dr. Charles: Ibid.

175 As of 2002, China: United Nations, "Country Fact Sheet–China," World Investment Report 2003.

175 At the beginning of 2001: United Nations, "Number of Parent Corporations and Foreign Affiliates by Region and Economy," World Investment Report 2003, p. 222, table A.1.15.

175 Its Ministry of Commerce: "China's Foreign Direct Investment Hits U.S. $53 Billion in 2003," People's Daily, January 15, 2004.

175 The Export-Import Bank of India: T. C. Venkat Subramanian, managing director and CEO of EXIM Bank (India), "Foreign Direct Investment and Manufacturing," February 24, 2003.

175 In two recent books: Edward Timperlake and William C. Triplett II, Red Dragon Rising (Washington, D.C.: Regnery, 1999); Edward Timperlake and William C. Triplett II, Year of the Rat (Washington, D.C.: Regnery, 1998).

176 In effect, the Chinese: Timperlake and Triplett, Year of the Rat, pp. 147–150.

176 In October 1999: U.S. Department of Commerce, "McDonnell Douglas, China National Aero Technology Import and Export Corporation and Others Indicted on Federal Charges for Making False and Misleading Statements in

Connection with Exporting Machinery to the People's Republic of China," news release, October 19, 1999.

176 In a similar case: Timperlake and Triplett, *Red Dragon Rising*, p. 176.

176 In February 2003, Scott: Scott L. Wheeler, "Missile Technology Sent to China," *Insight*, February 5, 2003.

177 Magnequench is the last: Ibid.

177 In January 1999: Report of the Select Committee of U.S. National Security and Military/Commercial Concerns with the People's Republic of China," 105th Cong., 2d sess., 1999, H. Rep. 105-851, available at www.gpo.gov/congress/house/hr105851-html/overbod.html.

177 Released with unanimous concurrence: Ibid.

177 The select committee: Ibid., pp. 23–24.

177 Not only has the Chinese government: Ibid., pp. 26–43.

178 The report also reveals: Ibid.

178 Among these are: Ibid., p. 8.

178 The technology on the used: Ibid.

178 In 2002, for instance: *China Facts and Figures 2003*, "Science and Technology: Summary," www.china.org.cn/english/.

179 What the Chinese wanted: Author interview with Edward Miller, Washington, D.C., December 2003.

179 Among China's government-specified: "China's Pillar Industries," China Economic Net, report, June 20, 2004.

179 The Chinese Academy of Sciences: Chinese Academy of Sciences, news release, http://english.cas.ac.cn/Eng2003/page/home.asp.

179 Any foreign company: Alysha Webb, "China Plans to Grab Imported Technology," *Automotive News*, June 9, 2003.

179 China also expects: Ibid.

180 The U.S. Commerce Department: Tom Brown, "Trade Official: China Car Imports by 2010," Reuters, Dearborn, Mich., June 23, 2004.

180 One Chinese manufacturer: "China Bogged Down in IPR Dilemma," *China Daily*, September 7, 2002.

180 Congressman James Sensenbrenner Jr.: "Editorial: Modern Piracy in China," *Milwaukee Journal Sentinel*, January 27, 2004.

180 Toyota was then fined: Freshfields Bruckhaus Deringer, *International IP Update* newsletter (winter 2003–2004).

181 China also agreed to: Embassy of the United States in Japan, "USTR Lists Outcomes of Commission Meeting on U.S.–China Trade," news release, April 21, 2004.

181 The United States has protested: Office of the U.S. Trade Representative, "U.S. Files WTO Case Against China over Discriminatory Taxes that Hurt U.S. Exports," news release, Washington, D.C., March 18, 2004.

182 According to the *San Jose Mercury News*: Kristi Heim, "Microsoft Hopes for Return on Costly Investment in China," *San Jose Mercury News*, March 16, 2004.

182 In March 2004: Peter Morris, "HP Launches Linux PCs, Asia Spurning Microsoft," *Asia Times,* March 19, 2004.

182 Dell and Oracle also: "Oracle, Dell Establish Strategic Partnership," *China View,* March 3, 2004.

182 In November 2003: Kristi Helm, "Microsoft Hopes for Return on Costly Investment in China."

182 Already Motorola and Nokia: "Motorola, Dell Lose China Market Share to Local Firms," *Taipei Times,* May 29, 2003.

183 By contrast, Dell and IBM: Ibid.

183 "The large numbers": U.S.–China Economic and Security Review Commission, "Trade and Investment Chapter," 2002 annual report, Washington, D.C., June 2002.

183 The National Science Foundation: National Science Board, *Science and Engineering Indicators, 2004,* vol. 1, NSB 04-1 (Arlington, Va: National Science Foundation, 2004) chap. 2, p. 30.

184 More than 26,500: Ibid.

184 The NSF also reports: *Science and Engineering Indicators, 2004,* vol. 2, NSB 04-2, "Plans of Foreign Recipients of U.S. S&E Doctorates to Stay in United States, by Field and Place of Origin: 1990–2001," appendix table 2-31.

184 They are helping build: *Science and Engineering Indicators, 2004,* vol. 1, "Overview," p. 2.

184 In 2000, they achieved more: *Science and Engineering Indicators, 2004,* vol. 2, "R&D Performed Overseas by Majority-Owned Foreign Affiliates of U.S. Parent Companies, by Selected NAICS Industry of Affiliate and Region/Country 2000," appendix table 4-25.

184 By the end of this: Of the $20 billion of R & D done outside the U.S. by American-controlled companies, almost $13 billion was done in Europe.

184 In 2002, the value of: U.S. Census Bureau, Foreign Trade Division, "U.S. Trade with China in Advanced Technology Products, Monthly and Cumulative Data," Washington, D.C., February 13, 2004.

186 China's State Intellectual Property Office: State Intellectual Property Office of the People's Republic of China, "History," 2002, www.sipo.gov.cn/sipo_english/default.htm.

186 In the 1980s: U.S. Department of State, International Information Programs, "Timeline of US and China IPR Developments: 1963–2002," 2003.

186 Beijing also enacted: Ibid.

186 With its accession: Ibid.

187 The International AntiCounterfeiting Coalition: International AntiCounterfeiting Coalition (IACC), "Submission of the International AntiCounterfeiting Coalition, Inc., to the United States Trade Representative: Special 301 Recommendations," Washington, D.C., February 13, 2003, p. 10.

187 The IACC documented: Ibid.

188 The International Intellectual Property Alliance's: IIPA, "IIPA 2004: Special 301 Recommendations to USTR," February 13, 2004.

188 The International AntiCounterfeiting: IACC, "Submission of the International AntiCounterfeiting Coalition, Inc."

189 In those same three years: Ibid., pp. 18–19.

189 However, it distributed: Ibid.

190 Meanwhile, the pirate kept: Luo Zhenghong, "Protection of Well-Known Trademarks in China," white paper, Peking University, pp. 18–20.

190 The European Union, which includes: European Commission, Taxation, and Customs Union, *Statistics Recorded at the External Borders of the EU, 2000–2003* (Brussels: European Commission, 2003).

190 The *New York Times* reports: Elizabeth Malkin, "Mexico Making Headway on Smuggling," *New York Times,* June 5, 2003.

190 Nevertheless, almost 58 percent: Jenalia Moreno and Ciudad Nezahualcoyotl, "China Tears at Mexico's Fabric: Illegal Imports Taking Thousands of Key Jobs" *Houston Chronicle,* May 15, 2003.

190 President Vicente Fox: Malkin, "Mexico Making Headway on Smuggling."

190 Still, that is down: Ibid.

191 The *Financial Times* reports: "Office Politics," *Financial Times,* June 24, 2002.

191 Many Westerners forget: Ibid.

191 "A system of state determination": William P. Alford, *To Steal a Book Is an Elegant Offense: Intellectual Property Law in Chinese Civilization* (Stanford, Calif.: Stanford University Press, 1995), p. 119.

CHAPTER 7: EVOLVING ENFORCEMENT

196 In the early 1980s: "Japan Inc." denotes Japanese corporations, cartels, and government working together to meet some specific industrial goal, such as achieving global dominance of a targeted industry. See Chalmers Johnson *MITI and the Japanese Miracle,* for a detailed explanation.

196 In *The Patent Wars:* Fred Warshofsky, *The Patent Wars* (New York: John Wiley & Sons, 1994), pp. 111–123.

197 In 1992, it won: Ibid., p. 1.

197 Subsequently, Honeywell licensed: Ibid.

197 Ten other Japanese: Ibid.

197 Gregory Aharonian, a writer: Gregory Aharonian, "Patent/Copyright Infringement Lawsuits/Licensing Awards," www.patenting-art.com/economic/awards .htm.

198 This dual system: U.S. Department of Justice, "The Protection of Copyrights," in *Federal Prosecution of Violations of Intellectual Property Rights,* manual, p. 2, www.usdoj.gov/criminal/cybercrime/intell_prop_rts/toc.htm.

198 Since most states: Ibid., pp. 2–10.

198 In 1992, Congress broadened: Ibid., p. 3.

198 The Justice Department defines: *The Lanham Act,* 1946, 15 U.S.C. §§ 1051–1127.

198 The Coca-Cola formula: Frederick Allen, *Secret Formula* (New York: Harper-Business, 1994), p. 105.

198 The formula is considered: Ibid.

198 when in 1977: Ibid., p. 370. Frederick Allen reports that a black market soon developed in which the price of a bottle of Coke smuggled into India fetched three times the old market price.

199 However, federal law does: U.S. Department of Justice, *Federal Prosecution of Violations of Intellectual Property Rights.*

199 Whether this is so: U.S. Department of Commerce, "Employed Civilians by Occupation, Sex, Race, and Hispanic Origin, 1983–2002," *Statistical Abstract of the United States, 2003,* Washington, D.C., 2003, p. 399, table 615.

200 In the decade before: Warshofsky, *Patent Wars,* p. 65.

200 Before the creation: Ibid., p. 68; William M. Landis and Richard A. Posner, *The Economic Structure of Intellectual Property Law* (Cambridge, Mass.: Harvard University Press, 2003) p. 338.

200 These certified patent: U.S. Patent and Trademark Office, "Attorneys and Agents," brochure, Washington, D.C., USPTO, 2004.

200 Alexander I. Poltorak: Alexander I. Poltorak and Paul J. Lerner, *Essentials of Intellectual Property* (New York: John Wiley & Sons, 2002), p. 145.

200 Of that one percent: Ibid., p. 47.

200 Only 4 percent: Ibid.

200 Of cases where: Ibid., p. 145.

200 When infringement is litigated: Ibid.

201 The commission is: United States International Trade Commission, "Section 337 Investigations at the U.S. International Trade Commission: Answers to Frequently Asked Questions," Washington, D.C., www.ustic.gov/webpubs.htm (accessed October 14, 2004).

201 Between the mid-1970s: United States International Trade Commission, "Investigations by Title," Washington, D.C., January 2004, www.ustic.gov/70ps/70ps/index.htm.

201 A multibillion-dollar: "Complaint and Jury Demand," *Cisco Systems and Cisco Technology, Inc. v. Huawei Technologies, Huawei America, Inc., and FutureWei Technologies,* U.S. District Court for the Eastern District of Texas, Marshall Division Civil Action no. 2:03-cV-027 TJW, January 22, 2003.

202 The software used: Ibid.

202 One was from a Cisco: "Declaration of Jack Flinsbaugh, Supplementing Cisco's Motion for Preliminary Injunction," civil action, *Cisco Systems and Cisco Technology, Inc. v. Huawei.*

202 According to the engineer: "Declaration of Chad Reynolds," ibid.

202 More explosive, a former: Ibid.

202 Independent experts would: Laurie J. Flynn, "Cisco Agrees to Suspend Patent Suit for 6 Months," *New York Times,* October 2, 2003.

203 The company's profits: Author interviews with Terry Dunlap. I attended parts of the GoVideo trial in the summer of 1991 and did extensive interviews with the participants, witnesses, and several jurors after the trial.

203 In September 1984, Dunlap: Dunlap continued to file patent applications, reinforcing his hold over the technology. See Patent No. 4768110.

205 They jointly carry: Author interviews with Joseph M. Alioto Jr. and Daniel Schulman. In addition to interviewing Alioto and Schulman in Phoenix during the trial, I did extensive interviews with each of them in their home offices. Those interviews are the basis for this story.

208 Then, he surrounds: Interviews with Terry Dunlap, April and May 2004.

209 Johnny, of course: Suzanne Smiley, "A Brief History of the Beatles," May 1, 2000, www.geocities.com/hollywood/Lot/2636/beatles.html.

209 In the early 1980s, an agreement: Associated Press, "Beatles' Company Sues Apple Computer," September 12, 2003.

209 Apple Corps, owned: Ibid.

210 Milliken holds copyrights: *Milliken & Company v. Haima Group Corporation and Weihai No. 1 Carpet Factory,* United States District Court, District of Nevada Case No. CV-S-02-1376-JCM-RJJ, October 17, 2002.

211 Subsequently, Haima: Ibid.

211 Haima exports to: Haima Carpet World, "Brief Introduction of Haima Group Corporation," 2003, www.haimacarpet.com/company_english.htm.

211 Then the regional office: *Milliken v. Haima,* op. cit.

211 The new catalog: Ibid.

211 In May 2003, the federal: Order Granting Motion for Default Judgment, *Milliken v. Haima Group Corporation and Weihai No. 1 Carpet Factory,* United States District Court, District of Nevada, May 14, 2003.

211 Timothy Monahan: Timothy Monahan, telephone interview with author, May 21, 2003.

212 Among its dozens: David Barbour, "Glow of Achievement," *Lighting Dimensions,* May 1999.

212 "Worldwide, neon sales": Ibid.

212 After Kingstone took back: "Former Distributor Stole Fiber Optic Firm's Trade Secrets," VerdictSearch, Case No. 96565, September 9, 2002.

213 Kingstone knew he was: Ibid.

213 Kingstone also learned: Ibid.

213 Wu, who had established: Brett M. Kingstone, *The Real War Against America,* unpublished manuscript read and quoted with the permission of Brett M. Kingstone.

214 The Chinese defendants: "Former Distributor Stole Fiber Optic Firm's Trade Secrets," VerdictSearch.

214 On September 22, 2002: Final Judgment, *Super Vision International, Inc., v. Wu et al.,* Circuit Court of the Ninth Judicial Circuit, Orange County, Florida, June 16, 2003.

214 The trial judge also: Ibid.

214 On February 25, 2004: Ric Keller (R.-Fla.), unpublished letter to the Honorable Grant Aldonas, Under Secretary for International Trade, United States Department of Commerce, February 25, 2004.

214 Reflecting on the case: Kingstone, *Real War Against America.*

215 In 1996, the director: Thomas R. Stutler, "Stealing Secrets Solved—Economic Espionage Investigations by the FBI," *Law Enforcement Bulletin,* November 2000.

215 To bring cohesion: The National Intellectual Property Law Enforcement Coordination Council, *NIPLECC 2003 Annual Report,* December 2003, p. 3.

216 Since June 2000, the USTR: The World Trade Organization, "Disputes, Chronologically," Geneva, June 23, 2004, www.wto.org/english/tratop_e/dispu_e/dispu_status_e.htm.

216 It also conducts training: NIPLECC, *NIPLECC 2003 Annual Report.*

216 It also provides training: Ibid.

217 The U.S. Copyright Office: Ibid.

217 The Department of Homeland Security: Ibid.

217 Out of more than: U.S. Census Bureau, *U.S. International Trade in Goods and Services,* annual report, October 2004; U.S. Customs and Border Protection, FY2004 Annual Report, December 17, 2004.

217 The Department of Justice investigates: NIPLECC, *NIPLECC 2003 Annual Report.*

217 In 2001, Justice strengthened: John G. Malcolm, Deputy Assistant Attorney General for the Criminal Division, U.S. Department of Justice, statement before the Committee on the Judiciary, U.S. House of Representatives, March 13, 2003.

217 They supplement the work: Ibid.

217 Since 9/11, almost all: Author interview with FBI official, Washington, D.C., May 2004.

218 Only four were sentenced: U.S. Department of Justice, "Intellectual Property Report," *FY 2003 Performance and Accountability Report,* www.usdoj.gov/ag/annualreports/ar2003/appendices.htm#cc.

218 On November 24, 2004, the day: *Conference Report on H.R. 4818, Consolidated Appropriations Act, 2005, Division B, Departments of Commerce, Justice, and State, the Judiciary and Related Agencies Appropriations Act, 2005,* U.S. House of Representatives, Washington, D.C., November 19, 2004, p. 124.

CHAPTER 8: A GLOBAL SOLUTION

222 The International Trade Commission: U.S. International Trade Commission, "Foreign Protection of Intellectual Property Rights and the Effect on U.S. Industry and Trade," Washington, D.C., 1988, p. H-2.

222 Brazil, Egypt, India: Stephanie Epstein and James Matthew Jones, "Intellectual Property at a Crossroads," report, Congressional Economic Leadership Institute, Washington, D.C., 1990, pp. 17–18.

222 The issue was: The Omnibus Trade and Competitiveness Act of 1988 authorized the Office of the United States Trade Representative to prepare an annual report that identified countries that deny adequate and effective protection for intellectual property rights or deny fair and equitable market access to persons that rely on intellectual property protection.

222 WIPO was a United Nations: Michael P. Ryan, *Knowledge Diplomacy* (Washington, D.C.: Brookings Institution Press, 1998), p. 68.

222 In the 1970s and 1980s: During that period, I did extensive work on trade and intellectual property matters with Congress. Associates who also worked in Congress during that period believe my estimate of five or ten may be too high. Certainly, it is not too generous.

223 These two men were: Peter Drahos with John Braithwaite, *Information Feudalism* (New York: New Press, 2002), pp. 67–68 and 73.

223 Beginning in 1949: IBM, "John R. Opel," IBM Archives, 2004.

224 In 1999, he donated: Pfizer Corporation, "Edmund T. Pratt, Jr.," Pfizer Archives, 2004.

224 IBM wanted minimal: Ryan, *Knowledge Diplomacy,* p. 68.

224 Pfizer, then a 130-year-old company: Ibid.

224 "What is distinctive": Edmund J. Pratt Jr., "Intellectual Property," speech at the U.S. Council for International Business, Conference on Intellectual Property, Washington, D.C., March 1995.

225 ACTPN members: Bruce Stokes and Pat Choate, *Democratizing U.S. Trade Policy* (New York: Council on Foreign Relations Press, 2001), pp. 53–59.

225 They organized congressional: Drahos with Braithwaite, *Information Feudalism,* pp. 72–73.

225 For example, Pfizer's general counsel: Ibid., pp. 69–72.

226 In the spring of 1983: I did TRW's staff work for participation in this organization and wrote the first draft of their report on competitiveness.

226 Its mission was to get: Ryan, *Knowledge Diplomacy,* pp. 69–70.

226 The objective was made: Ibid. pp. 73–79.

226 And Korean pirates were: Ibid.

227 A showdown was: Ibid.

227 In 1984, Opel commissioned: Drahos with Braithwaite, *Information Feudalism,* p. 73.

227 In March 1986, Pratt: Ibid., p. xii.

228 As Peter Drahos and: Peter Drahos and John Braithwaite, "Three Tests of U.S. Trade Policy on Intellectual Property Rights," Nth Position, www.nthposition. com/threetestsofustrade.php.

228 The Keidanren, whose membership: *Basic Framework of GATT Provisions on Intellectual Property: The Statement of Views of the European, Japanese, and United State Business Communities,* report by the Intellectual Property Committee, Washington, D.C., June 1988, pp. 4–5.

229 Finally, the U.S., Japanese: Ibid.

229 Consequently, John Beton: Duncan Matthews, "Trade-Related Aspects of Intellectual Property Rights: Will the Uruguay Round Consensus Hold?," CSGR Working Paper No. 99/02, Centre for the Study of Globalisation and Regionalisation, June 2002, www2.warwick.ac.uk/fac/soc/csgr/research/workingpapers/ 2002/wp9902.pdf.

229 In June 1988, the three groups: Ibid.

229 The USTR immediately distributed: Jacques Gorlin, interview with the author by telephone, Washington, D.C., 1998.

230 They write: Drahos with Braithwaite, *Information Feudalism,* p. 73.

230 The leading critics came: Drahos with Braithwaite, "Three Tests of U.S. Trade Policy," pp. 7–9.

230 India, Thailand, South Korea: Ibid.

231 Regardless of the name: Ryan, *Knowledge Diplomacy,* p. 92.

232 First, Mexico and Canada: See the text of the North American Free Trade Agreement.

232 Gorlin claims that they: Susan K. Sell and Aseem Prakash, *Globalization and Governance: Examining the Contest Between Business and NGO Agenda in Intellectual Property Rights,* report, Center for Study of Globalization, George Washington University, December 16, 2002, p. 6.

232 The other 5 percent: Ibid.

232 It covers four broad: World Trade Organization, "Intellectual Property Rights and the TRIPS Agreement," Geneva, Switzerland, June 2004.

232 Second, TRIPS ensures: Ibid.

232 TRIPS gave international protection: Ibid.

233 Integrated circuit layout: Ibid.

233 Most important, part 2: Ibid.

233 If any nation thinks: Ibid.

234 By the middle of 2004: U.S. Department of Labor, "Employment Statistics," Washington, D.C., June 2004, www.stats.bls.gov/webapps/legacy/cesbtabl.htm.

234 The resulting loss: *Statistical Abstract of the United States,* "U.S. Exports and General Imports by Selected SITC Commodity Groups, 1999–2002" (Washington, D.C.: 2003), table 1301.

234 The Labor Department estimates: U.S. Labor Department, "Displaced Workers by Industry and Class of Worker of Lost Job and Employment Status in January 2004," http://www.bls.gov/news.release/disp.t04.htm

234 Thus, the United States signed: "Testimony of Lori Wallach Regarding the WTO Dispute Settlement System: Powerful Enforcement of Unbalanced, Extensive Regulations Without Basic Due Process Protections," Senate Finance Committee, Subcommittee on International Trade, June 20, 2000.

235 The first administration: "Dispute Settlement: The Disputes," World Trade Organization, Geneva, January 10, 2005.

235 The eighth dealt with: Ibid.

235 In the entire year: Ibid.

235 Overall, U.S. federal: Administrative Office of the United States Courts, "Caseload Highlights, 2002," in *Federal Judicial Caseload Statistics,* Washington, D.C., March 31, 2002.

236 In an affidavit: Affidavit of Jacques J. Gorlin, May 28, 2002.

CHAPTER 9: THE PATENT BATTLE

238 The American is Jerome Lemelson: Bernard Wysocki Jr., "Royalty Rewards: How Patent Lawsuits Make a Quiet Engineer Rich and Controversial," *Wall Street Journal*, April 9, 1997.

239 Eventually, the patent office: Gabriel P. Katona, "The Myth of Submarine Patents," Intellectual Property Creators, May 15, 2001; Lewis J. Hoffman, "Why Patents Occasionally Take a Long Time to Issue," Intellectual Property Creators, December 26, 1995; Ronald J. Riley, "Louis J. Hoffman About Jerome H. Lemelson's Patents," www.rjriley.com/site-index/.

239 The ultimate result: "Louis J. Hoffman About Jerome H. Lemelson's Patents."

239 In thirty days: Wysocki, "Royalty Rewards."

239 The Japanese settlement: Ibid.

240 Finally, the basic machine: Katona, "The Myth of Submarine Patents."

240 In the 1980s, Hitachi: Pat Choate and J. K. Linger, *The High-Flex Society* (New York: Alfred A. Knopf, 1986), pp. 80–81.

240 In 1997, General Electric: Randy Myers, "Fighting Words: Growing Ranks of Litigants Are Putting Price Tags on Ideas," *CFO, The Magazine for Senior Financial Executives*, March 1998.

240 In 2003, Boeing was banned: John Kelly, "Air Force to Lift Ban on Boeing Bids," *Florida Today*, April 6, 2004. The Department of Defense assessed Boeing a penalty of approximately $1 billion but is allowing it to return to certain businesses, such as rocket launches, thereby creating a competitor for Lockheed.

241 Those systems were developed: Paul Heckel, "Innovation," Intellectual Property Creators, www.ipcreators.org.

242 And these blue ribbon: United States Department of Commerce, "The Report of the Presidential Commission on the Patent System (1966); and Advisory Commission on Patent Law Reform, "A Report to the Secretary of Commerce," Washington, D.C., August 1992. Two separate blue ribbon commissions have repeated these same recommendations.

244 Genentech sued one opponent: *Briefing Book for U.S./Japan Trade Framework Negotiations* (unpublished), U.S. Patent and Trademark Office, Washington, D.C., June 7–8, 1994, table 2.

244 This is remarkable testimony: Ibid.

245 The committee was composed: Advisory Commission on Patent Law Reform, "A Report to the Secretary of Commerce."

245 Small companies, independent investors: Ibid.

245 The article revealed: Andrew Pollack, "U.S. Agrees to Alter Patents' Period of Coverage," *New York Times*, January 24, 1994.

246 In 1969, President Nixon: "Helen Delich Bentley," Biographical Directory of the United States Congress.

246 The point man: Advisory Commission on Patent Law Reform, "A Report to

the Secretary of Commerce"; American Bar Association, "Proposed Resolution 157–4," Intellectual Property Law Section, May 3, 2002.

246 For nine years, Lehman: U.S. Department of Commerce, "Biography of Bruce A. Lehman," news release, November 21, 1997.

246 In the early 1980s: Ibid.

247 In exchange for: U.S. Patent and Trademark Office, "Mutual Understanding Between the Japanese Patent Office and the United States Patent and Trademark Office," letter of agreement, signed January 20, 1994.

247 With this, any third party: United States Department of Commerce News, "American Inventors Promised Swifter, Stronger Intellectual Property Protection by Japan," news release, Washington, D.C., August 16, 1994.

248 However, in March 1994: Committee of the Judiciary, "Oversight of the Patent and Trademark Office," hearing before the Subcommittee on Patents, Copyrights and Trademarks, United States Senate, 103rd Cong., 2d sess., 1994.

248 He made saving: Dana Rohrabacher (R.-Calif.), "Don't Add Baggage to GATT," extension of remarks in the House of Representatives, July 20, 1994.

248 Seventeen members, mostly: Unpublished letters from seventeen members of Congress to President William Jefferson Clinton, July 29, 1994.

249 Rohrabacher tore into: Proceedings of a joint hearing before the Subcommittee on Intellectual Property and Judicial Property of the House Committee on the Judiciary and the Subcommittee on Patents, Copyrights, and Trademarks of the Senate Committee on the Judiciary, Committee Print, U.S. Congress, August 12, 1994.

249 Finally, Lehman said: Ibid.

250 The other two were: Andrew Wheat, "A Year in the Life of the GATT Business Lobby," *Multinational Monitor,* 1994.

251 Steven Shore became: Beverly Selby to Pat Choate, "Chronology of Patent Issue," memo, November 6, 1998, supplemented by interviews, 1998–2000.

251 As much as anything: Author interviews with Steven Shore, 1994–1999.

251 "In that meeting": Selby, "Chronology of Patent Issue."

252 To most, he says: Ibid.

252 By December 1994: Ibid.

252 Riley created a Web site: "Biography of Ronald J. Riley," www.rjriley.com. Riley continues to follow the fight on patents, and his site has useful information for those wishing either to find background material or to be kept up to date.

253 *FDA Week* quoted an unnamed: "U.S. Patent Chief Negotiating to Give Chinese U.S. Patent Data Base," *FDA Week,* vol. 2, no. 14, April 5, 1996.

254 In one interview: Rory J. O'Connor, "Patent Proposal Stirs Up a Ruckus Vote Today: House Proposal Called Reform or a Path to Invention Thieves," *San Jose Mercury News,* April 17, 1997.

254 In mid-September 1997: Christopher B. Daly, "Nobel Laureates Speak Out Against Patent Bill," *Washington Post,* September 12, 1997.

254 On October 17, 1997: Editorial, "A Bad Patent Bill," *New York Times,* October 17, 1997.

255 Howard Coble: Author interviews with Dana Rohrabacher, Washington, D.C., September 2002.

255 Marcy Kaptur, a fierce advocate: Author interviews with Marcy Kaptur, Washington, D.C., July 2003.

256 The opponents rebutted: *Congressional Record,* U.S. House of Representatives (April 17, 1997) H 1629–1684.

256 The next round: Ibid.

256 Then Duncan Hunter moved that: *Congressional Record,* U.S. House of Representatives (April 23, 1997) H 1719–1742.

260 On August 2, 2004: U.S. Patent and Trademark Office, "Internet Access to Patent Application Files Now Available," press release, Washington, D.C., August 2, 2004.

CHAPTER 10: THE COPYRIGHT WARS

262 Congress then specified four factors: Association of Research Libraries, "A History of Copyright in the United States," an e-history, Washington, D.C., November 22, 2002, available at www.arl.org.

262 In another case, the court ruled: Ibid.

263 The Court's decision: Ibid., p. 269.

263 As the Congressional Budget Office (CBO) noted: Congressional Budget Office, "Copyright Issues in Digital Media," U.S. Congress, Washington, D.C., August 2004, p. vii.

263 Conversely, these same technologies: Ibid.

265 The IITF's mission: U.S. Patent and Trademark Office, "Final Report from the IPNII Working Group," press release, Washington, D.C., September 1, 1995.

265 Brown appointed a private: United States Advisory Council on the National Information Infrastructure, www.ibiblio.org/nii/NII-Advisory-Council.html.

265 Eighteen months later: Information Infrastructure Task Force, "Intellectual Property and the National Information Infrastructure: A Preliminary Draft of the Report of the Working Group on Intellectual Property Rights," *Report of the Working Group on Intellectual Property Rights,* 1994, www.uspto.gov/web/offices/com/iprii/.

266 In *Digital Copyright:* Jessica Litman, *Digital Copyright* (Amherst, N.Y.: Prometheus Books, 2001), pp. 89–100. Jessica Litman is a law professor at Wayne State University. During the copyright wars of the mid-1990s, she was an effective commentator, producing numerous papers that lucidly explained the nuances of the various proposals then under consideration. Most are still available on the Internet. In 2001, she published this book. It is a well-written, concise history of the fight surrounding the enactment of the Digital Millennium Copyright Act. Equally important, it is written for the general public, though all the legal citations and footnotes are available for lawyers and others wanting the technical background on this issue.

266 Soon its membership included: DFC, "A Description of the Digital Future Coalition," www.dfc.org/dfc1/Learning_Center/about.html.

267 In 1997, the MacArthur Foundation: Maurice M. Krochmal, "Fighting the Copyright Wars with a 'Genius Grant' in Hand," *New York Times,* June 28, 1997.

267 One of her most influential: Pamela Samuelson, "The Copyright Grab: A White Paper," *Wired,* January 1996.

267 She summarized: Ibid.

268 Samuelson then suggested: Ibid.

268 Samuelson's premise was dead on: Ibid.

269 His point is that: Pat Choate, *Agents of Influence* (New York: Alfred A. Knopf, 1990), p. 60.

269 Lehman moved quickly: "Request for Comments," *Federal Register,* vol. 61, no. 202, October 17, 1996, pp. 54159–54160.

270 Love, who holds degrees: James Love, biographical information, www.cptech.org./jamie.

270 Team owners could create: Ibid.

270 Billington urged: James H. Billington, librarian of Congress, letter to Laura D'Andrea Tyson, assistant to the president for economic policy, November 1996.

271 DiMario pointed out that the database: Michael F. DiMario, the public printer, letter to Bruce A. Lehman, commissioner of patents and trademarks, November 22, 1996.

271 Some companies: John Browning, "Africa 1, Hollywood 0," a report from the WIPO conference, www.wired.com.

272 On the last evening: Ibid.

273 The treaties set the minimum: WIPO press release no. 106, Geneva, December 20, 1996.

274 Three days later: *Digital Millennium Copyright Act,* 112 *Stat.* 2860, Public Law 105-304 (October 28, 1998).

274 The founding contributors: International Intellectual Property Institute Web site, www.iipi.org.

274 In 2001, Congress directed: *U.S. Congress Report 107-139,* Departments of Commerce, Justice, and State, the Judiciary, and Related Agencies Appropriations Bill, Fiscal Year 2002, July 13, 2001.

274 The fight was triggered: "Napster's High and Low Notes," *Business Week Online,* August 14, 2000; "Shawn Fanning," *Business Week Online,* May 15, 2000.

274 Napster, a corporate name: "Shawn Fanning," in People Who Mattered, *Time* magazine, December 17, 2000.

275 At this point, Napster claimed: "Napster's High and Low Notes," *Business Week Online,* August 14, 2000.

275 Napster went bankrupt in the fall: Napster was reorganized after bankruptcy. As of the summer of 2004, it was offering subscription-based access to more

than 700,000 songs, from 65,000 albums and 40,000 artists, for $9.95 a month.

275 In April 2003, Steve Jobs: "Invention of the Year: Coolest Inventions 2003," *Time,* December 21, 2003.

275 In its first year: Apple Computer, "iPod + iTunes," news release, May 17, 2004.

275 The purchased songs: Apple Computer, "iTunes Music Store Terms of Service," www.apple.com/legal/terms/itunes/service.html.

275 The Apple download license: Rob Pegoraro, "Sony's Connect Music Service Offers Fair Pricing, Little Else," *Washington Post,* May 9, 2004; Apple Computer, "iTunes Music Store Terms of Service."

275 Individual songs can be: Apple Computer, Inc., "The #1 Music Download Store," news release, May 17, 2004.

275 Several other companies: Pegoraro, "Sony's Connect Music Service Offers Fair Pricing, Little Else."

276 In September 2003: "Schoolgirl Settles with RIAA," *Wired News,* September 10, 2003.

276 The objective of these lawsuits: "RIAA Brings New Round of Cases Against Illegal File Sharers," Collegiate Presswire, March 23, 2004.

276 On March 23, 2004: Ibid.

276 Hart also reported that: Ibid.

276 A more appropriate name: "Copyright Extended for Mickey Mouse," Associated Press, October 16, 1998.

276 Rather than allow their valuable: *Eldred v. Ashcroft,* 537 U.S. 186, 208 (2003), footnote 2.

277 Then the Senate: Senate Finance Committee, *Clean Efficient Automobiles Resulting from Advanced Car Technologies (CLEAR ACT) Act of 2003,* 108th Cong., 1st sess., 2003, S. 505 IS.

277 Twenty days later: Ibid.

277 The Congressional Research Service: Edward Rappaport, "Copyright Term Extension: Estimating the Economic Values," CRS report for Congress, Congressional Research Service, Library of Congress, Washington, D.C., updated version, May 11, 1998, p. 3.

278 In addition, friend-of-the-court: *Eldred v. Ashcroft,* Open Law, Berkman Center for Internet Law and Society at Harvard Law School, Harvard University, www.cyber.law.harvard.edu/openlaw/eldredvashcroft/legal.html#amici.

278 Supporters of the Bono Act: Ibid.

278 Only 2 percent of the works: Lessig, *Free Culture: How Big Media Uses Technology and the Law to Lock Down Culture and Control Creativity* (New York: Penguin Press, 2004), pp. 220–221.

278 Jason Schultz, a staff attorney: Jason Schultz, "The Myth of the 1976 Copyright 'Chaos Theory,' " Electronics Frontier Foundation, 2002, www.cyberlaw.stanford.edu/lessig/blog/archives/jasonfinal.pdf.

279 Thus, by Schultz's count: Ibid.

279 Approximately half: Barbara and David P. Mikkelson, "Happy Birthday, We'll

Sue," Urban Legends Reference Pages, August 25, 2004, www.snopes.com/music/songs/birthday.htm.

280 To encourage voluntary action: Creative Commons, "About Us" and "Licenses Explained," www.creativecommons.org.

280 It requires the Register of Copyrights: H.R. 2601, Bill Summary and Status for the 108th Congress, at Thomas, Library of Congress. www.thomas.loc.gov.

280 It makes registering: Ibid.

282 These works, the knowledge they contain: Lawrence Lessig, *Free Culture*, pp. 220–228. In quick succession in the late 1990s and the early twenty-first century, Lessig wrote three important books on ideas, copyrights, and the Internet: *Code* (1999), *The Future of Ideas* (2001), and *Free Culture* (2004). In addition, he has provided important intellectual leadership in efforts to defeat legislation that would give major corporate media owners increased power over the content used on the Internet. For those interested in this general topic, I highly recommend his three books.

Over the past twenty-five years, I have written several books and in all instances have used one or more assistants to help with my research. However, for this book I relied on the Internet, interviews, and several online bookstores. As my footnotes reveal, I have used many references that were written before 1923, the backward limit on today's copyright law. Without the Net, without the digitalizing of those works by various universities around the world, and without those works being in the public domain, it is quite possible that I would never have known of their existence. Though those works are no longer commercially viable, the Net has brought them to life again, enabling their authors to send information and their observations across time and space to a new audience. Having access to the vast store of knowledge now needlessly frozen by existing copyright laws would be a boon of inestimable value to anyone doing research on virtually any topic.

EPILOGUE

284 At various times: Kenneth S. Davis, *FDR: The War President: 1940–1943* (New York: Random House, 2000) pp. 444–450. President Roosevelt appointed Arnold to the United States Court of Appeals for the District of Columbia, perhaps the most prestigious and important of the federal appeals courts. But after two years, Arnold resigned because "I'd rather speak to damn fools than listen to them." He then went into private practice.

284 The historian Kenneth S. Davis: Ibid.

284 Within twenty-four months: Ibid.

284 With great energy and publicity: Arnold, *Bottlenecks of Business*.

284 And then, as now: Choate, *Agents of Influence*, pp. xv–xxii.

285 In early 2003: The President's Council of Advisers on Science and Technology, The White House, "Sustaining the Nation's Innovative Ecosystems," Washing-

ton, D.C., January 2004; *Manufacturing News and Technology* 10, no. 18 (October 3, 2003): 1.

285 Released in January 2004: "Sustaining the Nation's Innovative Ecosystems."

285 Each benefits from proximity: Ibid.

285 The task force says: Council on Competitiveness, Task Force on the Future of American Innovation, "Industry, Academic Leaders Unveil Campaign on Economic Growth and Job Creation," Washington, D.C., April 20, 2004.

INDEX

Page numbers beginning with 289 refer to notes.

NOTE ABOUT THE AUTHOR

Pat Choate received his PhD in economics from the University of Oklahoma, which in 1994 named him the Arthur Barto Adams Alumni Fellow in recognition of his continuing scholarship. In 1996, Ross Perot chose him to be his vice presidential running mate. He is the author of *Agents of Influence*. His works have been published by the *Harvard Business Review*, *The Washington Post*, the *Los Angeles Times*, *The New York Times*, *The Atlanta Journal-Constitution*, *USA Today*, and other leading publications. He, his wife, Kay, and their English bulldog, Dolly, live on a farm near Washington, Virginia.

A NOTE ON THE TYPE

This book was set in Minion, a typeface produced by the Adobe Corporation specifically for the Macintosh personal computer and released in 1990. Designed by Robert Slimbach, Minion combines the classic characteristics of old-style faces with the full compliment of weights required for modern typesetting.

Composed by
Creative Graphics,
Allentown, Pennsylvania

Printed and bound by
Berryville Graphics,
Berryville Virginia

Designed by
Pamela G. Parker